Advance Praise

I have known Dr Agochiya for more than three decades. This Manual reflects his vast international experience as a trainer and an expert in youth empowerment, particularly in the field of life skills development. I am sure it will enhance the understanding and knowledge base of the facilitators in preparing youth to meet the challenges of life confidently.

—**P.K. Mishra**
Former Chief Secretary, UP, and ex-Member,
Union Public Service Commission

In the realm of training of trainers, this volume is a fine example of a researched guide. It is exceptional because of the inputs in terms of theory, application and innovation. Undoubtedly, it will prove valuable to all those engaged in personal development and the advancement of a flourishing humanistic society. In my professional opinion, no one is more qualified than Dr Agochiya to produce such a trainer's Manual.

—**Jitendra Mohan**
Professor Emeritus of Psychology, Panjab University

The Manual is a seminal piece of work in life skills education. If we have to produce confident, efficient and professional young workforce, it is necessary that vocational or entrepreneurial skills imparted by various training agencies are complemented by developing life skills as well. The Manual developed by Dr Agochiya who is an internationally acknowledged expert in youth development and training, provides this opportunity.

—**Jagadananda**
Mentor and Co-founder—CYSD; Chairperson:
Transparency International India (Odisha Chapter);
Member, State Audit Advisory Board; former
State Information Commissioner

Dr Agochiya has been associated with the IALSE programmes for nearly a decade. His rich experience as a trainer and his wide-ranging knowledge about life skills and human behaviour are evident in the contents of the Manual and the manner in which the material is presented. I am confident that his effort will give a significant boost to life skills education in India.

—Dr R.J. Solomon
President, Indian Association of Life Skills Education (IALSE)

LIFE COMPETENCIES

for

GROWTH

and

SUCCESS

LIFE COMPETENCIES
for
GROWTH
and
SUCCESS

A TRAINER'S MANUAL

DEVENDRA AGOCHIYA

Los Angeles | London | New Delhi
Singapore | Washington DC | Melbourne

First published in 2018 by

SAGE Publications India Pvt Ltd
B1/I-1 Mohan Cooperative Industrial Area
Mathura Road, New Delhi 110 044, India
www.sagepub.in

SAGE Publications Inc
2455 Teller Road
Thousand Oaks, California 91320, USA

SAGE Publications Ltd
1 Oliver's Yard, 55 City Road
London EC1Y 1SP, United Kingdom

SAGE Publications Asia-Pacific Pte Ltd
3 Church Street
#10-04 Samsung Hub
Singapore 049483

Published by Vivek Mehra for SAGE Publications India Pvt Ltd, typeset in 11/14 Adobe Caslon by Fidus Design Pvt. Ltd., Chandigarh and printed at Sai Print-o-Pack, New Delhi.

Library of Congress Cataloging-in-Publication Data
Name: Agochiya, Devendra, author.
Title: Life competencies for growth and success: a trainer's manual / Devendra Agochiya.
Description: Thousand Oaks, California : SAGE, 2018. | Includes bibliographical references.
Identifiers: LCCN 2017050110 (print) | LCCN 2017053704 (ebook) | ISBN 9789352805280 (Web PDF) |
    ISBN 9789352805266 (pbk : alk. paper)
Subjects: LCSH: Youth—Life skills guides.
Classification: LCC HQ796 (ebook) | LCC HQ796 .A337 2018 (print) | DDC 305.235—dc23
LC record available at https://lccn.loc.gov/2017050110

ISBN: 978-93-528-0526-6 (PB)

SAGE Team: Manisha Mathews, Sunil Koli, Madhurima Thapa and Ritu Chopra

In fond and eternal memories of my loving wife Anjali

*****

To
daughter Mahima, son Vipul and
daughter-in-law Manjari

*****

and, importantly, my two little gems—
granddaughter Ahaana and grandson Vivaan

Thank you for choosing a SAGE product!
If you have any comment, observation or feedback,
I would like to personally hear from you.

Please write to me at **contactceo@sagepub.in**

Vivek Mehra, Managing Director and CEO, SAGE India.

Detailed Contents

Section A: The Modules

Section B – Delivering an Effective Training Programme

Foreword

There is a great development potential in the Indian workforce conceived in demographic dividend in terms of population in the working age group (15–60). This has heightened the prospects for not just India but the entire world. While India sees the demographic resource as an aid in its economic development, the world sees it as a huge market and potentially global workforce. In the words of our Prime Minister Shri Narendra Modi Ji, 'Time has come to show India's strength to the world. Let us recognise our demographic dividend and present image of a Skilled India to the world'.

In view of the big gap between what the present training infrastructure and facilities can offer—in terms of both quantity and quality of training— and the requirements of skilled and semi-skilled workforce, skilling Indian youth has been adopted by the present government as the cornerstone of its economic policy. The National Skill Development Mission is a big step towards achieving this goal. For improving the chances of success, the agencies and institutes responsible for carrying out training in job-related or entrepreneurial skills should include a substantial component on life skills in their curriculum. Undoubtedly, those individuals who are equipped with life skills will be more effective in their work. They will not only be able to relate more appropriately with their colleagues at the workplace but also be in a better position to deal with the challenges that are innate to the job, thus raising the level of their performance.

Life skills have a unique position in the life of young women and men, regardless of whether they are in full employment in the private or public sector, job aspirants or seeking to become entrepreneurs. These skills also play a significant role in their day-to-day life—guiding their interactions, shaping their behaviour patterns, building their confidence and helping them make informed and pertinent choices in matters that impact their life.

The book *Life Competencies for Growth and Success: A Trainer's Manual* authored by Dr Devendra Agochiya will serve as a helpful guide to the trainers of life skills education and training. The modules in this Manual are extremely relevant, covering key aspects of the life of an individual. As mentioned in the introductory note by the author, the training institutes or the training teams have the option of choosing those modules that are considered suitable and useful for their specific groups of trainees.

The learned author of this book has put together his vast international experience as a trainer and his expertise in life skills to produce this valuable guide for trainers. He has to his credit a number of publications, including a bestseller *Every Trainer's Handbook* (SAGE). I compliment Dr Devendra Agochiya for this laudable and distinctive effort.

Dr Agochiya has been associated with the Rajiv Gandhi National Institute of Youth Development (RGNIYD) since its inception and has contributed substantially in its activities and programmes. He was a member of the high-profile Mentor Group that helped RGNIYD get the status of an 'Institution of National Importance' through an Act of Parliament (No 35/2012). This Manual will certainly supplement our efforts for organising training programmes in life skills for youth empowerment functionaries and trainers in entire India as an independent, non-violent democracy with integrity and amity. To provide roti (bread) and livelihood to the unemployed, we certainly need to increase Returns on Training Investment (ROTI).

Professor (Dr) Madan Mohan Goel
Director, Former Pro Vice-Chancellor,
VKSU (State University) Arrah, Bihar

Introduction

In a constantly changing environment, having life skills is an essential part of being able to meet the challenges of everyday life. The dramatic changes in global economies over the past five years have been matched with the transformation in technology, and these developments are impacting education, social life, the workplace and our family life. To cope with the increasing pace and change of modern life, young people need new life skills, such as the ability to deal with stress and frustration, and meet the challenges head-on.

In everyday life, the development of life skills helps young women and men to:

- Develop better insights into their actions and behaviour, and increase appreciation for others;
- Find new ways of thinking, problem-solving and decision-making;
- Analyse options, make decisions and understand why they make certain choices in their life—social as well as work-related;
- Build confidence in communication with people around, in establishing relationships and in group collaboration and cooperation; and
- Develop into more responsible and productive citizens of the country.

In the social networking-oriented world of today, it is important that you are amenable to others; else people tend to avoid you. Where there is an increased emphasis on interaction with people, soft skills have a big role. The world is more connected than ever before; therefore, these skills have acquired a new level of importance and cruciality.

Life skills have been defined as 'the abilities for adaptive and positive behaviour that enable individuals to deal effectively with the demands and challenges of everyday life' (WHO). 'Adaptive' means that a person is flexible in approach and is able to adjust in different circumstances. 'Positive behaviour' implies that a person is forward-looking and even in difficult situations can find a ray of hope and opportunities to find solutions.

LIFE SKILLS DEFINED

UNICEF defines life skills as 'a behaviour change or behaviour development approach designed to address a balance of three areas: knowledge, attitude and skills'. Life skills are essentially those abilities that help to promote physical, mental and emotional well-being and competence to face the realities of life.

The 10 core life skills identified by the WHO can be categorised as follows:

Social skills

- Self-awareness
- Empathy
- Effective communication
- Interpersonal relationship

Thinking skills

- Critical thinking
- Creative thinking
- Problem-solving
- Decision-making

Coping skills

- Coping with stress
- Coping with emotions

Social Skills

Self-awareness: It is the ability to introspect, analyse and accept one's thoughts, actions and feelings, recognising and acknowledging one's needs, likes, dislikes, strengths and weaknesses. Developing self-awareness can help us recognise when we are stressed or under pressure. It is also often a prerequisite for effective communication and interpersonal relations, as well as for developing empathy for others.

Empathy: It is the ability to be sensitive to another person's situation; to imagine what life is like for another person, even in a situation that we may not be familiar with, can help us to accept others and improve social interactions, especially in a pluralistic society like ours.

Interpersonal communication: Effective communication means that we are able to express ourselves, both verbally and non-verbally, in ways that are appropriate to our cultures and situations. This means being able to express opinions and desires, and also our needs and fears. And it may mean being able to ask for advice and help in a time of need. Listening skills and assertiveness are part of communication skill.

Interpersonal relationship: It helps us to relate in positive ways with the people we interact with. This may mean being able to make and keep friendly relationships, which can be of great importance to our mental and social well-being. It may mean keeping good relations with family members, which are an important source of social support. It may also mean being able to end relationships constructively.

Thinking Skills

Critical thinking: It is the ability to analyse information, experiences, situations, circumstances, etc. in an objective manner and rationally; to recognise and assess factors influencing our attitude and behaviour; and to make objective judgements about choices and risks.

Creative thinking: It is a novel way of seeing or doing things that is characteristic of four components—fluency (generating new ideas), flexibility (shifting perspective easily), originality (conceiving of something new) and elaboration (building on other ideas).

Problem-solving: It helps us to deal constructively with problems in our lives; significant problems that are left unresolved can cause mental stress and give rise to accompanying physical strain.

Decision-making: Decision-making helps us to take appropriate decisions about our lives; it can help us know how to actively make decisions about our actions in relation to healthy assessment of different options and what effects these different decisions are likely to have.

Coping Skills

Coping with stress: It means recognising the sources of stress in our lives, recognising how stress affects us and acting in ways that help us control our levels of stress by changing our environment or lifestyle and learning how to relax.

Coping with emotions: It means recognising emotions within us and others, being aware of how emotions influence behaviour and being able to respond to emotions appropriately.

LIFE SKILL EDUCATION

There is no age bar for education or training in life skills. It is there for all those who would like to enjoy, look for quality personal life and success, and seek growth and success in their personal as well as work-life. While it may be more prudent to integrate life skill education with the curriculum in schools, there is a need to provide structured opportunities to job contenders, especially those who wish to enter the corporate world, for training in life skills. As numerous studies have indicated, young job aspirants miss out on some excellent career opportunities with reputed business firms because they are found wanting in essential life skills. Possibly, there could be a private–public partnership (PPP) to set up 'career management' and 'guidance' centres that interlace life skill training with other career-related components. This will help them enhance their employment and entrepreneurial potential and capabilities.

Life skill education opens the door to knowledge and opportunities for young people by developing their psychosocial abilities; contributing to their physical, social and emotional well-being; enhancing their capacity to cope effectively with the multiple challenges of life; helping them in goal-setting and in shaping their aspirations; and making them more responsible and productive citizens of their country.

It should also be seen as a tool for empowerment of young women and men to bring them into the national mainstream and make them active partners in the national development agenda and decision-making processes.

In our culturally and socially diverse society, there is greater need for our young population to develop attitudes and values that are conducive to developing healthy bonds with people, regardless of their social or religious background, ethnicity or economic status. Training in life skills will be a step in this direction.

INTEGRATING LIFE SKILLS WITH TECHNICAL SKILLS

In our country, for the last few years, there is an increasing emphasis on skill development, and rightly so. However, the focus remains on developing vocational or technical skills. There is no doubt that given the curriculum of our educational institutions, especially in school education, there is tremendous scope to include life skill training to equip the youth to be able to confront the challenges of life more effectively. Young entrepreneurs—especially young beneficiaries of the start-up schemes of the Government of India—will have a greater chance of success in their business enterprises if they are fully equipped with life skills, dealing with people who they interact with in pursuance of their business activities. There is, therefore, a need to integrate vocational and technical skills with soft skills or people-oriented skills in all skill development programmes. Using vocational skills effectively and diligently is a measure of soft skills.

In today's world, there is a lot of emphasis on knowledge and technical skills. When two persons have the same or similar knowledge and technical skills base, what may set them apart is how well each can effectively use these skills and knowledge. Here is when 'people skills' step in. These skills improve interaction with bosses, colleagues and client groups, regardless of the field you are working in—business and trade, social development, academia, etc. These skills also play a crucial role in shaping perceptions of others towards us.

In a survey conducted by Global Management Consultancy, Hay Group, in India, 74 per cent (of the surveyed group of business leaders and HR professionals) said that they have hired graduates who lack the necessary 'people skills' due to a lack of opportunities and choice; 80 per cent of business and HR directors said that graduates who do not develop 'people skills' create toxic work environments. Ruth Malloy, global managing director—leadership and talent, Hay Group, said in the report

> Currently we are seeing an awkward generation joining companies across the globe. They have acquired the technical skills and qualifications to secure work but not the soft skills they need to succeed, once they are over the threshold. They find it difficult to fit in, struggle to build relationships, don't deal effectively with stress, or get their ideas across in the right way. This is a pronounced problem in the world's key markets.

One of the major attributes employers find lacking in young people seeking executive positions is soft skills. They have a very good level of technical and business skills but when it comes to soft skills—such as communication, interpersonal and management of stress—they are found wanting. Soft skills will not only enhance their employability but also contribute to make them more successful entrepreneurs. A few years back, I had a very interesting conversation with a director of a leading IT firm in the United States. He said, 'Young Indian IT experts who come to the US for work have excellent technical skills, but they remain at lower management positions and are not able to move up the ladder in management, because they lack soft skills, such as communication, interpersonal, leadership, etc.'. This, in a way, reaffirms the importance of soft skills in the corporate world, including IT firms.

Furthermore, most of our work done depends on how well we can network with others and how well we can get the work done from others. In professional as well as personal life, the people who cannot gel well with others often lag behind.

SKILL AND COMPETENCY

In some ways, a skill and a competency are similar. In fact, they are often used interchangeably. They both identify an ability that an individual has acquired through training and experience. However, though related, these terms are not identical. They differ in terms of their definitions or the functions, related to performance and outcomes.

Think of skills as one of three facets that make up a competency: the other two are knowledge and abilities. To succeed on the job, employees need to demonstrate the right mix of skills, knowledge and on-the-job ability.

Merely acquiring skills does not give us the 'how' of its use. How does an individual perform a job successfully? How does she behaves in the workplace environment to achieve the desired results? Competencies provide that missing piece of the puzzle by translating skills into on-the-job behaviours that demonstrate the ability to perform the job requirements competently.

Skill provides the base and can be translated into competency through application and consistent practice. There it is skill in 'action'. Therefore, it can be said that the ability to use an acquired skill in an efficient and effective manner is competency. For example, a person may learn driving skills from a driving school but the efficiency with which she negotiates her vehicle through the chaotic traffic of any big city in India, observing all safety and traffic rules, and reaches the destination will determine whether the skill has been transformed into a competency.

Therefore, we can discern three key ingredients for making a distinction between skill and competency: action, effective or efficient use of the skill and the desired or expected outcome in terms of performance.

Using the Manual

In view of the acknowledged significance of life competencies in our personal and professional life, it is expected that the Manual will be used in a variety of settings for diverse group of participants. Some of the groups may be as follows:

- Those working in the corporate or social development sectors
- Young entrepreneurs
- Job aspirants looking for training opportunities to enhance their employment potential by developing their social skills
- Young women and men looking for career-promoting and growth-oriented training opportunities
- Young girls and boys receiving technical or vocational training at different technical institutes under the skill development programme of the Government of India (life competencies should be regarded as complementary to vocational or technical skills)
- Incidentally, the Manual can also be used for self-training by all those who may not have access to formal training opportunities

It is, therefore, important that the trainers should contextualise the contents of the training programme to ensure that it is fully in sync with the background of the participants, their specific characteristics and needs.

The need for this Manual arose because most of the modules are of psychosocial nature and it is likely that all the trainers who are given the responsibility of delivering this programme may not have uniformly similar base of knowledge and expertise in the areas covered by the modules. This Manual will, to a large extent, ensure that the training across the country is standardised. Of course, there will be some variations due to the personal and the training styles of the trainers and the manner in which they use the material.

GENERAL GUIDELINES FOR THE TRAINERS

- Training in life skills is unique in many ways. Besides being intensely participatory and interactive, it has to be participant-centric as well.

In all sessions, the participants have to be constantly engaged in honest and sincere self-reflection and self-appraisal and helped to remain in regular contact with their thought processes, behaviour patterns and value orientation. They should also be encouraged to develop a path for self-improvement and self-growth. Only then, the training will be more consequential and valuable to them.

- On their part, the trainers have to be watchful of the responsiveness of the participants to the stimuli sent to them during the sessions, especially if they come from different socio-economic background. In such cases, the session will require very careful handling.
- While there are some common social and cultural features that transcend the boundaries of the states in our country, there may be some distinguishing facets that set each group apart from others. As this Manual will be used across the country, it is important that when discussing concepts, theories and premises, the trainers should tune the discussion to the local ethos.
- While the trainer's notes provide you with comprehensive material on all aspects of the topics covered under different modules, you may supplement it by drawing from your own experiences and areas of expertise. The important point is that all relevant sub-topics should be discussed during the sessions, ensuring that the training remains purposeful and relevant to the participants.
- You should use a variety of training aids and tools—transparencies, flip charts, power point illustrations, white board, etc.—for your presentation and inputs. You may also decide to prepare some handouts for the participants drawing from the material provided under the trainer's notes. They could use these handouts as post-training reference material or the 'takeaways' from the training.

SPECIAL FEATURES OF THE MANUAL

Modular Approach

- Though the nine modules are designed to provide an integrated, comprehensive programme in life skills training, each module can also be used as stand-alone one and delivered independent of the others. The user agencies, therefore, have the option of selecting any number of modules to develop a training programme package that is appropriate to the needs of their target groups. Though the modules have been numbered, the user organisations or the training team can follow its own sequential order.

Ready-to-use Format

- As indicated earlier, the Manual is designed in a ready-to-use format, inclusive in all aspects. It has trainer's notes for the facilitators and other users and training exercises for effective delivery of the modules. For greater focus, expected outcomes of the module have been specified before each one.
- To facilitate the effective delivery of the training programme, special exercises and instruments have been included in every module, keeping in view the practicable aspects of the sub-topics and issues under discussion. And for the conduct of each exercise, step-by-step process has been suggested. The materials for these exercises include worksheets, special instruments and, in some cases, future planners.

Trainer's Notes on the Modules

- By far, this is the most significant and distinctive section of the module. Trainer's notes are comprehensive and cover wide-ranging sub-topics and issues appropriate to the theme or the topic of the respective module. The objective of providing such exhaustive materials on each module is to enhance the understanding and knowledge base of the facilitators on all aspects of the topic. It is, therefore, imperative that the facilitators should go through the notes thoroughly. This will assist them in preparing for their presentations to the group and inputs during the delivery of the module. The notes are written in a reader-friendly and easy-to-assimilate language and style. In view of the psychosocial nature of the modules, professional words and phrases have been used only where it was absolutely unavoidable. Nevertheless, it is expected that those who are entrusted with the task of rolling out the training programme would have demonstrated their interest in the training of life skills.

- Different life skills cannot be completely compartmentalised. They are in some ways interrelated. Therefore, some overlaps are unavoidable. The user may find that certain concepts, ideas and issues have found reference in more than one module. However, the context in which these issues are discussed and the perspective they project will be different. While in one module, a concept or sub-topic may find brief mention, it is discussed in an elaborate way in another, consistent with the requirements of the overall theme of that module. We also need to be aware that each module is designed to be self-contained and inclusive, to the extent possible.

- It must be mentioned that, barring some specific context, in reference to an *individual* in the text, the pronoun 'she' has been used for both genders. This is to avoid the repeated and awkward use of he or she, him or her, or himself or herself that could have interfered with the flow of reading. Incidentally, this may provide a balance as most of the publications use the pronoun 'he' when referring to both genders.

Special Module on the Delivery of the Training Programme

Under Section B, some key areas crucial for effective delivery of the training programme have been discussed. It is suggested that the trainers should go through this section well before the programme so that they are fully prepared for delivering the training.

Section A
The Modules

Module 1

Self-awareness, Self-confidence and Self-esteem

This module deals with three key areas of self-development: self-awareness, self-confidence and self-esteem. These are not only interrelated areas of the personality of an individual, but these are also constantly interacting with one another to help develop an integrated and well-balanced *persona*. Working in unison, these three areas contribute immensely to defining the uniqueness of a person—her behaviour patterns, actions, relationships, dispositions, etc.

The module aims to widen the understanding of the participants with regard to these three important components and then takes them on a journey of self-discovery, self-analysis and self-appraisal through various training instruments and exercises on to becoming more confident, self-respecting, balanced and responsive persons.

Specifically, the module deals with the following sub-topics or sub-themes:

- Understanding self-awareness
- Need for self-awareness
- Instrument for developing self-awareness—Johari window
- Elements of self-awareness
- Understanding self-confidence
- General traits of a self-confident person
- How confident do you seem to others?
- Ways to improve self-confidence
- Understanding self-esteem
- Low and high self-esteem
- Conditional and unconditional self-esteem
- Characteristics of genuinely low self-esteem
- Improving self-esteem
- Self-confidence and self-esteem

Expected Outcomes from the Module

At the end of the session on the module, the participants will be able to:

- Enhance their conceptual understanding of various aspects of self-awareness, self-confidence and self-esteem
- Develop better insights into their own behaviour patterns, actions, attitudes, values, etc.
- Learn about the approaches and techniques they can adopt to boost their self-confidence and develop a rational and realistic level of self-esteem

SELF-AWARENESS

Understanding Self-awareness

To be happy is to be able to become aware of oneself without fright.

—Walter Benjamin

Self-awareness is one of those terms you hear thrown around a lot in the personal development world.

Who are you really? For most of us, this appears to be a simple question, but the truth is that it is a very complex one. There is an anecdote about Swami Dayanand Saraswati, the founder of the Arya Samaj sect. He was looking for a guru, and somebody directed him to a very prominent saint. He went there and knocked at the door. The saint asked, 'Who is there?' Swamiji thought for a moment about the answer but realised that he did not know himself well enough so how he could identify himself to the saint. He walked away to find the answer.

Self-awareness (sometimes also referred to as self-knowledge or intro-spection) is about getting unbiased insights into your own needs, desires, failings, habits and everything else that makes you tick. The more you know about yourself, the better you are at adapting life changes that suit your needs.

Most of us identify ourselves through our name, position, social or economic status, occupation or other such description or characteristics.

But if we look beyond these peripheral or evident features, we will realise that this is not what we really are. We are a lot more than this. There are several aspects of this puzzle. Many of us are thoroughly convinced that we know ourselves well and there is nothing more to it. If anyone suggests to us that we need to know more about ourselves, we just dismiss the idea as unnecessary or just a design to embarrass us. As a result, we do not make a sincere and earnest effort to know ourselves completely. Some people find it difficult to decipher and segregate key aspects of their *persona* simply because they do not have the ability to do so. They lack clarity about what and who they are, and, as a result, they are not able to fully realise their potential or growth. There is some ambiguity about their perception about themselves. In some cases, family or cultural factors contribute to this vagueness.

From the time you started understanding you and the world around, your parents, teachers, friends and members of the society gave you a lot of inputs, guidance and suggestions, conditioning your views, behaviour and actions of what you should or should not do; how you should or should not behave; what you should or should not be and who you should or should not associate with. If these views and exhortations are accepted and adopted by you without an objective analysis and evaluation, you may never be able to know your real identity and self. Undoubtedly, this will also affect your growth.

There are people who have better understanding of themselves, but they may not be willing to accept a number of facets of their *persona*, especially if these are negative or uncomplimentary to them, or not in harmony with their own perceptions about them. They project only that part that they are comfortable with and which people accept or appreciate. However, the problem begins when these people start believing in what they are showcasing as their true self and lose contact with other parts that they have been hiding from others. They are not prepared to see through their self-created camouflage or barriers.

For many of us, knowing ourselves can be a painful and complicated exercise. We are sometimes unwilling to dig deeper into us because we are somewhat apprehensive of what lies below the exterior that we know. There may even be fear of these hitherto unknown aspects of us. This view is highlighted in the aforementioned quote of Walter Benjamin. You have to become aware of you, overcoming fears, inhibitions or a sense of embar-rassment about who you *really* are. If there are grey areas that you feel may project a negative image of you, you need not feel guilty, but instead resolve to take necessary steps to come out of them.

So how do you identify who you really are? First, you must submit yourself to an honest scrutiny by reflecting and analysing different aspects of you. And to make this effort useful and helpful, you must do it as a complete individual, free from the confines and the opinions of others. This may mean that, sometimes, you need to be with your own self, detaching yourself from family and friends or removing yourself from the social life that you have established and are comfortable with. Take an independent view of you, and for some time do not let yourself be influenced by others as this may distort your own analysis and assessment. As mentioned earlier, you have been influenced, in one way or another, all your life, but now is the time to break this cycle. Of course, you will require considerable courage and determination, as well as purposefulness, to go through this process. However, you must remember that such an analysis has to take into consideration all the dimensions of your *persona*, including interaction with others, behavioural patterns, etc.

You need to discover yourself intimately and this will involve uncovering aspects of the inner you—layer by layer or part by part—and then building on these and getting an integrated and inclusive portrait of you. You may also be able to discern a relationship or similarities between different aspects of your *persona*. This will provide more harmony to your *self*.

The following set of questions may help you unravel some parts of you. It is, however, important that you answer these questions in a sincere and honest manner. The more you can answer honestly, the better chance you have to find out who you truly are. In preparing your response, you must be fully aware of your feelings, thought processes and other internal inhibitions. Talk to yourself intimately.

- What are your strong likes and dislikes?
- Do you feel responsible for your actions and behaviour or blame others for them?
- What motivates you and what are the demotivating factors that influence you?
- What are your desires, dreams or ambitions?
- What are your major strengths and weaknesses?
- What are your distinguishing abilities and competencies?
- How do you define success and happiness in your own context?

- Do you like working alone or as a team player?
- What are the bases for establishing close, personal relationships?
- Are you organised in your day-to-day activities and chores?
- Are you truthful, honest and trustworthy?
- Are you conniving, controlling or manipulative?
- What are your greatest fears and why?
- What makes you feel guilty and why?
- Do you feel angry or bitter—at you, at others, at society and why?
- Do you rely on others for guidance?

(Keeping in view your special situation, you may add more questions.)

Of course, going through this exercise can be a very challenging task, but it is also well worth your effort, because the rewards are unmatched by anything that you presently know or have experienced. There may be some areas that you may not like. You will have to come out of your 'comfort zone'. Once you are prepared to accept yourself completely, you will know what and who you really are. You will start living in truth, away from the facade that either you have created for yourself or people around have been instrumental for it. The fear factor or embarrassment will dissipate. You will then be expected to take some hard decisions to move forward and invoke your inner power to bring about desired changes in your *persona* leading you to the path of self-growth and success.

If we are aware of our authentic *self*, we feel the power of life flowing through us, we perceive the world differently and life becomes happier and more challenging. Awareness empowers you to see yourself and the world as they really are, without mental barriers, prejudices and judgements.

With awareness, you know where the boundaries lay between you and others, which emotions are yours and which belong to someone else, who is responsible for which problems and what you want versus what someone else wants for you. With awareness, you know what your truth is and what is not and whether the beliefs you have been carrying are based on your own search and analysis or on the conditioning and programming you have been raised with. Remember, borrowed beliefs and values will not take you far.

Awareness allows you to see the bigger picture, to let go of what is not you, to change what is not supporting you anymore and to create and manifest what you truly want to be in your life. Ask yourself this question: Are you ready to open your inner eyes and be more aware? If the answer is affirmative, go ahead and make a sincere effort for it.

However, knowing yourself completely is difficult, and it is impossible to remove every cognitive and affective bias that you have. But just because we suck at it does not mean we should not try. You cannot solve every problem in your life, but you can make some headway on minor changes. Once you start the journey, you will find the path to move from small changes to more profound ones.

Relationships are easy and uncomplicated until there is emotional turmoil. This is true about the work situation as well as your personal life. However, you will be in a better position to handle this somewhat unpleasant situation if you are fully aware of your behaviour patterns, values, predilections, etc. Having a clear comprehension of your thought processes and behaviour patterns helps you understand others as well. This ability to empathise facilitates better personal and professional relationships. A modification in the interpretation of a relationship will bring about change in its emotional quality. This opens up entirely new possibilities in your life.

To summarise, 'self-awareness' is having a clear perception of your personality—strengths and weaknesses; needs and desires; thoughts, beliefs and habits; motivation; and emotions and feelings. It allows you to understand other people, how they perceive you, your attitude and your responses to them in the moment. In essence, it means paying attention to:

- Your thoughts and thought processes
- What you speak and how you do it
- Your behaviour patterns and the reasons thereof
- Emotions and feelings, and what triggers them; what you do to manage them; how you express them
- General pattern of your responses
- How you make decisions; what the general process involved in your decision-making is
- Whether you carry a hidden agenda, and if so, what that is
- The patterns you see in your life
- Your body responses to various stimuli, positive and negative

Need for Self-awareness

As you develop self-awareness, you are able to make changes in the thoughts and interpretations you make in your mind. This will also have an impact on your emotions in a positive manner. Self-awareness is one of the attributes of emotional intelligence and an important factor in achieving success. The more you know about yourself, the better you are at adapting life changes that suit your needs and are in harmony with your life objectives.

As mentioned earlier, self-awareness is the key to self-improvement and personal growth. It is the first step in creating what you want and in mastering your life. Until you are aware in the moment of your thoughts, emotions, words and behaviour, you will have difficulty setting the direction of your life. It also allows you to take better control of your life, helping you to set realistic goals in life, carve out a path for their achievement and cope with difficult situations and circumstances in a more constructive manner.

Of course, self-awareness is a big part of both therapy and philosophy. It is also the basis of the quantified self-movement, which assumes that if you collect data about yourself, you can make improvements based on that data.

Self-awareness plays an important role in your communication with the outside world. As you communicate with others, it is important to be aware of who you are—your motivations, emotions, beliefs, faith, culture and inner thoughts. You frame messages and interpret them through the filters or noises that are your thoughts and your being.

Self-awareness is important because when we have a better understanding of ourselves, we are able to experience ourselves as unique and separate individuals. We are then empowered to make changes and to build on our areas of strength and also identify areas where we would like to make improvements.

Self-awareness also helps us in developing sound and healthy relationships, based on trust, mutuality of action and behaviour, and goodwill.

It lies at the root of strong character, giving us the ability to lead with a sense of purpose, authenticity, openness and trust. It explains our successes and our failures. And by giving us a better understanding of who we are, self-awareness lets us better understand what we need most from other people, to complement our own deficiencies in leadership and in other facets of life.

Essentially, the more you pay attention to your emotions and how you work, the better you will understand why you do the things you do. The more you know about your own habits, easier it is to improve on those habits. In most cases, this takes a little experimentation.

Instrument for Developing Self-awareness— Johari Window

Open Area or Known to Self and Others

This is an area of maximum psychic energy. It represents those things that are known to you and also to others—relatives, friends, colleagues, etc.—with whom you have regular interaction. This arena constitutes of those facets, traits, and bits and pieces about you and your life that you have shared with others and they have access to. It is all about how open you are about yourself. It is, however, important to remember that you do not reveal all about you to everyone. You are selective—both in terms of individuals and what you want to share and with whom. For instance, you may be more open with your colleagues or friends on certain matters but not with your family members or vice versa. The size of this quadrant varies with individuals, depending on the extent of your sharing and the feedback received from others.

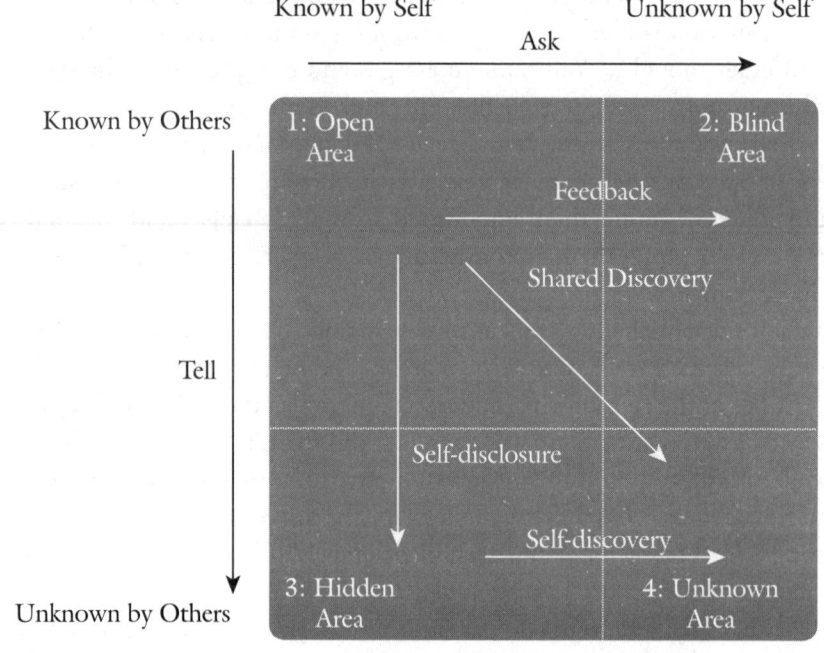

It is common knowledge that some people are more disposed to divulging a lot about themselves. They have less inhibition in talking about themselves. On the other hand, there are others who are more restrained and not too forthcoming in sharing their thoughts, actions, behaviour and emotions with others. The smaller the quadrant, the poorer is your communication with people around you. This is a reflection on your openness and transparency, affecting your relationships and social interactions.

Blind Area or Unknown by Self

This area represents all those things about ourselves that others know but we are either ignorant about them or are unsure. We often indulge in actions and behaviour in a subconscious way, and we are not even aware of these but others are able to see them and perceive them. The spectrum can be wide—stretching from simple things such as bad breath, nervous habits, unpleasant voice to more intense or significant actions and behaviour. Many a time, the extent to which we are insensitive to much of our behaviour and what it communicates to others can be quite surprising and sometimes even disconcerting to us. Some of us are even unaware of a number of our good qualities. Our goal, therefore, is to reduce this arena by creating an environment in which others are encouraged to give feedback to us.

(Cross-reference: for details, see the sub-section on 'Feedback').

Hidden Area or Unknown by Others

This area contains those elements of your *self* that you are familiar with but that are not known to others. They constitute part of your private domain. And you may justify it by convincing yourself that you are entitled to have your own 'private area'. You may either feel that these things need not be shared with others or make a conscious effort to hide them from their prying eyes. This is why this quadrant is called 'hidden or private self'. In this context, the following questions become relevant:

- Are these things occupying an area (in my *self*) that leaves very little for people to know about me?
- What is the nature of things that I am trying to hide or keep away from others?
- Is it worth hiding these things from others?
- Is this detrimental to my relationships with people and to what extent it is affecting my meaningful communication with them?
- Is this an impediment in my self-growth and self-improvement?

You should realise that people will not appreciate you if they do not know and understand you well enough. You can enhance their knowledge about you only if you provide them with accurate and factual information about you. If you do not share this information, they will form opinion and views about you on the basis of their own perceptions and there is a possibility that these may not truly reflect what you really are. Therefore, even for your own sake, self-revelation is important.

(Cross-reference: for more details, see the sub-section on 'Self-disclosure').

Unknown Area—Unknown by Self and Others

This area contains things that neither you nor those who are close to you know about you. Some of this material may be so far below the surface that you may never be able to access it or become aware of it. In Freudian terms, this may refer to the 'unconscious'. However, some part of this material may represent such things as intrapersonal dynamics, early childhood memories, latent potentialities and unrecognised resources.

Elements of Self-awareness

Sincere and Honest Self-assessment

Self-assessment, self-providing feedback to the *self*, helps to counter the negative effects of criticism, often a result of feedback. A self-assessment is the most productive form of assessment, where ratings on skills and qualities by others are better regarded as feedback. This feedback should be considered as inputs, information and data about you and help you in the rather difficult task of self-assessment. The act of self-assessing supports responsibility where it is needed most for effective action and improvement of performance.

Receiving Objective and Constructive Feedback

Feedback is a very important tool for enhancing your understanding and knowledge about you. An honest appraisal, appropriately delivered, helps you in the journey of self-discovery. It provides you with a window for getting an unbiased view of how others understand you as a person and how they perceive your interactive behaviour with the outside world—people, office colleagues, situations, problems, etc. This assumes considerable significance for an individual as it is not always possible for her to step out of her own self and get an objective and unimpassioned portrayal of her attributes, strengths and weaknesses, capabilities, actions and behaviour patterns. Others may be in a better position to provide you access to those areas of self that you have not fathomed earlier. They help you encounter those dimensions of your actions and behaviour that you were not able to experience or feel. This may trigger the process of more intensive self-investigation. Thus, you will be able to reduce your blind arena in the Johari window.

There is a general notion that feedback is often unfavourable, hurtful or even hostile. It is not so. An honest and objective feedback can help you become more aware of your strengths and indicate what you are capable of achieving. It helps you get in contact with realities of life, your immediate social environment and the outside world. In the process, you may get an affirmation of your self-image or an opportunity for a more analytical self-appraisal. This will persuade you to take necessary corrective steps for self-improvement and self-growth. However, a lot depends on the intentions of the person providing that feedback.

Perhaps, the most important factor that promotes the process of getting feedback from others is your willingness, your approach and your demeanour. The message you send to others determines, to a great extent, the nature, sincerity and objectivity of the feedback. You must create conditions that encourage others to tell you about yourself. However, many of us, wittingly or unwittingly, interact with others in a manner that dissuades them from giving objective appraisal of ourselves, their perspective and how they interpret or perceive our actions and behaviour. They may not communicate what they want to but, instead, tell you what you 'want to hear'. So watch out and cultivate a desire in you to solicit feedback from others. You must convey the message that you are open-minded and willing to receive feedback, regardless whether it is appreciative or depreciative. They must feel assured that you value their comments. This will stimulate them to be open and forthright.

In order to get a favourable appraisal, many of us are tempted to listen only to the views of those who, we believe, are inclined to give us the feedback we want. This negates the very purpose of the exercise. The problem is that you want to convince yourself that this is the authentic assessment of your actions and behaviour, and you want to go on with your life accordingly.

You may even persuade yourself to ignore the feedback that you find unpleasant and upsetting. This outlook will adversely affect your self-growth and keep you in a self-exalting mode. It is, therefore, important from whom you get the feedback and what you *wish* to believe or what you do not want to. It is, however, necessary to point out here that it is not incumbent upon you to accept all the feedback that you receive from others. You should undertake your own analysis of what people tell you about yourself and come to your own conclusions. But be sure that you take an unbiased view and remain open-minded and honest to yourself. Going through this process of deciphering the comments and views of others about you will also help in honing your self-appraising skills.

A key prerequisite for an authentic and objective feedback is the nature of relationship you are able to establish and nurture with most of the people with whom you have regular interaction. If this bonding is based on trust, mutuality of interests and reciprocity, the environment is conducive to genuine and reliable feedback. If the relationship has elements of trust deficit, doubts and suspicions, the process of giving and receiving feedback can become vitiated. Therefore, you must understand that the responsibility for generating favourable and helpful conditions for this transaction rests with you.

Do not prejudge the motive or intention of the other person who is giving you feedback that you find unpleasant and disconcerting. We tend to regard negative feedback as criticism and are thus inclined to dismiss such evaluative comments. Sometimes, we can be even very reactive and aggressive. We want to believe that this person has some ulterior design in disparaging us and tell ourselves that, perhaps, she wants to upstage us by showing us in bad light. Such frame of mind is unhelpful in self-analysis and self-growth. If you find the feedback unpalatable or are unsure, it is desirable to check with the person again just to confirm and where necessary, get clarification and elaboration. You will thus make the transaction more constructive.

Remember that in giving feedback that is not positive and could even be hurtful to you, the other person is taking certain risks. The relationship with you as also her image and reputation, in fact, the whole *persona* can be on the block. You must appreciate her courage and the spirit behind this. You must also realise that before giving shape to her feedback, she would have gone through a lot of reflection and contemplation, analysing your actions and behaviour. This could be a complex task. This is also indicative of her concern for you and a willingness to extend support and help in your growth and development. A word of gratitude will, therefore, be necessary from you. This will reinforce the process of receiving and giving feedback. This can strengthen emotional bond and relationship between you and the other person.

Essentially, feedback relates to past events. It is a key to learning and performance improvement. In many cases, feedback is not just about the action, behaviour or the results. It may be about the process itself that led to those actions or results. However, the focus should be on accuracy and providing a detailed description of results. We learn as much from actions taken that produce wrong results as we learn from those producing right outcomes.

Feedback can be in the form of personalised criticism or there can be judgemental comments by people who are closely associated with you, your actions and behaviour. This feedback is generally unsolicited by you. In most cases, this feedback can be situational, related to a particular event, episode or action. These critical remarks or observations do not provide you with the larger picture that will benefit you to become more aware of yourself and take positive action to apply course correction to your larger picture of actions behaviour, values, etc. You have to aggregate it to get the larger picture. Feedback can be immensely useful when you request it from those who are fully familiar with you, your actions and behaviour, and are willing to provide you with their frank views and opinions. These people can be your family members, your friends or work colleagues. This feedback is detailed and descriptive, not value laden or judgemental. This is an interactive feedback where you will also have an opportunity to seek clarifications and ask for elucidation. The value of this feedback will be enhanced when it takes place in a stress-free environment and the person giving the feedback and you are fully involved in the process.

Receiving Constructive Feedback—Some Guidelines

Do you find accepting constructive criticism difficult? No one likes to be made to feel inferior by an authority, a public figure or even a close friend. But constructive advice is intended to help a situation, not damage a working or professional relationship. If you find yourself in the position of accepting constructive criticism, the following are some guidelines for making the best use of someone's good intentions in providing you constructive and objective feedback:

Take the initiative: You do not have to wait for others to take the initiative in giving you constructive criticism. You can ask those whose opinions, views and expertise you trust for advice or suggestions to bring about necessary changes in your actions, behaviour, values or attitudes to improve your work performance, interpersonal relationships and general interaction with people. This feedback may help you avoid making same mistakes again. Let others know if you need help or are struggling before problems become apparent. Most people are more than willing to provide assistance or answer questions to help you do a better job. Ask someone you trust for a performance review at work or for an honest opinion in a friendship or interpersonal relationship. Then be willing to act on that information, if applicable.

Listen respectfully—be open: When a person is trying to tell you something negative, it is easy to get upset and focus only on the critical aspects of the discussion. You might be tempted to jump into the core of the conversation and deal with the negative points rather than wait to hear what the other person truly intended. It is best to hear her out, asking only brief questions for clarity, if needed. Give the person a chance to fully explain any concerns that are being described. Maintain a positive attitude with facial expression and body language. Try not to tune out the points you disagree with while staying focused on the entire message. Make a mental note of the point and plan to address it when it is your turn to speak. The person who is speaking to you will appreciate your willingness to get the whole story before responding too quickly.

Being open to constructive feedback is the single most important part of receiving it. Being open allows others to want to give it to us and allows them to feel more comfortable doing it. But it is not just to be open to feedback; you must follow it up with other key points.

Accepting the advice of others is the hallmark of an open mind and cooperative spirit. Accepting constructive criticism can make you a more effective friend, spouse or colleague at workplace.

Be sure you understand; seek clarification if needed: In accepting constructive criticism, you will need to understand fully what has been shared with you. You do not have to accept blame or responsibility for something that does not make sense or that is not clear. After hearing what the other person has to say, take time to ask questions or make comments to confirm your understanding of the situation being explained to you. This will give a message to her that you are interested in the feedback.

Acknowledge the speaker's point of view; do not argue or go into defence mode: As you listen, you may begin to disagree inwardly and eagerly await your chance to respond. Be careful that you do not get into a defensive mode and should be willing to own responsibility for your actions and behaviour. Just try to put yourself in the speaker's shoes. This cannot be easy for her. She may feel uncomfortable about confronting you with something that is potentially negative, or she may be counting on your intelligence and understanding to accept the situation for what it is, a reasonable approach to solving a problem. You would not respect this person if she hid her real feelings or allowed a more serious problem to develop into a failure.

It helps to realise that you have a valuable opportunity to learn from a negative outcome and become a better employee, partner, friend or family member. While you may indeed have useful information that will enlighten the speaker or at least explain your actions, do not share those facts in a self-righteous way. Instead, try to maintain a humble but positive outlook that will make it easy for others to communicate with you.

When discussing setbacks or limitations in a person's actions, the potential for escalating tensions is created. When we feel overly criticised or misunderstood, it becomes natural to bring up past issues or current problems that might otherwise have been overlooked. This is not the time to put all cards on the table, though. It is better to focus on the issue at hand and reserve any exchange of concerns for a later time, unless they are related to the current issue.

Of course, accepting constructive criticism does not mean that you should let yourself be belittled or harangued. Remember that a person who is willing to give you constructive feedback will not do these things. Look for the positive aspects of the feedback without trying to take the situation to the next level, or even conflict; avoid slipping into a tit-for-tat mentality.

All of us want to be accepted and appreciated for who we are. We are embarrassed and sometimes feel guilty or ashamed when others notice our problem behaviour or a mistake we have made. That is why it is, sometimes, difficult to come across as one who can accept constructive criticism. But being open to learning and growing is a desirable characteristic in any job position or relationship. Do not feel that you have to 'protect your turf' and go into defensive mode just for the sake of appearing right, or even perfect.

Just plain and simple: Do not argue! If you hear something and immediately disagree, do not voice it. It immediately makes the situation uncomfortable and creates a defence-attack scenario that is notoriously challenging. Try to just listen to what is being said. Try to believe as if the words are true without discounting them, immediately. If we do not take this personally, it is a lot easier.

Not arguing is a good practice, especially if we have asked for the feedback. Just imagine how frustrating it is for someone who put time and effort into coming up with feedback (because it was being solicited), for our benefit, only to have it shot down and disagreed with. Remember, we are trying to create an atmosphere to have an open, fluid communication regarding areas where we can improve. Would arguing with the person delivering it be conducive to future acts of delivering feedback?

Hearing anything bad (i.e., anything that does not tell us how wonderful and perfect and glorious we are) can be very uncomfortable. Who wants to hear that we suck at this and cannot do that properly or as well as others? Really, no one! But this type of feedback is incredibly helpful and allows us to use it constructively.

Consider the big picture: Any feedback cannot be taken as the gospel truth. What you get from one person is one angle. Just as much as we cannot possibly know every angle of our own self with complete accuracy, neither can another person. What may be true in one set of circumstances may not be true in another. What may be seen by one observer may not be seen by another. In fact, we really have no idea whether the feedback we are receiving is accurate or not. Therefore, you should realise that this feedback is information that is to be integrated into a larger picture. It should be received, digested, processed and integrated with existing knowledge and be used as the receiver desires.

Consider other experiences of formal or informal feedback you have received from others at different times and on different situations. Have you been given similar feedback before? Does it fit into a pattern? Is it time to change? What is your own honest assessment about you? Construct a comprehensive picture, covering all aspects of your *persona*.

Follow-up with positive action: After accepting critical comments graciously, accept the responsibility for making changes that will help matters improve. Some people will pretend to accept criticism, but then fail to make the necessary adjustments. Following up with suitable action will show others that you know how to accept criticism and can actually put it to good use, which enhances your professional image and potentially improve personal relationships. You might even want to keep a written record of any changes that you bring about to ensure that if the situation is revisited, later, you have documentation that demonstrates your willingness to follow helpful feedback.

Receiving feedback openly and using it constructively is a skill that we need to practise. That could mean putting ourselves in situations that require us to feel uncomfortable and to solicit feedback often (from multiple sources). We also need to practise our communication skills so we can ask good clarifying questions about the feedback in a way that is not argumentative, but rather is open and demonstrates our receptiveness. We need to practise not letting it all be personalised too much. We need to practise seeing the big picture.

Self-disclosure

Self-disclosure is a process of communication by which one person reveals information about herself to another. The information can be descriptive or evaluative and can include thoughts, feelings, aspirations, goals, failures, successes, fears and dreams, as well as one's likes, dislikes and favourites.[1]

Social penetration theory posits that there are two dimensions to self-disclosure: breadth and depth. Both are crucial in developing a fully intimate relationship. The range of topics discussed by two individuals is the breadth of disclosure. The degree to which the information revealed is private or personal is the depth of that disclosure. It is easier for breadth to be expanded first in a relationship because of its more accessible features; it consists of outer layers of personality and everyday lives such as occupations and preferences. Depth is more difficult to reach and includes painful memories and more unusual traits that we might hesitate to share with others. We reveal ourselves most thoroughly and discuss the widest range of topics with our spouses and loved ones.[2]

Self-disclosure is an important building block for intimacy and for establishing closer bond. We expect reciprocal and appropriate self-disclosure. Self-disclosure can be assessed by an analysis of cost and rewards, which

---

[1] https://en.wikipedia.org/wiki/Occupational_stress
[2] See note 1.

can be further explained by social exchange theory. Most self-disclosure occurs early in relational development, but more intimate self-disclosure occurs later.

Self-disclosure is an interpersonal process that has much to do with the receiver of the disclosure.

Self-disclosure Guidelines

- Disclose information that you want others to disclose to you
- Disclose information appropriate to the nature of relationship
- Disclose intimate information only when it represents an acceptable task
- Be sensitive to the other person's ability to absorb your disclosure
- Reserve intimate or very personal disclosures for ongoing relationships
- Continue intimate self-disclosure only when it is reciprocated

---

Reasons for Self-disclosure

Interestingly, recent research suggests that the pervasiveness of reality television, much of which includes participants who are very willing to disclose personal information, has led to a general trend among reality television viewers to engage in self-disclosure through other mediated means such as blogging and other social media.

When you share some information about you with others, there is an underlying assumption that the other person is interested either in you or in the information you are giving. The reasons may be the following:

Establish one's individual identity: You may share some basic information about you and your background just to establish your individual identity before those who matter to you or even with strangers.

Seek help or support in managing a problem: If you are faced with a difficult situation or a problem that you are unable to deal or cope with, you may seek assistance of someone who may be better placed, in terms of experience and competencies, to offer you guidance and help in working out an approach for more effective handling of the problem or the situation.

Communicate your views on issues of common importance: You may just want to share your thoughts or opinions on any issue or topic either in a one-on-one transaction or in a group. In a group situation, you may be driven by a desire to establish your credentials or position as a knowledgeable and competent person by presenting your views or opinion on the subject/issue or you may simply want to contribute to the discussion in the group as its member.

Self-disclosure as a response: Sometimes self-disclosure is unplanned. Self-disclosure can stimulate self-disclosure. If someone asks you a direct question or disclose personal information, you may be prompted to reciprocate and share your views or talk about your problems, feelings and emotions as a response to what the other person is telling you. For example, if a person comes to you and shares with you her situation, and difficulties, it is likely that as part of your empathetic response, you may also talk about similar situations that you had confronted in life hoping that this will, to some extent, alleviate her woes and soothe her nerves. Thus, self-disclosure can become reciprocal. In these instances, you may not manage your privacy well because you did not have time to think through any potential risks. The dynamics of fear (in the context of sharing) can be exchanged for the dynamics of trust and similarity of situation that makes you compatible.

Just to take it off your chest: Sometimes, people want to share their problems, feelings and emotions because they believe that sharing itself, with someone in whom you have trust and who is emotionally in harmony with you, will provide you some relief and succour and enhance your comfort level even though the person may not be in a position to extend any substantive support or help. Thus, self-disclosure may be driven by having a sense of relief or catharsis, clarifying or correcting information or seeking support.

Maintain trust and intimacy: Interpersonal reasons for disclosure involve desires to maintain a trusting and intimate relationship. Psychologists have long known that self-disclosure is one of the hallmarks of intimate relationships. Revealing your motives, intentions, goals, values and emotions can increase liking and feelings of intimacy.

Factors That Facilitate Self-disclosure

Bonding with people: Perhaps the most important factor that helps in self-disclosure and sharing of information about oneself is the relation-ship one enjoys with others. Evidently, this bonding is based on trust and confidence in each other. It is reciprocal and becomes more sustainable if the two persons involved have equal stakes in nurturing and strengthening it. The degree of trust that characterises the relationship will determine the nature and content of self-disclosure. If it is high, it provides the necessary stimulus and persuasion to a person to be open and frank in revealing her innermost feelings and emotions and not limit herself to sharing at the cognitive level. It unshackles one's inhibitions and innermost layer of self are unravelled. It will also help a person foretell precisely the response she is likely to get from the other person on her self-disclosure. Self-disclosure contributes to further strengthening the bonds because it reinforces mutual trust and assurance. It induces supportive behaviour.

Your communication skills: This is another key factor facilitating self-disclosure. It is important that people should be able to comprehend you fully and in the way you want them to receive your communication. If you do not possess the requisite communication skills, the message going out to others may be distorted and they may not be able to get the meaning and substance of what you are trying to convey. This will defeat the purpose of sharing. Therefore, you may be restrained.

Societal norms: It is seen that in some cultures, self-revelation is the usual norm and considered an important part of social transaction. Openness is encouraged. People grow up with this attitude. As a result, they have less inhibition in sharing their innermost thoughts and feelings. In India, of course, we are reluctant to share all information about ourselves, especially in areas such as emotions, feelings and values.

Lack of concern for rejection: As mentioned earlier, the extent of the fear of rejection from people forbids you from sharing and being open. You are concerned whether your revelations will be consistent with their expec-tations from you and their norms. There are individuals whose need for approval is overwhelming and they judge every act or behaviour accordingly.

On the other hand, there are people who are not overly concerned about the reaction of others and they are willing to share a lot about them even at the cost of rejection. Their desire for self-revelation overrides the fear of disapproval of others.

Reasons for Not Sharing Information

There are a number of reasons—some exaggerated and some real—why an individual will not open up and reveal about herself in a more forthright manner. These blocks to self-revelation will create a situation where you do not feel comfortable sharing about you. Some of these are indicated as follows:

Not of value to the other person: You believe that the information or the content of your disclosure may not be of any interest or value to the other person and, at best, she may be an uninterested listener. So why bother to share it.

Do not expect to be helped: You may not want to share your problems or difficult situations with others because you feel the other person is not in a position to help you out. This is either based on your earlier experience with the person or on your assessment of her capabilities in the context of your situation or problem and possible response from her. It is also possible that you consider the person unhelpful.

Fears, doubts and concern: There is an apprehension that the other person may use the information provided by you against you or to harm you. This is the reason why, sometimes, you share a lot more information about yourself with a stranger than with an acquaintance with whom you interact on a regular basis. You convince yourself that you will never meet the stranger again. Therefore, the threat component is not there.

Sometimes, you may feel that the other person is not trustworthy and will not protect the disclosed information, especially if it relates to feelings and emotions. There is a fear that she may share it with those who may not be favourably disposed towards you. In turn, they may use the information to harm you. For instance, you may not reveal a relationship with the opposite sex to those whom you do not trust.

You may be cautious or even have doubts and fears about sharing information with others if you believe that it may present you in a bad light, tarnish your image or hurt your interests. You might have projected a positive image of yours to the other person and you feel that sharing of this information will adversely affect that image. You are not sure of the reactions of others. As mentioned earlier, you may also have the fear of rejection from the other person if your revelations are not consistent with her norms, standards or expectations. Here, it is important to understand that we are careful about our image or fear rejection only for those who are part of our social circle or they have some value in our life. Young men and women who are in a relationship may not reveal everything about them for fear of losing the relationship.

You may even visualise others laughing at you or whispering about you.

There is also the fear of punishment. This environment of threat and uncertainties is a dampener to self-disclosure. This is particularly true of the adolescents who may not reveal everything about events in the school or friends, as they may fear reprimand from the parents.

Process of Self-disclosure

There are many decisions that go into the process of self-disclosure. We have many types of information we can disclose, but we have to determine whether or not we proceed with disclosure by considering the situation and the potential risks. First we must decide about the person to whom we should disclose than other crucial questions such as when, where and how much. Since all these decisions will affect our relationships, we should examine each one of them.

We usually begin disclosure with observations and thoughts, and then move onto feelings and needs as the relationship progresses. There are some exceptions to this. For example, we are more likely to share with others if we are going through a crisis situation. Although we do not often find ourselves in crisis situations, we may recall scenes from movies or television that show how people trapped in an elevator or stranded after a plane crash reveal their deepest feelings and desires. Interestingly, recent research has affirmed that the pervasiveness of reality television, much of which includes participants who are very willing to disclose personal information, has led to a general trend among reality television viewers to engage in self-disclosure through other mediated means such as blogging and other social media.

As indicated earlier, we may also disclose more than usual with a stranger if we think we will not meet the person again. Probably, we have all been in a situation where we said more about ourselves to a stranger than we normally would.

Once you have decided when and where to disclose information to another person, you need to figure out the best channel to use. Face-to-face disclosures may be considered more genuine or intimate given the shared physical proximity and possibility to engage in verbal as well as non-verbal communication. There is also an opportunity for immediate verbal and non-verbal feedback such as asking follow-up questions or demonstrating support or encouragement through a hug or a touch. The immediacy of a face-to-face encounter also means you have to deal with the uncertainty of the reaction you will get. If the person reacts negatively, you may feel uncomfortable or even fearful. However, you may be pressured to stay on. If you choose a mediated channel such as an e-mail or a letter, text, note or phone call, you may seem less genuine or personal, but you have more control over the situation in that you can take time to carefully choose your words, and you do not have to immediately face the reaction of the other person. This can be beneficial if you fear a negative or potentially aggressive reaction. Another disadvantage of choosing a mediated channel, however, is the loss of non-verbal communication that can add much context to a conversation.

There is considerable evidence that leaders who disclose their authentic selves to those working with them can build not only trust but generate greater cooperation and teamwork as well. Therefore, it is important that leaders should work towards developing the competency related to successful and strategic self-disclosure to team members and others working with them. However, they need to be cautious about it as used improperly, or in the wrong environment, self-disclosure can backfire.

Skilled leaders disclose information in ways that are authentic in that they can reveal relevant information about their thinking process, creating a shared mental model that facilitates communication and improves task performance. Perhaps, most importantly, skilful self-disclosure can humanise the leaders, connecting them with team members that increases feelings of trust and intimacy, and in an organisational context, a readiness to work together collaboratively to reach mutual task goals.

Of course, people have to walk a fine line when it comes to self-disclosure. Skilful self-disclosers choose the substance and process of their revelations, including the depth, breadth and timing of disclosure, with the goal of furthering the collective task rather than their personal agendas.

Too much disclosure might be met with revulsion, while, on the other hand, too little disclosure may result in your team members having feelings of uncertainty and suspicion, leading to trust deficit.

Generally speaking, some people are naturally more transparent and willing to self-disclose, while others are more opaque and hesitant to reveal personal information.

The process of self-disclosure involves many decisions, including what, when, where and how to disclose. All these decisions may vary by context, as we follow different patterns of self-disclosure in academic, professional, personal and civic contexts.

Whether it is online or face-to-face, there are other reasons for disclosing or not, including self-focused, other-focused, interpersonal and situational reasons.

Four Layers of Self-disclosure

There is a heap of information, data and facts about self that could be of interest to others or that is open for sharing with different persons with whom you interact. For ease of our discussion and understanding, we can segregate this mass of information into four layers or tiers as shown in the following figure:

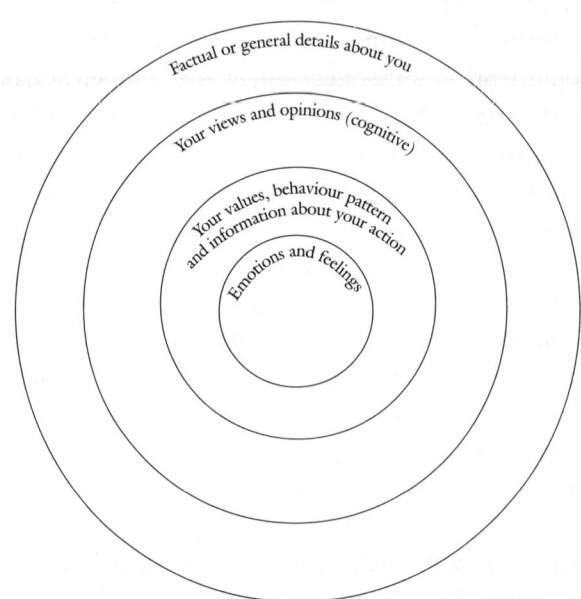

The *outermost layer* can be considered to comprise of factual or general details about you, such as educational qualifications, family background, your job and place of residence. This information sets you apart from others and helps you establish a distinct identity. Generally speaking, people are at ease sharing this information with others without inhibitions unless there are strong reasons for not doing so. As these are factual details, there is no apparent threat in sharing them. You may even be willing to talk about yourself to a stranger or those with whom you have a short, chance encounter.

As you *move inwards*, you encounter the next layer that consists of your views and opinions on different matters and issues, your thought process, your ideas, etc. In brief, this represents the entire domain of your cognitive processes. You could be hesitant to share your views, especially in a group situation, as you may not be sure of the value of your views to the group. You fear that others may not appreciate them. In some specific situations, you may also be concerned about free and frank expression of your views because this may have unpleasant consequences for you. But, by and large, there is no inevitability of threat to you or of any harmful consequences in sharing your thoughts. In fact, as mentioned earlier, you may be keen to share your views to get recognition of the group and qualify as an informed, thinking and knowledgeable person. Many are willing to share their views regardless whether they are pertinent or not. In a group situation, some members may like to share views just to convey a message that they could not be ignored.

The *third layer* is home to your values, behaviour patterns and actions. Understandably, there are apprehensions and uncertainties on sharing these. Generally, we all have positive and negative facets of our behaviour and actions. You may be willing to share those features about you that project you in favourable terms but hold back or even hide those aspects that present you in an unpromising manner. Sometimes, you deliberately present your negative aspects in a manner that they do not appear to be so negative. Thus, as we move deep inside the layers, you will notice that sharing becomes progressively more restrained and inhibitive, and there is a tendency to share in a selective manner. We tend to prejudge our actions and behaviour patterns on the basis of standards and norms set by the society, at the macro level, or by the family or the group with which we are associated, at the micro level. And accordingly, we take a decision what to share with others and what needs to be kept away from them. The selectivity is not just about the aspects of self but it is also about people. We may share some vital or sensitive information about ourselves with those who are close to us and have our trust but we may be unwilling to share same information with those who are not in harmony with us.

The *innermost*, but, perhaps, the most important layer of your self is the one that comprises of your emotions and feelings. This is generally a well-guarded region of your *self* and is open to a few chosen ones only. It may be worthwhile to understand the nuances of 'feelings' and 'emotions'. And here I wish to draw from an article by Neale Donald Walsch (2014) that appeared in a leading daily recently. According to him, 'your feelings are what you know about a thing. Your emotions are what you do with what you know'. Elaborating, he says, 'Your feeling is *your* truth, what *you* factually and intuitively *know*. A feeling is energy. An emotion is energy in motion. How you express your feelings is how you emote—or experience emotion. This is how you place energy in motion'. Evidently, we are not keen to share our feelings and emotions with all and sundry. There has to be a unique bonding with the person with whom we can share our feelings and emotions. Many a time, we manage our emotions in a manner that others are not even able to perceive them. We are not just inhibitive and careful in expressing our feelings and emotions but we even hide them behind a façade of calmness and composure. We are very careful that others should not even perceive them.

It is evident from the discussion that it is relatively easier for us to interact with others at the cognitive level and share our thoughts but as we move into the *personal* arena of values, behaviour and emotions, we are not that enthusiastic to be open and frank with others. In other words, your *cognitive* domain is more accessible to people than your *personal* or *affective* domain.

SELF-CONFIDENCE

Understanding Self-confidence

Self-confidence is a key, basic preparatory skill that precedes any assertive act. Without self-belief and self-confidence, it is very difficult for anybody to stand up for herself and her rights in an appropriate manner.

It is recognised that the path to self-confidence is built on self-knowledge, self-acceptance and self-esteem. A person who generally gives a non-assertive response is the one who suffers from a low self-esteem and for whom very uncomfortable anxiety is generated in nearly all social situations.

Self-confidence is gained through experience and interactions with others, but once you have acquired a certain level of it, you must constantly tend to it, augmenting it through conscious efforts. And you must take charge of the process of reinforcement.

There is a strong connection between self-confidence and self-esteem, on the one hand, and assertiveness, on the other. However, a person with low self-esteem is not necessarily non-assertive. Assertion techniques foster self-confidence because people take small successful steps rather than trying more than they can handle with a reasonable amount of risk.

Confidence is *quiet*. Remember, confidence is not bravado, swagger or an overt pretence of bravery. It is not some bold or brash air of self-belief directed at others. Confidence is a natural expression of ability, expertise and self-regard.

Self-confidence may relate to one particular competency or ability and also situational. A good dancer may be confident when she goes on stage to perform. But she may feel nervous and lack confidence if asked to speak before an audience. Similarly, a person may be confident speaking to a group of young people but may get overawed when she has to speak before an audience of professionals.

General Traits of a Self-confident Person

Self-confidence is the result of many inherited and acquired traits in a person.

Self-confident Persons:

- Are, simply put, positive people, whether they are engaged in tasks or interacting with people. They know how to assuage doubts or conquer fears. As they start with a positive mindset, they are able to find a silver lining even when they are confronted with failures or seemingly insurmountable problems. They do not easily give up even when odds are stacked against them. They believe that failure is a part of everyday life and it is always possible to make a fresh start.
- Are not hesitant to take risks to achieve their goals. They take risks because they are not afraid to lose or to be proved wrong. While they are confident in their abilities, they also know instinctively that nobody wins them all and that they will likely achieve success the

next time. In setting their objectives, they are prepared to raise the bar to redouble their efforts and are inclined to attempt those tasks that appear to be beyond their present capacity. They are willing to develop those competencies that will help them achieve their goals.

- Believe in their own abilities, strengths and powers, and are not burdened by doubts and low self-esteem. But they do not force their beliefs and ideas on others because they are good and creative in convincing others to their way of thinking. They do not seek the approval of others.

- Take a stand not because they think they are always right, but because they are not afraid to be wrong. They are not afraid of failure but take it as a challenge. They are not afraid of disapproval but use criticisms as constructive feedback. They respect differing views and position of others, even on issues that are crucial to them. They are also open to new ideas and are willing to discuss them even if the new idea is opposed to their own.

- Are ambitious in a realistic way and are open about their aspirations or goals. They believe in their plans and are not embarrassed at all to convince others about the benefits of joining them in reaching the goal. Any failure is considered as a temporary setback or challenge. A self-confident person loves challenges.

- Are proficient at finding their way through various social groups with which they are associated—in personal life or professionally— or social situations with seeming ease. This ease is borne of the belief that they belong in any environment. Confident people know how to endear themselves to others and how to take compliments and criticisms gracefully.

- Are often the most accepting people, taking others as they come, regardless of their shortcomings. They believe that everyone has her own strengths and weaknesses but this could not be the basis for putting down other people. They realise that the path forward is to connect with people and give them due recognition and regard.

- Are at ease in achieving their goals by taking help from others and drawing from other people's strengths and abilities. But they do not hesitate to acknowledge help and support of others in achieving their goals. Confident people know what they want. They easily define their goals and strive to achieve them. This could be the most significant trait of a confident person.

- Are good listeners. They listen and speak only when they feel it is required. Truly confident people are quiet and unassuming. They already know what they think; they want to know what *you* think. They do not brag.
- Accept compliments, praises and admiration with grace and humility.
- Have a good sense of humour and they refuse to be weighted down by the concerns and stress that they may face in their work situation or personal life.
- Realise they have substantial breadth and depth of knowledge but they are always willing to know and learn more and widen their horizons.

How Confident Do You Seem to Others?

Your level of self-confidence can show in many ways: your behaviour, your body language, how you speak, what you say and so on. Look at the following comparisons of common confident behaviour with behaviour associated with low self-confidence. Which thoughts or actions do you recognise in yourself and in people around you?

Confident behaviour	Behaviour associated with low self-confidence
Doing what you believe to be right, even if others mock or criticise you for it.	Governing your behaviour based on what other people think.
Being willing to take risks and go the extra mile to achieve better things.	Staying in your comfort zone, fearing failure and so avoid taking risks.
Admitting from them your mistakes and learning.	Working hard to cover up mistakes and hoping that you can fix the problem before anyone notices.
Waiting for others to congratulate you on your accomplishments.	Extolling your own virtues as often as possible to as many people as possible.
Accepting compliments graciously. 'Thanks, I really worked hard on that prospectus. I'm pleased you recognise my efforts'.	Dismissing compliments offhandedly. 'Oh that prospectus was nothing really, anyone could have done it'.

Source: Mind Tools, Essential Skills for an Excellent Career.

Ways to Improve Self-confidence

> Low self-confidence isn't a life sentence. Self-confidence
> can be learned, practiced, and mastered—just like
> any other skill. Once you master it, everything in
> your life will change for the better.
>
> —Barrie Davenport

Many people believe that self-confidence is an innate ability. However, this simply is not true. Self-confidence is not an attitude that one is born with. Even the most outwardly confident people feel insecure at times. It really can be learned and built on. For most people, it is developed from childhood. With practice, anyone can boost their confidence levels and command the workplace. And whether you are working on your own confidence or building the confidence of people around you, it is well worth the effort.

You have to constantly invest in building your self-confidence in all aspects of your personal and professional life. It is possible that you may be confident in a particular situation or in the context of a specific area of activities. A stage performer may exude all the confidence of a star performer while on stage but may not be confident to be a guest speaker in a symposium on Indian culture. Thus, you must constantly work—in terms of preparation, practice or experience—to widen the spectrum of the activities in which you feel confident.

Two main things contribute to self-confidence: self-efficacy and self-esteem. Confidence is the term we use to describe how we feel about our ability to perform roles, functions and tasks. We gain a sense of self-efficacy when we see ourselves (and others similar to ourselves) mastering skills and achieving goals that matter in those skill areas. Self-esteem is how we feel about ourselves, the way we look, the way we think—whether or not we feel worthy or valued. People with low self-esteem often also suffer from generally low confidence, but people with good self-esteem can also have low confidence. It is also perfectly possible for people with low self-esteem to be very confident in some areas. Thus, we see that confidence and self-esteem are not the same thing, although they are often linked.

Confidence is not a static measure; our confidence to perform roles and tasks can increase and decrease; some days we may feel more confident than others. In some situations, we may feel fully confident to deal with the situation or carry out certain tasks; while in some others, we may feel somewhat jittery and anxious, not sure of ourselves. It is our confidence that tells us that if we learn and work hard in a particular area, we will succeed; and it is this type of confidence that leads people to accept difficult challenges and persist in the face of setbacks.

Confidence is contagious and so is lack of confidence. Confident people inspire confidence in others: their audience, their peers, their bosses and their friends. And gaining the confidence of others is one of the key ways in which a self-confident person finds success.

If our mission is to enhance our self-confidence, remember, there is no quick fix or easy solution. However, with a firm commitment, focus and persistent efforts, it is something that is achievable. And what is even better is that the efforts you make to build your self-confidence will also help you in shaping your success. After all, your confidence will come from real, solid achievement. No one can take this away from you.

Self-confidence is about balance. At one extreme, we have people with low self-confidence. At the other end, we have people who may be overconfident. If you are under-confident, you will avoid taking risks and stretching yourself; and you might not try at all. And if you are over-confident, you may take on too much risk, stretch yourself beyond your capabilities and crash badly. You may also find that you are so optimistic that you do not try hard enough to truly succeed. Getting this right is a matter of having the right amount of confidence, founded in reality and on your true ability. With the right amount of self-confidence, you will take informed risks, stretch yourself (but not beyond your abilities) and try hard.

How do you build a sense of balanced self-confidence, founded on a firm appreciation of reality? The words 'balanced', 'firm appreciation' and 'reality' are significant. It is necessary that you must have a firm and honest reality check of your self-confidence that is balanced, not overconfidence that does not match with your *real persona*.

Know Yourself and Enhance Your Knowledge and Competence

> Know yourself and you will win all battles.
>
> —Sun Tzu

One big factor that contributes to your self-confidence is the faith in your knowledge and competence to face difficult situations, perform new tasks and take full advantage of the opportunities that come your way. If you are not fully assured of your abilities to handle situations, roles and tasks, you will lack confidence to venture into the unknown territory, regardless whether it relates to your personal or the professional life.

It is hard to be confident about yourself if you do not think you will do well at something. Beat that feeling by preparing yourself as much as possible. Think about taking an exam: if you have not studied, you would not have much confidence in your abilities to do well on the exam. But if you have studied and are fully prepared, you will be much more confident. Now think of life as your exam and prepare yourself.

When going into battle, the wisest general learns to know his enemy very, very well. You cannot defeat the enemy without knowing him. And when you are trying to overcome a negative self-image and replace it with self-confidence, your enemy is yourself. Get to know yourself well. Start writing a journal about yourself and about the thoughts you have about yourself and analyse why you have such negative thoughts. And then think about the good things about yourself, the things you can do well, the things you like. Start thinking about your limitations and whether they are real limitations or just the ones you have allowed to be placed there, artificially. Dig deep within yourself, and you will come out (eventually) with even greater self-confidence.

However, the first step for taking the journey to enhancement of your competencies is to have a genuine and honest appraisal of your strengths and weaknesses. Make a list of things that you are good at and things that you know need improvement. Get a feedback from your friends and family members who are likely to be more open with you and give you a candid assessment. Many of us are not fully aware of our latent talents and abilities, and also hide, consciously or subconsciously, some of our weaknesses. We should remember that in both cases, our self-confidence gets dented. While it is important that you ponder on the areas that need to be worked, make sure you spend a few minutes reflecting on your strengths and enjoying. This will give you confidence.

Empowering yourself, in general, is one of the best strategies for building self-confidence. You can do that in many ways, but one of the surest ways to empower yourself is by developing your knowledge and widening the range of your competencies—personal and professional or career related. People who are engaged in a vocation or income-generating activities generally focus more on developing profession-related competencies. Many of them do not realise that life competencies are equally, if not more, important. Life skills, or soft skills as they are also called, play an important complementary role and ensure that the professional competencies are used in an optimal way. It also gives you confidence in conducting transactions for developing personal relationships.

How do you become more competent? The path is simple and full of prospects but be prepared as the ride can be bumpy and arduous. You have to make a commitment to yourself to reach the destination. Just take small steps at a time but continue moving on. Make use of all available avenues to enhance your learning—through reading, studying and interaction with people who are competent and have achieved a lot in life through their abilities and hard work. Also take every opportunity to practise what you are learning. This experience will help reinforce the newly acquired learning and knowledge, boosting your confidence.

At the workplace, training may be provided for staff to teach them how to manage or work with new systems and procedures. During a period of organisational change, this is particularly important as many people will naturally resist changes. However, if those affected by the changes are given adequate information and training then such resistance can usually be minimised and the staff will be confident in adopting the changes.

People often feel less confident about new or potentially difficult situations. Perhaps the most important factor in developing confidence is planning and preparing for the unknown. For example, if you are applying for a new job, you would be wise to prepare for the interview. Plan what you would want to say in the interview and think about some of the questions that you may be asked. Practise your answers with friends or colleagues and gain their feedback.

Set Goals

Before you launch yourself on your journey to self-confidence, it is important to decide on where you want to go in your life—short-term and long-term goals. This will put you in the right mindset for your efforts—committing you to your endeavour and staying on course, regardless of the problems or the setbacks you may encounter. Goal setting is arguably the most important skill you can learn to improve your self-confidence.

However, one of the biggest problems people in our country have in setting clearly defined goals is lack of insights about where we want to go and what we want from life. In fact, the problem is compounded by the absence of an awareness even of our present position. Lacking a clear view of the path you want to take in your life makes it difficult to move on and decide on your efforts. The one thing all successful people have in common is that they are extremely focused and intensely goal oriented—in terms of their professional or personal life. They know what they want and they understand it takes setting firm and clear goals to achieve it.

There is a strong correlation between personal goals, self-motivation and achievement. In order to get properly motivated, and indeed to achieve, it helps to spend some time thinking about your personal goals and what you want to achieve in your life.

While setting goals, be aware that there are certain things that are beyond your control, and any efforts to change them will not yield any results, but, on the contrary, cause frustrations and distress to you. That is why it is said that your goals should be realistic.

Once you have set your goals in life, you should identify the competencies you need to achieve them. Set goals that exploit your strengths, minimise your weaknesses, realise your opportunities and control the threats you face. And then look at how you can acquire these competencies? Do not just accept a sketchy, just-good-enough solution—look for a solution, a programme or a course that fully equips you to achieve what you want to achieve and, ideally, gives you a certificate or qualification you can be proud of (inform your goal setting with your SWOT analysis).

If you feel that the goals appear to be too daunting or amorphous, try to break them into smaller, more manageable and achievable ones. Undertake a SMART analysis that underscores the need to have specific, measurable, achievable, realistic (or relevant) and time-bound goals.

Starting with the very small goals at this stage, just get into the habit of achieving them and celebrating that success. This is where you start, ever so slowly, moving towards your goal. By doing the right things, and starting with small, easy wins, you put yourself on the path to success—and start building the self-confidence that comes with this. Do not try to do anything clever or elaborate or reach for perfection—just enjoy doing simple things successfully and well. Also do not minimise your accomplishments, just enjoy them. Little by little, start piling up the successes. As your self-confidence starts to grow, you will develop self-belief in your abilities to take up bigger challenges. Slowly, you can make a foray into bigger and more difficult goals. Remember, this will not happen overnight. This will be a long-drawn effort but any life journey is complex and difficult. So persevere with your efforts and keep yourself motivated to pursue your mission.

SWOT ANALYSIS

	Helpful to achieving the objective	Harmful to achieving the objective
Internal origin (attributes of the organization)	Strengths	Weaknesses
External origin (attributes of the environment)	Opportunities	Threats

Gaining experience and taking the first step can, however, be very difficult. Often the thought of starting something new is worse than actually doing it. This is where preparation, learning and thinking positively can help.

Positive Thoughts

Positive thoughts can be a very powerful way of improving confidence. Self-confidence is not something that can be learnt like a set of rules; it is a state of mind. Positive thinking, practice, training, knowledge and talking to other people are all useful ways to help improve or boost your confidence levels.

Confidence comes from feelings of well-being, acceptance of your body and mind (self-esteem) and belief in your own ability, competencies and experience.

Low confidence can be a result of many factors, including, lack of knowledge and competence; fear of the unknown; apprehension of failure; criticism from family members or friends; being unhappy with personal appearance (self-esteem); feeling unprepared for a new task; poor time management and previous failures. For developing positivity, you must start managing your mind. Defeat the negative self-talk as it can destroy your confidence.

Low self-confidence is also caused by the negative thoughts running through our minds on an endless track. If you are constantly bashing yourself and saying you are not good enough, attractive enough, smart enough or athletic enough and on and on, you are creating a self-fulfilling prophecy. You are becoming what you are preaching inside your head, and that is not good. The next time you hear that negativity in your head, switch it immediately to a positive affirmation and keep it up until it hits the calibre of a self-confidence boost.

Think about your life so far, and list the 10 best things you have achieved in an 'achievement log'. Perhaps, you completed a project or activity; received commendation from your boss and colleagues; played a key role in your team's success; did something that made a positive difference in someone else's life and so on. You can take the option of recording some important things that helped you achieve success in your endeavour. Do not just file away this document but spend a few minutes each week to go over the list and compliment yourself. Do not consider it a childish act. Put your heart into it.

More than just thinking positively, you have to put it into action. Actually, action is the key to developing self-confidence. It is one thing to learn to think positive, but when you start acting on it, you change yourself, one action at a time. You are what you do, and so if you change what you do, you change what you are. Act in a positive way; take action instead of telling yourself you cannot be positive. Talk to people in a positive way, put energy into your actions. You will soon start to notice a difference. Optimism is the faith that leads to achievement. Nothing can be done without hope and confidence.

And on the other side, learn to handle failure. Accept that mistakes happen when you are trying something new. In fact, if you get into the habit of treating mistakes as learning experiences, you can (almost) start to see them in a positive light. Succeeding through great adversity is a huge confidence booster. There is a solution to everything, so why would you want to throw in the towel? After all, there's a lot to be said for the saying 'if it doesn't kill you, it makes you stronger!'

Do something you have been procrastinating on. What is on your to-do list that has been sitting there? Do it first in the morning, and get it out of the way. You will feel great about yourself.

Be Assertive but Not Arrogant

Assertiveness means that you stand up for your beliefs and principles even in the face of disagreements and criticism. However, it does not mean that you are stubborn and arrogant. While asserting your thoughts, opinions and convictions, you should be open to change, not under pressure from somebody but you feel convinced of the change and you believe it is the right thing to do. Assertiveness, confidence and self-esteem are all very closely linked—usually people become more assertive as they develop their confidence.

It is, however, important that as you achieve success and grow in confidence, you do not become arrogant, acting superior to others. Remember—nobody is perfect, there is always more that you can learn. Be willing to give others credit for their work—use compliments and praise sincerely. Be courteous and polite, and show an interest in what others are doing, ask questions and get involved.

(For details on 'assertiveness', see Module 2 on 'Interpersonal Communication').

Your Body Language

Your body language can instantly demonstrate self-assuredness, or it can scream insecurity. Present yourself in a way that says you are ready to master or take command of any situation. If you look confident and act the part you aspire to reach, you not only feel in control, people show much more confidence in you as well.

Stand tall, stretching to your full height. Hold your head high, sit up straight, gently bring your shoulders back to align your spine and look directly at the other person when interacting. Avoid a limp or casual handshake and maintain good eye contact while someone is speaking to you.

Speak slowly, emphasising every word, with necessary pauses. Do not sound rushed in expressing yourself. Such a simple thing, but it can have a big difference in how others perceive you. A person in control of herself and of the situation speaks slowly. It shows confidence. A person who is not confident of what she is saying is of any value to the other person will speak quickly. Even if you do not feel the confidence to speak slowly, try doing it a few times. It will make you feel more confident. Of course, do not take it to an extreme, and make the other person impatient and frustrated. Research has proved that those who take the time to speak slowly and clearly not only feel more self-confident but also appear more self-confident to others. The added bonus is they will actually be able to understand what you are saying.

Appear cheerful with a positive outlook to life. Offer compliments to others and congratulate them on their successes. If someone pays you a compliment, do not feel embarrassed; accept it with a courteous 'thank you'.

Just the simple act of pulling your shoulders back gives others the impression that you are a confident person. Smiling will not only make you feel better but will make others feel more comfortable around you. Imagine a person with good posture and a smile and you will be envisioning someone who is self-confident.

Look at the person you are speaking to, not at your shoes or floor. Maintaining eye contact when you interact with another person shows confidence.

Groom Yourself

If you dress nicely, you will feel good about yourself. This will automatically increase your self-esteem. Now dressing nicely means something different for everyone … it does not mean that you wear a costly outfit. It only means that you are dressed for the occasion, something that makes you look nice and presentable. Remember, you can look good even in casual clothes.

Our self-image means so much to us, more than we often realise. We have a mental picture of our physical attributes and this is a determining factor how confident we are in ourselves. But this picture is not fixed and immutable. You can change it. Figure out what changes are possible and find a way to bring about the desired changes.

Self-confidence at Workplace

Surveys have demonstrated 'a strong correlation between confidence and occupational success'. Maintaining a positive workplace attitude can, in many cases, lead to better performance and quicker promotions. However, success at the workplace can be harder to come by for people who lack confidence. Insecure workers often find themselves passed over in favour of more self-assured colleagues.

Confidence is primarily undermined by stress, which professionals define as when the demands on an individual 'exceed the personal and social resources that the individual is able to mobilise'.

At the workplace, you may feel stressed when faced with:

- New and unfamiliar tasks
- Tasks you have struggled with in the past
- Unrealistic deadlines
- High-handed boss
- Difficult colleagues
- Unexpected disruptions
- Critical comments

These and, possibly, many other such situations often occur in the workplace and can rapidly chip away our self-confidence.

A lack of confidence often stems from being unsure of how to do something or carry out a task. As a result, many people feel a rising sense of panic when faced with an unfamiliar task. You have a few options. If you feel that asking for help will demonstrate your failure, think twice because this is not true in all cases. Try hard to work out a logical approach to go through this challenge. But do not give up. Inaction or shying away from the task is likely to further erode your confidence. You may even face a knock from your boss and colleagues.

When faced with an unfamiliar task, some people instinctively react negatively. When you are struggling to master a new skill or get into a new role, it is too easy to believe you will never succeed. However, practice makes you perfect—envisaging yourself mastering the task in the future can provide you with a confidence boost. Remember those who are now competent in this task had also gone through similar predicament when they tried it for the first time.

Positive energy leads to positive outcomes, so set your mind to the can-do side of any situation, avoiding the negative self-talk that can make you feel less confident. Smile, laugh and surround yourself with happy, positive people. You will feel better and the people with whom you work will enjoy your company.

The fear of repeating previous failures is a powerful force and can prevent people from realising their true potential. If you find yourself dwelling on past mistakes, remember that you now have the benefit of experience on your side. Firmly remind yourself that one failed enterprise or action does not mean you will necessarily fail in the future.

Criticism can be difficult to hear—even when delivered in a constructive manner. For some people, a critical comment can completely destroy their self-confidence. If you are due to have a discussion about your work, arm yourself with a record of your thought processes and be prepared to talk through your decisions.

Unfortunately, we cannot control external influences. For some people, this lack of control can cause confidence to rapidly crumble away. If you fear the unknown, build your confidence back up through thorough preparation. Decide how you will deal with unexpected issues in advance, and draw up an 'emergency plan of action' to fall back on.

Sometimes, it is necessary to take time to really evaluate your inner circle, including friends and family. This is a tough one, but it is time to seriously consider getting away from those individuals who put you down and shred your confidence. Even a temporary break from such people can make a huge difference and help you make strides towards more self-confidence.

Do not get intimidated by people who are loud and appear to be over-confident. This will shake your self-worth. Remember loudness does not necessarily indicate competence.

SELF-ESTEEM

Understanding Self-esteem

Self-esteem is one of the most significant dimensions of self-concept. It can be defined as 'the evaluation that an individual makes about herself'. It is a realistic, appreciative opinion of oneself—realistic means accurate and honest, and appreciative implies position feeling and liking. It may also be understood as a personal judgement of one's worthiness as a person, indicating to the extent to which she believes herself to be capable, important to others and successful.

Self-esteem affects our daily life and is reflected in our interaction with people, the way we establish and sustain our relationships with others—parents and other family members, peers, colleagues at workplace, superiors, etc.—and our ability to cope with a specific situation, accomplish a particular task assigned to us or take on a demanding challenge.

It is also associated closely with our rational thinking, objectivity, initiative and risk-taking behaviour. It also helps us in managing changes in our life and influences our willingness to engender changes as part of our self-growth. It also helps us to overcome or minimise fear of the unknown.

Self-esteem is not a transient state but relatively more enduring with a person. It is an inclusive, all-pervasive feeling or demeanour of self-worth and confidence in dealing with problems, situations and people. Self-esteem is not something that a person is born with. It is developed through a process of interaction with people—family members to start with and later with teachers, peers, colleagues and others. It is also shaped by the situations that a person confronts in life and her responses. Thus, it is dynamic and can be changed through a conscious effort on the part of an individual, by cultivating a desire to change through other interventions such as, training, counselling, etc. It may get further reinforced when an individual is able to carry out the tasks or confront difficult situations effectively. It also gets charged when she is able to manage effectively her fears and concerns about herself. An individual has to constantly nurture it because in some cases, persistent failures in dealing with situations and problems she encounters in life can erode it.

Self-esteem also gets enhanced when you *choose* to do something good for yourself rather than do what you are told to do. Your initiative and proactive behaviour and success in your efforts will raise your self-esteem. You are willing to do things on your own rather than wait for someone to tell you what to do and how. You have confidence in your abilities in making right choices in the context of your life; in achieving goals and objectives you set for yourself and in upholding the values you cherish.

Your ability, both to develop interpersonal skills and to use them for your growth, development and maturity depends, to a great extent, on the quality and level of your self-esteem.

A person with healthy and rationally developed self-esteem respects and likes others. In contrast, a person with irrational and unrealistically high self-esteem displays some degree of arrogance and is self-centred. She can even be disrespectful to others. She may have difficulty forming close, trusting, equal relationships with others.

Everybody is different. Some people are naturally positive and optimistic, maintaining equilibrium when faced with constant difficulties, while others are less so. Some people are good at appearing to be positive and optimistic on the outside while they struggle with low self-esteem and feelings of self-doubt on the inside.

Self-esteem may vary from situation to situation, sometimes even from day to day. Some people feel relaxed and positive with friends and colleagues, but uneasy and shy with strangers. Others may feel totally in command of them at work but struggle socially (or vice versa).

Low and High Self-esteem

Irrationally Low Self-esteem

Those with low self-esteem and self-confidence tend to raise doubts about their own worth and their ability to develop skills for assertive response. They suffer from self-defeating shame or humility. Self-defeating humility is an abject lack of self-respect, spineless submissiveness and contemptibility. People with low self-esteem tend to view people in a hierarchical position and see themselves at the bottom of the ladder.

Unrealistically High Self-esteem

As a person can have irrationally low self-esteem, it is also possible to have unrealistically high self-esteem. As mentioned earlier, persons with irrationally high self-esteem display some degree of arrogance and are self-centred. They suffer from self-defeating pride. Self-defeating pride is the attitude that one is superior, more valuable or more important as a person than others. It is often rooted in insecurity and fear, and reflects a need to defend oneself. Such people also perceive themselves as more capable, self-sufficient or infallible than they actually are. Thus, they are haughty, arrogant, conceited, pretentious and vain (with an excessive desire to be admired). They can even be disrespectful to others. Therefore, they may have difficulty forming close, trusting, equal relationships. Their view of others is vertical or competitive. They consider themselves to be on top, meaning that others must be below them. They are insensitive to the needs and feelings of others and exploit other people for their own purposes. When they are criticised or confronted, they meet with rage or with feelings of shame.

Rational, Realistic Self-esteem

Persons with healthy and rationally developed self-esteem respect and like others. They do not view people vertically, but horizontally. There is no relative comparison. They are not afraid to admit their mistakes and are always prepared to take necessary corrective action for improvement. Healthy pride and healthy humility are indicative of rational self-esteem. Healthy pride is realistic sense of one's dignity or worth, self-respect, gratitude and delight in one's achievements; and healthy humility involves an absence of self-defeating pride, the recognition of one's imperfections and weaknesses, and consciousness of one's shortcomings and ignorance. Healthy pride and healthy humility coexist in a person with realistic self-esteem.

Conditional and Unconditional Self-esteem

Self-esteem can be conditional or unconditional. When you base it on a particular situation, event or position, it is referred as conditional self-esteem. Alternately, you can make your self-esteem unconditional, not linked to situational aspects of your life.

Conditional Self-esteem

Self-esteem should not be based on a particular situation, event or position. This linkage is not appropriate. When people with conditional self-esteem fail or do not conduct themselves according to their set standards and norms, their self-esteem is undermined or threatened. Thus, you make yourself dependent on circumstances and situations.

It is likely that there may be a phase in your life when you confront difficult situations or problems and regardless of how hard you may try, you are not able to come out of them successfully. You may not measure up to the criteria you have set for yourself. Then you will be vulnerable to anxiety and despair. Instead of thinking, 'I have failed' and trying to learn from the situation, you may think, 'I am a failure'. Some people base their self-esteem on being successful at work, in educational pursuits or in relationship with others. Then when we lose our job or get rejected by someone we love and care for, we may feel devastated and lose our self-esteem. Now, in contrast, you work hard and experience outstanding success for a period of time. Are you now more worthwhile then what you were when you were going through a difficult phase? The answer is: No. Those who have rationally high self-esteem are not deterred by failure and they do not measure their worth against a let-down or disappointment. Self-esteem cannot be considered transitory. It has to be more stable and secure. You cannot make yourself or your self-esteem dependent on circumstances. You should not lose control on yourself and give control (of your self-esteem) to people, situations, events or circumstances.

Conditional self-esteem has its benefits as well. If you base your self-esteem on your hard work and accomplishments, it may motivate you to work hard and do your best.

Unconditional Self-esteem

By contrast, people with unconditional self-esteem feel secure in their worth. They realise that many desirable traits and behaviours express their worth and serve as reminders of their worth. They do not let their poor performance in one area define them. As they mature, they learn that humans express themselves in varied and complex ways, and they discover more and more ways by which they express their own core worth. They realise that few people can achieve extreme levels of fame and recognition, and even the most successful people experience many failures along the way.

On the other hand, unconditional self-esteem is not measured on the basis of achievements or success but on the basis of:

- Your efforts and not results
- Optimising your abilities
- Desire to grow and improve
- Commitment to a course and not necessarily to action or results
- Your perseverance
- Your determination
- Your qualities as a good human being (love and respect for others)
- To be helpful to others (desire to be helpful to others)

Advantages of Unconditional Self-esteem

- You will always know that you are worthwhile, even if you are having tough times.
- You will not be afraid of failure or rejection. You will be willing to take more risks with your career and personal life.
- Although you may feel disappointed and down when you encounter failure but you will not be out, feel ashamed or inferior.
- You will always feel equal to other people, never superior or inferior. This will make your personal relationships more rewarding.
- You will not get defensive when you are criticised because your self-esteem will not be on the line.
- You can enjoy life more because you would not use up your energy worrying about whether you are good enough or whether people appreciate you.
- You will face your shortcomings more honestly and openly.
- You will have greater capacity to love others and accept yourself.

Disadvantages

- You may be complacent and less motivated to do your best.
- You may become self-centred and insensitive to the needs of the other people.
- You may not try to listen to others and learn from them.

Characteristics of Genuinely Low Self-esteem

- Social withdrawal
- Anxiety and emotional turmoil

- Lack of social skills and self-confidence. Depression and/or bouts of sadness
- Less social conformity
- Eating disorders
- Inability to accept compliments
- Incapability to see yourself 'squarely'—to be fair to yourself
- Accentuating the negative and playing down the positive
- Exaggerated concern over what you imagine other people think about you and your actions
- Self-neglect
- Treating yourself badly but 'not' other people
- Worrying whether you have treated others badly or done something wrong to others
- Unwillingness to take on challenges
- Reluctance to put yourself first or anywhere
- Lack of enthusiasm to trust your own opinion
- Expecting little out of life for yourself

Boosting Your Self-esteem

There are ways to boost your self-esteem, even if you feel that you are struggling to do so. It is normal for us to, sometimes, have wavering self-esteem where we may feel insecure and inadequate. Building healthy self-esteem is an ongoing task that requires effort, but is a practice that is worth the energy and effort. It requires constant investment. You cannot achieve everything in a day, but you can start taking steps to enhance the way you feel. However, you must always try and stay in touch with how you feel as you progress.

Know Yourself—Take a Measure of Your Strengths and Weaknesses

Our self-image means so much to us, more than we often realise. We have a mental picture of ourselves, and it determines how confident we are in ourselves. But this picture is not fixed and immutable. If it is not a very good one, change it. Use your mental photoshop skills, and work on your self-image. Figure out why you see yourself that way, and find a way to fix it. Keep adjusting your self-image and self-esteem to match your current abilities and competencies, not those of your past.

Self-esteem is not worthwhile if it is based upon an older version of you that no longer exists. You might have been good at something but this is no longer the case; on the other hand, you have developed new competencies and knowledge that did not exist earlier. On the way, your belief about yourself and your strengths might have improved. You might have identified areas that you need to work on to improve your performance and relationships. So constantly update your self-image with *here and now* situation.

Know yourself: 'know thyself' is an old saying passed down through the ages to encourage us to engage in self-exploration. Usually the most well-adjusted and happiest people are those who have gone through this exercise. It is not just about knowing your strengths and weaknesses but also opening you to new opportunities, new thoughts and viewpoints, trying out something new and developing new relationships.

Sometimes, when we are down on ourselves and our self-esteem has taken a big hit, we feel like we have nothing to offer to the world or others. It may be that we simply have not found out the value of what we can do or offer to others—things we have not even considered or thought of yet. Learning what these are is simply a matter of trial and error. It is how people become the people they have always wanted to become, by taking risks and trying things they would not ordinarily do.

Work on your self-empowerment. Empowering yourself will lead to high level of self-esteem. You get empowered when you feel more competent to deal with challenges of life. It is hard to be confident in yourself if you do not think you will do well at something. Beat that feeling by preparing yourself as much as possible. And how do you become more competent and empowered? By gathering more information and expanding the spectrum of your knowledge and competencies, in areas that are important to you or for your life. So study and practice; interact with people who are good in the areas relevant to you. Take small steps at a time before you take a long leap.

Avoid Comparing Yourself with Others

Comparing yourself to others can be extremely detrimental to building healthy self-esteem. In our society, it is quite easy to compare ourselves to others, but it is something we must learn to move away from. When we compare ourselves to others—whether it is about looks, money, personality or job status, we may end up feeling inadequate. We start to feel that we are just not good enough. There is always someone who has more or is better than you at something in the world; there are always people ahead of you. Nothing can hurt our self-esteem more than unfair comparisons. You can see how this might have an impact on our feelings about ourselves, the more we do this sort of thing. Comparing yourself to others is often linked to negative self-talk, which is another thing you must be mindful of.

There is another dimension to this. These comparisons may not be fair because you do not know about the lives of these people as much as you think you do; or what it is really like to be them. You think it is better, but it may be many times worse than you can imagine. It is not always possible to get into the shoes of others. Remember the saying: 'If you think the other person is happy, that means you do not know him'.

Instead of comparing yourself to others, it is important to remind yourself of all the positive qualities you possess. When you recognise that you are a unique person who has a lot to offer to the world, you will feel your sense of self-esteem rising. Perhaps, the only person you should be competing against is *yourself*. Focus on you. Look at how far you have come so far instead and what you would like to do more to bring in better results. Compare yourself to yourself. This will both motivate you and raise your self-esteem.

You cannot base your happiness on the parameters decided by someone else. Everyone defines happiness according to him or her, so why borrow someone else's ideas on that. Some people may opt for money and opulence; some may want position and power; and yet some others may opt for sound health and physical well-being. Create your own standards and criteria of happiness.

When you compare your life, yourself and what you possess to other people's lives and what they have, then you have a destructive habit on your hands. So replace that habit with something better.

Often when we compare ourselves to others, we develop negative self-talk. For example, if you meet someone who has the dream job you have always wanted, you may start to feel inadequate and perhaps even insecure. For many people, this is the time when the issue of negative self-talk begins.

Instead of feeling happiness for that other person, you compare yourself to them and begin a very unhealthy dialogue of negative-self talk in your head. 'I am not good enough' and 'they are better than me' are examples of things you might tell yourself at such times. Unfortunately, when you speak to yourself like this, your self-esteem also starts to suffer. You feel completely down and maybe even depressed. Avoid it.

Do Not Run After Perfection—It is Elusive

Few thoughts can be so destructive in daily life as the desire to pursue perfectionism. It can paralyse you from taking action because you become so afraid of not living up to some standards. And so you procrastinate or ponder what to do and you do not get the results you want; or you take action but are never or very rarely satisfied with what you accomplished or with your own performance. And so your opinion and feelings about yourself become more and more negative and your motivation to take action plummets. This will make your self-esteem sink.

While we pursue perfection, you must realise that it is simply unattainable for any of us. Let it go. You are never going to be perfect. You are never going to have the perfect body, the perfect life, the perfect relationship, the perfect children or the perfect home. We revel in the *idea of perfection*, because we see so much of it in the media. But that is simply an artificial creation of society. It does not exist. Instead, grab a hold of your accomplishments as you achieve them. Acknowledge them to yourself for their actual value (do not devalue them by saying, 'Oh, that? That was just so easy for me, no big deal').

It may even help to keep a little note or list of things you accomplished. Some people might even do this on a daily basis, while others might feel more comfortable just noting them once a week or even once a month. The key is to get to your smaller goals and move on from each one, like a connect-the-dots game of life.

It is just as important to take something away from the mistakes you make in life. It does not mean you are a bad person, it simply means you made a mistake (like everyone does). Mistakes are an opportunity for learning and for growth, if only we push ourselves out of the self-pity or negative self-talk we wallow in after one, and try and see it from someone else's eyes.

Set Realistic Goals and Expectations

Setting goals for yourself will allow you to reach milestones in your life that will help you to feel more confident and inspired. When we reach goals, we are able to truly believe in ourselves, which in turn helps us to boost our self-esteem. It is important, however, that we set realistic goals that we are able to achieve. By making your goals realistic and specific, you are setting yourself up for success and ultimately boosting your self-esteem. Nothing can kill our self-esteem more than having unrealistic expectations from our actions and then feeling dejected when we are not able to realise them. This may also help you to stop the cycle of negative thinking about yourself that reinforces your negative self-esteem. When we set realistic expectations in our life, we can stop berating ourselves for not meeting some idealistic goal.

There are people who make the mistake of shooting for the moon, and then when they fail, they get discouraged. Instead, shoot for something much more achievable. Set a goal you *know* you can achieve, and then achieve it. You will feel good about that. Now set another small goal and achieve that. The more you achieve small goals, the better you will be at it, and the better you will feel. Soon you will be setting bigger (but still achievable) goals and achieving those too.

Sometimes our expectations are so much smaller, but still unrealistic. You may wish that your boss will never criticise you. That may not happen, but that is no reason to let that criticism affect your own view of yourself, or your own self-worth. Check your expectations if they keep disappointing you. Your self-esteem will thank you.

Turn Negative Self-talk into Positive Self-talk

Negative self-talk can be about anything from trying to lose weight or starting a new hobby. This is why it is important for you to find ways to reframe the negative self-talk into positive self-talk.

Instead of telling yourself that 'you are not good enough', you can tell yourself that you have room to improve and grow. Or if you think someone is better than you, you can learn to compliment them and learn from them. When you find ways to reframe your negative self-talk, you will start to see your self-esteem improve as well. In order to truly develop healthy self-esteem, you need to be mindful of and monitor the dialogue you have with yourself. Positive internal dialogue is a big part of improving your self-esteem.

Instead of saying things like 'I'm not good enough' or 'I'm a failure', you can start to turn things around by saying 'I can beat this' and 'I can become more confident by viewing myself in a more positive way'.

To begin with, you will find yourself falling back into old negative habits, but with regular effort you can start to feel more positive and build your self-esteem as well.

(For details of positive self-talk, see Module 6 on 'Positive Thinking').

Surround Yourself with Positive People

Our self-esteem is not only limited to our own internal feelings but is also linked to the types of people we surround ourselves with. When we have positive people in our life, people who will support our goal and life journey, we also feel positive and motivated. This, in turn, helps us to develop healthy self-esteem. Remember, like self-confidence, self-esteem is also communicable.

When we want to develop healthy self-esteem, we need to surround ourselves with the type of people who will help us to feel good about ourselves. Find people who will support you and help you reach the goals you set in your life. These types of people are the ones who will help you to boost and build healthy self-esteem.

Create a List of the Wonderful Things You Have Done

This is something that can be done on slips of paper or within a journal you keep. Every time you have a moment of feeling good about yourself, you should jot it down in writing. On the days when you are not feeling so great about yourself, you can take a look at this list. This list will serve as a reminder that you are capable of doing great things in your life. In turn, this will help you to feel more confident and positive, and help boost your self-esteem.

Be Mindful of Your Body Language

Body language plays a significant role in how we feel about ourselves, even if we are not consciously aware. Becoming aware of our body language is an important realisation we must make if we want to develop healthy self-esteem. It is important to walk and sit with your posture upright, with your shoulders rolled back. You should also try not to cross your arm when speaking to others, because this can make you appear guarded. With positive body language, not only will you appear more confident but also feel more confident.

Eye contact is another thing that helps you to develop healthy self-esteem. Low self-esteem is often connected with looking away from others when speaking. Do not worry if you struggle with this now. It is something you can learn to do over time. To begin with, you can start to maintain eye contact with close friends and colleagues you are comfortable with. Over time, it will become a natural habit. Maintaining eye contact will make you appear more confident to others, which should help you to feel more confident about yourself as well. In turn, this boosts your self-esteem.

Practise Self-forgiveness to Experience Self-love

In order to develop healthy self-esteem, we must be able to truly forgive ourselves for things in our life that did not turn out the way we expected. This may be about regrets we have or goals we were not able to reach. Talk to yourself as you would to a friend who had experienced a failure; committed a mistake or had suffered a setback in job or relationships. Normally, you would counsel your friend and prop her up or boost her morale with words of consolation, encouragement and support. Talk in the same way to yourself.

Life is a journey and we should not see our failures, setbacks or mistakes as negative experiences, because they help us to learn what to do right the next time. When we are able to forgive and assure ourselves, we can develop self-love. This sense of self-love helps us to develop healthy self-esteem that cannot be shaken by extrinsic factors. It allows us to feel empowered and confident in our lives.

Try Something New and Different

Learning something new is often accompanied by feelings of nervousness, lack of self-belief and high stress levels, all of which are necessary parts of the learning process. The next time you feel under-confident, remember to remind you that it is perfectly normal—you are just learning.

When you try something new, when you challenge yourself in a small or bigger way and go outside of your 'comfort zone', then your opinion of yourself goes up. You might not have done whatever you did in a spectacular or great way but you at least tried instead of sitting back and doing nothing. And that is something to appreciate about yourself and it can help you come alive as you get out of a rut. So go outside of your 'comfort zone' regularly. Do not follow a routine; just tell yourself that you will try something different and special. Later on you can do the same thing a few more times and improve your own performance. In case you find it somewhat scary to come out of your 'comfort zone', do not get angry with you. Try a smaller step forward by nudging yourself into motion. Soon you will find that you are getting comfortable outside your 'comfort zone'. This whole effort will boost your self-esteem.

Another thing that you can do is to attend to something that you have been postponing for some time for a variety of reasons—something that involved taking a decision that you have been reluctant to take or doing something of which you were not sure.

Another thing that will help boost your self-esteem when you engage in something that you are good at. If possible, it should be something that holds your attention and requires enough focus to get you into that state of 'flow' where you forget about everything else. You will feel more competent, accomplished and capable afterwards, great antidotes to low self-esteem!

Learn to Be Assertive

Stand up for what you believe in, and do not be pressured by others. (See the module on 'Interpersonal Communication'—Assertiveness).

Self-esteem and Self-confidence

Genuine self-esteem is not the same as self-confidence. Self-confidence is based on the knowledge that you are likely to be successful at an activity because you have been successful at similar activities in the past. In cases, where you have not carried out similar activities earlier, you still feel that you have the necessary capabilities and motivation to carry out the task in an effective manner. However, there may be situations when you are not able to measure up to yours or others' expectations. In such cases, your self-confidence may be somewhat dented but your self-esteem can still be intact. Despite this failure, you may continue to 'like and respect you' and consider you as a worthy and capable person. Thus, while self-confidence may be related to particular task, activity or area of work, self-esteem is far more enduring and deep-rooted than self-confidence.

Self-confidence usually refers to a belief in one's abilities related to competence and self-efficacy. As one's capabilities increase, so does self-confidence. Competence and confidence correlate with self-esteem but are not causal. If we base our feelings of worth on competence and achievements, then if we fail there is no worth. In the broader and deeper sense, self-confidence is a belief in oneself as a person, leading to a general sense of 'I can do it'.

The concept of a 'worthwhile person' and 'worthless person' is relative to certain situations, problems or circumstances. Do not label yourself. One person may be good at certain things but not so good in others. Similarly, someone may be good at certain point in time but fail in same or similar activity at some other time.

Our worth is also relative to people. If we compare ourselves with more successful people, we may feel 'worthless' or 'inferior'. However, if we compare ourselves with people who are less successful or with less achievements or qualifications, or career, you may feel that you are a worthwhile person, a superior human being. In this way, everyone is worthwhile or worthless.

SUGGESTED GUIDELINES FOR THE TRAINERS

Before you take up Exercise 1, you should elucidate on Johari window and how it works as an important instrument for enhancing self-awareness and explain the concepts of self-disclosure and feedback in this context. It is likely that some of them might not be familiar with the use of Johari Window, and, therefore, they may have several queries and clarifications to seek. You must respond to all of them to ensure that they fully understand the application of this instrument for enhancing self-awareness.

Exercises 2, 3 and 4 aim to provide opportunities to the participants to assess their levels of self-confidence and self-esteem and learn about ways that will help them improve the levels of these two crucial aspects of the personality of an individual. However, before you take up these exercises, you should make detailed presentations on different aspects of self-confidence and self-esteem, of course, ensuring that the participants are constantly engaged in the discussion. To the extent possible, contextualise your discussion and indicate how these can be boosted to make life of an individual happier and more successful.

You may decide on the time frame for all your inputs, keeping in view the time allocation for the three exercises.

Consistent with the suggested overall approach to the training programme, you must always engage the participants in active discussion, even while you are providing the inputs.

EXERCISE 1

SELF-AWARENESS (JOHARI WINDOW)

Objective

At the end of the exercise, the participants will be able to:

- Fully appreciate the value of self-disclosure to others and feedback from them, for enhanced self-awareness, so crucial for personal and professional growth and success.

Time allocation

About 1 ½ hours

Materials required

Training aids required for your elaboration on the exercise; copies of Johari window model handout (to be taken from the trainer's note) and worksheets Part I and Part II (one for each participant); flip charts and writing markers for displaying key points emerging out of the sharing by the participants and discussion, and your summing-up; white board and markers.

Steps in conducting the exercise

- Recall your discussion on self-awareness and your illustration of the Johari Window.
- Introduce the exercise, emphasising the important goal for individuals should be to enhance the level of self-disclosure and to

encourage others to give them honest and objective feedback. This exercise should result in reducing the areas of 'hidden self' (private self) and 'blind self'.

- This is an individual exercise and has two parts and accordingly each participant receives two worksheets—for Part I and Part II—and a handout of the Johari Window model.
- Distribute copies of worksheet Part I and ask the participants to complete it after going through the instructions. Give them enough time as they may have to reflect and also recall their experiences with others to record their responses.
- After all the participants have completed the worksheet Part I, distribute copies of worksheet Part II and ask them to complete it on the basis of the instructions.
- After the participants have completed both worksheets, initiate discussion by providing opportunities to those who wish to share their responses.
- Sum up and provide your inputs, drawing from participants' responses. Close the exercise.

SELF-AWARENESS (JOHARI WINDOW)

Worksheet Part I

Instructions for completing the worksheet:

- **Open area:** Write down three key positive and three key negative points about you—qualities, attributes, competencies, etc.—that are part of open self. It means that you know them and so do others with whom you interact on a regular basis.
- **Hidden area:** List three positive and three key negative points about you—qualities, attributes, competencies, etc.—that you are aware of but others with whom you interact on a regular basis are not.
- **Blind area:** Indicate three key positive and three key negative points about you—qualities, attributes, competencies, etc.—of which you were not aware earlier but now you know them because others with whom you interact on a regular basis told you about them.

Open area:

_____

_____

_____

Hidden area:

_____

_____

_____

Blind area:

_____

_____

_____

SELF-AWARENESS (JOHARI WINDOW)

Worksheet Part II

Receiving feedback from others

The following scale provides you an opportunity to rate to what extent you have *actually* engaged in soliciting feedback from your peers, parents and teachers on your actions, behaviour and attitudes. *Do not* base your rating on how many times you *felt* the need for feedback or *thought* of asking for feedback but give the rating on how often you *actually* asked for feedback.

Never   0   1   2   3   4   5   6   7   Always

What prompted or encouraged you to solicit feedback?

_____

_____

What prevented you from soliciting feedback?

_____

_____

Being open or self-disclosure

The following scale provides you an opportunity to rate to what extent you have *actually* engaged in self-disclosure on your weaknesses, strengths, actions, behaviour, feelings and emotions with your peers, parents or teachers. Do not base your rating on how many times you *felt* like sharing these things with them, but give the rating on how often you *actually* engaged in self-disclosure.

Never   0   1   2   3   4   5   6   7   Always

What prompted or encouraged you to be open or engage in self-disclosure?

_____

_____

What prevented you from sharing these things with others?

_____

_____

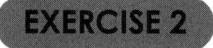

EXERCISE 2

ENHANCING MY SELF-CONFIDENCE

Objectives

At the end of the exercise, the participants will be able to:

- Understand various aspects of self-confidence in their personal context
- Identify areas in which they need to take action to enhance the level of their self-confidence

Time allocation

About 1 ½ hours

Materials required

Training aids and tools required for explaining key aspects of self-confidence as part of your introductory talk and for summing-up: worksheet on 'Enhancing Self-confidence'; flip charts and writing markers for displaying key points emerging out of the sharing of the participants of their individual responses in the subgroups; white board and markers.

Steps in conducting the exercise

- Give a brief introductory talk on self-confidence. Explain the exercise and distribute the worksheet on 'Enhancing My Self-confidence', and explain the procedure for completing it.
- As this is an individual exercise, give the participants adequate time to complete Part I of the worksheet.
- After all participants have completed the exercise, ask the group to complete Part II of the exercise (action planner).
- Invite volunteers to share their responses to the worksheet (Parts I and II). Write key points on the flip chart for discussion and your summing-up and inputs.
- Sum up the discussion bringing together the points highlighted by the participants supplemented by your inputs.

ENHANCING MY SELF-CONFIDENCE

Worksheet

Part I
Key strengths
List at least five key qualities or characteristics you think have contributed most or have supported your present level of self-confidence (example: I am willing to take up tasks that challenge me; I persevere regardless of success I achieve: I can work under pressure)

1. _____

2. _____

3. _____

4. _____

5. _____

6. _____

7. _____

Key weaknesses or limitations

Similarly, list at least five key weaknesses or negative traits that tend to undermine or destabilise your self-confidence (example: I give up easily; I am not able to give practical shape to my thoughts and plans)

1. _____

2. _____

3. _____

4. _____

5. _____

6. _____

7. _____

Part II

Action Planner

(Go over the above list carefully and mark with 'N' those weaknesses, limitations or negative qualities that you cannot change; also mark 'Y' those that you feel you are in a position to change if you make sincere efforts. Transfer those marked as 'Y' in the table below)

Serial number	Weaknesses, limitations or negative traits you wish to change	Difficulties or hurdles you are likely to confront in this task	How you propose to overcome these difficulties? (Refer to the list of your strengths)

EXERCISE 3

WHAT I LIKE ABOUT MYSELF AND DO NOT LIKE ABOUT MYSELF

Objective

At the end of the exercise, the participants will be able to:

- Reflect on different aspects of their personality and identify those affirmative qualities and traits they possess that contribute to enhancing their self-confidence and self-esteem.

Time allocation

About 1 ½ hours

Materials required

Training aids and tools for your inputs and summing-up: worksheet on 'What I Like About Myself and What I Do Not Like About Myself'; flip charts and writing markers for displaying key points emerging out of the discussion (in the subgroups) based on the sharing by the participants of the data generated through the exercise and their views on the two elements; white board and markers.

Steps in conducting the exercise

- Introduce the topic, explain the exercise and distribute the 'What I Like About Myself and What I Do Not Like About Myself' worksheet. Go over the instructions given in the worksheet for completing the exercise. Offer clarifications, if necessary. Remind the group that this is an individual exercise and let the participants complete the task.
- After everybody has completed the exercise, divide the group into subgroups of 8–10 participants. In the subgroup, every member is expected to share five (5) highest ranking items from each table. She must also explain the reasons behind the ranking.

- Bring the group together and initiate discussion, giving opportunities to the participants to express their views on the relationship they see in the selected items and their self-esteem.
- Sum up the discussion, based on the sharing by the participants and your inputs.

Worksheet

'What I Like About Myself and What I Do Not Like About Myself'
(This is an individual exercise and its outcome will depend how honest you are in identifying the items in both tables. You must reflect on each item before putting it down in the table. Do not consult anyone)

A. In the table below, in the first column, write down 10 most important things/traits/qualities that you like about yourself (examples: I look for the good in other people; I am capable of working hard when required; I am friendly with my peers). After you have completed the list, go over it again and rank these items from 1 to 10 with '1' being the highest positive value item for you in your life. There is no duplication of ratings.

What I like about myself	Rank
1. _____	_____
2. _____	_____
3. _____	_____
4. _____	_____
5. _____	_____
6. _____	_____
7. _____	_____
8. _____	_____
9. _____	_____
10. _____	_____

B. In the table below, in the first column, write down 10 key things/behaviour/habits that you do not like about yourself (examples: I lack self-confidence and self-belief; I am not capable of taking initiative; I do not trust people). After you have completed the list, go over it again and rank these items from 1 to 10 with '1' being the item you do not like the *most* in your life. There is no duplication of ratings.

What I do not like about myself	Rank
1. _____	_____
2. _____	_____
3. _____	_____
4. _____	_____
5. _____	_____
6. _____	_____
7. _____	_____
8. _____	_____
9. _____	_____
10. _____	_____

EXERCISE 4

IMPROVING YOUR SELF-ESTEEM

Objectives

At the end of the exercise, the participants will be able to:

- Understand the concept and scope of self-esteem as applicable to their day-to-day life.
- Develop insights into their own behaviour, beliefs, attributes, etc., that contribute to the building of their self-esteem or self-image,

etc., appreciate the value of self-disclosure and feedback from others, in personal growth and for personal and professional success and achievement.

Time allocation

About 1 ¼ hour

Materials required

Training aids required for your elaboration on the exercise; copies of worksheet (one for each participant); flip charts and writing markers for displaying key points emerging out of the sharing by the participants and discussion, and for your summing-up; white board and markers; and white sheets for the participants to respond to the questions in the worksheet.

Steps in conducting the exercise

- Give a brief introduction to the exercise and emphasise the importance of being open and honest in responding to the questions in the worksheet.
- This is an individual exercise and each participant has to respond recalling the events and situations of their life, interaction with others and their own assessment about themselves. Tell them that they should record their responses to the questions given in the worksheet on separate sheets of paper.
- Assemble the group and provide opportunities to those participants who wish to share their responses in the group.

IMPROVING YOUR SELF-ESTEEM

Worksheet and Handout

You and your self-image

How you see yourself determines the state of your happiness and success. You are who you think you are, period. The beliefs you have about yourself—positive and negative images—determine the level of your self-esteem. These beliefs and images are the source of your behaviour and your results in life. The beautiful thing is that you can change and choose what you believe. And by changing those long-lasting thoughts, you were once so certain about, you change everything.

Please respond to the following:

Include everything no matter how small, insignificant, modest or unimportant you think it is.

Write brief responses on a separate sheet of paper for sharing once the worksheet is completed.

Strengths

What do I like about who I am? _____
What are the skills and talents that I am good at? (Personal and professional) _____
My positive characteristics or qualities _____
What are my significant achievements and successes in life? _____
Why do I consider them significant? _____
What are some of the key challenges that I have overcome? _____

Make compliments

What do others say they like about me? _____
What are some attributes I like in others that I also have in common with? _____
If someone shared my identical characteristics, what would I admire in them? _____
How might someone who cared about me describe me? _____
What do 1 think my friends like best about me? _____
What compliments would I make myself? _____

Source: Adapted from 'Growing' from self-esteem.com

HANDOUT FOR THE PARTICIPANTS

Exercise (for the Participants to Complete in Their Free Time)

The following set of questions may help you unravel some parts of you in the process of becoming aware of you. It is, however, important that you answer these questions in a sincere and honest manner. The more you can answer honestly, the better chance you have to find who you truly are. In preparing your response, you must be fully aware of your feelings, thought processes and other internal inhibitions. Talk to yourself intimately.

- What are your strong likes and dislikes?
- Do you feel responsible for your actions and behaviour or blame others for them?
- What motivates you and what are the demotivating factors that influence you?
- What are your desires, dreams or ambitions?
- What are your major strengths and weaknesses?
- What are your distinguishing abilities and competencies?
- How do you define success and happiness in your own context?
- Do you like working alone or as a team player?
- Are you organised in your day-to-day activities and chores?
- Are you honest and trustworthy?
- Are you conniving, controlling or manipulative?
- What are your greatest fears and why?
- What makes you feel guilty and why?
- Do you feel angry or bitter—at you, at others, at society and why?
- Do you rely on others for guidance?

Keeping in view your special situation, you may add more questions.

Note for the participants

Going through this exercise can be a very challenging task, but it is also well worth your effort, because the rewards are unmatched by anything that you presently know or have experienced. There may be some grey areas that you may not like. You may have to come out of your 'comfort zone'. Once you are prepared to accept yourself completely, you will know what and who you really are. You will start living in truth, away from façade that either you have created for yourself or people around have been instrumental for it. The fear factor or embarrassment will dissipate. You will then be expected to take some hard decisions to move forward and invoke your inner power to bring about desired changes in your persona leading you to path of self-growth.

Module 2
Interpersonal Communication

While the module discusses various aspects of interpersonal communication, it aims to help the participants become aware of their own communication profile and suggest ways for improving their interpersonal communication skills.

Specifically, the module focuses on the following sub-topics or sub-themes:

- Understanding interpersonal communication
- What is effective communication?
- Skills in interpersonal communication
- Barriers to effective communication

Expected Outcomes from the Module

At the end of the session on this module, the participants will be able to:

- List and discuss key components that contribute to effective communication.
- Become aware of their communication profile and learn about ways for enhancing their communication skills.
- Gain knowledge about various aspects of assertive behaviour and assertive communication and become versed in improving skills in these areas.

UNDERSTANDING INTERPERSONAL COMMUNICATION

Interpersonal communication, as the term signifies, indicates communication between two persons, regardless whether the objective is to establish a relationship or common understanding; convey a message; discuss an issue or simply to engage in a casual conversation. In fact, interaction between two individuals gets initiated not necessarily through spoken words but also through signs, gestures, facial expressions or body language. A key aspect of interpersonal communication is that it is not completed unless the person, at whom it is directed, does not signal that she has received it.

There are five basic elements in interpersonal communication:

1. Source or speaker
2. Receiver or listener
3. The message or the contents of the communication
4. Channel that is used for communication
5. Environment in which the transaction takes place

Communication Process

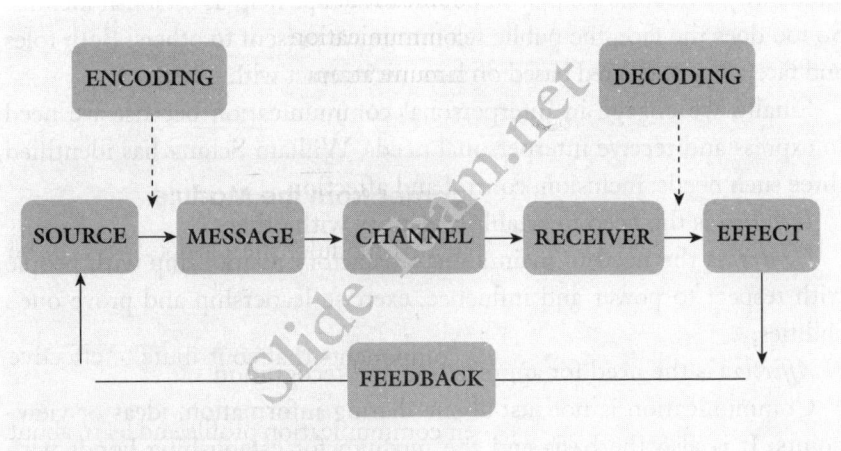

By specifying the roles, 'sender (source)' and 'listener (receiver)', we simply imply that when an interaction is initiated, one who starts it can be referred to as the source of the communication. The one who receives it for the first time is termed receiver or the listener. However, when the listening party responds, she becomes the source and the one who initiated the interaction takes the role of the receiver or the listener. And in this way, the transaction continues, the two individuals alternating between the role of a sender or a receiver.

Encoding means the creation of a message based on your thoughts, views and intention. It is, therefore, necessary that the message should be so designed that it is not only clear and accurate but also conveys the meaning you want to put across to the listener. Once the message is received by the other party in the communication transaction, she starts decoding it. Decoding is a skill the listener uses to interpret the message according to her perception or understanding of the source and also her own frame of mind, experience and context. Therefore, any communication is successful when the encoded message is accurately decoded by the listener.

One of the reasons for which we engage in interpersonal communication is to get information about the other person or to get acquainted with her. Some of this information can be obtained in a passive way, through observation; actively, by having others engage them or interactively, through one-on-one communication with her. Self-disclosure is often used to get information from another person.

Another reason we engage in interpersonal communication is to establish an identity. The roles we play in our relationships help us establish identity. So too does the face, the public self-image we present to others. Both roles and face are constructed based on how we interact with others.

Finally, we engage in interpersonal communication because we need to express and receive interpersonal needs. William Schutz has identified three such needs: inclusion, control and affection.

Inclusion is the need to establish identity with others.

Control is the need to maintain a satisfactory relationship with people with respect to power and influence, exercise leadership and prove one's abilities.

Affection is the need for appreciation and recognition.

Communication is not just about sharing information, ideas or viewpoints. It is also the basis and the medium for establishing bonds with people. These transactions constitute the contents of communication between the two parties. However, sometimes, the communication may not have a defined purpose or a definite message to convey. There are occasions when people interact and talk without any predetermined purpose or objective in mind. It is a casual conversation with no particular direction or topic as the base, such as a conversation with fellow travellers or guests at a social function.

Communication does not take place in a vacuum. There is always a physical environment that not only influences the process but also, sometimes, adds substance to the communication. The people involved can become oblivious of the environment only when they are so focused on what is being shared or discussed that everything else recedes into background. But even here environment has a facilitative role. People engaged in communication find the environment so congenial that they are able to get into high concentration mode. There are, however, situations when physical environment can be distracting or even disruptive to communication. Distraction is more for the listener rather than the speaker. The thought process of the speaker may be disturbed but the listener may be so disconcerted that she may even stop listening and get drawn more to the interfering audio and visual distractions.

Interpersonal communication differs from other forms of communication in that there are few participants involved; those who are engaged in interaction are in close physical proximity to each other; there are many sensory channels used and feedback is immediate.

Thus, some researchers have proposed an alternative way of defining interpersonal communication. This is called the developmental view. From this view, interpersonal communication is defined as communication that occurs between people who have known each other for some time. Importantly, these people view each other as unique individuals, not as people who are simply acting out social situation.

WHAT IS EFFECTIVE COMMUNICATION?

In most cases, communication is more than mere exchange of information. It is about understanding the other person and providing access to her to know you—the *persona*, behaviour, emotions, etc., that lies behind that information. Effective communication is also a two-way swap. It is not only how you convey a message so that it is received and understood by someone in exactly the way you intended, it is also how you listen to gain the full meaning of what is being said and to make the other person feel heard and understood.

More than just the words you use, effective communication combines a set of skills including non-verbal communication, engaged listening, managing stress in the moment, the ability to communicate assertively and the capacity to recognise and understand your own emotions and those of the person you are communicating with.

Effective communication is the glue that helps you deepen your connections to others and improve teamwork, decision-making and problem-solving.

It enables you to communicate even negative or disagreeable messages without creating conflict or undermining trust.

While effective communication is a learned skill, it is more effective when it is spontaneous rather than formulaic. A speech that is read, for example, rarely has the same impact as a speech that is delivered (or appears to be delivered) spontaneously or extempore. Of course, it takes time and effort to develop these skills and become an effective communicator. The more effort and practice you put in, the more natural and unprompted your communication skills will become.

Self-concept is a critical factor in a person's ability to be an effective communicator with others. A person with a strong self-concept does not experience any difficulty in communicating with others. She is able to express herself clearly and emphatically, and with a lot of confidence. She is able to comprehend and appreciate the views of others, especially in relation to her own views and perceptions. On the other hand, an individual with a weak self-concept finds it difficult to engage in meaningful interaction with others, partly because of her lack of self-confidence and partly because she is unsure of the response of others. She is reluctant to express her feelings and views, especially in cases where they are at variance with those of others. Therefore, while on the one hand, a person's self-concept affects her ability to communicate, on the other, the limited exchange she has with others shapes her self-concept. There is no doubt that if an individual has to develop her self-concept, she must continue to work on her communication competencies and create opportunities to interact with others in a significant way.

Self-disclosure is another factor that contributes to effective communication. The ability for an individual to express truthfully and fully about herself is necessary for effective communication. A person's willingness and capability to engage in self-revelation is a symptom of a healthy personality. An individual cannot really communicate with another person or get to know that person unless she herself is willing to engage in honest self-disclosure. If you are prepared to reveal some hitherto unexpressed details about you, others may also be encouraged to do so. There is, therefore, some degree of reciprocity about self-disclosure. It works on the maxim, 'the more you know about me, the more I know about you; together we can make the communication smoother and effective'.

(Cross-reference: for more details on 'Self-disclosure', refer to Module 1).

SKILLS IN INTERPERSONAL COMMUNICATION

Active Listening

If we were supposed to talk more than we listen,
we would have two tongues and one ear.

—Mark Twain

In communication, listening has often been relegated to a less consequential position in comparison with skills in expressing oneself clearly and fully. Though listening is crucial to all effective communication, people tend to spend far more energy considering what they are going to say rather than wanting to listen to what the other person is trying to convey. Without the ability to listen effectively, messages can be easily misunderstood; there may be a breakdown of communication and possibility of interpersonal animosity looms large as the sender may become upset or enraged.

Listening is the ability to accurately receive and interpret messages in any interpersonal communication. However, it is a much more intricate and complicated process. We often tend to think that hearing and listening are synonymous terms. It is not so. Hearing is a physical or biological process and refers to the sounds you receive or hear. On the other hand, listening is an intellectual and emotional process that integrates physical, emotional and intellectual inputs in a search for meaning, purpose and substance. It requires considerable focus and commitment on the part of the receiver of the message. Listening means paying attention not only to the words or views being expressed but how the message is being conveyed—the use of language and voice, the emotions behind the words and the body language. In other words, it means being aware of both verbal and non-verbal messages and clues, including subtle enunciation and articulation. It is only then that the transaction is complete and the purpose of communication is realised.

There is a clear distinction between *engaged* listening and simply hearing. When you really listen, when you are engaged with what is being said, you will understand the intonations in someone's voice that tell you how that person is feeling and the emotions that are being transmitted. When you are an engaged listener, not only will you better understand the other person you also make that person feel listened to and understood. This can help build a stronger, deeper connect between you and the other person.

By communicating in this way, you will also experience a process that lowers stress and supports physical and emotional well-being. For example, if the person you are talking to is calm, listening in an engaged way will help to calm you too. Similarly, if the person is agitated, you can help in making her relaxed and comfortable by listening in an attentive way and making her feel understood and recognised.

Seven Levels of Listening

1. **Not listening:** Not paying attention to or ignoring the other person's communications. You are simply not part of the transaction.
2. **Pretend listening:** Acting like or giving the impression that you are paying attention to other person's communication, but in actuality not really paying attention to that individual. You are either mentally distracted, your thought process is taking you away or you are paying attention to things in the surroundings.
3. **Partially listening:** Only focusing on part of the other person's communication or only giving it your divided attention. Sometimes you are in the conversation and at other times, you are out of it. So you get part of the message but not the complete one.
4. **Focused listening:** Giving your undivided attention to the other person's communication.
5. **Interpretive listening:** Interpretive listening goes beyond the words and enters the domain of emotions and feelings; you try to give meaning and substance to the message by making an extra effort to understand what the person is saying.
6. **Interactive listening:** By getting actively involved in the communication process, you become part of it. You seek clarifications through questions and respond not merely through words but also through non-verbal language.
7. **Engaged listening:** Being fully engaged in communications involves listening to the other person's views, feelings, interpretations, values, etc., concerning the communication and sharing yours as well with the other person(s). In engaged listening, both parties are given the opportunity to fully express their views, feelings and ideas. There is no desire to compete.

Improving Your Listening Skills

If there is one communication skill you should aim to master then listening it is. The following guidelines may help.

Get ready for the transaction: The first thing you should do is to prepare yourself fully to engage in a meaningful communication. Focus on the speaker and get into an eager mode to receive the message. It is easy to get distracted by other thoughts but make a conscious effort to put other things out of mind. Get yourself ready to concentrate on the speaker and the message.

Put the other party at ease: It is important to remember that others also have their concerns, anxieties, apprehensions and needs. They also may be experiencing a certain level of discomfort and unease. Your endeavour should be to make the environment as easy and relaxed as possible. Use words, gestures and body language to convey that you are keen to be a part of this communication. Maintain eye contact but avoid *staring*.

Be patient: When the other party is speaking, show patience. A pause or even a long pause does not necessarily mean that the other person has finished. Be patient and let her continue in her own time. Remember some people take time in formulating what they want to convey and in deciding how to say it. Do not interrupt or complete a sentence for the other person.

Set aside judgement initially: Do not rush to start evaluating the views, opinions and values of the other person. By seeming to criticise or impute motives to the communication without objectively trying to get its meaning, you may create a mental block, thus, losing access to real meaning and substance of what is being conveyed. In order to communicate effectively with someone, you do not have to agree with all that is being expressed but wait for an opportunity to express your views and opinions, regardless whether they are contrary to what is being expressed. Do not allow your biases and attitude towards the speaker or your own views on the issues to blur the communication and vitiate the environment.

Pause before responding: It is desirable for you to wait until there is a clear signal—look for verbal or non-verbal clues—from the other person that she has finished. Too prompt a response reduces listening effectiveness. Ideally, there should be a time gap between listening, deciphering and grasping the meaning of the communication, formulating the response and your views and expressing them to complete the communication process. This makes the communication more meaningful to both parties.

Avoid formulating your response before the other party has finished: Sometimes we start formulating our response while the other person is still speaking. This is contrary to active listening. You will not be able to concentrate on what is being said if you start forming what you are going to say next. In fact, you may even stop listening to what she is communicating. In such cases, your response may only relate to the part to which you paid full attention and not to the complete message or communication. In most of such cases, the other person will be able to read your facial expressions and know that your mind is somewhere else and you have stopped listening. This is not good for a healthy communication.

Pay attention to non-verbal signals: When we communicate things that we care about, we use a lot of non-verbal signals. Non-verbal communication, or body language, includes facial expressions, body movement and gestures, eye contact, posture, the tone of your voice and even your muscle tension and breathing. The way you look, listen, move and react to another person tells them more about how you are feeling than words alone ever can. Developing the ability to understand and use non-verbal communication can help you connect with others, express what you really mean, navigate challenging situations and build better relationships with people, at home and work.

Communication Through Non-verbal Signals

Interpersonal communication is much more than the *explicit* meaning of words, the information or message conveyed. It also includes *implicit* messages, whether intentional or not, which are expressed through non-verbal behaviours. These non-verbal signals can give clues and additional information and meaning over and above spoken (verbal) communication.

Non-verbal communications include facial expressions, the tone and pitch of the voice, gestures displayed through body language, such as crossing of the arms, use of hands and shifting of sitting or standing positions and the physical distance between the communicators.

Unfortunately, interpreting non-verbal communication is not that simple. It is not a language with a fixed meaning. It is influenced and driven by the context in which it occurs. This includes the place and the people concerned, as well as the cultural nuances.

We learn to interpret non-verbal communication as we grow up and develop. It is a normal part of how we communicate with other people, and most of us both use it and interpret it without a conscious effort. It is just there.

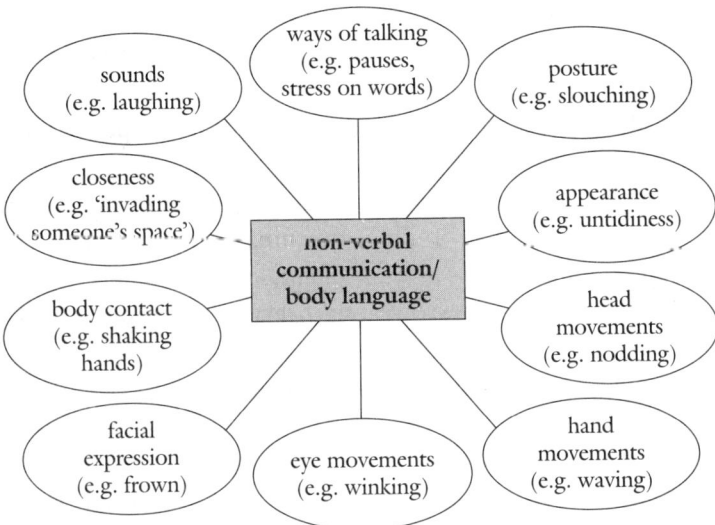

When we communicate, non-verbal cues can be as important, or in some cases *even more* important, than what we say. Non-verbal communication can have a great impact on the listener and the outcome of the communication, indeed on the emotional connect between the two persons.

Non-verbal messages allow people to:

- Reinforce or modify what is said in words. For example, people may nod their heads vigorously when saying 'yes' to emphasise that they agree with the other person, but a shrug of the shoulders and a sad expression when saying 'I'm fine thanks' may imply that things are not really fine at all.
- Convey information about their emotional state.
- Define or reinforce the relationship between people.
- Provide feedback to the other person.
- Regulate the flow of communication, for example, by signalling to others that they have finished speaking or wish to say something.

There are many different types of non-verbal communication. They include:

Body movements: Hand gestures or nodding or shaking the head.

Posture: How you stand or sit, whether your arms are crossed and so on.

Eye contact: The manner and intensity of eye contact often determines the level of trust and trustworthiness; sincerity of what you are saying.

Paralanguage: Aspects of the voice apart from speech, such as pitch, tone and speed of speaking.

Closeness or personal space: This may reflect the level of intimacy.

Facial expressions: Smiling, frowning, twitching of the mouth and even blinking.

Physiological changes: Sweating, heavy breathing or abnormal blinking.

Improving Your Non-verbal Communication

You can enhance effective communication by using open body language—arms uncrossed, standing with an open stance or sitting on the edge of your seat and maintaining eye contact with the person you are talking to.

You can also use body language to emphasise or enhance your verbal message—patting a friend on the back while complimenting her on her success, for example, or pounding your fists to underline your message.

Tips for Improving Non-verbal Communication

Be aware of individual differences: People from different parts of the country tend to use dissimilar non-verbal communication gestures. Therefore, it is important to take age, culture, religion, gender and emotional state into account when reading body language signals.

Look at non-verbal communication signals as a whole: Do not read too much into a single gesture or non-verbal cue. Consider all of the non-verbal signals you receive, from eye contact to tone of voice to body language. Anyone can slip up occasionally and let eye contact slip, for example, or briefly cross their arms without meaning to. Consider the signals as a whole to get a better understanding of the person and the message.

Use non-verbal signals that match up with your words: Non-verbal communication should reinforce what is being said, not contradict it.

If you say one thing, but your body language says something else, your listener will likely feel you are being dishonest. For example, you cannot say 'yes' while shaking your head, suggesting a 'no'.

Adjust your non-verbal signals according to the context: The tone of your voice, for example, should be different when you are addressing a child than when you are addressing a group of adults. Similarly, take into account the emotional state and cultural background of the person you are interacting with.

Use body language to convey positive feelings: Even when you are not actually experiencing them. If you are nervous about a situation—a job interview, important presentation or first date, for example, you can use positive body language to signal confidence, even though you are not feeling it. Instead of tentatively entering a room with your head down, eyes averted and sliding into a chair, try standing tall with your shoulders back, smiling and maintaining eye contact and delivering a firm handshake. It will make you feel more self-confident and also help to put the other person at ease.

Some Cautions

Interpretation of non-verbal language can be subjective, dependent on your own physical, mental and emotional state and your understanding of the other person.

Non-verbal communication can have a great impact on the listener and the outcome of the communication.

People tend to have much less conscious control over their non-verbal messages than of what they actually say. This is partly because non-verbal communication is much more emotional in nature, and, therefore, much more instinctive.

If there is a mismatch between the two, you should probably trust the non-verbal messages, rather than the words used.

A lack of non-verbal message may also be a signal of sorts, suggesting that the speaker is carefully controlling her body language and may be hiding her true emotions.

Sometimes, interpersonal communication can get further complicated as it is not always possible to interpret a gesture or expression accurately on its own. Non-verbal communication consists of a complete package of expressions, hand and eye movements, postures and gestures, which should be interpreted along with speech. It is likely that you may not be able to fully get the meaning of the non-verbal language if you rely only on one of the non-verbal expressions.

Cultural context of the gestures and expressions should also be taken into consideration.

Management of Emotions

'Let me manage my emotions and not let my emotions manage me!'

Emotions are an essential component of any communication. They give the communication a human dimension. However, your ability to manage and deal with them in a manner that does not take away from the message that you wish to convey is a measure of effective communication. In fact, emotions should be managed in a way that they are supportive of your communication and reinforce it. It does not, however, mean that you should suppress or hide them from others or feel guilty about them. The exercise of managing emotions involves becoming aware of them, understanding them in the context of the present transaction and the situation, and exploring ways of integrating them with your words and body language, and the relationship with the other person. The aim is to convey the message you want to without hurting the relationship or the person with whom you are communicating, with due deference to the emotions of the other person. A sound transaction between two individuals, therefore, will also mean harmony of emotions between them.

It is likely that during communication, there may be situations that may create stress and you may feel emotionally disturbed. Under such circumstances, it is important that to continue communicating effectively you need to be aware of and in control of your emotions. And that means learning how to manage stress and emotions. When you are stressed, you are more likely to misinterpret the message of the other person, send confusing or even repulsive non-verbal signals and lapse into unhealthy knee-jerk patterns of behaviour. Your facial expressions and body language may give away your psychological and mental state.

It should, therefore, be your endeavour to manage your emotions and return quickly to a state of calmness and self-composure. Remember the times when you felt stressed during a disagreement or arguments with your spouse, kids, friends or co-workers and then you said or did something that you later regretted. If you can be in command of your emotions, quickly relieve stress and return to tranquillity, you will not only avoid a replay of that situation and such regrets but in many cases, you will also help to soothe the other person as well. It is only when you are in a composed, relaxed state that you will be able to know whether the situation requires a response, or whether the other person's signals indicate it would be better to remain silent. It is, therefore, necessary for you to learn to manage your emotions and stay unruffled under pressure and difficult situations.

When things start to get worked during a conversation, you need to act quickly to bring down the emotional intensity. By learning to promptly reduce stress in the moment, you can become skilled at facing strong emotions you may experience with others, regulating your feelings and behaving appropriately. When you know how to maintain a relaxed, energised state of awareness even when something upsetting happens, you can remain emotionally stable and engaged.

The following tips may be helpful:

Recognise when you are becoming stressed: Your body will let you know if you are stressed as you communicate. Are the stomach muscles stretched and/or sore? Are your hands clenched? Is your breath shallow? Are you 'forgetting' to breathe?

Own your stress: It is also important that you own your emotional state and do not blame the other person for your stress. If you feel that the source of your stress is the other person—her words, views, opinions, body language, etc.—your response is likely to be challenging and even argumentative. This can lead to more tensions, thus vitiating the environment.

Pause to collect your thoughts and regain control of your emotions: Remember brief silence and a pause do not necessarily signal a break in communication. A pause will give you enough time to regroup your thoughts and get back control of your emotions. At this time, it will not be advisable to rush your response.

Deliver your words clearly: In most cases, how you say something can be as important as what you say. Part of managing your emotions will be to speak clearly and slowly, maintain an even tone and make eye contact. Keep your body language relaxed and open.

Make one point at a time: Do not get entangled in a number of points at the same time. Try to pick up the point that is least contentious and build on that before you bring in the point that was the source of stress. Try to be brief and to the point. If your response is too long or you waffle about a number of points, you risk entering an arena where you may lose control of your emotions. By dealing with one point at a time, you will be in a position to gauge the listener's state of mind and her possible reaction, and this will give you a signal whether you should proceed to make a second point. This will also help you gain precious moments to think of what point to put next and how you should do it. In this way, you will not only soothe your nerves but also make the other person feel relaxed. This will help keep the environment congenial for the communication to continue in a healthy manner.

Be willing to see other person's point of view: If disagreement on an issue or divergence of views with the other person is the cause of your stress, you can reduce it by making a sincere and conscious attempt to see her point of view. Try to find some point which even obliquely helps you locate a common ground that reduces the stress levels for both of you. If you realise that the other person cares much more about something than you do, this approach may be easier for you and a good investment in the future of the relationship. If necessary, agree to disagree as this can calm both parties and the situation. The communication can then move on.

Bring your senses to the rescue: Take a few deep breaths; change your posture; lean back; find a little distraction; let your muscles relax; do a little self-talk and find things that are soothing to you.

Clarity of Expression—Using Proper Language and Words

If you can't explain it simply, you don't understand it well enough.

—Albert Einstein

Sometimes, we are either compelled to or opt to speak in a language in which we do not have full facility or are not comfortable. This can make communication somewhat complicated or difficult. We may choose wrong words and may not have facility to express ourselves fully.

Many people find it difficult to say what they *actually* mean or to express what they *actually* feel. Either they are not able to find appropriate words to convey their message or they do not have the necessary skill or the ability to put across to the other person the intended meaning and purport of their communication. Some of them assume that the other person understands what they mean, even if they are unclear about their own words or expressions. There are times when the speaker herself is not sure of what she wants to convey and what could be the most effective way of doing it. This further complicates the situation.

A poor communicator leaves the listener to guess or infer what she means, while she herself assumes that her communication is clear and proper. The listener, in turn, proceeds to respond on the basis of her own understanding of the message, regardless of the intentions of the speaker. Thus, the speaker and the listener operate at two different levels and from two diverse positions, each unaware of the level and position of the other. This may lead to miscommunication and mutual misunderstanding.

Being Assertive

Assertion can be defined as self-expression through which one stands up for one's own basic human rights without violating those of others involved in the transaction. On the other hand, non-assertion response style represents an inability to maintain adequately the boundaries between one person's rights and those of another. Non-assertion occurs when one allows one's own boundaries to be restricted.

Direct, assertive expression makes for clear communication and can help boost self-esteem and decision-making. Being assertive means expressing your thoughts, feelings and needs in an open and honest way, while standing up for you and respecting others. It does *not* mean being hostile, aggressive or demanding. Effective communication is always about understanding the other person, not about winning an argument or forcing your opinions on others.

'Wisdom is knowing when to have the courage to speak up and the courage to sit down and listen.'

Assertion, non-assertion or aggression can be viewed as either a generalised pattern of behaviour or a situational response. Generalised pattern of behaviour means that a person demonstrates consistency in certain demeanour and is generally identified with that style in interaction with people. On the other hand, when we speak of situational response, we are classifying response to a particular situation as assertive, non-assertive or aggressive and not categorising people as assertive, non-assertive or aggressive. Situational response means that it is not part of an overriding general pattern. If non-assertion or aggression becomes a broad pattern of behaviour of a person, it is likely that she has some emotional problems or lacks interpersonal skills. If we accept this premise, our earlier assumption that people can develop assertion skills becomes credible and valid.

In assertion theory, the underlying assumptions are that all people have certain basic human rights. These rights include such fundamentals as:

- The right to refuse requests without having to feel guilty or selfish
- The right to consider our own needs as important as those of other people
- The right to make mistakes
- The right to express ourselves as long as we do not violate the rights of others

It is important that these rights are respected by all those who interact with you.

Assertiveness in Communication

Verbal Language

A way of differentiating between assertion, non-assertion and aggression is to pay attention to the type of verbal language used. Certain words tend to be associated with a particular response style.

Assertive words may include 'I' statements ('I think', 'I feel', 'I want'); cooperative words ('let's', 'how can we resolve this') and emphatic statements of interest ('what do you think', how do you see this moving').

Non-assertive words can include qualifiers ('may be', 'I guess', 'I wonder if you could', 'would you mind very much', 'only', 'just', 'I cannot', 'don't you think'); fillers ('uh', 'well', 'you know', 'and') and negators ('it is not really important', 'don't bother').

Aggressive words include threats ('you'd better', 'if you do not, watch out'); put downs ('come on', 'you must be kidding', 'you don't mean that, do you').

Evaluative comments ('I do not think you understand'; 'you are wrong in assuming that'; 'your behaviour is not appropriate').

Non-verbal Behaviour

For effectively conveying the message, each of the three response styles is characterised by certain non-verbal or body language cues. Emotional, non-verbal and verbal cues are, therefore, helpful keys in recognising response styles, but they should be understood as general indicators and not as means of labelling behaviour.

Assertion faces up to a situation and demonstrates an approach by which one can stand up for oneself in an independent or interdependent manner. When being assertive, a person generally establishes good eye contact, stands comfortably but firmly on two feet with hands loosely at her sides and talks in a strong and steady tone of voice. When sitting, she is relaxed in her posture, maintains good eye contact and uses gestures to express her.

A non-assertive response, on the other hand, is self-effacing and depend-ent; she moves away from the situation. This response may be accompanied by such mannerisms as downcast eyes, shifting of weight, a slumped body, wringing of hands or a whining, hesitant or giggly tone of voice.

Aggression represents a non-verbal 'moving against' situation; it is either effacing or counter-dependent. This response may be expressed through glaring eyes, by leaning forward or pointing a finger or by a raised, snick-ering or haughty tone of voice.

Am I Assertive?

To improve assertiveness, take the following test and find out how assertive you are.

- I am comfortable meeting new people in social situations
- I am able to say no without feeling guilty or anxious
- I can express strong feeling such as anger, frustration and disappointment
- I can easily request help or information from others
- I feel capable of learning new things and performing new tasks
- I am able to acknowledge and take responsibility for my own mistakes
- I can discuss my beliefs without judging those who do not agree with me
- I am able to express my honest opinion to others even if they do not agree with me
- I tell others when their behaviour is not acceptable to me
- I can speak confidently in group situations

- I believe my needs are as important as those of others and should be considered
- I can assert my beliefs even when the majority disagrees with me
- I can express anger or disappointment without blaming others
- I am comfortable in delegating tasks to others
- I value my own experience and wisdom

Source: Mutual of Omaha Insurance Company (2016).

Assertive, Non-assertive and Aggressive Behaviour

Assertiveness is often confused with aggressiveness. Aggression takes place when one person invades the other's boundaries of individual rights. On the other hand, assertive response style recognises boundaries between one's individual rights and those of others and operates to keep these boundaries stabilised. An assertive response means that the person is in a position to express herself clearly and calmly, does not back down in the face of disagreement and is prepared to express views even on controversial issues. The response needs to be also honest and appropriate to the culture, the situation and the other people involved.

Functionally, assertive responder seeks a solution that equalises the balance of power and permits all concerned to maintain their dignity and self-respect. Non-assertion and aggression are dysfunctional not only because they use indirect methods of expressing wants and feelings and fail to respect the rights of *all* people but also they create an imbalance of power and position. In refusing to stand up for her rights, the non-assertive responder creates a power imbalance by giving out everyone else more rights than she gives to herself. On the other hand, the aggressive responder creates a power imbalance in her favour by giving herself more rights than the other person.

But if there were a yardstick to measure human behaviour, assertiveness would fall right in the middle, with passiveness at one end and aggressiveness at the other. Few of us are exactly in the middle of this yardstick, but all of us can benefit from consciously practicing assertive behaviour. Very passive and very aggressive people often have an underlying issue of self-esteem—unrealistically low or high self-esteem. If you find yourself usually at one extreme or the other, self-esteem may be a concern for you to explore further.

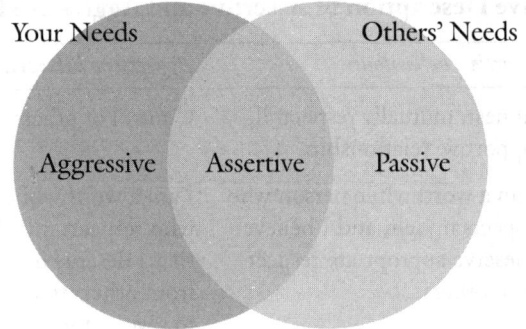

Here are some of the ways that passive, assertive and aggressive people are perceived by others.

Passive people	Assertive people	Aggressive people
Have trouble saying 'no'	Are firm and direct	Are loud, bossy and pushy
Do whatever others ask, even if it is very inconvenient	Do not blame others but take full responsibility for their own feelings	Get their way, no matter what
Get stepped on a lot	Concentrate on the present	React instantly
Talk softly and do not stand up for their rights	Can express their needs and feelings calmly and easily	Like to get even
They are not even sure whether they have any rights	Are confident about who they are	Do not care about feelings of others
Do anything to avoid conflict	Speak firmly and make eye contact.	Give vice-like handshakes
Are taken advantage of. They get resentful but do not tell anyone	Respect others' rights and expect the same in return	Believe that winning is everything

Comparative Description of Assertive and Aggressive Behaviour

	Assertive behaviour	*Aggressive behaviour*
Results	Honest, mutually respectful, supportive relationship	Control of others
Values	I am a worthwhile person who respects myself, and I believe I deserve appropriate respect from others	I am a worthwhile person who respects myself and feels that I deserve more respect from others than I am willing to give to them
	I am in control of myself and secure in myself	I am in control of myself, secure in myself and I have a right to control others
	I have rights and this includes the right to assert them	I have rights more than the other people have
	It is important that I should and I can express my feelings towards others	I need not express my true feelings towards others and I do not need to know how they feel about me
	It is important that others should know that I am sensitive to their needs and I expect them to be sensitive to mine	It is important for others to be sensitive to my needs and I do not need to reciprocate this
	Confrontation can be positive, non-judgemental and constructive	Confrontation must always have a positive result for me regardless of how people come out of it
Language	Marked by 'I' language, that is	'I' language usually self-centred: 'I want...' 'You' language is
	Reporting something about you	Judgemental
	Not imposing your beliefs or feelings on anyone else	Harsh
	Leaving room for differences of opinions or judgements	Demanding
	Open to discussion and dialogue	Emotional

Reasons for Not Being Assertive

- Early training, grooming and family environment diminished your capacity to stand up for yourself. You did not have appropriate opportunities to discover whether you can be assertive. Now you are reluctant to test your limits.
- You have not clearly established the standards that you should adhere to or the values you should follow in your social interactions or in developing relationships. You may also be unsure of what you actually want from life, a person, a situation or a relationship.
- You are afraid that your assertive behaviour may evoke angry or negative response from the other person. You feel that the risks involved are too great and the consequences can be very damaging for you, your career or the relationship.
- You suffer from low self-esteem. You do not feel that you have the right to stand firm and demand correct and fair treatment from others.
- You are not sure how your behaviour will be perceived or interpreted by the other person. You may be seen as being aggressive or rude.
- You think that it is not worth the while to be assertive. You let the situation pass.
- Your self-expression tends to be vague, unimpressive, confusing or emotional. You are not sure how your words or emotions will come out as a response. Therefore, you take a safer and easier route of being non-assertive.

Developing Empathetic Understanding

(Cross reference: this topic has been discussed in detail under Module 8 titled 'Empathy').

Reflecting, Seeking Clarification and Clarifying

Reflecting and its Techniques

Reflecting is the process of paraphrasing and restating both the feelings and words of the speaker. The purposes of reflecting are to:

- Provide an opportunity to the speaker to listen to her own thoughts and to focus on what she said or how she felt
- Make her feel understood and important

- Show the speaker that you are trying to perceive the world as she sees it and that you are doing your best to understand her messages. This sends a positive vibration to her
- Encourage her to continue expressing her without restraint
- Help her to focus on her ideas

Reflecting does not involve asking questions, introducing a new topic or leading the conversation in another direction. Its techniques are mirroring and paraphrasing.

Mirroring

Mirroring is a simple form of reflecting and involves repeating almost exactly what the speaker says.

Mirroring should be short and simple. It is usually enough to just repeat keywords or the last few words spoken. This shows you are trying to understand the speaker's terms of reference and acts as a prompt for her to continue. Be aware not to over-mirror as this can become irritating and, therefore, a distraction from the message.

Paraphrasing

Paraphrasing involves using other words to reflect what the speaker has said. Paraphrasing shows not only that you are listening but that you are attempting to understand what she is saying.

It is often the case that people 'hear what they expect or want to hear' due to assumptions, stereotyping, prejudices or self-interest. This is often referred to as selective hearing. When paraphrasing, it is of utmost importance that you do not introduce your own ideas or question the speaker's thoughts, feelings or actions. Your responses should be non-directive and non-judgemental.

It is very difficult to resist the temptation to ask questions and when this technique is first used, reflecting can appear to be very stilted and pretentious. You need to practice this skill in order to feel comfortable.

Clarifying and Clarification

Seeking clarification from the speaker and clarifying your own message are important communication skills. Clarification is important in many situations especially when what is being communicated is difficult in some way. Communication can be *difficult* for many reasons: perhaps sensitive emotions are being discussed; the speaker is sending highly complex message involving many issues or people, or some important information or instructions are being passed on to you. As an extension of reflecting, clarifying reassures the speaker that the listener is attempting to understand the messages.

When using clarification, follow these guidelines to help aid communication and understanding:

- Admit if you are unsure about what the speaker means
- Ask for repetition
- State what she has said as you understand it, and check whether this is what she really said
- Ask for specific examples
- Use open, non-directive questions, if appropriate
- Ask if you have got it right and be prepared to be corrected

Seeking clarification can involve asking questions or occasionally summarising what the speaker has said. When you are the listener in a sensitive environment, right sort of questioning enables her to describe her viewpoints more fully or make the message more comprehensible. Of course, asking the right questions at the right time can be crucial and comes with practice.

The best questions are *open-ended* as they give the speaker choice in how to respond, whereas closed questions allow only very limited responses. Some examples of non-directive, open-ended questions are:

- 'I'm not quite sure I understand what you are saying'.
- 'I don't feel clear about the main issue here'.
- 'When you said .... what did you mean?'
- 'Could you repeat ...?'

On the other hand, *closed* questions usually elicit a 'yes' or 'no' response and do not encourage speakers to be open and expand on their thoughts. Such questions often begin with 'did you?' or 'were you?' For example:

- 'Did you always feel like this?'
- 'Were you aware of feeling this way?'

BARRIERS TO EFFECTIVE COMMUNICATION

There are many things that get in the way of active listening and in effective communication. It is necessary that you are aware of these personal or environmental barriers. While some of these personal barriers may be part of your behaviour patterns and even bad habits, others may be specific to the situation or the person, with whom you are in communication. However, in order to become an active and engaged listener, you need to be fully conscious of these habits and the manner in which you behave with people to enable you to take control of the situation and facilitate effective communication. You must continue trying to reduce their impact by continually checking understanding and by offering appropriate feedback. Remember, if you are not watchful, these barriers may even lead to a breakdown in communication, affecting even your relationship with the other person.

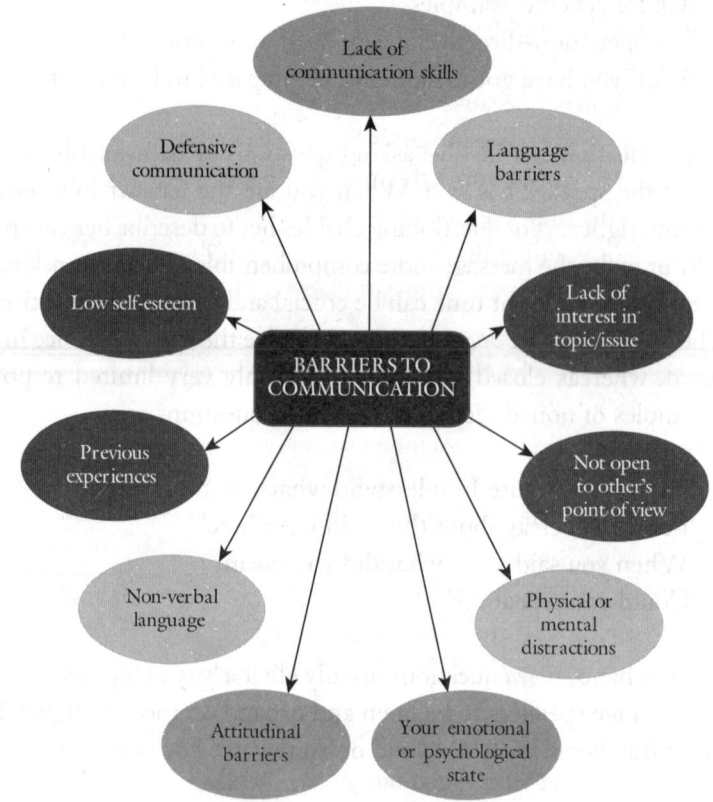

Lack of Communication Skills

Your lack of verbal skills or ability to articulate or present your thoughts and ideas in a coherent and logical manner acts as a barrier to your active and meaningful participation in the conversation or discussion. This can also distort your message, making it open to misinterpretation. You risk getting misunderstood. Also, if you are acutely sensitive to your inadequacy in expressing yourself properly, you may become a disinterested or passive listener or participant in the transaction.

Language Barriers

Sometimes the message may become over-complicated because of the use of technical terms and jargons. If the listener is not familiar with the terminology, she may not fully understand the message, and, as a result, there may be annoyance and frustration. This could be a cause of breakdown in communication.

In our country, because of a plethora of languages and regional colloquialisms and expressions, it is likely that in some situations, the communication may not be correctly understood or interpreted. Some regional colloquial terms may even be considered offensive. We are all aware that even when communicating in the same language, there may be difficulty in understanding different or unfamiliar accents.

Lack of Interest in the Topic

If the topic or subject does not interest you or you have aversion to it, you will cease to be an active participant in the conversation or discussion. You are liable to switch off and withdraw, seeking distractions in the environment that can engage your attention. Depending on the relationship with those who are part of that transaction, you may not make it so apparent but, nevertheless, you will stop listening. In other words, you cease to be part of the communication.

It is also likely that you lack comprehensive knowledge about the topic or the issues being talked about. This will also distract you from the conversation and affect your listening.

Not Open to Others' Point of View

If you have preconceived ideas or viewpoints on the topic or issues and you are not open or willing to listen to any other viewpoint or perception, you may become closed to what others are saying and this serves as a barrier to effective communication. We all have ideals and values that we believe to be correct and it can be difficult to listen to the views of others that contradict our views on these. The key to effective listening and interpersonal skills more generally is the ability to have a truly open mind—to understand why others think about things differently to you and use this information to build a better connect with the speaker. This does not, however, mean you have to agree with whatever is being said but what is more important is to listen and attempt to comprehend and acknowledge.

As most of us have a lot of internal self-dialogue, we spend considerable time on listening to our own thoughts and feelings. Sometimes, it can be difficult to switch the focus from 'I' or 'me' to 'you' and 'them'. Effective listening involves opening your mind to the views of others and attempting to feel empathetic.

Physical or Mental Distractions

An example of a physical barrier to communication is geographic distance between the speaker and the receiver(s). This may make listening an uncomfortable exercise for the receiver. Physical distance may also make it difficult for you to observe the non-verbal cues, gestures, posture and general body language. This can make communication less effective.

Also, you cannot communicate effectively when you are not focused. If you are planning what you are going to say next; daydreaming, checking text messages, fiddling with your hair, fingers, pen, etc., or gazing out of the window, you are almost certain to miss non-verbal cues in the conversation. You need to stay focused on the moment-to-moment experience.

While you are engaged in a conversation, there may be distracting sounds in the immediate environment, such as television or radio, someone else having a conversation within your hearing distance or some other dominant noises. Trying to listen to more than one voice at a time will distract you from your main communication, lessening your listening capability.

It is also likely that you may find the other person attractive/unattractive and you pay more attention to his or her physical appearance and how you feel about the communicator than to what he or she is saying. Perhaps, you simply do not like the speaker—you may mentally argue with the speaker and be fast to criticise, either verbally or in your head.

Some other distractions may be: you are feeling unwell or tired, hungry or needing to use the toilet.

Your Emotional and Psychological State

Emotional and psychological state of the communicators will influence how the message is sent, received and perceived. If you are preoccupied with something that is extraneous to the communication or the person, your listening abilities will be affected. If you are stressed, emotionally overwhelmed or worried about other issues, you may be too busy concentrating on what you are thinking about and your mind may get blurred. In such situations, you may only listen in such a way that none or only a little of the message comes through, making it difficult for you to grasp completely the intent or meaning appropriately. You are more likely to misread other people, prompting you to send confusing or off-putting non-verbal signals and lapse into unhealthy knee-jerk patterns of behaviour. Sometimes, your lack of attention becomes apparent to the other person, affecting good communication.

Keep a watch on your emotions; otherwise, they may so overwhelm you that you are not able to think rationally and objectively. You may lose contact with reason and your sense of judgement. Wittingly or unwittingly, you may be trapped in a situation in which the process of thinking and expression is impaired. The words that come out of you may become emotionally charged and your listening may also get influenced.

Your emotions can be supportive of your communication only if you are able to keep them in control. Therefore, take a moment to calm down before continuing the conversation.

Attitudinal Barriers

For a meaningful, sincere and open interaction with others, your disposition towards the person(s) and your interest in the communication are important elements. If you are indifferent or resentful to the person with whom you are communicating, consciously or subconsciously, you have already raised barriers for a proper, meaningful and productive communication. You will have difficulty in getting your message across to the other person and the communication you receive also gets distorted or vitiated. You will be inclined to give your own meaning and interpretation to the message you receive. Your perceptions will become subjective. It is, therefore, important that you should attempt to overcome these attitudinal barriers to facilitate effective communication.

Sometimes, your expectations and prejudices may lead to false assumptions or stereotyping. For instance, you may make a judgement that the other person is not very bright and, perhaps, not qualified, so there is no point to listening to what she has to say. Also, people often hear and comprehend what they expect to hear and comprehend rather than what is actually said and jump to incorrect interpretations and conclusions. Similarly, attitudinal barriers are behaviours or perceptions that prevent people from communicating effectively.

Non-verbal Language

Non-verbal communication should reinforce what is being said, not contradict it. If you say one thing, but your body language says something else, your listener is likely to feel that you are being dishonest. For example, you cannot say 'yes' while shaking your head in a 'no' gesture.

If you disagree with or dislike what is being said, you may use negative body language to rebuff the other person's message, such as crossing your arms, avoiding eye contact or tapping your feet. You do not have to agree, or even like what is being said, but to continue communicating effectively without irritating or making the other person defensive, it is important to avoid sending negative signals.

Previous Experiences

We are all influenced by previous experiences in life. We respond to people based on personal appearances, how initial introductions or welcomes were received and/or previous interpersonal encounters. If we stereotype a person, we become less objective and, therefore, we are less likely to listen effectively.

Your not-so-pleasant experiences with those who are to be part of the transaction can put you in a frame of mind where you are inclined not to be active participant. You may be convinced that it is not worthwhile to be part of the discussion where these people are present. As a result, you may completely desist from participating in the discussion.

The negative emotions from previous experiences, if not released, continue to haunt us and get expressed when we expect less. They are triggered by similar situations that show up in our life, without us consciously recognising them. Did it occur to you that, sometimes, we get upset, engage into an argument or raise the tone of our voice for something that is trivial or not really a big deal? It is likely that our previous unreleased or unexpressed emotions are finding an outlet through a trigger that is seemingly trivial or insignificant. Keep a check on such situations, taking care that they do not affect your communication as well as your relationships.

Low Self-esteem

Low self-esteem of any of the participants impacts interpersonal communication. More generally, people with low self-esteem may be less assertive and, therefore, may not feel comfortable communicating—they may feel shy about saying how they really feel or read negative subtexts into messages they hear. Not having the courage to express your ideas (because you believe they are not worthy or relevant) could send a different message than the one you want to. It might mislead other people, leaving them to believe whatever they want (which might be different from what you want). Low self-esteem could also show up as lack of confidence in continuing the conversation.

Defensive Communication

Defensive communication is a manifestation of defensive behaviour. Defensive behaviour is defined as that behaviour which occurs when one perceives a threat or challenge to her viewpoints or position. Thus, defensive communication is when a person deliberately and continually refracts messages received. If you are insecure, you tend to distort questions into accusations and your replies into justifications. You view others and their communication with apprehensions and doubts. Trust, a cornerstone of communication, is absent. This can create an environment that is not conducive for a healthy and useful exchange of ideas, thoughts and feelings.

SUGGESTED GUIDELINES FOR CONDUCTING THE SESSION

Before the group takes up Exercises 1 (Interpersonal Communication Profile) and 2 (Listening Bad Habits), give a brief introduction to communication, highlighting its importance in our day-to-day life. It is suggested that at this point in time, you do not go into substantive discussion on various aspects of communication or the skills involved in interpersonal communication otherwise you are likely to influence their responses to the two exercises.

Next, administer Exercises 1 and 2, using the guidelines provided with each of them. Once the participants have completed the two exercises, it is time for you to give your substantive and comprehensive inputs on various aspects of communication, including the skills involved in the process (for now, do not deal with 'Assertiveness in Communication'). You may draw from the extensive material provided under trainer's notes. Your discussion should also analyse data generated through the participants' responses for the two exercises. This is very important as the participants will be keen to know about their own communication profile. To discuss 'Statements' under Exercise 1, you may use the 'Tool for the Trainer for Discussion', given as part of the exercise.

After you have given inputs on all other aspects of communication, now you open discussion on 'assertiveness', as this by itself is important not only in communication but also in interpersonal relationships. Before going to Exercise 3, the participants should fully comprehend the distinguishing nuances between *assertive*, *non-assertive* or *passive*, and *aggressive behaviour*. After these inputs, the group is now ready for Exercise 3. Provide a copy of the handout on the three types of behaviour to assist them in completing the exercise.

After you have wrapped up discussion on Exercise 3, you may discuss 'barriers to communication'. You may start by eliciting participants' experiences in interpersonal communication and then build on their responses, reinforcing the discussion with your inputs.

You may decide on the time frame for all your inputs, keeping in view the time allocation for the three exercises.

Consistent with the suggested overall approach to the training programme, you must always engage the participants in active discussion, even while you are providing the inputs.

EXERCISE 1

INTERPERSONAL COMMUNICATION PROFILE

Objectives

At the end of the exercise, the participants will be able to:

- Get insights into their own communication profile—how they express themselves and how they listen and respond to others; stimulating them to take corrective action to improve their communication skills
- Understand key aspects of interpersonal communication

Time allocation

About 1 ½ hours

Materials required

Training aids and tools for your inputs on the exercise and summing up; flip charts for highlighting key points as the participants share their responses and the statements are discussed, with paper markers; worksheet on 'Interpersonal Communication Profile' (each participant gets a copy); white board and its markers.

Steps in conducting the exercise

- Introduce the exercise to the group, emphasising the importance of effective communication. You must ensure that your introductory talk does not go into more substantive details.
- Distribute the worksheet—Interpersonal Communication Profile. Emphasise that this is an individual exercise and the participants are expected to go through each statement carefully and record his or her responses. Give the participants some time to go through the worksheet and the instructions carefully and provide clarifications, if required. However, remember that at this point in time you should

only offer clarifications for better understanding of the statements. Refrain from entering into any specifics as this may influence or condition their responses.

- Provide enough time to the participants to complete the exercise in accordance with the instructions indicated in the worksheet.
- Once the participants have completed the exercise, invite some of them to share their responses. However, you must limit the discussion to the minimum as you will give your substantive inputs on all aspects of communication after the participants have completed Exercise 2—Listening Bad Habits—as well. Sum up the session, making it clear to the group that detailed discussion will follow after the next exercise.

WORKSHEET ON INTERPERSONAL COMMUNICATION PROFILE

This exercise offers you an opportunity to make an objective appraisal of your interpersonal communication skills. It will help you understand how you interact with others in your day-to-day contacts and activities.

Instructions for completing the worksheet

- The exercise refers to persons 'other than your family members or relatives'.
- The responses should be spontaneous reflecting the 'real manner or pattern' in which you conduct your interpersonal communication.
- If you wish to get a realistic assessment of your competency in interpersonal communication, you should be 'frank and honest' in your responses.
- The responses are confidential and you will not be required to share them 'if you do not wish to'.
- Against each statement, indicate by circling the appropriate number on a scale of 1–7 (where 1 is the lowest and 7 is the highest), how you rate yourself in the context of that specific statement.

Statements

1. When engaged in a conversation, do you feel that your words are coming out the way you want them to?

   1   2   3   4   5   6   7

2. When someone makes a comment or asks a question that is not clear to you, do you ask the person to clarify, elaborate or explain the meaning?

   1   2   3   4   5   6   7

3. Do you merely assume the other person fully understands your comments or question without your attempting to explain what you really wish to convey?

   1   2   3   4   5   6   7

4. In a discussion, do you find it difficult to express your views or give your comments when you feel that they differ from those of others or challenge them?

   1   2   3   4   5   6   7

5. Do you find it difficult to think clearly when your feelings or emotions enter the discussion or conversation?

   1   2   3   4   5   6   7

6. Do you feel greatly upset or angry when someone disagrees with your views or challenges you?

   1   2   3   4   5   6   7

7. Do you worry and feel low for a long time if someone upsets or hurts you?

   1   2   3   4   5   6   7

8. In conversation, do you let the other person finish talking before responding or expressing your views?

   1   2   3   4   5   6   7

9. While speaking, are you able to perceive how others are receiving your views and how they are likely to react to what you are saying?

   1   2   3   4   5   6   7

10. Do you pretend and give others an impression that you are listening to them when actually you are not?

    1   2   3   4   5   6   7

11. In conversation or discussion, do you attempt to understand the meaning of what others are trying to say or merely listen to the words and respond?

    1   2   3   4   5   6   7

12. In a discussion, is it difficult for you to view things from the other person's perspective?

    1   2   3   4   5   6   7

13. In a discussion or conversation, do you make an effort to find out about how others feel about the point you are trying to put across?

    1   2   3   4   5   6   7

14. Do you find it difficult to compliment and praise others?

    1   2   3   4   5   6   7

15. In conversation, are you in a position to distinguish between communication through words and what is being conveyed through emotions and feelings?

    1   2   3   4   5   6   7

16. Do you deliberately try to conceal your faults from others?

    1   2   3   4   5   6   7

17. Do you refrain from saying something that you know will only hurt others or make matters worse?

    1   2   3   4   5   6   7

18. When you find that someone has hurt your feelings, do you make an effort to convey this to the person and discuss this with him or her?

    1   2   3   4   5   6   7

19. Do you become very uneasy when someone pays you a compliment?

    1   2   3   4   5   6   7

20. If you feel that others are not able to get the intended meaning, do you make an effort to explain yourself and convey what you think, feel or believe?

    1   2   3   4   5   6   7

TOOL FOR THE TRAINER FOR DISCUSSION

Interpersonal Communication Profile

Note for the facilitators

This tool is to assist in discussing the statements in the context of the responses of the participants. To help you in this task, six statements covering four key elements of effective communication are discussed here by way of illustration. However, feel free to choose any statements that you consider appropriate for the group.

Statement 1

Clarity in expression: This statement relates to effective expression. If the words are not coming as you want them to, it can lead to miscommunication. What you mean to convey will not reach the receiver. Incidentally, it is quite likely that you may not even realise that the words are not coming the way you intended them to. You may feel that the communication has reached the listener but it has not. And the response (of the receiver) will be based on the comprehension of the receiver. Therefore, your endeavour should be to develop the competency that will help you to make the expression consistent with the thinking.

Statement 3

Clarity in expression: This assumption can lead to miscommunication and, in some cases, even misunderstanding between the two people in interaction with each other. It is possible that your notion may be wrong but you may continue the conversation believing that you are being fully understood by the other person. It is, therefore, important for you to check whether he or she is receiving your communication with its intended meaning and substance. There may be non-verbal signals from him or her but, at times, you may have to confirm it verbally from her/him.

Statement 5

Managing of emotions: This statement refers to your ability to cope with emotions during a conversation. It is not always an easy task as often we can get overwhelmed by the emotions and, as a result, our communication can get vitiated. We may lose objectivity, our ability to think clearly gets affected and we may not be able to focus on the issue at hand. It is, therefore, important that we should be fully conscious of our emotions and feelings during our interaction with others and learn to manage them.

Statement 8

Active listening: This is a problem with many of us. We start formulating our response in a conversation even before the other person has finished speaking. This means that without fully hearing out him or her, we are getting ready to respond. As we start forming our views or comments, we cease to listen to him or her. It is, therefore, likely that we may miss out on some substantive point being made by the other person. In such cases, our response will be based only on the part of the conversation when we were engaged in active listening. This results in miscommunication or distortions. It is, therefore, important that when in conversation we should listen carefully and respond only when we have fully comprehended the meaning and essence of the communication received from the other person.

Statement 11

Active listening: Communication is not merely through words. A lot is conveyed through body language and feelings. Unless you are sensitive to these clues, you may not be able to fully understand the meaning and substance of the message being conveyed to you. So you have to develop the ability not only to listen to the words but also to grasp what lies behind the verbal communication. You have to alert yourself to read between the lines by honing your listening competencies.

Statement 16

Self-disclosure: It is important that you are not just honest and open in your conversation but are also perceived to be so. If you try to engage in cover-up operations with regard to your faults and shortcomings, you will not be able to acquire the confidence of the person with whom you are in conversation. If he or she is assured of your genuineness and straightforwardness, you will be able to build a bond of mutual trust that facilitates meaningful and sincere conversation. It is, therefore, necessary that while you should be proud of your strengths, you need not be ashamed of your shortcomings.

EXERCISE 2

LISTENING BAD HABITS

Objectives

At the end of the exercise, the participants will be able to:

- Identify areas in which they need to improve their listening skills
- Take action to remove deficiencies

Time allocation

About one hour

Materials required

Training aids required for your briefing on the exercise; copies of handout on Listening Bad Habits (one for each participant); flip charts and writing markers for displaying key points emerging out of the sharing by the participants and discussion, and for your summing-up; white board and markers.

Steps in conducting the exercise

- Give a brief introduction to the exercise and emphasise the importance of being open and honest in checking the appropriate responses
- This is an individual exercise and the responses of the participants should be based on the assessment of their usual listening habits, in the context of their interaction with family members and friends
- Distribute the worksheet and ask them to complete the exercise

- After the participants have completed the exercise, invite some of them to share their responses and also indicate what they propose to do to remove deficiencies, if any
- Summarise the points and tell the group that your inputs will deal with the points emerging out of the participants' responses.

LISTENING BAD HABITS

Worksheet for Participants

Following is a list of 12 bad habits of listening. Check those listening bad habits that you are sometimes guilty of committing when communicating with others. Be honest with yourself!

( ) I interrupt often or try to finish the other person's sentences
( ) I jump to conclusions
( ) I make up my mind before I have all the information
( ) I am impatient
( ) I lose my temper when hearing things I don't agree with
( ) I try to change the subject to something that relates to my own experiences
( ) I think more about my reply while the other person is speaking than what he or she is saying
( ) I get easily distracted during a conversation
( ) I listen only to facts
( ) I prejudge people on the basis of their comments
( ) I ignore non-verbal clues
( ) I assume the other person already knows what I am

Suggestions for action to remove one or two key deficiencies, if any

_____

_____

EXERCISE 3

ASSERTIVE BEHAVIOUR AND COMMUNICATION

Objectives

At the end of the exercise, the participants will be able to:

- Understand different aspects of assertive behaviour and distinguish between assertive, non-assertive and aggressive behaviour.
- Develop appropriate responses consistent with assertive behaviour to some common situations one confronts in life.

Time allocation

About 1 ½ hours

Materials required

Training aids and tools required for explaining key aspects of 'assertive behaviour' as part of your introductory talk and for summing up: flip charts and writing markers for displaying key points emerging out of the sharing of the participants of their individual responses; white board and markers; the following materials for each participant:

- Identifying Assertion Response Worksheet
- Handout for the participants for reference
- Identifying Assertion Response—Discussion Tool

Steps in conducting the exercise

- Recall the discussion you had on 'assertive behaviour' and explain the purpose of the exercise. Check if they have any clarifications to seek or some questions. Respond to them before you go to the next step. However, you must ensure that you do not condition their responses.
- Distribute copies of the Identifying Assertion Response worksheet and handout for the participants for reference to the participants

and explain the task. Make it clear that as it is an individual exercise, each of them must complete the worksheet independently.

- When all the participants have completed the worksheet, distribute the 'Identifying Assertion Response—Discussion Tool' and ask the participants to compare their responses with the ones provided in the tool. They should also get ready for the following discussion.

- Invite some participants to share their responses and lead a discussion based on the Discussion Tool. Clarify the responses for all situations given in the exercise, answering questions of the group, if any.

- Sum up the discussion by highlighting the points that might have emerged from the sharing of responses by the participants. Also, reinforce your earlier elaboration on assertive, non-assertive or passive, and aggressive behaviour by putting into context the situations presented in the worksheet. You may also add some examples appropriate to the local context.

(Note for the trainer: In the following worksheet, the names mentioned in the situations may be changed consistent with the cultural context).

Worksheet

Identifying Assertion Response

Instructions: Following are some situations that you may encounter in your day-to-day life when interacting with your friends and others around you. For each situation, three possible responses are given. The task before you is to go through the situations carefully and then examine the options for your response that is indicative of assertive behaviour. You may draw clues from the discussion you had before this exercise and the handout for the participants.

Tick your response in the space provided after the statement.

Situation 1

You invited your friend, Nikhil, for a formal get-together at your place. He has just arrived, about an hour late. He did not call to let you know that he would be delayed. You were, evidently, annoyed. You say to him:

1.1 Come on, Nikhil, all is ready. We can start the party _____
1.2 We have been waiting for you for an hour. I wish you would have
called to let us know that you were being delayed _____
1.3 You kept us waiting. You think we are all fools. It is highly irresponsible
of you _____

Situation 2

Your friend Jyotika has always been taking your help in writing her
assignments and in her homework. Consequently, often, you find it difficult
to attend to your own tasks and studies. You have decided to put an end to
this. She has just asked you to do some of her assignments. You tell her:

2.1 I am somewhat busy now. If you are not able to do it, I guess I can
help you _____
2.2 I am sorry I cannot do it anymore. I am sick and tired of it all. It is
time that you do it yourself. You are very inconsiderate and selfish
_____
2.3 No, Jyotika. Please do not expect me to continue doing this for
you. My own work is getting neglected and I no longer want to do it.
Hope you realise that it is time for you to handle your work on your
own _____

Situation 3

A friend has just complimented you on your securing excellent grades in
the examination. You are indeed happy at your performance. Your response:

3.1 Thank you very much. I greatly appreciate your gesture _____
3.2 Oh! This. It is nothing special. Others have also got good grades
_____
3.3 Well _____ Well _____ I do not know whether
I deserved these grades _____

Situation 4

You are out with a group of friends. You are all deciding which disco to go
for the evening. One person has just suggested a particular joint. You are
not happy with the suggestion. You say:

4.1   You always seem to be making the choice on the basis of only your interests. You do not care for what others want. You are very selfish _____

4.2   I am not inclined to go there. How about considering other options acceptable to all? One possibility is 'Evening Joy' _____

4.3   Well, I am not keen to go there but I guess if you want it, I will go along with the suggestion _____

Situation 5

A classmate has criticised your close friend, Jayant. You feel the criticism is unjustified and unfair. You are face-to-face with the classmate. You say:

5.1   I think you should stop all this rubbish. You are just a bully. You seem to be prejudiced against him _____

5.2   Well...I see what you mean _____

5.3   I feel that your criticism is unfair. I know him well. He is not like that _____

Situation 6

You are at a department store to return a piece of garment that is faulty. You bought a shirt from the store but when you took it home, you found a stitching defect in it. You do not want the item as it is. The counter attendant has just told you that no one would notice it. Your response is:

6.1   Well, I would still like to return it or exchange it for another one. I do not want this one _____

6.2   Look, I want my money back. You gave me a defective piece. I have wasted my time. I do not wish to spend any more time on this _____

6.3   Well, are you sure no one will notice it? Let me have a second look _____

IDENTIFYING ASSERTION RESPONSE—DISCUSSION TOOL

Responses to Situations

Situation 1

1.1 Non-assertive: Because you are pretending that the late arrival does not mean much though you were earlier quite annoyed. You neither make an attempt to express your displeasure to Nikhil nor make him realise that his behaviour was not appropriate.

1.2 Assertive: Because you make him aware that he is late. You also tell him about his responsibility of calling you about the delay. You expressed your feelings without getting into a confrontation with Nikhil.

1.3 Aggressive: Here you are accusing him of being irresponsible. You are confronting him with words and phrases that can lead to a very unpleasant situation.

Situation 2

2.1 Non-assertive: You do not tell your friend that helping her is affecting your own work. You are keeping the window of helping her open when the truth is that you no longer want to help her. You are not helping yourself.

2.2 Aggressive: Your response is rude and you are engaged in making accusations that are not consistent with the nature of the situation.

2.3 Assertive: You are able to put across your problem without getting into a confrontation with Jyotika—helping her is affecting your own work. You are urging her to redefine her expectations from you and telling her that hereafter she should look after her work.

Situation 3

3.1 Assertive: You accept the compliment and express appreciation of your friend.

3.2 Non-assertive: You do not accept the compliment. In fact, you appear to be belittling your achievement by pointing out that others have also got good grades though you are happy with your performance. You are not expressing your feelings.

3.3   Non-assertive: Here also you are not inclined to accept the compliment. You go even further and doubt whether you deserved the grades. This is not humility but indicates unwillingness to celebrate your success.

Situation 4

4.1   Aggressive: Instead of being reasonable, you attack not just the suggestion but also your friend calling him or her selfish. This response of yours could trigger an unhappy situation.

4.2   Assertive: You not only make your views clear to the group but also come out with a suggestion that the group should consider other options. Your stand may help the group take a decision where everyone feels comfortable.

4.3   Non-assertive: You do express your unhappiness with the choice but are unwilling to go any further. In fact, you are ready to go along with the suggestion. You appeared to be almost backtracking.

Situation 5

5.1   Aggressive: You behave in a confrontationist manner. You call the classmate a bully and accuse him or her of being prejudiced against Jayant.

5.2   Non-assertive: Although you do not agree with your classmate but you do not make this clear. You are reluctant to express your views openly and explicitly. In fact, you give an impression that you do not disagree.

5.3   Assertive: You express how you feel and even your assessment by saying that the criticism was unfair. You reinforce this by saying that you know Jayant well and he does not deserve this criticism.

Situation 6

6.1   Assertive: While you do not disagree with the counter attendant but you still insist that you want to either return the defective shirt or get another one in exchange. You are categorical in conveying to the attendant that you do not want this piece.

6.2   Aggressive: You are strong in your language. You accuse the attendant (or the store) of giving you a defective piece of garment. You also communicate your anger by saying that this whole thing has resulted in wasting your time. And you make it clear that you are not willing to waste any more time.

6.3   Non-assertive: You appear to be agreeing with the attendant although you are well aware that the piece is defective. You also admit that you could be wrong by saying that you want to have a second look.

Handout for the Participants for Reference

Passive people (Non–assertive)	Assertive people	Aggressive people
Have trouble saying no	Are firm and direct	Are loud, bossy and pushy
Do whatever others ask, even if it is very inconvenient	Do not blame others but take full responsibility for their own feelings	Get their way, no matter what
Get stepped on a lot	Concentrate on the present	React instantly
Talk softly and do not stand up for their rights	Can express their needs and feelings calmly and easily	Like to get even
They are not even sure whether they have any rights	Are confident about who they are	Do not care about feelings.
Do anything to avoid conflict	Speak firmly and make eye contact	Give vice-like handshakes
Are taken advantage of. They get resentful but do not tell anyone	Respect others' rights and expect the same in return	Believe that winning is everything

Source: Will Schutz, xxxx, Chapter 7.

Module 3
Interpersonal Relationships

Establishing and nurturing relationships is an important part of our life. Healthy, harmonious relationships—personal or professional—contribute a lot to our physical, social and emotional well-being and help us realise our objectives, personal or work-related. Underscoring this importance, this module aims to provide opportunity to the participants of the programme to discuss various aspects of this crucial life skill, including the skills required to build meaningful and enduring relationships within the family, in social circles and at workplace.

Specifically, the module focuses on the following key areas:

- Understanding interpersonal relationship
- Interpersonal relationship at workplace
- Personal qualities that influence interpersonal relationships
- Skills in interpersonal relationship

Expected Outcomes from the Module

At the end of the session on the module, the participants will be able to:

- Understand various aspects of interpersonal relationships in personal and professional life
- Specify and elaborate on various qualities that are at the basis for establishing and nurturing healthy bonds with people
- Identify, through a process of self-assessment, the areas and skills that they need to work on to enhance their abilities to establish and develop affable and mutually constructive relationships

UNDERSTANDING INTERPERSONAL RELATIONSHIP

It is generally acknowledged that we cannot live by ourselves even if we want to. All of us have an intense desire, whether expressed or unexpressed, to interact with people and establish and maintain relationships that are productive and cordial.

There are always a number of things in our life that we cannot carry out without help or support from others. Our first realisation comes in early childhood when even for our basic physical needs, such as food and clothing, we are dependent on our immediate family. This process continues as we grow up. Our relationship with family members grows stronger (generally) and as we move from school to institutions of higher education, and then to the workplace, we establish new relationships and expand our social network.

Routinely, you interact with a number of people, some casually and others with a greater sense of purpose and meaning. If you are travelling in a public transport, you may interact with co-passengers—with some because you want to and with others simply out of courtesy. You may engage in discussions on topics and issues of mutual interest but this interaction may last only up to our respective destinations. We are reconciled to the fact that we may never see them again. And we move on with our lives (though in a few cases, this interaction may be the beginning of a more enduring and closer relationship, extending well beyond the travel). Even when we commute regularly on a particular route using the same mode of transport, we may strike a more enduring relationship with at least some commuters. Sometimes, regular morning walkers also develop rapport and become buddies. It is, therefore, not unusual to see even casual or chance meetings resulting in more durable and productive relationships. But in all such relationships, we may make the choice whether to pursue them or not and also decide on the nature and strength of the bonding.

Interpersonal relationship may, thus, be understood as social association or affiliation between two people. It is a positive and constructive outcome of regular and more stable human interaction with others. Relationships vary in levels of intimacy and sharing, implying the discovery and establishment of shared ground. Some relationships are short-term but some are more enduring, depending on the people with whom we relate, the situations, the circumstances and the nature of these relationships.

Relationship is built on the motto of 'give and take'. It is always a two-way transaction. Therefore, it has an element of mutuality. If either of the parties is indifferent or unresponsive, a relationship may not even take off or it may become fragile, leading to a possible parting of ways.

However, there are some relationships or associations in which we do not have choice. We do not choose our parents, siblings or relatives, or even neighbours though we may opt for a particular neighbourhood. We do not have any option with regard to our classmates or teachers. At the workplace also, we have no freedom to pick our bosses or colleagues. There is certain inevitability about this situation and we have to accept their companionship and association.

Two individuals in a relationship must be compatible with each other. There should be no scope of conflicts and misunderstandings in a relationship. Individuals from similar backgrounds and similar goals in life do extremely well in relationships. People with different aims, attitudes, thought processes find it difficult to adjust and hence fail to carry the relationship to the next level.

INTERPERSONAL RELATIONSHIP AT WORKPLACE

In the life of a working individual, interpersonal relationship at workplace assumes considerable importance. She spends about eight to nine hours in her organisation, and it is practically not possible for her to work all alone. Working in isolation can induce boredom and make the task uninteresting. Fatigue may set in early and she may also become prone to stress and anxiety.

Also, human beings are not machines who can work at a stretch without any human interaction. We need people to talk to and share our views, thoughts and emotional state. Imagine yourself working in an organisation with no friends around. You will shudder at the thought. We are social animals and we need people with whom we are able to interact on a person-to-person level on a regular basis.

It is essential to have trustworthy fellow workers around with whom you can share your problems and feelings without the fear of them getting passed on to others in the organisation. Also, we must have friends at the workplace who can give us honest feedback on our performance and behaviour.

The work of the organisation also requires us to interact with other colleagues as part of our job profile. A prerequisite for effective and functional team in an organisation is sound, working relationship among its members. They must be able to relate to one another in order to realise the goals of the team and produce the best outcomes from their efforts. In some cases, an individual needs the support of fellow workers to complete tasks or job assignments within the stipulated time frame for better results. In most cases, roles and responsibilities of different employees in an organisation are complementary. This necessitates regular interaction.

Collective decision-making requires employees to discuss various issues, evaluate pros and cons, and reach to solutions benefiting not only the employees but also the organisation on the whole. If the relationships are not cordial and functional, the process can become very complicated and the work of the organisation will get adversely affected. Collective decision-making assumes that the employees will brainstorm together and reach to better strategies and ideas. Strategies must be discussed on an open platform where every individual has the liberty to express his or her views. The management must take measures to promote free communication. Interaction on a regular basis is important for healthy relationship.

Interpersonal relationship has a direct effect on the organisational culture. Misunderstandings and confusions lead to negativity at the workplace. Conflicts lead you nowhere and, in turn, spoil the work environment. Employees working together ought to share a special bond for them to deliver at their best level. It is essential for individuals to be honest with each other for a healthy interpersonal relationship and eventually positive ambience at the workplace.

We need people around who can extend support when we face difficult situations in our work, appreciate our hard work and its outcomes and guide and motivate us from time to time. Therefore, it is essential to have some trustworthy colleagues at the workplace. We need colleagues to fall back on at the times of crisis. In some cases, one needs to have people at the workplace who are more like mentors than mere colleagues.

PERSONAL QUALITIES THAT INFLUENCE INTERPERSONAL RELATIONSHIPS

Certain personal qualities are the prerequisites of effective interpersonal relationships. They constitute the bedrock for all productive and sound human relationships. They get manifested in your demeanour and actions in the context of establishing and nurturing healthy bonds with people with whom you interact on a regular basis. In certain other situations, they get translated into skills that are helpful in promoting warm, healthy and productive relationships.

Warmth

Warm people are likely to get along better with others than those who are rather cold or indifferent to others. Warmth is reflected in a pleasant and cordial demeanour that is not faked but genuine. In a relationship, it means sending a message to others that you are approachable and willing to interact with them. However, do not expect that your warmth will also be reciprocated in the same measure. You must be prepared for these situations and should not feel discouraged by a somewhat adverse or indifferent response of others. You have control on your behaviour and actions but you do not exercise the same level of control over others.

Being Open and Frank

Openness means that you are open to ideas and suggestions coming from others. It also means that you create a threat-free and congenial environment that facilitates free sharing of views, feelings and emotions. Being sincere and candid also mean that you do not carry a hidden agenda in your interaction with others and you are also open to receiving feedback from others on your actions and behaviour, and value it. Generally, people who are open and frank are also genuine. They are transparent and have no pretensions. They do not create facades or build defences.

Treating Others with Respect and Dignity

Regardless of his or her social or professional status or position, an individual deserves respect and regard from you. As people say, 'Respect begets respect'. Remember, warm and enduring relationships can be established only if we treat others with regard they deserve as human beings. We should recognise the dignity of others.

Empathetic Understanding of Others

Establishing bonds with people requires understanding their perceptions as objectively as possible without attempting to bring your own context into play. This is empathetic understanding. You need to be able to empathise with others in order to understand them. Empathy is the term used to convey the idea of the ability to enter the perpetual world of the other person to see the world as she sees it.

(Cross reference: for more details on 'Empathy', refer to Module 8).

Unbiased Attitude

For a meaningful, sincere and open relationship, it is important that you become conscious of your biases and mental blocks not only towards others but also how you look at situations and circumstances that guide and regulate the relationships. If you continue to harbour these biases and do nothing about them, you will be inclined to interpret and perceive the other person and the events impinging on the relationship through these biases, thus losing objectivity. Consciously or subconsciously, you will distort behaviour and actions of the other person to affirm these biases and justify your attitude. In the process, you may lose contact with reason and rationality. This will amount to betraying the trust of the other person.

SKILLS IN INTERPERSONAL RELATIONSHIP

Communication

Communication is said to be the basis of every interpersonal relationship. In fact, effective communication is the key to a healthy and long-lasting relationship. If individuals do not communicate with each other effectively, problems are bound to come. Communication also plays a pivotal role in reducing misunderstandings or removing minor aberrations, eventually, strengthening the bond between individuals. There is no doubt that a relationship will lose its meaning and value if individuals do not express and reciprocate their feelings through various modes of communication. A healthy interaction is essential for a healthy relationship.

(Cross-reference: 'Interpersonal Communication' has been discussed in considerable detail under Module 2).

Assertiveness

Assertiveness is part of effective communication, which itself is crucial in establishing and sustaining a strong interpersonal relationship. Being assertive means that you are able to stand up for your own rights, views and values without being aggressive or passively accepting what others say or do, even when knowing that they are 'wrong'. However, an important part is that you do not undermine or disrespect the rights, views or values of others who are in a relationship with you.

(Cross-reference: for more details, see Module 2).

Building Trust

> Whoever is careless with the truth in small matters
> cannot be trusted with important matters.
>
> —Albert Einstein

> To be trusted is a greater compliment than being loved.
>
> —George MacDonald

Trust in Interpersonal Relationship

In dictionaries, trust has been defined as:

- 'Reliance on and confidence in the truth, reliability, etc., of a person or thing' (*Collins Dictionary*)
- Belief that someone or something is reliable, good, honest, effective, etc. (*Merriam-Webster Dictionary*)

Trust has also been defined as 'a psychological state comprising the intention to accept vulnerability based upon positive expectations of the intentions or behaviour of another'. Similarly, Lewicki, McAllister and Bies (1998) describe trust as 'an individual's belief in, and willingness to act on the basis of, the words, actions, and decisions of another'.

We may wonder that if we have an inherent trust in society, is it necessary to build trust in relationships. After all, if we trust our general society, would not we also trust the people with whom we have relationships? Well, not necessarily. It is important to understand that trust as a general social concept is somewhat different from the trust we build in interpersonal relationships with friends, family, co-workers or other people with whom we have a connection or bond.

Genuine and enduring relationships are built over a long period as people get to know and try out one another, gradually building up mutual trust. While on the one hand, this trust gets reinforced through difficult and challenging situations, it can also get shattered and relationships can collapse if they fail this test. Nothing can go right when there is no trust between spouses; children and parents; an employer and employees; friends; the state and its citizens or between institutions. In such cases, people cannot realise their full potential, cannot express their positive and negative feelings, cannot share their joys and sorrows, and cannot work efficiently. This may also block the way to growth, development and maturity.

The need for trust arises from our *interdependence* with others. There are numerous instances in our life when we depend on others to help us get what we want, to support us when we need it, to guide us when we are beset with problems or crisis. Sometimes, rather than expecting support, we just want them not to frustrate us or multiply our woes. As our interests with others are intertwined, we also must recognise that there is an element of *risk* involved insofar as we often encounter situations in which we cannot compel the cooperation or help we seek. Therefore, trust can be very valuable in social interactions. Trust has also been identified as a key element in conflict resolution, problem-solving and decision-making. It is the bedrock for teamwork.

You must recognise that to remain trustworthy for others, especially those who are close to you, you need to constantly invest in maintaining trust. Remember that it takes a lot of efforts and time to establish trust and your reputation as a trustworthy person but it may take just one small incident or aberration in your behaviour to bring down the edifice of trust you so assiduously built.

So why do these relationships require a different type of trust? The trust that you place in general society is kind of a general or abstract concept; you trust that people will come to your help if you are mugged by a stranger; a driver will not hit you while you are crossing the road from the zebra crossing. It is more about your safety and security. On the other hand, trust in interpersonal relationships is more specific and has concrete applications within the relationship between you and the other person. In simple terms, the trust you place in a friend or family member has clear meaning because it comes with certain easily identifiable risks or situations. Unlike the subconscious trust we place in our general society, the trust we have in our interpersonal relationships is something that must be built and maintained.

People need to feel secure in opening up their feelings and thoughts to others, so that they are able to establish a good relationship. Expressing ourselves freely, opening up to somebody else, is in direct proportion with the degree of sincerity and trust between that person and you. Undoubtedly, we cannot simply open up to everyone we meet. Opening up to someone means that there is a sense of trust between you and the other person although it must have taken time to build and maintain it at that level. Generally, the person who is able to open up inspires trust in the other and receives the message 'I trust you' in return. The trusted person may also be encouraged to open up and this leads to a deeper and closer relationship.

People share information with others in proportion to the trust they repose in them. Self-disclosure is directly proportional to the trust people have in others.

Building Trust in Interpersonal Relationship

Know yourself and your intentions: To be honest with someone else, we must know ourselves. We have to understand what we really think and feel about the world around us. Very often in life, we are either influenced by or conforming to certain *expectations* of people around us. Here it is important to differentiate between our 'real self'—what we really are and want—and 'assumed self'—what people want us to be and what we want because of people's expectations. When we are true to ourselves in this way, we are in a position to be more honest with the people around us. We are less likely to just tell people what they want to hear or try to cover up things about ourselves of which we feel ashamed. Instead, we can be truthful and candid about who we are and what we want in a relationship. This kindles trust.

Engage in open and transparent communication: Communication is one of the most important factors in building trust in interpersonal relationship. It is desirable that to the extent possible, communication should be face to face, as physical proximity will generate trust, by making it more personal and direct. Avoid doing it through e-mails or phone calls. Do not hold back when faced with issues that may impact relationship. When you have something to tell the other person, do not defer it but take the earliest opportunity to convey it. Through open communication in relationships, you set out on the pathway to trust.

Be honest and transparent in your communication. Do not have a hidden agenda. Sooner or later, truth is going to come out and this will shatter trust and the relationship may also crumple. Remember, being open and sincere in your communication makes you trustworthy. You will be trusted only if you are found to be worthy of it.

The way we communicate with others is a primary way we build trust. Along with specific behaviours and actions, communication serves as the vehicle for building trust in relationships. What we say, how we say it and how we respond to what others communicate can make or break trust. That is why it is important to develop your interpersonal communication skills.

Another aspect of interpersonal communication that builds trust is respecting confidentiality and privacy when requested by your friends on the information conveyed to you in good faith.

(Cross reference: for more details, see Module 2—'Interpersonal Communication').

Be transparent and show vulnerability: Establishing trust in a relationship requires one person to make the first move in extending it. Someone has to make herself vulnerable to another and one way to do that is to be transparent (appropriate for the context of the situation) in sharing information. A lack of transparency or vulnerability breeds suspicion in the relationship and is usually the result of one party wanting to minimise risk and maximise control.

Do not cave in when the boundaries of the relationships are tested: This is really crucial in building trust in the relationships. You cannot expect the relationships to be smooth sailing all the way. Without going through all those rocky terrains, it will be impossible to see how much strain the relationships with your friends can sustain before they reach *breaking point*. That is not to say that you should go out and create problems just to test how your friends react. Be aware that every relationship comes with its ups and downs, and that it is totally natural. In some cases, a relationship will meander through difficult terrains due to circumstances beyond your control. These situations are great for gauging one another and will lead to a greater sense of mutuality and understanding.

Do not hesitate to disagree: You do not have to agree with everything that your friends say or do and approve of their every behaviour or action. If you find something that does not agree with your thought process, views and values, simply express your differences, at an appropriate time and place and in a proper manner. You can express yourself clearly and explicitly without undermining the trust or affecting the relationship. In fact, these divergences will promote better appreciation of each other's positions, thus reinforcing trust. When you contribute to establishing a relationship based on reciprocity, the path becomes easier.

Make your actions match your words: Often, relationships lose their spark when people in a social relationship replace *substance* with *form*. To avoid this dishonest way of relating and to build trust, it is important to maintain consistency and integrity to make our actions match our words. This is when trust truly begins to form. Consistency is the primary ingredient of trust. When we observe consistency in honest words and actions in someone, we are inclined to reciprocate. We will let our guard down and this trust can lead to deeper levels of relational intimacy. Your credibility will be reinforced by 'walking the talk'. However, it will be rapidly lost if there are discrepancies between what you say and the actions you take.

Be open to feedback: Just as we should be straightforward with our friends, we should be open to receiving honest feedback directed at us. We should always be willing to listen to our friends and to see things from their point of view as well. What are they trying to tell us about how they are experiencing us and feeling towards us? Rather than argue every small detail, we should look for the kernel of truth in what our friends tell us. It is important not to be defensive, reactive or punishing for feedback. If we get victimised or fall apart when we hear criticism, then we emotionally manipulate our friends and encourage them to sugar-coat their words and expressions or even deceive us in the future. Such cases or situations will give rise to trust deficit.

Accept the other person as a separate person: No matter how connected we may *feel* to someone else, we will always be two separate people with two independent minds. If the other person does not see things the same way you do, there is no reason to feel hurt or offended. It just means that you are two people who view the world and issues from different perspectives. Remember the more we accept this reality, the more comfortable we can feel in accepting that we would not agree on everything. Indicate your acceptance and even respect of these individual differences. By being honest with each other, we can know and accept each other for who we actually are, not who we *want* each other to be. In this scenario, neither of us has to pretend to be someone else or try to fit an image or expectations. This becomes the basis of trust.

Be positive and respectful: Right or wrong, people will judge the quality of your character by how you speak about and treat others. If you are positive and respectful in your words and actions, people will trust that you are likely to treat them in similar manner. The opposite is also true. If you speak disparagingly about others or treat others as 'less than' yourself, you will become suspect in the eyes of those with whom you want to establish intimate relations. They will feel that today it is the turn of others and tomorrow they could be the target of your unfavourable and adverse remarks. They will doubt that you would act with fairness and integrity in your dealings with them.

Look for opportunities to build up the other person: Your words, behaviour and actions can go a long way in helping your friends learn, grow and build themselves. Look for every opportunity to make an effort in that direction. Your genuine action in this regard will assure others that you have their best interests in mind, a key driver of deciding to place their trust in you.

Demonstrate care and sincere interest for the other person: You must continually invest care and sincere interest in the relationship to cultivate trust. You should be fully involved in ensuring that the relationship grows and does not stagnate.

People can see right through a phony. If you do not genuinely care for the other person in the relationship, it will show in your words and actions. If it is important for you to build trust with someone, then you should find ways to genuinely care about them. Focus on every aspect of the relationship in an authentic way.

Cooperation and shared commitment: In relationships, shared commitment to certain cause, mutual interests, well-being and agenda will contribute to building trust. In many cases, commitment becomes the defining factor of trust. In working together for a common task, mutual cooperation and support also help to build trust among team members or colleagues. People intuitively trust people who are similar to themselves.

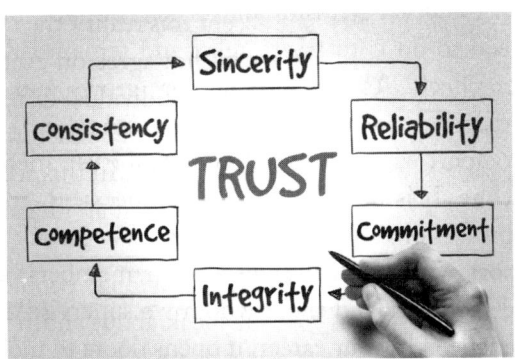

Building Rapport

What is Rapport?

- Rapport is a relationship of mutual respect, responsiveness and influence
- It is an ongoing process
- It is an honest attempt to understand another person from their world
- A willingness to be open—it is not agreement
- It is possible to have good rapport and strongly disagree

Rapport is a state of harmonious understanding with another individual or group that enables greater and easier communication. In other words, rapport is getting on well with another person or a group of people. It is about making a two-way connection. The task of building rapport becomes easier if we are able to find some common ground—shared interests or traits. However, there are occasions when you experience a genuine sense of trust and respect with another human being. You easily engage with them, regardless of how different the two of you may be. You feel like you are listening and being listened to. That is rapport.

The first task in successful interpersonal relationships is to attempt to build rapport. Building rapport is all about matching ourselves with another person. For many, starting a conversation with a stranger is a stressful event; we can be lost for words and feel awkward with our body language and mannerisms. Creating rapport at the beginning of a dialogue with somebody will often make the outcome of the conversation more positive. However stressful and/or nervous you may feel, the first things you need to do is to try to relax and remain calm and keep the tension under check. As a result, rapport grows and communication becomes easier.

You build rapport when you develop mutual trust, friendship and affinity with someone. It is often a long-term process. Rapport is important in both our professional and personal lives. We need to establish good working rapport with our colleagues, team members, superiors in the organisational hierarchy and those whom we supervise. Building rapport can also be beneficial to your career; it opens doors to more opportunities.

Sometimes, rapport happens naturally; you 'hit it off' or 'get on well' with somebody else without having to try; this is often how friendships are built. However, in most cases, rapport has to be assiduously built and developed; being empathetic helps in that process.

The First Interaction—Breaking the Ice

When meeting somebody for the first time, some simple tips will help you reduce the tension in the situation enabling both parties to feel more relaxed and thus communicate more effectively:

- How you dress is a key component of making a great first impression and establishing rapport with someone. Your appearance should help you connect with people, not create a barrier. A good rule of thumb is to dress just a little bit 'better' than the people you are about to meet. Whenever possible, find out about this in advance. If you arrive and see that you are overdressed, you can quickly 'dress down' by taking off your jacket or tie and by rolling up your shirtsleeves.
- Use nonthreatening and 'safe topics' for initial small talk. Talk about how you travelled, the weather, general issues. Do not talk too much about yourself and avoid asking direct questions about the other person. Make sure she feels included in the opening dialogue. Do not give an impression that you are interrogating.
- Listen to what the other person is saying and look for shared experiences or circumstances. This will give you clues to take the conversation forward in a positive way. Put her at ease, this will also enable you to relax and help the conversation to take on a natural course.
- Try to inject an element of light-hearted humour. Having a bit of fun together breaks the ice quickly and creates harmony. Engage in harmless bantering; talk about a funny episode or situation involving you. However, avoid making jokes about others. This is likely to place you in bad light.
- Be conscious of your body language and other non-verbal signals you are sending. Try to maintain eye contact as much as is appropriate, without making the other person uncomfortable. Relax and occasionally lean slightly towards the other person to indicate that you are listening, nothing more, especially if the other person is of opposite gender.

- Show some empathy. Demonstrate that you can see the other person's point of view. Remember rapport is more about finding similarities and 'being on the same wavelength' as somebody else— so being empathic will help to achieve this.

Non-verbal Rapport Building

Although initial interaction can help us to relax, most rapport building happens without words and through non-verbal communication channels. We create and maintain rapport subconsciously through matching non-verbal signals, including body positioning, body movements, eye contact, facial expressions and tone of voice with the other person. Watch two friends talking when you get the opportunity and see how they subconsciously replicate each other's non-verbal communication.

It is important that appropriate body language is used; we read and instantly believe what body language tells us, whereas we may take more persuading with vocal communication. If there is a mismatch between what we are saying verbally and what our body language is conveying, then the person we are communicating with is likely to trust the body language more. Building rapport, therefore, begins with displaying appropriate body language—exuding warmth, friendliness and openness.

As well as paying attention to and matching body language with the person we are communicating with, it helps if we can also match her words. Reflecting back and clarifying what has been said are useful techniques for reiterating what has been communicated by her. Not only will it confirm that you are listening but also give you opportunity to use her words and phrases of the other person, further emphasising the existence of common ground.

The way we use our voice is also important in developing rapport. When we are nervous or tense, we tend to talk more quickly. We can vary our voices, pitch, volume and pace in ways to make what we are saying more interesting. We will also come across as more relaxed, open and friendly. Try lowering your tone, talk more slowly and softly, this will help you develop rapport more easily.

Helpful Rapport-building Behaviours

- If you are sitting, then lean slightly forward towards the person you are talking to, with hands open and arms and legs uncrossed.

This is open body language and will help you and the person you are talking to feel more relaxed

- When listening, nod and make encouraging sounds and gestures; smile, when appropriate
- Use the other person's name early in the conversation. This is not only seen as polite but will also reinforce the name in your mind so you are less likely to forget it
- Ask the other person open questions. Open questions require more than a yes or no answer. This helps her in better engagement in the conversation
- Use feedback to summarise, reflect and clarify back to the other person what you think she said. This gives opportunity for any misunderstandings to be rectified quickly
- Talk about things that refer back to what the other person has said. Find links between common experiences
- When in agreement with the other person, openly say so and say why
- Build on the other person's ideas
- Be non-judgemental towards the other person. Let go of stereotypes and any preconceived ideas you may have about the person
- If you have to disagree with the other person, give the reason first then say you disagree
- Be genuine with visual and verbal behaviours working together to maximise the impact of your communication
- Offer a compliment, avoid criticism and be polite

Strategies for a Quick Rapport

Find common ground: Think of how comfortable you might feel if, while living thousands of miles from where you grew up, you met someone from your hometown. That sense of connectedness creates an instant rapport between two people.

When you meet someone new, do your best to find something you have in common. Engage the person in conversation to find out about her background, some personal information that may help you find some points of convergence, some common interests, roots, hobbies, education, friends, similar beliefs, values, etc. It is important to be sincere here; do not make up an interest in something just to create rapport. Not only can this seem desperate, it can dent your credibility.

Be empathic: Empathy is about understanding other people by seeing things from their perspective and recognising their emotions. Once you achieve this, it's easier to get 'on their level'. To be more empathic, develop your emotional intelligence so that you can understand others better. You can also use Perceptual Positions[1]—a technique for seeing things from other people's perspectives.

(Cross-reference: for details, see Module 8 titled 'Empathy').

Mirror the other person: Mirroring is when you adjust your own body language and spoken language so that you 'reflect' those of the person you are talking to. Carefully watch the person's body language, including gestures and posture. If the person is sitting down with both hands folded, then copy the person's posture. As the person grows more comfortable with you, she may relax and sit back; mirror this change in posture as well.

Mirror the other person's language. If she uses simple, direct words, then you should too. If the person speaks in technical language, then match that style, if appropriate. When you respond, you can also reiterate keywords or phrases that she used.

Also, copy the other person's speech patterns, such as vocal tone and volume. For instance, if she speaks softly and slowly, then lower the volume and tempo of your voice. It is very subtle, but it makes the other person feel comfortable and, most importantly, it makes them feel that they are being understood.

While mirroring is useful in building rapport, do not match every word and gesture. Also, do this on a subtle level—being too overt can be counter-productive, as the person may feel that you are just mimicking her.

Observe the basics: In developing rapport with others, you should also use the tried and true basics of good communication:

- Making a crisp gesture of greeting acceptable in the culture, using the name
- Looking people in the eye
- Walking briskly to the person; holding your head up and maintaining good posture.
- Appearing upbeat and pleasant with a smile; indicating that you were looking forward to meet the person

---

[1] Retrieved 27 October 2017, from https://www.mindtools.com/pages/article/newCS_93.htm

- Facing the other person instead of getting distracted by things around
- Carrying yourself in such a way that is easy-going, friendly and confident

Influencing

Understanding Influencing

Right from our childhood, we are continually being influenced by what happens around us—people, events, places, situations, etc. Some of these influences are internalised by us and have profound and lasting effect on us. They bring about changes in the manner we think and conduct our lives and shape our values, beliefs, behaviour patterns and our attitude towards life. On the other hand, there can be situational influences that may not have an enduring value and may wear off within a short period of time.

So what is influencing? Influence is when you automatically make someone do something without trying or making a conscious, directed effort. A dictionary definition suggests that it is when we change someone's views, attitudes, decisions, perceptions or beliefs to produce an effect on them—in a positive way. It involves adapting your words and behaviour subtly through an awareness of the effect you are having on someone else. Thus, influence is the ability to have others take a desired action while building and maintaining the relationship.

Influence is where you do something, and it indirectly affects other people's behaviours, thoughts, physical demeanour, working style, etc.

Through this skill, you can move things forward and gain agreement or change someone's mind and, importantly, you can achieve this without pushing, forcing or telling them what to do. In short, it is applied common sense blended with high-level communication skills and a subtle game plan.

You may influence others not necessarily through words but through your actions, behaviour and body language as well. Some leaders in a group situation or at workplace exercise this influence. Group or team members may get influenced by their leaders merely by observing them *in action*—how they communicate or interact with their members or work colleagues; style of leadership; their behaviour patterns.

There is no right way, nor is there only one way to influence others. Everything that you do and say in your interaction with others can be turned into a factor for influencing people. It all depends on how strong and appealing are the vibes coming from an individual and how these subtle messages are perceived by others. This perception, in part, may also depend on the situational factors of others, their mental, emotional and physical state. For example, someone going through a difficult phase of life may be vulnerable to the influence of so-called 'god-men'; someone struggling with her self-confidence may be easily influenced by someone who appear to her as a very confident person.

Though, sometimes, influencing may appear to be one way, the primary relationship is two way, and it is about changing how others perceive you. You try to influence and the other person is, in a way, 'willing to be influenced'.

At the workplace, you influence others and also get influenced by those with whom you work. And this happens all the time, not necessarily limited to the confines of the workplace but may even extend after working hours. This influence may take the form of gaining support or help in carrying out job-related tasks, inspiring others through the manner in which you accomplish your assignments, informal communication, taking a stand in favour of a wronged colleague, establishing relationships or simply engaging someone's imagination through your personal attributes. Whatever form it takes, if you are an excellent influencer, your job becomes easier and you are able to establish good rapport with your colleagues and bosses. However, be careful not to stretch this skill too far.

Effective leadership today relies more than ever on influencing others—impacting their ideas, opinions and actions. While influence has always been a valuable managerial skill, today's highly collaborative organisations make it essential. Consider how often you have to influence people who do not even report to you in order to accomplish your objectives. Success depends on your ability to effectively influence both your direct reports and the people over whom you have no direct authority.

Influencing Factors

Everyone has a natural style of influence. Truly effective influence does not just happen. So how do you get people to buy into your views, behaviour pattern and style of living? Being able to accurately read situations, individuals and groups, and applying the appropriate type of influence behaviour contribute to becoming successful at influencing.

To be an effective influencer, you need both substance and style. Without a solid foundation of credibility, even the most interpersonally adept leaders will fall short. On the flip side, highly credible people can struggle with influence if they do not understand the interpersonal dynamics that are at play.

Some of the key factors are discussed below. These factors may either work as unique and solitary factor or in certain combinations.

Charisma and inspiration: By far, the most successful trait-driven influence is due to the charisma of a person. Charisma is really a complex process—an interaction between the qualities of the charismatic person or leader, people around them or the followers, their needs, level of identification with the person/leader, and the situation, that may have inherent need for change. The emphasis is, of course, on how they communicate with the people, appeal to them and build trust for them to get influenced.

Charisma is related to inspiration and the strength of their moral and dynamic personality. Generally, they have a vision for life or a cause that appeals to the people. There is one problem though. Once the charismatic leader or person goes away, the influence may start wearing off, unless the baton is passed to another person, with equal or even less charismatic qualities.

Becoming charismatic involves paying careful attention to how you interact with other people and ensuring that you develop the traits that make up charisma, positive and appealing to others. Charismatic people use their skills to get people on their side, perhaps from a professional, ideological or social point of view.

Position or authority: There are times when we 'buy' ideas, opinions and behaviour patterns from those whose position or authority we value. This authority or position may not be hierarchical or power-driven but can also be in a field—professional, personal or ideological—that is of interest to us. At the workplace, many of us do not always get influenced by those who are in the top position in our organisations but by those whom we consider as very competent and accomplished in their work. It is the power of their proficiency and the manner in which they conduct themselves that become the source of influence.

Identification: Identification is a psychological process whereby the subject assimilates an aspect, property or attribute of the other and is transformed, wholly or partially, by the model the other provides.

We are more inclined to follow the lead or learn from someone who is similar to us rather than someone who is dissimilar. These similarities may be in terms of profession, age, interests or background. Peer influence is a major factor in shaping the values, behaviour patterns and lifestyle of young people. That is the reason why mirroring is an important factor in building rapport as that could be a precursor to influence. We are more likely to interact with people who dress like us, are the same age as us or have similar backgrounds and interests. We even prefer people whose names are similar to ours. For this reason, sales trainers teach trainees to mirror and match the customer's body posture, mood and verbal style. A lot of advertisements use celebrities to draw on the identity factor for influencing people to buy certain products, especially those that are part of personal grooming.

When we speak of role models, we are, in fact, talking of subtle influence that the *persona* of an individual has on others—his or her lifestyle, actions, beliefs and values, behaviour patterns, etc. In some cases, this influence may bring about changes in the life of others, despite being there no physical proximity.

Relationships: Relationships are a strong factor that influences people. People who value relationships want to belong. And in many cases, this desire to belong becomes an important reason for people to emulate behaviour and other traits. This influence is greatly visible in family and social relations. Parents have a strong influence on the growing children. While, on the one hand, relationships stimulate changes in behaviour, on the other hand, influence further reinforces bonding.

Law of social proof: We view certain behaviour as more likely to be correct when we see a lot of people engaging in it. We assume, sometimes wrongly, that if a large number of people are doing the same thing, they must know something that we do not. We give them the benefit of more wisdom. This is particularly the case when we are in a situation of indecision or dilemma, and are floundering. We are more likely to trust in the collective wisdom and knowledge of a group (or crowd). This explains herd or lemming behaviour. For example, in the case of tremors, everybody rushes out following others, without pausing to think whether there is a real case for that fright or whether rushing out is the best option for safety. When there is a panic in the stock market, everyone follows everyone else and sells. When there is a scarcity of a food item or any other household commodity, everyone starts hoarding because others are doing it.

Law of commitment and consistency: People tend to follow those who, in their view, are more consistent in their behaviour, actions and thinking because consistency is often associated with confidence, strength, honesty, stability and logic. Inconsistent people may be seen as two-faced, indecisive and unreliable. They are not considered worth emulating.

Persuasion

Persuasion is the process when you consciously and directly seek to get someone to change or adopt certain views, behaviour, values or actions in your desired way. In some ways, it can be termed as a conscious and planned attempt to influence, along with an accompanying awareness that the person whom you are trying to persuade has a mental state that is susceptible to change. It is a type of social influence, a broad process, in which the behaviour of one person alters the thoughts or actions of another.

Researchers and scholars have defined persuasion in different ways. According to them, it is a:

- Communication process in which the communicator seeks to elicit a desired response from another person
- Conscious attempt by one individual to change the attitudes, beliefs or behaviour of another individual or group of individuals through the transmission of some message
- Symbolic activity whose purpose is to effect the internalisation or voluntary acceptance of new cognitive states or patterns of overt behaviour through the exchange of messages
- Successful intentional effort at influencing another's mental state through communication in a circumstance in which he or she has some measure of freedom

Persuasion is about creating an environment that lets two or more people find common ground and beliefs. The fine line between persuasion and manipulation revolves around intent. Typically persuasion has a very positive connotation while manipulation does not.

—Dave Lakhani (2011)

Some people are born with natural talent to influence and persuade others. For many people, this skill is helpful and may play a key role in their lifestyle. Its usefulness may remain confined to them and they may use it in largely rational and ethical ways. Unfortunately, some people with whom we interact, especially the ones with natural persuasive skill, may misuse their skill to exact undue levels of influence and achieve goals that may be harmful to you or others. It is common knowledge that many young people are persuaded into unhealthy practices and anti-social activities such as drug or substance abuse or even crime by their peers. On the other hand, persuasive influence of the family members or other well-meaning friends can dissuade young people from falling prey to these harmful ways.

In relationships, persuasion is a constant. We persuade people, including those whom we love, into loving us, into loving or accepting others, into behaving certain ways, into telling certain things and so forth. Although there are individuals who prefer to pretend as though persuasion is not present and is not necessary, it very often is. But persuasion is not always a bad thing. While we try to make positive and loving decisions for those that we care about, we also have to make positive and loving decisions for ourselves. When these two things come into conflict, whether in large or small ways, persuasion is often necessary to rectify the situation. Persuasion can save jobs, marriages, friendships and more. The trick is usually making sure that the methods we use are ethical and positive and that the reasons that motivate us are worthy.

Four Key Elements of Persuasion

Persuasion is the Transmission of a Message

In interpersonal relationship, persuasion is a communicative activity; thus, there must be a message for persuasion, as opposed to other forms of social influence, to occur. This message may relate to views and opinions on certain issues; desired changes in behaviour, actions and values or adopting a course of action. The message may be verbal or non-verbal.

Persuasive communication can bring about three recognisable effects:

1. Shaping: Attitudes, values and behaviour patterns may be shaped through association with a person, group or ideology
2. Reinforcing: Contrary to popular opinion, many persuasive communications are not designed to transform or convert people, but to reinforce a position they already hold

3. Changing: This is perhaps the most important persuasive impact and the one that comes most frequently to mind when we think of persuasion. Communications can and do change views and opinions, attitudes, values, etc.

Persuasion is an Attempt to Influence

Persuasion does not automatically or inevitably succeed. However, persuasion does involve a deliberate attempt to influence another person. The persuader must intend to change another individual's attitude or behaviour, and must be aware (at least at some level) that she is trying to accomplish this goal. Thus, persuasion represents a conscious attempt to influence the other persons, along with an accompanying awareness that they are in a situation or state that is susceptible to change. Thus, persuasion occurs within a context of intentional messages that are initiated by a communicator in hopes of influencing the recipient.

People Persuade Themselves

One of the great myths of persuasion is that persuaders convince us to do things we really do not want to do. They supposedly overwhelm us with so many arguments or such verbal ammunition that we acquiesce. They force us to give in. This overlooks an important point: people persuade themselves to change attitudes or behaviour. Communicators provide the arguments. They set up the bait. We make the change or refuse to yield. In the words of Whalen (1996), 'You cannot force people to be persuaded— you can only activate their desire and show them the logic behind your ideas'. Self-persuasion means that people have the choice of bringing about the desired changes or refuse to do it.

Persuasion is Not Coercion or Compulsion

How does persuasion differ from coercion and compulsion? Persuasion deals with reason and verbal appeals, while coercion is a technique for forcing people to act as the coercer wants them to act and presumably contrary to their preferences through use of authority, force or threats. Compulsion is when people are constrained to change their views, beliefs, etc., because of their own circumstances, inabilities, benefits or other vulnerabilities.

Philosophers define coercion as a technique for forcing people to act as the coercer wants them to act and presumably contrary to their preferences. It usually employs a threat of some dire consequence if the actor does not do what the coercer demands (cited in Perkoff, 2003). Ramesh's boss, Anjana's professor and Rohit's classmates pushed them to act in ways that were contrary to their preferences. The communicators employed a direct or veiled threat. They might have also employed coercion to some extent.

Things get murkier when you look at scholarly definitions that compare coercion with persuasion. Smith (1982) takes a relativist perspective, emphasising the role of perception. According to this view, it is all a matter of how people perceive things. Smith argues that when people believe that they are free to reject the communicator's position, as a practical matter, they are free, and the influence attempt falls under the persuasion umbrella. When individuals perceive that they have no choice but to comply, the influence attempt is better viewed as coercive.

Deciphering Influencing and Persuasion in Interpersonal Relationship

Both influence and persuasion have the common objective of making a change in a person's behaviour or attitude. However, their methods differ. Whereas persuasion requires you to communicate, in most cases, influence works silently without you having to make any effort.

Though persuasion is a handy technique in any circumstance, influence is preferred by most leaders as it is essentially based upon trust and credibility. This may not always be the case in persuasion. There are situations where influence would be a better option. If persuasive techniques are used there, the leader is often seen as a manipulator and any compliance on the part of the team members or employees is temporary, at best. Regardless, persuasion and influence are great tools in the hands of any leader.

While we are talking of persuasion and influence, it may be helpful to briefly refer to other related concepts—conformity and compliance. Conformity is a type of social influence involving a change in behaviour, belief or thinking to align with those of others or to align with *normative* standards of a group to which you belong. In the case of peer pressure, a person is convinced to do something (such as illegal drugs) which they might not want to do, but which they perceive as *necessary* to keep a positive relationship with their friends or keep a sense of belongingness to the group. Conformity from peer pressure generally results from identification within the group members or from compliance of some members to appease others. Conformity can be in appearance or it may be a complete conformity that impacts an individual, both publicly and privately. On the other hand, compliance (also referred to as acquiescence) demonstrates a public conformity to a group majority or norm while the individual continues to privately disagree or dissent, holding on to their original beliefs or an alternative set of beliefs differing from the majority. Compliance appears as conformity but there is a division between the public and the private self.

Process of Influencing and Persuasion

Although influencing and persuasion have some dissimilarities, it is possible to discuss the process involved in both in an integrated way. We can also identify skills that help in both the processes, though some may be more relevant in one case, while some others in the other. There may be variations in terms of how we apply them and the extent of their efficacy. Both have the undertones of interpersonal relationship, as cause and also as effect. Also, in both cases, another key factor is communication, whether verbal or non-verbal or both.

Influencing and persuasion are about assessing and understanding you and other people. Through these skills, you can move things forward and gain agreement or change someone's mind and, importantly, you can achieve this without pushing, forcing or telling them what to do. It involves personal as well as professional relationships. In short, it is applied common sense blended with high-level communication skills and a subtle game plan.

Do not assume that on day one you would head out and persuade or influence anyone and everyone and get things done your way. The art of persuasion and influence is a hard nut to crack. It takes practice and experience before you can really get the process going your way.

Understand Yourself and Your Influencing Style

It all begins with self-awareness. What is your dominant style? Do you assert, convince, negotiate, bridge or inspire? Do you tend to apply the same approach to every situation and individual? Understanding your natural inclination is a good place to start. If you are not sure, consider taking a quick assessment.

Sometimes, you can get so used to your own personal style, way of being or pattern of communicating that you do not think of how it is being received, and you do not think of behaving in any other way. It is, therefore, important to periodically take a reality check and find out what styles are working and with whom and bring about changes, where necessary. It is also likely that one style may work with one and not with others; may work in certain situations and not in all circumstances.

Take another assessment. What are your special qualities that are likely to work with people—charisma, lifestyle, background or values? Identify and nurture them if you wish to engage in persuasive and influencing techniques.

Know the People Whom You Wish to Influence

It is 'them' *not* 'you': Strive to understand before being understood. Learn as much as you can about the people you want to influence or persuade. Ask well-designed questions to get a sense of what issues your peers and counterparts believe are important and must be addressed. Use this information to tailor your strategy and style.

You also need to know where the person is located at present in terms of her work, performance and achievements or social life and where she wants to be tomorrow, how much she is keen to reach the new destination and what is her present mental or emotional state. This will determine the scale and nature of your efforts in influencing or persuading her.

Always think why the other person would be influenced by you. It is not always about how good you are at persuasion but how you assess the needs of the other person, her interests and receptiveness to be influenced for a particular work or situation. Do the groundwork first. A thorough study on how they are likely to be benefitted from what you are offering or suggesting—your solution to their problems, your views, new thinking, or ideology, etc.—would go a long way in making the persuasion exercise personal and effective.

Gain Their Trust and Establish Your Credibility

People will automatically be wary of anyone who is trying to change their minds. This is why it is paramount to gain their trust by convincing them that you are sincere and know what you are talking.

Authenticity and credibility are two important ingredients for effective persuasion and influence. Before you are able to persuade others, think how credible you are to that person or situation. Why would they listen to you? Are you knowledgeable enough to persuade others to act according to your idea? If not, first act on this checklist item before approaching others. Credibility comes from your experience—your past and present achievements. Work on how you can present these before the persuasion *session* or meeting, and during your presentation.

Enhance their identity with you. Show them that you are in tune with them and your views and ideology enmesh with their own. Again, you need to put yourself in their shoes, understand their concerns and be empathetic to their feelings.

Construct and Communicate Your Message

Persuasion is essentially a communicative activity. It involves the transmission of a well-defined message, unlike other forms of social influence. The message may be verbal or non-verbal. It occurs within a context of intentional messages that are initiated by a communicator in hopes of influencing the recipient.

Influence and persuasion cannot be a one-way communication. Listening and reading the body language of the recipient is an important part of the process. And note that not only the words that are exchanged but the body language says a lot about how you finally get persuasion and influence to work. Show patience and empathy towards what others have to say and change your persuasion style accordingly. We all are different and there is no universal style of persuasion that works for everyone. As mentioned earlier, as part of your preparation for the session, you should assess how others are likely to respond to your views or ideas, or to your influencing style.

You could have constructed a brilliant message and developed an exceptional strategy to convey it but if you are not able to take the other person(s) with you, the efforts are wasted. So it is not about the authenticity and relevance of the message to others but how you reach out to them and shake them will determine whether your objective of influencing them has been realised. Yet again, you cannot be in a win-win situation because, remember, not you, they are first.

Weigh the pros and cons of your ideas, as doing so will make you seem fair and reasonable to others. However, your strategy should be to emphasise the pros and underplay the cons, while still making a reference to them. Explain why the cons are not so bad, or how the benefits outweigh the drawbacks. Never hide or lie about the cons because people may question you on the other side of your arguments and this may expose you to an avoidable situation. It is likely that you lose their trust.

Getting your message through is all about getting on the same wavelength as the other person and gearing your pace and timing to theirs. If you articulate clearly the direction in which you are taking the conversation, you will keep them on board and save them some of the trouble of working out what you mean. This will be very helpful in the process of persuasion or influencing.

Skills in Influencing and Persuasion

Interpersonal communication:

- The ability to think rationally, to analyse problems and situations, and identify logical solutions to them
- Being creative and innovative; the ability to see alternatives and solutions where others have not; skill at 'thinking outside the box'
- Skill at asking and responding to insightful questions that can lead both you and other person to the heart of the problem or issue
- The ability to engage people in casual conversation; skill at conversing on a number of topics; being a skilled conversationalist
- Bringing energy and enthusiasm to interactions and situations; being naturally energetic and engaged; the ability to get others energised
- Skill at actively listening to others; being engaged in others when they are speaking and accurately listening and retaining the essence of their thoughts

(Cross-reference: for more details, refer to Module 2 titled— 'Interpersonal Communication).

Assertiveness skills:

- Skill at stating an opinion with confidence or force; presenting ideas strongly and affirmatively; maintaining one's position without becoming aggressive.

- Skill at enduring steadfastly; continuing on one's course despite opposition or resistance; being resolute and tenacious.
- Having faith in one's own judgment, abilities and rights; projecting firmness and steadfastness in one's purpose, directions and goals.
- Skill at projecting authority; behaving as though one has the legitimate right to use authority; clearly stating a decision, conclusion or course of action.
- Having a strong, firm and resonant voice; the ability to command attention when one speaks.
- Skill at using strong and confident gestures, facial expressions and body language; projecting confidence and assurance through all the non-verbal aspects of communication.
- The ability to command others and use legitimate authority without being overbearing, clumsy, oppressive or harsh. A key skill in using the influence technique stating.

(Cross-reference: for more details, refer to the section on 'Assertive in Communication' under Module 2).

Interpersonal skills:

- Skill at opening up to and engaging with people one does not know; being outgoing and conveying warmth, acceptance and interest in strangers. A critical skill in the influence technique of socialising.
- Skill at conveying genuine interest in other people; being authentic in showing care, concern and curiosity in other people; skill at making others feel important. A critical skill in socialising and appealing to relationship.
- Having a strong, intuitive understanding of other people and what is important to them; skill at discerning what others value without them having to say what it is; interpersonal perceptiveness.
- Skill at understanding others' emotions and empathising with them.
- Skill at building harmonious and sympathetic relationships with others; skill at conveying trust in others as well as causing them to feel that one can also be trusted; establishing trustful connections with others.

- The ability to create trusted friendships and close relationships with other people; skill at sustaining intimate and friendly relationships with others over a period of time.
- Skill not only at helping and encouraging others but conveying that attitude as well; giving aid or assistance to others and promoting, advancing, inspiring or stimulating others and encouraging them to forge ahead.

(Cross-reference: for more details, refer to earlier sections of this module).

Negotiation

Negotiating skills are important for arriving at an agreed solution whenever you are confronted with interpersonal conflicts in interpersonal relationships.

(Cross-reference: for details on negotiation, see Module 4—'Skills for Resolving Interpersonal Conflicts').

Resolving Interpersonal Conflicts

In any interpersonal relationship, personal or work-related, there will be disagreements that may turn into conflict situation. In order to maintain the relationship, you should be willing to discuss the conflict with the other person and work together to resolve it. There are only a few interpersonal conflicts that cannot be resolved through collaboration, discussion and sincerity of purpose.

(Cross reference: for details on 'Interpersonal Conflicts', see Module 4).

SUGGESTED GUIDELINES FOR CONDUCTING THE SESSION

Four exercises have been designed for this module. However, before you take up Exercise 1, engage the participants in discussing the concept of interpersonal relationship and its importance in our daily life—in the family, at workplace and in our social circle. You may initiate the discussion through a brief brainstorming exercise.

Exercise 1 will help you bring out the qualities required for a healthy interpersonal relationship. You have the opportunity to supplement the responses generated through the exercise. Through Exercise 2, the participants will be able to assess to what extent they possess different elements that form the basis for establishing sound and mutually beneficial interpersonal relationships.

Trust is a crucial component of interpersonal relationship. Therefore, an exercise (Exercise 3) has been specifically included. You may elaborate on the participants' responses, extracting from the trainer's notes.

Exercise 4 will help you generate considerable material on the skills required to establish and promote healthy interpersonal relationships. This area has been dealt with at considerable length in the trainer's notes and, therefore, you will be in a position to give comprehensive inputs on this sub-topic. However, you must ensure that the group is kept fully engaged in the discussion. You may consider giving the participants brief on-the-spot exercises. Also, encourage them to share their experiences as you proceed with your presentation.

EXERCISE 1

QUALITIES IN INTERPERSONAL RELATIONSHIP

Objectives

At the end of the exercise, the participants will be able to:

- Assess their qualities that are important in establishing and sustaining interpersonal relationships
- Indicate what special qualities they look for in others for developing interpersonal relationships

Time allocation

About 45 minutes

Materials required

Training aids and tools for your inputs; flip charts and writing markers for listing qualities that are crucial for interpersonal relationships, based on the participants' response, for your summing up; copies of worksheets I and II (one copy for each participants of the two worksheets); white board and its markers

Steps in conducting the exercise

- Give an introductory talk, indicating some key qualities that can help us promote healthy relationships
- Introduce the exercise and distribute copy of worksheet I, asking the participants to complete it as per the instructions
- Collect the completed worksheets I from the participants and distribute worksheet II. Ask the participants to complete the second worksheet as per the instructions
- After they have completed worksheet II, return worksheet I to the respective participants (the worksheet carries the name of the participant)
- Ask them to compare their responses in the two worksheets. Invite some participants to share their responses, strictly on voluntary basis. Highlight the point that while we consider certain qualities as important in others, we may not have the same yardstick when we assess us as worthy of having good relationships
- Sum up and close the exercise

QUALITIES IN INTERPERSONAL RELATIONSHIP

Worksheet I

Instructions for completing the exercise:
Below are given 20 key qualities that are important in establishing healthy interpersonal relationships. Pick up 10 you consider as very crucial for interpersonal relationship. Then, on a scale of 1 to 5—5 being the highest and 1 the lowest—indicate the level you possess these selected qualities. Although your responses are confidential, write your name at the bottom of the worksheet.

Patient _____	Reasonable _____
Helpful _____	Good listener _____
Ambitious _____	Cooperative _____
Understanding _____	Sincere _____
Committed _____	Social _____
Independent _____	Responsible _____
Friendly _____	Organised _____
Interesting _____	Polite _____
Calm _____	Relaxed _____
Careful _____	Thoughtful _____

Name _____

QUALITIES IN INTERPERSONAL RELATIONSHIP

Worksheet II

Instructions for completing the exercise:
Below are given 20 key qualities that are important in establishing healthy interpersonal relationships. Pick up 10 you consider as very important 'for the people to possess' with whom you want to have positive and stable social relationships. Then, rate these qualities from 1 to 10—10 being the least important of these selected 10 qualities and 1 as the most important.

Patient _____	Reasonable _____
Helpful _____	Good listener _____
Ambitious _____	Cooperative _____
Understanding _____	Sincere _____
Committed _____	Social _____
Independent _____	Responsible _____
Friendly _____	Organised _____
Interesting _____	Polite _____
Calm _____	Relaxed _____
Careful _____	Thoughtful _____

EXERCISE 2

ELEMENTS OF INTERPERSONAL RELATIONSHIPS

Objective

At the end of the exercise, the participants will be able to:

- Grasp broad understanding of different elements that constitute the basis of warm and congenial interpersonal relationships.

Time allocation

About 1 ¼ hours

Materials required

Training aids and tools for your initial briefing on the topic and inputs, and summing-up; flip charts and writing markers for highlighting key points as the participants share their ratings; copies of the worksheet on Interpersonal Relationship Self-rating Scale (one worksheet for each participant); white board and its markers.

Steps in conducting the exercise

- Recall some of the key points you made in your inputs on the importance of establishing and nurturing warm and harmonious relationships. Introduce the exercise emphasising the need to be frank and honest. Inform the participants that it is an individual exercise and there is a need to be honest and open in completing the worksheet
- Distribute copies of the worksheet for Interpersonal Relationship Self-rating Scale. Provide time to the participants to complete the exercise
- Get the group together. Give opportunities to the members to share their ratings; display key points on the flip chart for further discussion

- Sum up the discussion based on the points highlighted by the participants' sharing. This is also the time for giving your own inputs on key aspects of interpersonal relationship

INTERPERSONAL RELATIONSHIP SELF-RATING SCALE

Worksheet

The responses to the following statements should be completed quickly without thinking too much. You have to give the rating considering what response describes you fully in a *here and now* situation. Do not think of the *ideal* situation otherwise you will not get correct rating. Be honest and frank in rating yourself.

For each of the following items, circle the number that best describes the degree to which the statement fits you

1. Level of awareness of your strengths and positive qualities

   (Low) 1—2—3—4—5—6—7 (High)

2. Ability to listen to others in an understanding and empathetic way

   (Low) 1—2—3—4—5—6—7 (High)

3. Being open to influence or persuasion of others

   (Not at all) 1—2—3—4—5—6—7 (Fully open)

4. Willingness to acknowledge and appreciate strong points, good qualities and abilities of others

   (Unwilling) 1—2—3—4—5—6—7 (Willing)

5. Level of being honest and frank about your inadequacies and negative qualities

   (Low) 1—2—3—4—5—6—7 (High)

6. Ability to have constructive interaction with others at the feeling and emotional levels

   (Low) 1—2—3—4—5—6—7 (High)

7. Receptivity or openness to opinions and views of others even when they differ from yours

    (Low) 1—2—3—4—5—6—7 (High)

8. Willingness and ability to repose trust in others

    (Unwilling) 1—2—3—4—5—6—7 (Willing)

9. Ability to influence (or persuade) others in terms of views, behaviour and actions

    (Low) 1—2—3—4—5—6—7 (High)

10. Level of tolerance of opinions and views of others that are at variance with yours or challenge you

    (Low) 1—2—3—4—5—6—7 (High)

11. Awareness and appreciation of the feelings and emotional state of others

    (Low) 1—2—3—4—5—6—7 (High)

12. Ability to promote trust of others in you through your actions and behaviour

    (Low) 1—2—3—4—5—6—7 (High)

13. Competency to express your views and thoughts with clarity and candour

    (Low) 1—2—3—4—5—6—7 (High)

14. Reaction to conflicts and antagonism from others

    (Low tolerance) 1—2—3—4—5—6—7 (High tolerance)

15. Ability to manage emotions during interaction with others

    (Low) 1—2—3—4—5—6—7 (High)

16. Level of physical and mental energy

    (Low) 1—2—3—4—5—6—7 (High)

EXERCISE 3

WHAT TRUST MEANS TO ME?

Objective

At the end of the exercise, the participants will be able to:

- Develop understanding of the concept of trust and recognise its value in interpersonal relationship

Time allocation

About 45 minutes

Materials required

Training aids and tools for your inputs; flip charts and writing markers for listing the responses of the participants and your summing up; one card each for the participants (about 3" × 4"); white board and its markers.

Steps in conducting the exercise

- Give a brief introduction to the concept of trust. Do not elaborate otherwise you will influence the thinking of the participants
- Introduce the exercise and brief the participants as under:
  - o This is an individual exercise
  - o Each participant should write a sentence—about 12–15 words—describing what *trust* means to him or her in the context of interpersonal relationship
  - o Write clearly and legibly on the card provided for the purpose
  - o You have 10 minutes for the task
  - o Do not write your name on the card
- Distribute the card, one each to the participants

- After the participants have completed writing, collect the cards and take the help of a participant to read each card loudly. List keywords of each response on the flip chart
- Using the responses, elaborate on the concept, keeping the participants engaged in the discussion

EXERCISE 4

SKILLS IN ESTABLISHING AND PROMOTING INTERPERSONAL RELATIONSHIPS

Objective

At the end of the exercise, the participants will be able to:

- Catalogue the skills that are crucial in developing healthy interpersonal relationships

Time allocation

About 1 ½ hours

Materials required

Training aids and tools for your initial briefing and inputs at the conclusion of the exercise; flip charts and writing markers for the presentation of reports of the subgroups and for your elaboration and summing-up.

Steps in conducting the exercise

- Give a brief introduction to the role skills can play in helping one to develop healthy and enduring relationship with others—family members, friends, colleagues at workplace, etc.
- Divide the group into subgroups of 6–8 participants each and brief them about the task as follows:
  - ○ As a subgroup, you will identify and discuss the skills that help an individual develop healthy relationships with others

- o While this is a group exercise but every member must be given opportunities to express her or his views
- o As a group, you need to arrive at an agreed listing of the skills and prepare a report for presentation to the larger group ·
- o You have 30 minutes for this task
- Call back the subgroups and give each of them time for presentation of the report. After all the groups have made the presentations, initiate the discussion, elaborating on the material generated by the subgroups, where necessary
- Sum up the discussion and close the exercise

Module 4

Conflict: Dimensions and Resolution

In the context of life skills, we are intently connected with intrapersonal, interpersonal, intra-group and intra-organisational conflicts. The other two levels of conflicts—inter-group and intercommunity—fall within the domain of social conflicts and are, therefore, outside the scope of this Manual. Interpersonal conflicts are part of our day-to-day life. They can challenge us in our relationships with family members, friends and office colleagues. For resolving or, at least, mitigating their adverse impact on our life, we need to understand their dynamics in different contexts. Keeping this in view, the module puts greater emphasis on interpersonal conflicts, whether in intra-group or intra-organisation settings.

Specifically, the module focuses on the following areas:

- Understanding conflict—definition and meaning
- Intrapersonal conflicts (personal dilemmas)
- Interpersonal conflict and its dimensions
- Preventing interpersonal conflict
- Styles for management of interpersonal conflicts
- Interpersonal conflict resolution strategies
- Skills in resolving interpersonal conflicts
- Resolving interpersonal conflict—suggested steps
- Intra-group conflict
- Sources of conflict in an organisation

Expected Outcomes from the Module

At the end of the session on the module, the participants will be able to:

- Enhance their knowledge and understanding of the geneses and dynamics of intrapersonal, interpersonal, intra-group and organisational conflicts
- Learn about the process involved in working out solution to interpersonal conflicts
- Understand the skills that one should possess for resolving interpersonal conflicts
- Become aware of their styles in resolving interpersonal conflicts

UNDERSTANDING CONFLICT—DEFINITION AND MEANING

In every society, while there may be agreements on certain issues or areas or bonding between two individuals, groups or communities, there are bound to be disagreements or acrimony as well. These differences can be at a personal level, within a family or group, or between different groups or communities. Thus, conflict is an inevitable and, perhaps, unavoidable part of everyday life—in the family, within our social circle, at the workplace or with other groups or communities.

As per the *Collins Dictionary*, conflict is defined as 'state of opposition between ideas, interests, etc.: disagreement or controversy'.

A conflict is a lot more than a mere disagreement. It is a situation in which you perceive something or someone as a threat to some areas that are crucial to your well-being and life—physical, emotional, power, status, etc. As such, it is a meaningful experience in people's lives, not to be shrugged off by a mere, 'It will pass…' or 'It does not matter'.

Conflicts do not occur in vacuum. There cannot be an enduring conflict between two individuals or groups who are not connected with each other in some ways. You cannot imagine of a conflict with a stranger whom you meet at a party, during travel or casually at other places. You interact with them, share views and even if there are differences, you just ignore the situation as a one-off one. Evidently, there has to be some level of inter-dependence, relationship or common area(s) of interaction for the conflict to take shape. It also occurs when competitive individuals or groups consciously attempt to oppose, resist, defeat or subordinate each other in an effort to achieve certain objectives or avail of limited opportunities or resources.

Conflict occurs between two or more people who disagree on an issue that threatens their respective goals, values or needs. In the manner the participants in a disagreement perceive this threat determines, to a great extent, how intense the conflict can become. With only so many resources and opportunities available within any social setting, it is not uncommon for conflicts to arise.

Threats typically trigger emotional or psychological responses. When this happens, your ability to view and approach the situation in an objective manner is hampered. This, in turn, makes it seem like there is a limited number of solutions to a particular problem. Once perspective is hampered by emotion, communication becomes difficult, and resolvable disagreements and differences may transform into conflicts.

People involved in a situation that has the potential of developing into a conflict view it differently. They tend to understand it on the basis of their perceptions, rather than taking an objective review of it. For instance, some may consider diversities in views, opinions and viewpoints as a potential source of conflict, while others may take them in the stride and accept these differences as normal. One party may feel they are in a conflict situation, when the other party feels that they are just discussing opposing views. However, there is always a possibility of conflict when emotions are associated with these disagreements and a challenge to ideas and views is perceived as a confrontationist attitude. A lot depends on our personal *take* of the situation.

There is a conflict when there are *differences or disagreements* in the positions of the two (or more) parties involved in the conflict. These disagreements or differences may be real, based on hard evidence or based on information or perceptions that may lack validity or authenticity. There are cases when perceived differences are considered as real. In fact, conflict tends to be accompanied by significant levels of misunderstanding that exaggerates the perceived disagreement considerably. If we can understand the true areas of disagreement, this will help us solve the problems and manage the true needs of the parties.

People respond to the *perceived threat*, rather than the true threat, facing them. Thus, while perception does not become reality *per se*, people's behaviours, feelings and ongoing responses become modified by that evolving sense of the threat they confront. If we can work to understand the true threat (issues) and develop strategies (solutions) that manage it (agreement), we are acting constructively to manage the conflict.

Functional Conflict

Although there is a general belief that conflicts have damaging outcomes not only for the participants involved in the conflict but it also affects others around and immediate environment, conflicts are not necessarily dysfunctional or damaging. Functional conflict is a healthy, constructive disagreement between two or more people. It can arise from someone putting different points of view in the organisational functioning or someone challenging old, established policies and practices of working. Thus, functional conflicts are very often cognitive in nature. It is, therefore, evident that such conflicts can produce new ideas, learning and growth among individuals, thus helping in the development of the organisation.

When individuals engage in constructive conflict, they develop a better awareness of themselves and others. In addition, functional conflicts can improve working relationships because when the two parties work together through the issues that are at the root of the conflict, they emerge with the feeling that they have worked and achieved something together. This, of course, assumes that the conflict was not due to clash of personalities but its genesis was essentially in issues and views.

Functional conflict can also result in a desire for excellence and creativity, and take the form of healthy interpersonal or inter-group competition. Positive form of conflict can release energy that can be translated into increased productivity. Thus, functional conflict can lead to innovation and positive change for the organisation. It enhances the vitality of the organisation. As such, conflict need not always be a problem, but it can become one only if it is handled ineffectively or allowed to last so long that it begins affecting the working environment adversely.

Sometimes, an interpersonal conflict that has genesis in personal agenda or in pursuance of goals may help in better understanding between those involved in the conflict. However, there is a condition to this. Both of them should have the desire to understand each other better and they see this as an opportunity to realise this goal.

If appropriately expressed, functional conflict can serve as a safety valve to the bottled-up feelings of frustration, resentment and animosity.

These conflicts also help individuals and groups establish their own identity and this can help the organisation as it raises the level of self-esteem of the individuals and the groups, so necessary for effective functioning of the organisation.

Dysfunctional Conflict

On the other hand, dysfunctional conflict is an unhealthy, destructive disagreement between two or more people. The danger is that it can take the focus away from work and put emphasis on the conflict itself or the parties involved. Excessive or prolonged conflict drains energy not only of the parties involved but also of those who are helping to resolve it.

Such conflicts are rarely cognitive in nature although, sometimes, the parties may pretend it is so. They are more affective or behavioural (these aspects of an interpersonal conflict are discussed in a later section of this module).

A fallout of such conflicts is that there is a breakdown of meaningful and direct communication between the feuding parties. This type of conflict gets manifested in the form of personalised anger and resentment directed at individuals rather than on issues or ideas. This increases aggressive posturing and behaviour.

The parties approach the conflict with their fixed agenda and intransigence, often unwilling to see other's standpoint on matters and issues that are central to the conflict. This, obviously, affects the organisational climate. Thus, in dysfunctional conflicts the losses to both the parties, indeed to the organisation, outstrip gains, if any.

INTRAPERSONAL CONFLICT (PERSONAL DILEMMAS)

When conflict occurs within an individual, it is called intrapersonal conflict. It arises when a person faces two incompatible demands, opportunities, needs or goals. While it is usually possible to resolve the conflict through careful analysis of the competing demands or goals, there are occasions when there is no complete solution to such conflicts. In latter situations, the individual must give up one of her goals, needs or demands; modify one or both; delay one for a later day or learn to live with the fact that neither can be fully satisfied. Intrapersonal conflict arises from frustration, numerous roles, which demand equal attention but the individual is not able to fulfil effectively.

Geneses of Intrapersonal Conflict

Inter-role Conflict

Inter-role conflict occurs between different roles that one individual assumes. As you take on multiple roles, they will, sometimes, conflict with one another. That is, one role expects one thing of you while another role expects something else of you. Perhaps the most common inter-role conflict that many of us experience is the conflict between our work responsibilities and our family obligations. It is not just about the expectations and responsibilities but also demands on time.

Intra-role Conflict

Intra-role conflict can be triggered off when you receive conflicting messages from two equally important people about how to carry out your responsibilities or some specific tasks. For instance, at your workplace, your immediate supervisor may want you to perform a task in a particular way but the manager or colleagues may want it in another way; at home, you may be torn between how your spouse wants you to carry out a certain job and the path your parents or elders in the family want you to take. This conflict has both functional and dysfunctional aspects. You may feel confused and even frustrated affecting your motivation and performance at your workplace and family harmony at home. On the other hand, this conflict may help in bringing out certain ambiguities regarding the role and thus lend more definiteness and clarity to the roles, at workplace and at home. The outcome is reduction in the potential of role conflict.

Person-role Conflict

You may realise that in the discharge of your responsibilities, you are expected to engage in behaviour and actions that are not compatible with the values you hold important for your life. This conflict also has workplace and family dimensions. This conflict has a positive side as well. You may get better insight into the values you believe in and you may also learn to modify them rather than insist on doing what you want to do. This can become an important source of growth and maturity. Also, your decision-making skills may also get honed. The values may get crystallised and contribute in shaping your identity.

Forms of Intrapersonal Conflicts and Strategies to Resolve Them

Approach/Approach

Kurt Lewin (1935) described conflict in terms of two opposite tendencies: *approach* and *avoidance*. When something attracts us, we want to approach it but if something frightens us, we try to avoid it. The first he called approach–approach intrapersonal conflict. The individual is simultaneously attracted to two desirable goals. For example, a woman may want to pursue a career but also want to raise a family. As a rational person, she considers the alternatives. She could accept a job now and delay having children, or she could have children now and look for a job later when the children are of an age that permits her to leave them in someone's else's care and pursue a career. Alternatively, she could modify both goals by hiring a housekeeper and working part-time. Or she and her husband could share childcare duties. Here the solutions are numerous. However, this may not always be the case.

Avoidance/Avoidance

The reverse of this dilemma is avoidance–avoidance conflict when a person is face to face with two undesirable or threatening possibilities. When faced with an avoidance–avoidance conflict, people will usually try to escape from the situation. If escape is not possible, they will try to cope with the situation in a number of ways depending on the severity of the factors influencing the conflict. The choice is not always easy. People caught in avoidance–avoidance conflicts often vacillate between one threat and the other. In no-exit situation, many people sit down and wait for the things to change so as to reduce their dilemma or the situation may improve facilitating exit or helping them to make a choice. Or the conflict may resolve itself.

Approach/Avoidance

Approach–avoidance conflict is when you are both attracted and repelled by the same goal. The desire to approach a desired goal grows stronger as you get nearer to it. But the desire to avoid the goal also becomes stronger when you get closer to it. The avoidance tendency usually increases in strength faster than the approach tendency. Thus, in an approach–avoidance conflict, you will approach the goal until you reach the point where the two gradients intersect. Afraid to go further you are likely to stop, fall back, approach again, continuing to vacillate until you are forced to make a decision either way or the situation changes and making a choice becomes easier. For example, you are offered a promotion in your job but this will involve your moving to another station. Now you have settled yourself well here, in terms of your spouse's job, children's education, social circle, etc. You will be in a dilemma whether to accept the transfer or not.

Managing Intrapersonal Conflicts

As part of managing intrapersonal conflict, the first task for an individual is to ask a question to herself—is the dilemma real or a creation of my own weaknesses, frailties and limitations? Once this question is answered satisfactorily, the following action is suggested for resolving the dilemma.

Engage in Objective, Realistic and Purposeful Self-analysis

This analysis should include level of expertise, especially with regard to the tasks or goals that are at the centre of the dilemma; mapping of career graph and the plan of action for self-improvement; core values on which you are not willing to compromise and others that could be open to negotiations and change; your biases, norms and patterns of behaviour; propensity for change; risk-taking behaviour, etc. Objective self-reporting is a key factor in resolving your internal conflicts. You should also be sensitive to your own personal struggles to avoid projecting problems on others and creating external conflict with others.

Situational Analysis

Undertake an intensive analysis of the situation(s) in the context of the dilemma. What have been the factors that have contributed to producing the dilemma? Every situation has a nucleus and there are also some factors that may either contribute to make it more helpful for you or more difficult and complex. Investigate them.

You may be in a better position to take up the task of diagnosing the situation that will help you resolve the dilemma if you have complete and factual information about different aspects of the situations that are confronting you and the options that are available to you.

Role Analysis

Role analysis is a good tool to manage role conflicts. Therefore, besides undertaking a thorough assessment of the role and responsibilities in the context of the dilemma you are facing, you must be fully aware of different roles that you are expected to play in relation to your family, the workplace or as a member of the community where you live. A comprehensive analysis will give you insights into consistencies or the contradictions in these roles and forewarn you of the possible intrapersonal conflicts that you may face in the future. The outcomes are reduction in ambiguity and indecision, thereby preparing you better for resolving the conflicts.

Self-expectations and Expectations of Others

There are three sets of expectations that impact your efforts to resolve the intrapersonal conflict you are facing—your expectations from those who are associated with the situation; their expectations from you, emanating from your relationship with them and the level and nature of their stakes in the situation or your decision; and your self-expectations. A harmonious integration of these three sets of expectations will help you in resolving the conflict. You must, however, ensure that these expectations are reasonable and based on realities. You should realise that you may not be in a position to fulfil all the expectations others have from you or your own self-expectations. Any overzealousness on your part can make your task of resolving the conflict more difficult.

Enhance Your Problem-solving and Decision-making Competencies

Among the key competencies that help you resolve the dilemma in a satisfactory manner are those related to problem-solving and decision-making. The situation that you are confronting will test the level of your competencies in these areas, and, therefore, as part of your preparation for effective resolution of the conflicts you should hone your competencies in these areas.

INTERPERSONAL CONFLICT AND ITS DIMENSIONS

Interpersonal conflicts occur when two persons have different perceptions of a situation; identity or self-image is challenged; there is a perceived or real breach of trust in a relationship; lack of respect; clash of personalities or egos; a perceived threat to your well-being; blocking or interfering with the achievement of personal or professional goals and so on.

Cognitive Conflicts

Some conflicts arise out of differences in views and opinions on issues that are of importance to both the persons. It is not unusual for people to have divergent views on an issue or topic, but most of the times we just take these dissimilarities in the stride and let them pass, without getting too concerned about them. However, there are occasions when these views are very significant and valuable to us. For instance, when you are in a discussion where important decisions are to be taken by the group. In such cases, your whole *persona*—competencies, intellect and quality of views—is at stake. In a way, the views and opinions expressed by you represent you and your interests. Therefore, you will be inclined to be less tolerant of those who are in conflict with them. There are situations when we identify so much with our views that any challenge to them or expression of differing views can offend us so much that we perceive it as a conflict with those who have expressed differing views.

People see or perceive things differently as a result of their knowledge, needs, prior experiences and expectations. Since their perceptions are very real to them, they, sometimes, fail to realise that others may hold contrasting perceptions of the same situation, issue, circumstances or event.

Thus, two people in an interpersonal or group situation may have different views and opinions on the same issue or situation. If these differing views and opinions remain at the cognitive level, there is little possibility of any conflict. In fact, one-on-one dialogue or discussion in an open forum may get enriched and result in better decision- making with regard to a problem or situation. However, there is always a possibility that these seemingly divergent views may not remain at that level. As mentioned above, some people may identify so strongly with their opinions and views that any opposing views are considered a challenge to them, personally. They may not express their feelings openly but resent those who disagreed with them. Sooner or later, this situation may translate into conflict.

Personality Differences

This is often a key factor in interpersonal conflict. Whether in an interpersonal relationship or in a group situation, people bring with them a baggage of their values, attitudes, predilections, likes and dislikes, etc. Abrasive persons often tend to ignore the interpersonal aspects of a relationship or group life and the feelings and concerns of other person or group members. They fail to appreciate the fact that every individual is different and right in her own way. They cannot easily accept these differences. They may also have a style of functioning that impinges on the rights of others and make them feel unimportant and worthless. They are the people with whom it is difficult to work or relate with. These personal attributes will create stress and strain for those around and this can lead to serious interpersonal conflicts in a one-to-one relationship or within a group. Personality differences can also take the form of ego clash. In such cases, conflicts arise simply because of inflated egos of two people, each constantly trying to play a game of one-upmanship with the other and wanting to get into a position of dominance and power.

Some people are generally aggressive by nature. They demonstrate little concern for the needs and feelings of others. For them, the dignity of others has no meaning. They want to get their way, regardless of its merit or the interests of the group or other members. Their motto is 'My way or the highway'. If others submit to their whims and fancies, it is fine but if there are people who resent this attitude, the possibility of conflict looms large.

Affective Conflicts

These conflicts arise when one person's emotions, feelings or attitudes are incompatible with the other person. Affective conflicts are among the most difficult to manage as these are often not based on logic and reason. People in affective conflict are usually not very reasonable and, sometimes, the outsider cannot see any reason why the conflict should exist at all. Strong personal, cultural, moral or religious values, attitudes and beliefs fall into this category. In some cases, individual differences get expressed through groups, leading to clashes between two groups or communities. In cases where one or both are willing to make adjustments or compromises, it is possible to find a solution to the conflict. However, in most cases, very little can be done effectively to put an end to this conflict and often parting of ways is the only recourse to resolve it.

People often have personality differentials but we regard them as unique to an individual and do not get unduly concerned about them. However, if there is a situation or event where two persons have common stakes or interests, and both take the positions based on their values and attitudes and these get expressed in actions or behaviours, there is likelihood of a conflict as the other person may find these actions and behaviour offensive, insensitive or unacceptable. These differences may not surface immediately and may simmer for some time before they take the shape of a conflict.

Behavioural Conflicts

There are situations where one person behaves in a manner that is unacceptable to another. This is seen in social relationships and also in group situations. If the perceptibly undesirable behaviour takes place in a group, it is frequently resolved within the group itself. Other group members may intervene and diffuse the situation. Also, it is likely that the person whose behaviour or actions have triggered the conflict may be amenable to the suggestions of the group members because she values the membership of the group. In some cases, however, she may continue to sulk and this can damage her relationships with others though the threat of an overt conflict might have blown away for the present. On the other hand, in the context of personal or social relationships, behavioural problems can easily escalate into a conflict. These interpersonal conflicts are not amenable to easy solutions unless the feuding parties decide to take a step forward or there is an intervention from a third party—a common friend or a family member.

Relationship Conflicts

When one puts faith and trust in another, and that confidence is broken, it can create an emotional response that elevates to conflict. To trust someone is to place a high confidence level that the relationship will not be compromised in any way; that I can expect you to *do* what you *say* or *profess*. A trusting relationship leads to feelings of confidence and security. A *breach of trust* or *betrayal* unleashes our strongest emotions that frequently lead to conflict.

PREVENTING INTERPERSONAL CONFLICT

Most people have no interest in creating conflict with others. Generally speaking, it is in our interest to establish and maintain good relations with people with whom we come into contact in the family, neighbourhood, workplace or social settings. We all want the relationships to be healthy, sincere and mutually enhancing. The problem occurs when we fail to use cooperative approaches consistently in our interactions with others. This may not be a deliberate failing but on many occasions we do not realise that our behaviour (in relation to the relationship) is being monitored by the other person. It is not just about how we behave and act but how the other person perceives our behaviour and actions. If these perceptions stay with her as realism, it can give rise to bitterness. Thus, many times, we may not be aware how our own behaviour contributes to interpersonal problems in different settings, but we find ourselves in conflict, still wondering what has happened. Remember many relationships are damaged not due to the actual actions and behaviour of the two individuals but because of perceptions and assumptions about them.

To prevent conflict from happening in the first place, it is important to identify the ways in which we contribute to the disagreement. One way of doing this is to identify a specific, recent conflicted situation, recall what you said and then think specifically about how you could have used more effective language or acted in a different manner. Think about ways in which your communication could have set a more trustful tone or reduced defensiveness. Once you have identified your part in the conflict, such as blaming, practice working on that particular behaviour for a day or a week. At the end of the time period, evaluate your progress. Did you succeed? In what situations did you not succeed? (While it may be the other person who created the conflict, you are the other half of the interaction and it is your own response that you have control over and you can change).

The climate in which conflict is managed is important. The two individuals involved in the conflict should not contribute to creating a defensive environment. In order to avoid conflicts, we should be conscious of our defence mechanisms that could contribute to damaging relationships. Some of these are as follows.

Evaluation

Many people have the tendency of judging others' actions and behaviour all the time. They base their response on these judgements. A corollary of this unhealthy trait is that these people generally engage in fault-finding behaviour. This predilection is an inhibiting factor in developing mutually valuable relationships. As Mother Teresa said, 'If we are constantly judging people, where is the time to love them'. This message has a lot of substance for all of us.

Control

Another important point is that we should not be looking to control the relationship and the other person. There should be enough scope for both individuals to grow in the relationship. If we aim to impose our views and choices on others, there will be time when they see through our game and may shy away from the relationship or the conflict could be on the cards. Trying to dominate the relationship and using it to serve our own self-interests is being insincere and dishonest to others. If the views of one prevail on one occasion, at other times it should be the turn of the other to dominate. This mutuality in control and domination contributes immensely to developing a healthy and sound relationship.

Hidden Agenda

Some of us enter a relationship with a hidden agenda. We aim to manipulate others and the relationships with them for serving our self-interests. We use subterfuges to hide our real motives and *schema*. We can use these tactics for some time but once we are exposed, the damage will be severe and we can land ourselves in a crisis situation. Sincerity of purpose and transparency of actions and behaviour provide the bedrock for a healthy, enduring relationship.

Commitment

Relationships thrive on commitment and earnestness. If we are indifferent and lack allegiance to the relationship, we are already putting it at risk. Commitment does not, however, mean surrendering your interests and self-dignity but viewing and assessing them in the context of a relationship as also respecting other person's interests and dignity.

STYLES FOR MANAGEMENT OF INTERPERSONAL CONFLICTS

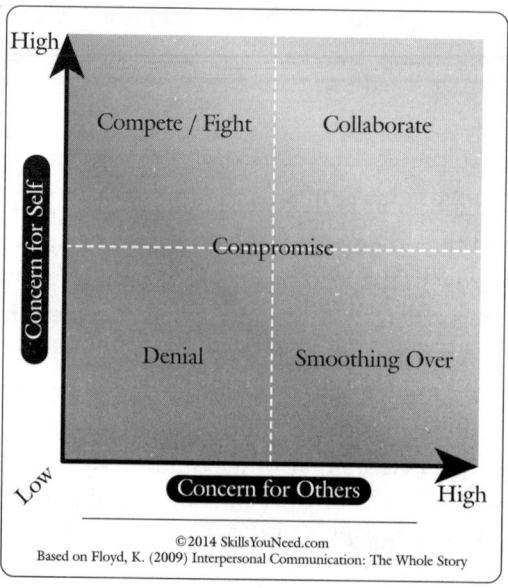

©2014 SkillsYouNeed.com
Based on Floyd, K. (2009) Interpersonal Communication: The Whole Story

Compete or Fight

Motto: 'It's not enough that I win—you must lose'.

It is characterised by the need to win at all costs. It reflects a desire to meet one's own needs and concerns, completely ignoring the concerns and the position of the other person. Winning and that too decisively is the only metric, and any concession to the other side is seen as a sign of weakness. There is a strong need to dominate and overwhelm the other person. If you use this style, you have no concern about the other side's feelings or how they will live with the decisions. You may just shrug your shoulders and say, 'It is their tough luck'. As the model suggests, the aggressive and least cooperative people use the competitive style. To achieve the desired outcome, the competitor uses whatever power is available and acceptable, for example, position or rank, information, expertise, persuasive or influencing abilities, economic sanctions or coercion. If the stakes are high enough, a very competitive person's use of power may well be limited only by some greater external power such as the law or social taboos.

Some advocate the use of the competitive style in all actual or potential conflict situations, which is not surprising given the endless models and reward systems that foster and support competition in our society. Others condemn this style as a win-lose strategy. Competing is neither good nor bad, but one of many styles that may be appropriate and effective or otherwise, depending on the situation.

Life-threatening situations requiring quick, decisive action may require a power-oriented competition style. A competitive style may also be necessary at times to protect oneself from others who tend to take advantage of non-competitive behaviour.

The competing style can be appropriately used when the goal is quick action, or when there is little hope of consensus ever being reached. To use this style, you had better be sure of your ability to make certain the other side accepts your decision and acknowledges your authority, wisdom or power.

The disadvantage of the competing style is that it may cause the other side not to voice important concerns because they are convinced that these will be ignored anyway. In this way, domineering bosses or co-workers can get their way, but possibly at the expense of important information or views which could alter the decision, perhaps for better outcomes. People using the competing style can be surrounded by *yes men*, and since their concerns are always ignored, their loyalty does not run very deep.

In brief, those who use this style:

- Defend their position
- Want to win at all costs; have little concern for the other person
- Seek immediate resolution of the conflict; have little concern for the process
- Make quick decisions about what needs to be done
- Put forward views and arguments forcefully, even aggressively
- Use authority and position for resolving differences

If this is your preferred style, attend to the following:

- Consider whether you really care about the issues—or just care about winning
- Assess whether your need to win is damaging your relationships
- Practise giving in on issues unimportant to you (this will be hard for you)
- If both sides in a conflict are using a competing style, watch out. The struggle will be long and hard, and the result is likely to be ugly

Avoid or Deny

Motto: 'I'll think about that tomorrow'.

This style is characterised by attempts to distract attention from the issue or ignore it completely. The goal of this style is to avoid making a decision at whatever cost. Neither your concerns nor the concerns of the other party need to be satisfied. Obviously, this style is only appropriate when the issues are of low importance, or it is clear to both parties that the consequences of delay in making a decision will be minimal (or perhaps more information is forthcoming). It may also be appropriate when you are being pressed to negotiate a peripheral issue and there is a much bigger—and more important—conflict looming.

An avoiding style should be used sparingly and only when something is going to change: you, the other person, or the situation. For example, it is okay to avoid a conflict with a co-worker or your boss if you know you are likely to quit your job soon.

Use this style carefully, and only if you are certain that you are not employing it as a way to escape an unavoidable conflict. The avoiding style is only a delaying tactic and if you use it too often, you will be labelled as 'passive–aggressive' and the decisions will be made without your inputs.

In brief, those wanting to use this style:

- Want to avoid creating unpleasant situations
- Let others take responsibility for resolving conflicts
- Encourage others to delay direct confrontation
- Accept the situation
- Suppress own feelings and needs
- Deny there is a problem to be solved
- Look for ways to avoid taking a stand that might lead to disagreement

If this is your preferred style, attend to the following:

- Maintain an awareness of your tendency to withdraw in tense or difficult interpersonal situations and work to overcome it
- Learn to move a conflict from confrontation to collaboration
- Ask questions if you are uncomfortable making assertions: instead of 'I deserve a raise', try 'Do you think I am being fairly paid?'

Collaborate

Motto: 'Let's find a solution that works for all of us'.

It is characterised by a desire to get into a *win-win* situation. Satisfaction of both parties is the prime consideration. Collaboration involves the maximum use of both cooperation and assertion. Those using a collaborative style aim to satisfy the needs and concerns of both parties. Collaborating means: acknowledging that there is a conflict; identifying and acknowledging each other's needs and concerns; exploring alternative solutions and their consequences for each person; selecting the option that meets the needs and concerns, and accomplishes the goals of each party and implementing the alternative selected and evaluating the results. This requires open and frank discussion, and honesty and commitment from both parties.

Both of them should have opportunities to surface concerns in a nonthreatening way and think imaginatively.

Collaborating requires more commitment than the other styles and takes more time and energy. It follows that such commitment must be warranted by solutions in which the needs and concerns of the parties are extremely important and cannot be ignored. Collaboration is also the best style to use when it is essential that the parties to a conflict are committed to the resolution, because an outcome that meets the needs of both parties is more likely to have the required mutual support and enduring commitment to maintain relationship. Going through the collaboration process can also lead to personal growth as the parties involved explore and test their values, assumptions and potential solutions.

Be sure you understand the difference between a compromising style and a collaborating style: compromising is 'horse-trading', giving up things you want in the hope that the other side will do the same and that you can live with the outcome. On the other hand, in collaboration, both sides are trying to find a solution which truly satisfies the needs of each.

The downside of the collaborating style is that it is not always possible to realise it. It requires close attention to the issues at hand (concerns, not just positions) and to the emotional state of the other side.

In brief, those wanting to use this style:

- Seek to identify underlying issues and concerns
- Offer creative and innovative alternatives
- Work for win-win situation
- View conflict as an opportunity for team growth
- Help others verbalise their issues and concerns
- May push for win-win solutions even when impractical and not feasible
- Encourage others to work together

Compromise

Motto: 'You win some, you lose some'.

It is described by meeting the conflict at mid-point. Both parties in a dispute achieve moderate but incomplete satisfaction.

If you use a compromising style, then you are both assertive and cooperative. You are willing to trade some of your needs in order to win concessions from the other side. This style can be effective when both parties are equally powerful and willing to cooperate, and they want to preserve the relationship for the future.

One of the challenges to the compromising style is that options have to be evaluated fairly—and they may be valued differently by each side.

The biggest problem with the compromising style is that both parties may end up giving away too much and neither ends up satisfied. You have to be careful in a compromise that you are not giving away something you cannot live without. Because each side goes into the negotiation with the expectation they will have to give something away, they may start with extreme positions, which make it harder to reach a reasonable compromise. This we see often in negotiations.

In brief, this style signifies that:

- Goals are important but not worth the effort of disruption
- Opponents with equal power are committed to different means to a similar end
- You want to achieve temporary settlement to complex issues
- You want to strive at an expedient solution under time pressure
- You need backup because collaboration or competition is not working

If this is your preferred style, attend to the following:

- Evaluate carefully the things you agree to give up during a compromise
- Make sure the other party is not giving up something they will regret later
- Be aware that both sides may be starting out with an exaggerated position in order to have something to give up
- Try to identify things that mean a lot to the other side, but not as much to you. Give these up first

Accommodate or Smooth Over

Motto: 'Whatever'.

It is characterised by the desire to please others at the expense of a person's own needs. The accommodating style is one of sacrifice, selflessness and low assertiveness. You are willing to give up just about everything in order to preserve the relationship with the other party. It is certainly reasonable to use this strategy when the issue at hand is something of little importance to you. If you are trying to pick a movie to watch, and you really do not care, it is fine to say 'Whatever you want is ok with me'.

This strategy may also be useful when you are hopelessly outmatched in power and the other side is using a competing strategy and you are going to lose anyway. It is possible to overuse this strategy, however. If you feel that your concerns are never acknowledged and your opinions are ignored, you may become too accommodating. However, this will dent your self-esteem.

In brief, those wanting to use this style:

- Opt for a conciliatory approach
- Are ready to listen and understand others' point of view
- Want to help others get what they want
- Neglect own concerns in favour of others
- Work towards maintaining a harmonious relationship
- Respect all points of view
- Tend to defer too much to others and minimise their ability to influence the outcome

If this is your preferred style, attend to the following:

- Focus on learning collaborative approaches to conflict resolution and negotiation.
- Practise being assertive by saying 'My needs are not being met'.

INTERPERSONAL CONFLICT RESOLUTION STRATEGIES

WIN-WIN	**WIN-Lose**
Lose-WIN	**Lose-Lose**

Win-lose strategy can be deceiving. The conflict is actually solved on the surface, but the losing side in the equation is not really satisfied. Over a period of time, resentment begins to build and as it surfaces, conflict is expressed again.

Win-lose situations result when only one side perceives the outcome as positive. Thus, win-lose outcomes are less likely to be accepted willingly.

This strategy imposes a solution on the disputing parties, which sets someone up to lose. This strategy is not recommended unless there is an ongoing conflict that the parties themselves cannot resolve and that interferes with the actual work performance of the organisation.

Lose-lose strategy means that all parties end up being worse off. In some lose-lose situations, all parties understand that losses are unavoidable and that they will be distributed in a balanced way to both parties to the conflict. In such situations, lose-lose outcomes can be preferable to win-lose outcomes because no party gains an advantage as benefits and losses are distributed fairly and evenly.

Lose-lose strategy is found in three different scenarios:

- There is a compromise by everyone involved. Each of the parties must give up something that they wanted
- The parties involved use an arbitrator. She may suggest a solution that does not make either of the parties 100 per cent happy
- The parties are forced to stick to the rules with no room for flexibility. Both parties lose as the rules are strictly adhered to

Lose-lose strategy is used when you need a speedy solution. In this case, there is generally not enough time for any negotiations. This is a 'quick fix' and does not address the root cause of the conflict.

Both *lose-lose* and *win-lose* strategies set up the parties involved in the conflict for an adversarial relationship. Those involved tend to think in terms of winning and how much they are losing. The problem itself becomes secondary. There is seldom concern for the actual causes of the problem.

Win-win strategy addresses the root problem that is creating the conflict. The implementation of this strategy requires patience and flexibility on the part of the mediator. Finding the win-win solution requires trust and the ability to listen. The parties cannot be competitive and are not focused on winning. It requires creative thinking and a move away from the concept of winning versus losing.

Win-win outcomes occur when each side of a dispute feels they have won. Since both sides benefit from such a scenario, any resolutions to the conflict are likely to be accepted voluntarily. The process of integrative bargaining aims to achieve win-win outcomes through cooperation.

SKILLS IN RESOLVING INTERPERSONAL CONFLICT

Diagnostic

Diagnosing the nature of a conflict is the starting point in any attempt at resolution. The most important issue that must be decided is whether the conflict is an ideological (value) conflict or a 'real' (tangible) conflict—or a combination of both. Value conflicts are exceedingly difficult to negotiate. A difference of values, however, is really significant only when our opposing views affect us in some real or tangible way. There will be situations when neither of the opposing parties needs to change its values to come to a mutually acceptable resolution of the real problem. If each of the parties stands on its principles—maintaining the value conflict—no headway is possible. But if, instead, they concentrate on the

tangible effects in the conflict, they may be able to devise a realistic solution. It is, therefore, important to determine whether the conflict is a real or a value conflict. If it is a conflict in values resulting in non-tangible effects on either party, then it is best tolerated. If, however, a tangible effect exists, that element of the conflict should be resolved.

Communication

In the process of resolving the conflict, communication can be difficult and emotional. It is, therefore, important that you take recourse to all your communication skills before entering into the process of conflict resolution and making the course productive for both parties.

Make sure you have all your facts straight before you begin. Also, mentally go through what you are going to say, how you are going to express it and also the why of it. Try to anticipate any questions or concerns others may have and think carefully about how you will answer questions.

Once you are sure that something needs to be communicated then do so in an assertive way. Do not find yourself backing down or changing your mind mid-conversation, unless, of course, there is very good reason to do so.

Be empathetic. Put yourself in the other person's shoes and think about how they will feel about what you are telling them; how would you feel if the roles were reversed? Give others time to ask questions and make comments.

Often a difficult situation requires a certain amount of negotiation. So be prepared to negotiate. When negotiating, aim for a win-win outcome, that is, some way in which all parties can benefit. This is not a one-upmanship game.

When communicating, use appropriate verbal and non-verbal language, speak clearly, avoiding phrases or words that other parties may not understand; give eye contact and try to sit or stand in a relaxed way. Do not use confrontational words or body language.

When stressed, we tend to give a pass to active listening. It is, therefore, important that you try to relax and listen carefully to the views, opinions and feelings of the other person. Use clarification and reflection techniques to offer feedback and demonstrate that you were listening through body language and verbally.

Stay calm and remain focused when speaking and listening. Communication becomes easier when we are composed, take some deep breaths and try to maintain an air of composure. In most cases, you can be sure that the other party will mirror this demeanour. Keep focused on what you want to say, do not deviate or get distracted from the reason that you are communicating.

(Cross reference: for more details, see Module 2 on 'Interpersonal Communication')

Interpersonal

Interpersonal skills will include effective verbal communication, listening skills, communication, rapport building, assertiveness, problem-solving reflection and clarifying, and influencing.

(Cross-reference: for more details, see Module 3 titled 'Interpersonal Relationships')

Negotiation

It is inevitable that, from time to time, conflict and disagreement will arise as the differing needs and wants, aims and beliefs of people are brought together and expressed. Without negotiation, such conflicts may lead to argument and resentment resulting in one or both the parties feeling dissatisfied. The point of negotiation is to try to reach agreement without causing future barriers to communications that may lead to accentuation of disagreements and conflicts in future. Thus, negotiation is a method by which people settle differences. It is a process by which compromise or agreement is reached while avoiding argument and dispute. It is, therefore, important to develop negotiation skills.

Remember negotiation is about finding an agreeable solution to a problem, not an excuse to undermine others. Therefore, ensure that negotiation does not degenerate into arguments. It is helpful to consciously separate the issues under dispute from the people involved in the conflict.

All too often, disagreement is treated as a personal affront. Rejecting what an individual says or does is seen as rejection of the person. Because of this, many attempts to resolve differences worsen into personal battles or power struggles with those involved getting angry, hurt or upset. By not allowing 'disagreements over issues' to become 'disagreements between people', a good relationship can be maintained, regardless of the outcome of the negotiation.

Stages of Negotiation

In order to achieve a desirable outcome, it may be useful to follow a structured approach to negotiation, regardless whether the conflict is between two people or groups. The process of negotiation includes the following stages:

Preparation: This stage involves ensuring all the pertinent facts of the situation are known in order to clarify your own position. Undertaking preparation before discussing the disagreement will help to avoid further conflict and unnecessarily wasting time during the negotiation session.

Discussion: During this stage, individuals or members of each side put forward the case as they see it, that is, their understanding of the situation. It is extremely important to listen, as when disagreement takes place it is easy to make the mistake of saying too much and listening too little. Each side should have an equal opportunity to present its case.

Clarification of goals: From the discussion, the goals, interests and viewpoints of both sides of the disagreement need to be clarified. It is helpful to list these factors in order of priority. Through this clarification, it is often possible to identify or establish some common ground. Clarification is an essential part of the negotiation process, without it misunderstandings are likely to occur which may cause problems and barriers to reaching a beneficial outcome.

Negotiate towards a win-win outcome: This stage focuses on what is termed a *win-win* outcome where both sides feel they have gained something positive through the process of negotiation and both sides feel their point of view has been taken into consideration. A win-win outcome is usually the best result. Although this may not always be possible through negotiation, it should be the ultimate goal. Suggestions of alternative strategies and compromises need to be considered at this point. Compromises are often positive alternatives which can achieve greater benefit for all concerned compared to holding to the original positions.

(Cross-reference: for more details, see the section on 'Styles for Management of Interpersonal Conflicts')

Agreement: Agreement can be achieved once understanding of both sides' viewpoints and interests have been considered. It is essential that to reach an agreement everybody involved keeps an open mind in order to achieve an acceptable solution. Any agreement needs to be made perfectly clear so that both sides know what has been decided.

Implementation of a course of action: From the agreement, a course of action has to be implemented to carry forward the decision.

Always be aware that negotiation is not an arena for the realisation of individual achievements. It is also likely that those in authority may not like to enter into any negotiations. They may be inclined to have their way, under any circumstances. For them, their need to maintain feelings of self-worth is more important than the particular point of disagreement. In some cases, the process of negotiations may influence a person's behaviour, for example, some may become more defensive.

The Win-lose Approach to Negotiation

Negotiation is sometimes seen in terms of 'getting your own way', 'driving a hard bargain' or 'beating off the opposition'. The *win-lose* approach means that while one side wins, the other loses and this outcome may well damage future relationships between the parties. It also increases the likelihood of relationships breaking down, of people walking out or refusing to deal with the *winners* again and the process ending in further increase in the differences, escalating the conflict.

The Win-win Approach to Negotiation

In this case, the parties try to reach an agreement in which both of them feel satisfied with the outcome. This involves looking for resolutions that allow both sides to gain. Such resolution helps in maintaining healthy relationship between the parties, as neither feels aggrieved or disgruntled. It focuses on interests and not positions.

Assertiveness

Being assertive involves taking into consideration your own and other people's rights, wishes, wants, needs and desires. Assertive behaviour includes:

- Being open in expressing wishes, thoughts and feelings, and encouraging others to do likewise
- Listening to the views of others and responding appropriately, whether in agreement with those views or not
- Accepting responsibilities and being able to delegate to others
- Regularly expressing appreciation of others for what they have done or are doing
- Being able to admit to mistakes and apologise
- Maintaining self-control
- Behaving as an equal to others

Those who struggle to behave assertively may find that they behave either aggressively or passively.

(Cross-reference: for more details, see Module 2 on 'Interpersonal Communication'; section on 'Assertiveness')

Emotional Intelligence

Daniel Goleman divided emotional intelligence into 'personal' and 'social' competences, which broadly split between personal and interpersonal skills. Within each of these sections are a range of skills which are the elements of emotional intelligence.

Personal skills or competencies (How we manage ourselves)	Social skills or competencies (How we handle relationships with others)
Self-awareness	**Empathy**
Emotional awareness	Understanding others
Accurate self-assessment	Developing others
Self-confidence	Service orientation
	Leveraging diversity
Self-regulation	Political awareness
Self-control	
Trustworthiness	**Social Skills**
Conscientiousness	Influence
Adaptability	Communication
Innovation	Conflict management
	Leadership
Motivation	Change catalyst
Achievement drive	Building bonds
Commitment	Collaboration and cooperation
Initiative	Team capabilities
Optimism	

Source: Goleman (1998).

Problem-solving

Another skill necessary to successful resolution of interpersonal conflict is the use of the problem-solving process to have a dialogue and reach a negotiated and consensus decision. The steps in this process are simply stated and easy to apply:

- Clarifying the problem; what is the tangible issue? Where does each party stand on the issue?
- Generating and evaluating a number of possible solutions. Often these two aspects should be dealt with separately. First, all possible solutions should be identified in a brainstorming session. Then each proposed solution should be evaluated
- Deciding together on the best solution. The one solution most acceptable to all should be chosen
- Planning the implementation of the accepted solution. How will the solution be carried out? Why?
- Finally, planning for an evaluation of the solution after a specified period of time

(Cross-reference: for more details, see Module 9)

Tact and Diplomacy

It is the ability to assert your ideas or opinions, knowing what to say and how to say it without damaging the relationship by causing offence.

> Tact is the art of making point without making an enemy.
>
> —Isaac Newton

> Diplomacy is the art of letting somebody else have your way.
>
> —David Frost

Tact and diplomacy are skills based on an understanding of other people and being sensitive to their opinions, beliefs, ideas and feelings. Effective use of such skills means that you are able to sense accurately what another person is feeling or thinking at any given time, and then responding in such a way as to avoid bad feelings or awkwardness, whilst at the same time asserting or reflecting your own ideas and feelings back in a delicate and well-meaning fashion.

The effective use of tact and diplomacy in the process of conflict resolution relies on some other key skills, namely:

Attentive listening: You need to be able to listen to not just what is being said but also how it is being said in order to understand and respond appropriately to others.

Emotional intelligence: People with higher emotional intelligence are able to use tact and diplomacy more naturally in communication. Emotional intelligence is a measure of how well we understand our own emotions and the emotions of others.

Empathy: As an extension to emotional intelligence, empathy is your ability to see the world from another person's perspective.

Assertiveness: The reason for using tact and diplomacy is very often to persuade or influence others to think or behave in a certain way. Assertiveness is fundamental to this process and a skill that many people lack.

Rapport: Rapport is closely linked to tact and diplomacy as well as emotional intelligence and good manners.

Politeness: Being polite and courteous, respecting other people's viewpoints and cultural differences is important in many interpersonal relationships.

(Cross-reference: for more details, see Modules 2, 3 and 8 on 'Interpersonal Communication'; 'Interpersonal Relationship' and 'Empathy', respectively)

Strategies for Tact and Diplomacy

Understanding what is the most appropriate behaviour and in any given situation what can be problematic; this is due to the unpredictable nature of communication and of human relations generally.

Sometimes, the most appropriate action may be to withhold your opinion, or it may be possible to introduce an idea, or a favoured outcome in such a way that the other person can take ownership of it. In other situations, it may be the best option to take a direct stance, stating exactly what you want and how you intend to achieve it.

We all know people who are capable of talking their way out of difficult situations or who are more likely to be successful at negotiating. Although a certain amount of luck may be attributed to isolated incidents, long-term success is based on strong communication skills, planning, self-control, confidence and emotional intelligence.

While using tact and diplomacy for conflict resolution, the following points may be kept in view:

- When you are planning a difficult conversation, you should first focus on knowing what you want to achieve; what is your favoured outcome

- Consider what could be the objections from the other person or what could be their line of arguments
- Do not enter into a process when you are stressed or angry
- When communicating, listen to what other person has to say
- Negotiate
- If possible, turn your statements into questions that will make the other person think about
- If there is a possibility of emotions getting out of control, play the calming influence rather than inflaming it
- Always keep an eye on your preferred outcome; do not get distracted

Managing Your Own Response

> Every person you fight with has many other people in his life with whom he gets along quite well. You cannot look at a person who seems difficult to you without also looking at yourself.
>
> —Jeffrey Kottler, Psychologist

That is because the only person you can truly manage during conflict is yourself. During conflict conversations, many people focus attention on the other's behaviour, on the other's transgressions and on what they demand. If that worked, you would not be going through this process. So let us have you stop doing what is not working and disempowering yourself in the process. When you make the fix to a conflict entirely the other person's job, you hand all power to them for how the future unfolds.

The way you act in conflict is heavily influenced by the way you think about conflict and its resolution, and by the narrative, you tell yourself and others about the situation. By choosing a certain kind of narrative, you create opportunity to change the conflict and its impact on the relationship. The narrative you choose to tell yourself and others about the conflict will determine your words and actions.

Identify 'stoppers', quick mechanisms to help you stop doing something you know would not serve you well but is still a habit that is hard to break. Stoppers are a mental shortcut to help you bridge the gap between what you know and what you actually do.

Notice the narratives you tell yourself and others about this conflict. Is it helping you or blinding you to a fuller understanding of the problem?

If a conversation gets tense or begins to go downhill in another way, stop until you have your balance back. Proceeding when you have lost your cool serves no one well.

RESOLVING INTERPERSONAL CONFLICT—
SUGGESTED STEPS

Conflicts run all the way from minor, unimportant differences to disputes which can threaten the existence of a relationship. Conflicts with a loved one or a long-term friend are, of course, different from negotiating with someone who does not care about your needs, like a stranger or a salesperson. However, there is an underlying principle that underscores all successful conflict resolution, that is, both parties must view their conflict as a problem to be solved mutually so that both parties have the feeling of winning—or, at least, finding a solution which is acceptable to both. Each person must participate actively in the resolution and make an effort and commitment to find answers, which are as fair as possible to both. This is an easy principle to understand, but it is often difficult to put into practice.

Where communication ends, conflict begins. So long as there is communication between two individuals, and there is sharing, chances of the conflict getting out of control are minimal. However, when there is no or reduced communication, there is a possibility that each one will interpret the situation in her own way with little opportunity to check up with the other person. As a result, live images will be formed on the basis of these perceptions and these act as further deterrent for initiating a dialogue for resolving the conflict. Therefore, you need to be fully aware of these perceptions if you are desirous of working out resolution of the conflict.

The following steps are suggested to help you resolve the conflict. However, in following the steps indicated below, it is important to remember that the manner you conduct yourself and how you arrive at solutions for resolving the conflict will be heavily influenced by the level of your *interpersonal* and *conflict resolution skills*.

Prepare Yourself

As an individual involved in the conflict, if you accept responsibility to do something about it, can anything be done? A decision has to be made as to whether this conflict can be resolved and whether you want to resolve it.

In deciding, consider these questions: Are the issues central to the conflict important enough for me to work on? Is the person with whom I have the conflict important to me? Will having a dialogue to address the issues and resolve the conflict improve our relationship? Am I willing to spend the time necessary to resolve it? Am I in a mental and emotional state to work on it at this time? If answers to most of these questions are affirmative, you are ready to proceed.

However, if in considering the above questions some of your answers are in the negative, you may decide to avoid the issue at this point in time or take other action to address it. There are situations when you may feel that it is not prudent to spend time and energy to resolve the conflict and, instead, choose to manage it as best as you can for the present. There are occasions when all of us do this. However, there is an equal chance for resentment and acrimony to get reinforced it there is total inaction to resolve the conflict. So be watchful.

In understanding the problem and defining it, pause for a minute and reflect whether the problem is real or the result of your subjective perception or imagination. This step may appear to you as apparent or irrelevant but it is an important step in the resolution of the conflict. You might be exaggerating the issue or the problem. There are a number of situations when the problem is the result of our perception and exists only in our mind, though we are inclined to assure ourselves that it is real. So it is important to be convinced that there is a problem situation and is of the dimension that it is affecting the relationship. It is not unusual when an unintended or casual behaviour, action or remark is interpreted to be deliberate and designed to cause you hurt when it is not the case.

Once you are convinced that the problem is real, it is necessary to think in specifics. You need to precisely pinpoint what particular behaviour, action or situation is at the heart of this conflict and why it is upsetting you or causing you distress and also its nature and level in terms of its intensity. You must be clear on this point before you take the first step to enter into a dialogue with the other person.

When we have a difference with someone, it is not unusual for us to think something like: 'We have a problem here, and the problem is YOU!' Usual or not, this attitude will not get us moving down the road to mutual problem-solving. Think about it the other way around. If someone tells you that you are the problem, you will tend to be defensive. You may send the message, verbally or through body language or simply through the vibes, 'Well if I am the problem, then what is the big deal? Let us not discuss it anymore because I am not going to change in the near future'.

It is often difficult to treat another person with respect when we are in conflict with her. However, if we hope to resolve the conflict, we will need to work very hard at looking beyond the current difficulties and see the person as another human being, just like us, with needs like our own. We should recognise the human being in the other and extend to her the respect that we would wish others to extend to us. If we do not follow this simple principle, we might be killing the dialogue before it has even started.

Plan ahead of time what you think the other person will say and what you will say in response. Additionally, plan the desired changes you would like to see the other person implement. Also, be willing to bring about changes in you as well. Remember that conflicts are never one-sided. You have to look at the other person's side of things and find out what you can do to make work easier for her too.

As you enter into the process, some basic beliefs about conflict resolution should be kept in mind: belief in cooperation rather than competition; belief that everyone is of equal value; belief that the views of others are legitimate statements of their position; belief that differences of opinion are helpful and belief in the trustworthiness of those involved.

Create a Supportive Environment

A dialogue to resolve the conflict cannot take place in a hostile or unhealthy environment. It needs a supportive environment for its progress. And you have an equal responsibility to create a setting based on goodwill and a sincere desire to find solution to the conflict. It is, therefore, important that you do not show any sign of contempt or bitterness. Appear calm and confident without a hint of self-importance or acrimony at the other person. The first few words you say to the person will set the tone for the rest of the meeting. Therefore, make sure you do not start by accusing the other person, by using *you* statements. You will put her on the defensive and the result will be early closure of the session.

Diffuse the Situation

In every conflict, there are feelings and these *must* be dealt with *before* the problem can be solved. Therefore, to resolve conflict, it is important to focus first on the emotional aspects—the anger, distrust, defensiveness, resentment, fear and rejection. It is likely that the other person might be agitated and even angry and she may come to the discussion armed with a number of arguments describing how you are to blame for her unhappiness. Your goal is to address the other's anger—and you do this not by reacting in a similar manner but countering it by your calm conduct, assuring her that you understand the anger. When you take this position, it is difficult for the other person to maintain an angry demeanour. At the very least, we need to acknowledge that individuals have different ways of seeing things. This does not mean that we have to compromise our own basic principles or self-respect. We simply validate the other's stance so that we can move on to a healthier resolution of the conflict. This may be hard to do in a volatile situation, but a sign of individual strength and integrity is the ability to postpone our immediate reactions in order to achieve positive goals.

Convey Your Sincerity for Finding a Solution

You must convey an unmistakeable message to the other person that you are not here to score a point and engage in a 'win' situation but for a 'win-win' result. Your conduct and the words that come out of your mouth should be consistent with this approach. In such cases, the other person is more likely to respond in a similar way. On the other hand, if you are perceived otherwise, the other person may also adopt a similar stance, and the dialogue will come to nothing.

Identify the Issues

The most effective way to approach conflict resolution is first to discuss the problem and then come to its resolution. However, a common mistake we make in trying to resolve conflict is to focus immediately on solutions to the issues or the problem. We spend our time debating the pros and cons of each possible way of resolving the problem even before the underlying issues are clearly stated or understood by both parties. Therefore, it is necessary to clarify and understand the issues that are at the centre of the conflict, from the perspectives of both parties. Remember, effective problem solvers spend proportionately more time in problem definition and knowing its dimensions than in problem-solving. It is equally important to focus on issues rather than on persons. In doing so, the goal is to say what you want and to listen to what the other person wants. Be open and try to be a good listener.

Define the things that you both agree on, as well as the ideas that have caused the disagreement. At this stage, it may not be prudent to go into frivolous details of the conflict situation that may not be any help in resolving it. Sometimes, by going into its history—who said and did what—the issues can get more complicated, making the task more difficult for both the parties.

Share Positions on the Issues

When we are engaged in resolving interpersonal conflict, we are eager to state our position or own point of view. We tend not to listen to the other person. Therefore, it is important to attend fully, listen to the content (ideas, needs, proposals, position), listen and comprehend the feelings and try to understand the situation from the point of view of the other party. We do not have to agree with everything she tells you, but we should make every effort to arrive at an honest understanding of her position.

Having done that part, now it is time for you to state your own perspective to the issue, needs and feelings. This usually takes the form of an assertive but unemotional and matter-of-fact statement. Remember, there are situations when you may not even feel the need to put forward your point of view, as the problem may get to near resolution on the basis of respectful and careful listening to the other person's point of view.

In formulating your response, use the following guidelines:

- Be brief and direct; do not ramble or mince words
- Avoid loaded words (words that are emotional or judgemental)
- Be honest and say what you mean
- Describe your feelings and how they affect you

Maintain Clarity of Purpose

As you are engaged in the exchange, be sure that you set out common goal and objectives that will not only lend direction to the process but also serve as the reference point for both persons. Clarity of purpose will help you maintain focus, necessary for a productive dialogue. Be consistent with this goal. Do not let yourself be distracted. You must keep the dialogue going even under pressure or difficult circumstances. However, if by modifying this goal, you enhance the chances of reaching a solution, be willing to do that. Be flexible and not rigid.

Avoid Blame Game

You should be open to taking part of the blame and responsibility for the conflict. There are people who refuse to acknowledge their mistakes or faults even when they are fully aware of them and of the consequences that followed. They feel that they can never go wrong and are unwilling to admit their mistakes. Do not go into that mode and make a sincere effort to find a way out of the present difficult situation. If you do that, the other person will also be encouraged to accept her part in the conflict.

Take responsibility for your own thoughts and actions rather than shifting it to the other person and attributing motives to her. This decreases the chance of resolution as she may become defensive. For example, 'I feel pretty upset that this thing has come between us'. This statement is much more effective than saying, 'You have made me feel very upset'.

Manage Your Emotions

Evidently, during the dialogue there will be exchange of emotions and feelings, especially if the issues are emotive. It is, however, important that you manage your emotions in a way that they do not overwhelm you and instead of becoming a support turn out to be a barrier to effective communication of your position and the line of reasoning. However, you should not lose the opportunity to convey how the conflict has upset you and affected you emotionally. Speak of it as a matter-of-fact situation in a sincere and honest way, and not in an insinuating manner. Do not try to dramatise it. Convey them in a manner that is appropriate to the overall framework of the dialogue and only in the context of the conflict.

Once you find yourself in a conflicted situation with someone else, it is important to reduce the emotional charge from the situation so that you and the other person can deal with your differences on a rational level in resolving the conflict.

(Cross-reference: for more details on management of emotions, see Modules 2 and 3—'Interpersonal Communication' and 'Interpersonal Relationships')

Empathise

Another important point is that you must constantly attempt to understand the context of the actions and behaviour of the other person. Empathetic understanding of the issues, her views and position will help in building an environment that contributes to resolving the conflict and in finding solutions to the problems that have been at the centre of the conflict.

Try to put yourself into the shoes of the other person. See the world through her eyes. Empathy is an important listening technique which gives the other feedback that she is being heard. There are two forms of empathy. *Thought Empathy* gives the message that you understand what the other is trying to say. You can do this in conversation by paraphrasing the words of the other person and getting her endorsement. For example, 'I understand you to say that your trust in me has been broken'. *Feeling Empathy* is your acknowledgment of how the other person probably feels. It is important never to attribute emotions which may not exist for the other person (such as, 'You are confused due to the emotional stress you have been undergoing'), but rather to indicate your perception of how the person must be feeling. For example, 'I guess you probably feel pretty mad at me right now'.

By listening to the other person and attempting to express our understanding of her point of view, we can enhance the communication between us. This will help us reach a sound level of understanding. This is empathetic understanding.

(Cross-reference: for more details on 'Empathy', see Module 8)

Decide on the Best Solution

Look for a 'win-win' solution. Maintain a perspective. Relationships are not destroyed but can even be enhanced by working towards a mutually satisfactory solution to a conflict. Select the solution(s) that will best meet both parties' needs and check possible consequences. If needed, develop a mutually agreed plan of action with a follow-up procedure. Make sure all of the details are agreed upon and, if necessary, write them down.

Select the solution that seems mutually acceptable, even if it is not perfect for either party. As long as it seems fair and there is a mutual commitment to work with the decision, the conflict has a chance for resolution. It is also useful to set out the manner in which the decision will be implemented, including the responsibilities of the two parties.

Full expression of feeling is an essential part of the problem clarification process. If the emotions get too high, either take a break or set another time, but they should not be ignored.

INTRA-GROUP CONFLICTS

Conflicts between people in work groups, committees, task forces, teams and other forms of face-to-face working are inevitable. Intra-group conflict is distinctive in that it occurs between members of the groups who share common goals, interest and other identifiable characteristics.

Intra-group conflicts are marked by cognitive (views, opinions, etc.), behavioural, affective (attitudes, values, etc.) and performance-related disagreements; unhealthy competitions and personal feuds between group members. While some of these factors may result in fracturing the group into distinct and opposing subgroups, others may affect productivity and performance or show delayed progress in achieving group objectives. Behavioural and affective differences can also create a number of interpersonal conflicts within a group. In all such cases, appropriate and timely interventions by the leadership may help in improving the situation.

Like all other conflicts, intra-group conflicts may be destructive or constructive. Though conflict is generally regarded as a problem, one involving a group can also serve as a valuable tool in some contexts. In some cases, conflicts bring to the surface the simmering discontent between members. Through constructive dialogue and open sharing of deep-seated views and feelings, it can result in enhanced communication between the members that could translate to better performance of the group. Functional intra-group conflict promotes careful discussion of a variety of ideas that can yield greater or more effective outcomes for the group.

Prevention of intra-group conflict depends on the degree to which team members are equipped to identify, manage and navigate conflict situations. All group members should receive training in conflict management that aims to develop skills in active listening and clear communication and helps in establishing effective feedback loops that promote growth rather than chastise for slip-ups and lapses. Some intra-group conflicts require management from an external third party that provides guidance and inputs during group conflicts.

As mentioned earlier, while in some cases, conflict has a destructive effect on the individuals and groups involved, at other times, however, conflict can increase the capacity of those affected to deal with problems. Therefore, in the latter cases, it can be used as a motivating force towards innovation and change.

Areas of Conflict

There are broadly five areas in which there is potential for conflicts in group settings. It must, however, be remembered that this categorisation is not absolute. There is always interplay between these areas, impacting one another. For instance, if two people are having difficulty in relationships, they may have problems working together on a common project, affecting the project-related work adversely.

(Note: As a group comprises of individuals, there are interpersonal conflicts in the group. Therefore, the sources of interpersonal conflicts discussed earlier are equally relevant in the group situation. However, the context and implications for the group, as a whole, and for the individuals involved in a conflict situation are different. It is, therefore, suggested that if there are any overlaps, they should be located within the framework of a group in the following discussion.)

Relationships Between Members and Leadership-members Relations (Relationship Conflict)

In an intra-group relationship conflict, members of the group struggle with interpersonal relationships regardless of the task or objects of the group. In either type of intra-group conflict, members are at risk for damaging personal relationships and failing to achieve goals or objectives. Intragroup conflict can distract group members from producing valuable results as outlined by the group or the leadership, which can place their position at risk. Conflicts within work groups are often caused by struggles over control, status and scarce resources.

Reasons for intra-group conflicts in the context of relationship may be varied. There may be *personality differences* as indicated by the following table:

Some people are	While others are
Extrovert; outgoing, very communicative; keen to interact with other members of the group	Introvert; happy to keep to themselves; not very communicative; reluctant to share their views and feelings
Logical; base their feelings on reason and fact; straightforward attitude	Emotional; sensitive; may get upset by even small problems or differences with others in the group; may not be in a position to manage emotions
Concerned with group goals and objectives; work- and result-oriented	Concerned for people; people-oriented; warm in their relationships
Structured; organised; believe in proper planning; love for details	Flexible; less faith in planning; wants to go with the flow

Another reason may be *different value system*. From the moment we are born, we begin acquiring our value system. Our values are the beliefs we hold that help us to make decisions about what is right or wrong, good or bad, normal or not normal. These values may have been derived from our family, religion, ethnic group, peers, previous experiences, etc. No two people ever have the same life experiences, so we, ultimately, have different sets of values and beliefs that guide our decisions and behaviour. There are people who are unwilling to compromise on their values and, on the other hand, there are others who are not so rigid. For the former, value system becomes a strong driver of behaviour and of interaction with group members and this becomes a potential source of interpersonal conflict in a group.

Ego is another strong driver of our behaviour and decisions. Ego wants us to believe and assert that we are always right and moves us into defending our position, regardless of the merit of our views or reasons. We are often unwilling to admit our mistakes or faults, as there is a strong misplaced conviction that we can never go wrong. While some members of the group may get intimidated by this behaviour, others may not accept this behaviour and respond strongly. If not handled early, this attitude can create rifts in the group and escalate into conflicts. One of the quickest ways to diffuse an argument or conflict is to admit one's mistakes. At a minimum, move out of ego and attempt to see the situation from the other person's point of view as well. There is a saying that *it takes a big person to admit his mistakes*. Consider this the next time you are defending yourself and not sure why.

These problem areas may create a number of interpersonal conflicts within a group, leading to its polarisation and division into subgroups and even cliques that can break up the group.

Roles and Responsibilities with Regard to Group Goals and Objectives (Task Conflict)

If the goals and objectives or its working methods are either not clearly defined and leave scope for divergent approaches, there is a possibility of conflict situations as each one may interpret them in her own way and evolve her role accordingly.

If a group is experiencing a task conflict, members of the group disagree about the best practices for achieving an objective or struggle to agree even at the stage when objectives are being established for a particular task or project.

Behavioural scientists, sometimes, describe a work group as a system of position roles. Thus, the group can be considered an association of individuals who share interdependent tasks and perform formally defined roles. These roles may be further influenced by the expectations of others, by one's own personality and by self-expectations. Though interdependence recognises that differences will exist, there are cases when these differences get translated into acrimonies between two persons and, if not resolved at an early stage, can lead to conflicts. In some cases, interdependence itself leads to conflict situations because there may be members who value independence and, therefore, resist the need for interdependence. Further, each may have her own style of working that may not be compatible with that of others, working on the same task. On the other hand, through interdependence, members may learn to accept others' ideas, value openness and realise the need to share a mutual problem-solving attitude to ensure the exploration of all facets of a problem facing the group.

Conflicts also occur when the roles and responsibilities are not properly defined; there are overlaps or some members feel that they are carrying an overload of work in comparison with other members. This may lead to rancour, which, if not checked in time, can degenerate into conflicts.

Another area that can lead to conflicts in a group relates to mutual expectations of the members. These expectations may be unrealistic and not always related to the group goals and objectives; the role and responsibilities of others; level of their abilities and expertise in the tasks allotted to them or the overall framework of the group functioning.

Exercise of Power and Control in the Group (Leadership Conflict)

People whose primary motivation is to seek power and status in the group are in constant competition with the existing leadership. Their actions and behaviour converge on this objective. They show disregard for the existing leaders and find opportunities to lower their position with other members of the group. These people are potential source of conflicts in the group and if not properly handled they can damage the group relationships. Another aspect of leadership that can create conflicts is the incompetence of leaders and their inability to manage the group affairs effectively.

Group may have its own norms of behaviour and standards for the performance of tasks. Some members may find them unacceptable for various reasons. People may also resist conformity to group norms and other forms of regulatory procedures in the group simply because they feel that their freedom is being curbed. They want more options for their behaviour and actions, regardless of group objectives and its culture of functioning. They may respond to these pressures by defensive reactions such as hostility or aggression against the leaders or other members of the group. While the need for order and control in the group has to be recognised, the norms have to be implemented with due regard to individual initiative and growth opportunities.

These types of conflict in the workplace are also fuelled by emotions and perceptions about somebody else's motives and character. For example, a team leader jumps on someone for being late because she perceives the team member as being lazy and inconsiderate. The team member sees the leader as out to get her.

Rewards and Recognition for Work and Performance (Resource Conflict)

Conflicts may also arise when rewards and recognition are perceived as insufficient and improperly distributed, and members are inclined to compete with each other for these prizes. There are cases when this competition can become acrimonious leading to conflicts.

Personal Problems

Our lives today place enormous demands on our time and energy, but frequently those demands exceed our capacity to deal with them. Nevertheless, we come to work and attempt to function normally with our team members. Too often, however, this underlying stress surfaces at the slightest provocation, and we find ourselves in conflict.

One of our greatest lessons is to understand that a person's angered response to us may have nothing to do with us at all. They may simply be reflecting other stresses in their lives. Knowing this makes it easier to respond in a more tempered, appropriate and responsible manner. If we do not understand this important principle, we may react to their anger with similar or even aggravated anger, elevating the situation to one of conflict.

Negative Effects of Intra-group Conflicts

Intra-group conflicts can impact the functioning of the group in many adverse and destructive ways. Some of these are indicated as follows:

- Divert time and energy from the main issues
- Delay decisions
- Create deadlocks
- Drive inhibited and quiet group members to the sidelines; they may become resentful or indifferent to the group activities or even leave the group
- Interfere with listening
- Obstruct exploration of more alternatives because of the fear of conflict
- Decrease or destroy sensitivity
- Cause members to become indifferent to the activities of the group or leave it altogether
- Arouse anger and acrimony that prevent proper discussions on important issues
- Interfere with empathetic understanding among members

- Provoke personal abuse
- Encourage defensiveness in members for all actions and behaviour

SOURCES OF CONFLICT IN AN ORGANISATION

In an organisation, conflict can have varied sources. There are organisational factors that have their genesis in the system of the organisation, the way an organisation functions. In addition, there are personal factors that can lead to conflict situations, factors that can accentuate differences among the individuals.

(Note: There are some factors that cause intra-group or interpersonal conflicts, which are also relevant to this discussion. It is, therefore, suggested that while understanding the sources of conflict in an organisation, the reasons for intra-group and interpersonal conflicts should also be kept in mind.)

Goals and Direction

It is possible to look into this aspect at different levels. One, when the goals of an individual are in conflict with those of others in the same department or unit, giving rise to the possibility of interpersonal conflict. Another aspect is when the goals of an individual are incompatible with the goals of the organisation. It is also possible that in an organisation, two work groups have different, incompatible goals. Regardless of its origin and nature, goal conflicts are perhaps the most dangerous to the organisation as a whole. Groups or individuals within the organisation who no longer hold its goals as their own may well develop alternative goals that could be at odds with those of the organisation. Goal conflict can have another implication. If the organisation is planning changes in its structure and functioning, and people hold differing views over the direction to go, the routes to take and their likely success, the resources to be used and the probable outcomes, conflicts can get escalated. And with the pace of technological, political and social change increasing and with the compulsions of globalisation and free markets, organisational changes will ever be present.

It may also refer to the group, where one person or one group desires a different outcome from others. In an organisation, it is important that individuals have knowledge of another department's objectives, especially those directly connected with the work of that department. Some people may see these goals as conflicting and against the interests of others.

The introduction of new ideas and systems is frequently met by just this kind of conflict. In fear of changes that are to come, the group develops goals that are at odds with the changes proposed by the new system and they, instead, try to thwart the induction of these changes in the organisation.

Power/Authority and Accountability

Power or authority can become a potent source of conflict. To understand and manage interpersonal conflicts arising out of power and authority, it is necessary to become aware of power networks or equations existing in an organisation. Based on these power relationships, certain kinds of conflict tend to emerge.

The most common power network seen in any organisation is the relationship between a more powerful versus a less powerful, the traditional boss–subordinate relationship. This is very much in evidence in countries like India. This relationship is often defined by the power one holds on the other. However, for many employees, this relationship is not a comfortable one, because this implies that another person has a right to tell them what to do. No one really likes control. However, some people resent authority more than others. This can create conditions for conflict. Therefore, conflicts that emerge here take the basic form of the powerful individuals trying to control others, with the less powerful people trying to resist extra control and wanting to become more autonomous or enjoy more freedom in the discharge of their responsibilities, though in many cases this may not have overt manifestations because the employee sees the adverse consequences of entering into an open conflict with the superior. However, the simmering discontent and resentment can damage the working relationship, affecting the work of the organisation. It is also possible that the disgruntled employee may seek to widen the scope and area of the conflict by lobbying with the colleagues against the boss. In such cases, there can also be conflicts within the group of employees, some supporting the employee and others supporting the boss.

There is another dimension to this power network. If an individual feels that the exercise of power is legitimate and does not work against the interests of the individual, she may not resist much and there will be no conflict. Organisations typically respond to these conflicts by setting out rules in a clear and unambiguous manner and defining lines and extent of control and accountability. However, a more enduring and healthy approach in tacking these conflicts is to encourage the emergence of styles of leadership or to change the structure to a more decentralised one. But this depends on the perception and attitude of the less powerful. In such situations, there is also a problem of motivation.

Another power equation is among peers or equals. In a normal situation, there is a balance of power contributing to harmonious and working relationship among peers. However, there are situations, not uncommon in an organisation when an individual attempts to maximise the area of influence and power at the expense of others in the department or unit. This is sought to be done either through the favourable intervention and support of the manager/supervisor or through her own covert and overt efforts. There is no holds barred competition for acquiring positions of importance. The balance of power thus gets disturbed. And this gives rise to interpersonal conflict among the individuals or within the group. Interventions like improving coordination between the parties and working towards common interests can help manage these conflicts.

For the middle-level manager, there is another source of conflict. There are situations when conflicting expectations are placed on her by senior managers, on the one hand, and by subordinate employees, on the other. There is also a possibility of intrapersonal conflict due to role ambiguity and lack of clarity of the expectations of the senior manager. Improved communication among all parties can reduce role conflict and ambiguity. In addition, middle managers can benefit from education in positive ways to influence others.

Jurisdictional Ambiguities

This means unclear or undefined lines and boundaries of responsibilities, accountability and authority within an organisation. When lines are blurred, conflict is most likely to result when new situations and relationships develop. In case of ambiguity on responsibilities, there is a tendency to pass the buck if something goes wrong and claim credit if things go well. There can also be resentment by an employee when someone whom she does not consider to be its genuine repository exercises authority or she feels that the supervisor is going beyond the limits of her authority.

Work Interdependence

Organisational activities or tasks that are interdependent require groups or individuals to depend on one another to accomplish targets or goals. Everything is fine if the process works smoothly. However, when there is a problem, it becomes very easy to blame the other department or party and conflict escalates. In a garment manufacturing plant, for example, when the fabric cutters get behind in their work, the workers who sew the garments are delayed as well. Considerable frustration may result when the workers at the sewing machines feel their efforts are being blocked by the cutters' slow pace. Conflict can be avoided if the two units or departments understand and appreciate the problems and difficulties of each other. This is the task of the manager or supervisors.

Common Resources

In an organisation, there are situations when multiple parties must share resources, especially with regard to the manpower, and here is potential for conflict. The potential is enhanced when the resources become scarce. One resource often shared by managers is secretarial support. This puts a lot of pressure on the secretaries and leads to potential conflicts in prioritising and scheduling work. They may become the targets for perceived preference for work of one or the other.

Status Inconsistencies

Some organisations have strong status differences between management and non-management workers. Managers may enjoy privileges—such as personal phone calls at home, better meals, flexible hours, etc. This can cause resentment among some and consequently conflict, though it may simmer and not become overt. It is also likely that some people are more status-conscious than others are and they expect others in the organisation to respect their views, as they enjoy superior status. This can lead to conflict situations.

SUGGESTED GUIDELINES FOR CONDUCTING THE SESSION

This module deals with different aspects of conflict and its resolution.

Two exercises have been prepared for this module. The first one will help you bring out some important aspects of conflicts by engaging the group in discussion. It is, therefore, suggested that after initial introduction to the topic and some general inputs on how conflicts are an integral part of our lives, you should carry out Exercise 1. This exercise is designed to generate enough material for you to build on that and make an elaborate and comprehensive presentation on various aspects of intrapersonal, interpersonal and intra-group conflicts. To a large extent, you can draw from the trainer's notes to prepare your inputs. However, it is necessary for you to integrate your inputs with the material generated through the exercise. This will help to make the discussion more interactive and participatory.

Exercise 2 deals with 'conflict management styles'. Therefore, you should avoid giving any substantive inputs before the exercise. However, before the group takes up this exercise, it is necessary to introduce the participants to the concept of conflict resolution styles. Therefore, give a general talk but avoid going into an area that will condition their responses during the exercise. However, you must prepare for a comprehensive presentation on 'Conflict Management Styles' after the exercise is completed.

After completing Exercise 2, you will be in a better position to deal with this topic in an elaborate manner. While you can once again draw from the trainer's notes, the exercise will also provide you substantial material for your presentation. Explain in what circumstances these styles are most effective.

To further involve the participants during your presentation and making the session highly interactive, you may consider giving brief on-the-spot exercises to the participants on areas such as: skills required for conflict resolution, meaning and importance of negotiation in resolving interpersonal conflicts and the process for sorting out interpersonal conflicts. You may consider brainstorming, using individual cards for their responses or setting up dyads for sharing experiences and views on these aspects of conflict management.

While the causes of conflict in an organisation have been discussed, you must note that strategies and processes for resolution of conflicts discussed under the sections on interpersonal and intra-group conflicts will also be relevant in the case of an organisation. Therefore, this topic has not been discussed separately.

EXERCISE 1

CONFLICT—HOW DO YOU SEE IT AND ITS IMPLICATIONS?

Objectives

At the end of the exercise, the participants will be able to:

- Have a better understanding of the concept of conflict through shared perspectives
- Learn about how individuals respond to interpersonal conflicts
- Know about the positive and negative aspects of conflict in a group situation
- Learn about the techniques in handling conflict

Materials required

Training aids required for your elaboration on the exercise; copies of the worksheet 'Conflict: How Do You See It and Its Implications? (one for each participant); flip charts and writing markers for each subgroup and for displaying key points emerging out of the sharing by the subgroups and your summing-up; white board and markers.

Time allocation

About 2 hours

Steps in conducting the exercise

- Give a brief presentation on 'conflict' and its importance in our life. However, at this point in time, avoid going into any elaborate discussion as this may influence the views of the participants for the subgroup discussions.
- Introduce the exercise and divide the group into subgroups of 5–7 participants; distribute the worksheet on 'Conflict—How Do You See It and Its Implications?

- Give the following instructions to the subgroups:
    - ○ Each subgroup discusses responses to the questions posed in the worksheet
    - ○ While in most cases, the subgroup records the general consensus on different aspects of conflict, in some cases, it may be necessary to include the views and responses of individual participants. Each subgroup will prepare a report on key points for presentation in the larger group through flip charts or any other suitable aid
    - ○ Time allocation for discussion in subgroup and preparation of the presentation is about 1 ¼ hours
- Recall the subgroups and ask them to make presentations. Inform them that each presentation will be followed by brief discussion but the data generated by them will be used for more substantive discussions on various aspects of conflict.
- Give necessary inputs, taking into consideration the points emerging from subgroup presentations. Close the exercise.

WORKSHEET FOR SUBGROUPS

Conflict—How Do You See it and its Implications?

The following questions relate to different aspects of conflict. Once you have described 'conflict', you must shift to the context of interpersonal conflict situations. Your task, as a subgroup, is to discuss these and prepare a report for presentation in the larger group. Please note that in some cases, it may be necessary to record individual responses.

- What do you understand by the term 'conflict'?
- What are the key features of an interpersonal conflict?
- When an interpersonal conflict is resolved, what are the outcomes you expect from it?
- What is an individual's greatest strength in dealing with conflict?
- What is an individual's greatest weakness or inadequacy in dealing with a conflict situation?
- What can an individual do to prevent a conflict?
- When an individual realises that he or she is in conflict, what would be his or her typical response?

- What can an individual do to avoid conflict?
- What are some key reasons for an individual to choose to avoid conflict?
- What is the difference between an interpersonal conflict outside a group setting and within a group?
- List three key positive and three negative outcomes of a conflict in a group or an organisation?
- What are the measures a leader can put in place to prevent interpersonal conflicts in a group?

HANDOUT FOR THE PARTICIPANTS

Resolving Interpersonal Conflicts

Create a supportive environment

- You are responsible for creating an environment that will help in resolving the conflict. Convey sincerity of purpose and action to the opposite party.

Diffuse the situation

- Even if the other party is angry and expresses his or her annoyance in clear terms, you counter it by maintaining a calm demeanour and poise. This is the test of individual strength and integrity, and your ability to achieve positive results out of a seemingly volatile situation.

Convey your sincerity for exploring solution

- The message must go to the other party that you are not looking to 'win' result but for a 'win-win' situation.

Identify the issues

- Let the issues be placed on the table with understanding of the perspective and views of the other party.
- Be a good listener.

- Do not go into frivolous details as this may blur the issues and make resolution of the conflict difficult.

Maintain clarity of purpose

- Establish common objective and maintain clarity of purpose throughout the dialogue. Do not let yourself be distracted.

Avoid blame game

- Be willing to take responsibility for the situation, your actions. Acknowledge your mistakes, where appropriate.
- Do not engage in blame game.

Manage your emotions

- As you proceed with the dialogue, there will be exchange of emotions and feelings. Be frank in expressing them but in a rational and matter-of-fact manner.
- Do not let your emotions overwhelm you or overtake reason and objectivity.

Empathise

- Empathetic understanding of the issues is vital to finding a 'win-win' solution.
- Express appreciation of the position of the other party.

Decide on the best solution

- Select the solution that is mutually acceptable, realistic and workable.

EXERCISE 2

CONFLICT MANAGEMENT STYLES ASSESSMENT

Objectives

At the end of the exercise, the participants will be able to:

- Assess their conflict management style
- Know about the implications of the styles with regard to their use

Time allocation

About 1 ¼ hour

Material required

Training aids and tools required for presentation by the trainer; flip charts and writing markers for displaying key points emerging out of the sharing of the data generated by the participants; copies of the worksheet of Conflict Management Styles Assessment, and the Scoring Sheet and Interpretation, and handout on Description of the Styles (one for each participant) and white board and markers.

Steps in conducting the exercise

- Give a brief introduction to the topic 'Conflict Management Styles'. However, you must not elaborate on the conflict management styles as this may influence the participants' responses to the statements that constitute the exercise
- Distribute copies of the worksheet and ask the participants to complete the worksheet in accordance with the instructions
- After all of them have completed the exercise, distribute the Scoring Sheet and Interpretation and ask the participants to score as per the instructions

- Once all of them have scored their responses, invite them to share their data on a voluntary basis. You may pose the following questions to those who volunteer:
  - o What was your dominant style?
  - o Do you agree with the results of the assessment?
  - o Were there any surprises in the results?
  - o Do the results help explain how things have gone in different conflict situations you have encountered in your personal and professional life?
- Distribute copies of Description of the Styles. Give them time to go over the description and understand the implications of their dominant style. Respond to queries, if any
- Sum up and inform the group that more elaborate discussion on different conflict management styles will follow

Worksheet

Conflict Management Styles Assessment

We each have our own way of dealing with conflict. The techniques we use are based on many variables such as our basic underlying temperament, our personality, our environment and where we are in our professional career. However, by and large, there are five major styles of conflict management techniques in our toolbox. In order to address conflict, we draw from a collaborating, competing, avoiding, accommodating or compromising style of conflict management. None of these strategies is superior to the others. How effective they are depends on the context in which they are used and the outcomes.

Instruction for Completing the Exercise

Each statement below provides a strategy for dealing with a conflict. Rate each statement on a scale of 1 to 4 indicating how likely you are to use this strategy. 1: Rarely; 2: Sometimes; 3: Often and 4: Always.

It is suggested that you should keep in view one reference point—personal conflicts or those at your workplace.

Be sure to answer the questions indicating how you *would* behave rather than how you think you *should* behave.

1. I explore issues with others so as to find solutions that meet everyone's needs _____
2. I try to negotiate and adopt a give-and-take approach to problem situations _____
3. I try to meet the expectations of others _____
4. I would argue my case and insist on the merits of my point of view _____
5. When there is a disagreement, I gather as much information as I can and keep the lines of communication open _____
6. When I find myself in an argument, I usually say very little and try to leave as soon as possible _____
7. I try to see conflicts from both sides. What do I need? What does the other person need? What are the issues involved? _____
8. I prefer to compromise when solving problems and just move on _____
9. I find conflicts challenging and exhilarating; I enjoy the battle of wits that usually follows _____
10. Being at odds with other people makes me feel uncomfortable and anxious _____
11. I try to accommodate the wishes of my friends and family _____
12. I can figure out what needs to be done and I am usually right _____
13. To break deadlocks, I would meet people halfway _____
14. I may not get what I want but it's a small price to pay for keeping the peace _____
15. I avoid hard feelings by keeping my disagreements with others to myself _____

SCORING SHEET AND INTERPRETATION

As stated, the 15 statements correspond to the five conflict resolution styles. To find your most preferred or dominant style, total the points in the respective categories. The one with the highest score indicates your most commonly used strategy. The one with the lowest score indicates your least preferred strategy. However, if you are in a position in which you are required to deal with conflict on a regular basis, you may find your style to be a blend of different styles.

Style Corresponding Statements: Total:

Collaborating: 1, 5, 7 _____
Competing: 4, 9, 12 _____
Avoiding: 6, 10, 15 _____
Accommodating: 3, 11, 14 _____
Compromising: 2, 8, 13 _____

Brief Descriptions of the Five Conflict Management Styles

Collaborating Style: Problems are solved in ways in which an optimum result is provided for all involved. Both sides get what they want and negative feelings are minimised.

Pros: Creates mutual trust; maintains positive relationships; builds commitments.

Cons: Time consuming; energy consuming.

Competing Style: Authoritarian approach

Pros: Goal oriented; quick.

Cons: May breed hostility.

Avoiding Style: The non-confrontational approach

Pros: Does not escalate conflict; postpones difficulty.

Cons: Unaddressed problems; unresolved problems.

Accommodating Style: Giving in to maintain relationships

Pros: Minimises injury when we are outmatched; relationships are maintained.

Cons: Breeds resentment; exploits the weak.

Compromising Style: The middle ground approach

Pros: Useful in complex issues without simple solutions; all parties are equal in power.

Cons: No one is ever really satisfied; less than optimal solutions get implemented.

HANDOUT FOR THE PARTICIPANTS

Description of the Styles

What Are You Like?

The Turtle (Avoidance)

The turtle withdraws into its shell to avoid conflicts. They give up their personal goals and relationships. They stay away from the issues over which the conflict is taking place and from the persons they are in conflict with. Turtles believe it is hopeless to try and resolve conflicts. They feel helpless. They believe it is easier to withdraw (physically and psychologically) from a conflict than to face it.

The Shark (Competition)

Sharks try to overpower opponents by forcing them to accept their solutions to the conflict. Their goals are highly important to them and relationships of minor importance. They seek to achieve their goals at all costs. They are not concerned with the needs of the others. They do not care if others like or accept them. Sharks assume that conflicts are either won or lost and they want to be the winner. This gives them as sense of pride and achievement. Losing gives them a sense of weakness, inadequacy and failure. They try and win by attacking, overpowering, overwhelming and intimidating others.

The Teddy Bear (Accommodation)

To teddy bears, the relationship is of great importance while their own goals are of little importance. Teddies want to be liked and accepted by other people. They think that conflict should be avoided in favour of harmony and that people cannot discuss conflicts without damaging relationships. They give up their goal to preserve relationship. They like to smooth things over.

The Fox (Compromising)

Foxes are moderately concerned with their own goals and their relationships with others. They give up part of their own goals and persuade others in a conflict to give up part of theirs. They seek a conflict solution in which both sides gain something—the middle ground between two extreme positions. They compromise; they will give up part of their goal and relationship in order to find agreement for the common good.

The Owl (Collaboration)

Owls highly value their goals and relationships. They view conflicts as problems to be solved and seek a solution that achieves both their own and the other person's goals. Owls see conflicts as a means of improving relationships by reducing tension between two people. They try to begin a discussion that identifies the conflict as a problem to be solved. By seeking solutions that satisfy everyone, owls maintain the relationship. They are not happy until a solution is found that both satisfies everyone's goals and resolves the tensions and negative feelings that may have been present.

Module 5

Management of Stress

This module deals with different aspects of mental stresses that seem to be increasingly becoming part of our daily life—in the family, personal relationships, workplaces, etc. The aim is to provide the participants with an opportunity to discuss the dynamics of stress by going down to the very sources that cause stress. The module also suggests some measures that could assist them in honing their skills to prevent or cope with stress in a more positive way. Undoubtedly, if an individual is able to cope with stress in an effective manner, she can lead a happier and more successful life.

Specifically, this module focuses on the following areas:

- Stress and people
- Internal stressors
- External stressors
- Causes of stress at workplace
- General strategies to manage stress
- Things you can do to avoid or manage stress

Expected Outcomes from the Module

At the end of the session on the module, the participants will be able to:

- Identify and describe the key sources of stress—external and internal, and those arising out of the changes on life;
- Discuss general strategies that one can adopt to manage stresses and
- List activities that one can serve as stress busters

STRESS AND PEOPLE

There's going to be stress in life, but
It's your choice whether to let it affect you or not.

—Valerie Bertinelli

Although we all talk about stress, it often is not clear what stress is really about. Many people consider stress to be something that happens to them, an event such as an injury or a job loss. Others think that stress is what happens to our body, mind and behaviour in response to an event. While stress does involve events and our response to them, what is critical is our thought process about the situations that decides whether we are under stress or not.

Stress is best seen as pressures and demands put on an individual's maladaptive responses, for example, anxiety, irritability, aches and pains. It is an interaction between situational demands and the resources of the individual to cope with them; a reaction that can be positive or negative, depending on the person and the situation; a transactional process, whereby the ability of a person to prevent stress is determined by that person's appraisal of threat and her assessment of her coping abilities.

Stress is the way human beings react both physically and mentally to changes, events and situations in their lives. When something happens to us—personal or work-related problems; unhappy situations, sorrowful events, etc., we automatically evaluate the situation mentally in terms of the nature and level of concern or threat, and the manner it impacts us, consequences, etc. On the basis of this analysis, we mentally explore the options of dealing with the situation, then we assess our abilities and skills for effectively coping with it. If we find that our coping skills outweigh the demands of the situation, then we do not see it as *stressful*. However, if we realise that we are not competent enough to deal with the situation in an effective manner—in terms of our abilities and resources that we possess or can muster, as also our mental preparedness—we label the situation as *stressful* and react with the classic *stress response*. Thus, stress is a physical and psychological response experienced on encountering a situation when we find that we are not able to cope with it.

Stress can come from any situation or thought that makes one feel frustrated, angry, anxious or concerned. However, people experience stress in different ways and for different reasons. No two people will respond in an identical manner even when confronted with same or similar situation. A number of factors are at play in developing a response to a given situation: previous experience, abilities, support system, resources available, etc. For instance, if somebody loses her job, she would carefully weigh up her own liabilities and assets, the likely support she can receive from family members or friends and her chances of getting another job soon. If she finds the circumstances favourable, she may not feel the level of stress another person will feel if she is the sole earner and has a family to support with no backup resources, and the job market not offering much hope. Evidently, in the latter case, the stress level will be very high.

Another key factor that determines the response to stress is the nature of stress and its implications for the life of the individual. If the impact of the situation that has caused the stress is serious, the individual may be severely affected. On the other hand, if the implications are not very damaging for her, the stress may be less.

What enables some individuals to not only effectively cope with but also thrive in the face of trouble, and what makes others crumble? The answer, perhaps, lies in the way people perceive the situation that can cause stress. Given the same set of circumstances, one person may visualise a crisis where another finds it a challenge. Therefore, the key to controlling stress is learning to see things in a specific way. If viewed in the proper perspective, some may find in stress an opportunity for growth and excitement. There is another factor: people who successfully cope with stress are usually very committed to what they do in life. Some overriding goal or belief gives them purpose, one that gets them through life's inevitable difficulties and crises. Stress-resistant people are able to exercise greater control over their life than those who fall apart. They also manage internal stresses such as worry and guilt within controllable limits.

It is not stress that kills us, it is our reaction to it.

—Hans Selye

All stresses are not negative although in daily life, we often use the term 'stress' to describe negative situations. This leads many people to believe that all stress is bad for you, which is not true. It has some positive functions as well. Positive stressor can act as driver for that extra bit that can help in progress and growth of an individual. In its positive form, stress helps you rise to a challenge and can be an antidote to boredom because it engages focused energy. It is also possible that a positive stressor for one person can be a negative stressor for another. Many people regard public speaking or airplane flights as very stressful, with its attending physical and mental reactions, while some look forward to the event. It is often a question of perception.

Many professionals suggest that there is a difference between what we perceive as positive stress (also called eustress) and what we experience as negative stress (also called distress).

If you view a situation negatively, you will likely feel *distressed*—overwhelmed, oppressed or out of control. Distress is the more familiar form of stress. The other form, *eustress*, results from a 'positive' view of an event or situation, or something new happening in your life for which you are not fully prepared. This is why it is also called 'good stress'.

Some examples of eustress or positive stress are:

- Receiving a promotion at work
- Starting a new job
- Marriage or commitment ceremony
- Buying a home
- Having a child
- Moving your residence to a new location
- Giving a presentation to a group; appearance before an audience
- Retiring

Eustress has the following characteristics:

- It is generally short-term and affects you temporarily
- It is perceived as within our coping abilities
- Motivates or invigorates, focuses energy
- Feels exciting

Some examples of distress or negative stress are:

- The death of a partner or family member
- Losing job, job insecurity or unemployment

- Excessive job- or performance-related demands
- Separation from a spouse or committed relationship partner
- Conflicts with office colleagues, supervisors or bosses
- Financial problems
- Long-term health problems (oneself or a family member)
- Conflict in interpersonal relationships
- Losing contact with loved ones
- Being abused or neglected

Distress (negative stress) has the following characteristics:

- Causes anxicty, concern or worry
- It can be short-term or long-term
- It is perceived as outside our coping abilities
- It demotivates and drains our energy
- It feels very unpleasant
- It can lead to mental and health problems
- It decreases performance

INTERNAL STRESSORS

Anger

One of the emotions that can cause a lot of stress is anger, although it is completely normal, usually healthy, human emotion. However, when it gets out of control and turns destructive, it can lead to multiplicity of problems. It can sour relationships at home, at workplace and with friends. Your quality of life gets affected. It also has severe physical and emotional implications for you. Though researches have not conclusively proved that there is a correlation between anger and its physical and biological effects, it is widely acknowledged that when you get angry, it has a number of physical reactions—your heart rate and blood pressure go up, your ability to hear properly, think objectively and speak coherently gets severely affected.

Anger can be viewed as a natural, adaptive response to threats. When we are faced with a situation that threatens our very survival, it inspires a powerful, often aggressive feelings and behaviour urging us to fight and defend ourselves.

When you are angry, you experience a powerful emotion is overwhelming and controlling you. The irony, however, is that you feel that by yelling at people and gesturing wildly you are controlling people and situations. The truth, however, is the opposite.

All of us at one time or the other got angry. It could have been irritation, annoyance at something or full-fledged rage, an outburst at some body or in response to a situation. As life gets more complicated, you interact with more people on a daily basis. Inevitably, you are engaged in more incidents and situations that have the potential of irritating, annoying, provoking and enraging you. The stage is set for you to get angry.

Anger can be caused by both external and internal factors and events. You could be angry at a specified person—a friend, family member or office colleague; or situation—a traffic jam or someone splashing rainwater on you as you walk on the street. You could also get angry by worrying about a personal problem or by sulking over something that happened earlier. Memories of traumatic or enraging events can also trigger angry feelings.

Why do some people get angry more easily than others? This is the question often asked. People who are prone to getting angry easily and more intensely generally have a low tolerance of frustration. They want to have everything their way. They are the people with high expectations from others. When these are not fulfilled, instead of being more realistic and understanding, they get frustrated and disappointed. If not controlled, these emotions can quickly turn into anger or rage. These people would not like to be told what to do and what not to do. They cannot be corrected.

We express anger in different ways, depending on the environment and the person(s) at whom we are getting angry. We are also restrained by social norms or by awareness of the consequences of our angry response to a situation or person. Nevertheless, aggression is the underlying factor.

People use a variety of conscious and subconscious processes to deal with their anger. You can express it in an unrestrained manner, regardless of the consequences, sometimes, to regret, later. Shouting, gesticulating wildly, blaming people, giving threats or calling names are all aggressive responses. Some people may suppress their anger in a given situation or with a particular person but then redirect it to someone, who appears to be more vulnerable or easy target. For example, you may be angry with your boss or colleagues but take it out on your spouse, children or friends. You may either show your anger in a more demonstrable way by throwing things around or turn inwards by withdrawing and sulking. There are also people who can direct their anger to other positive things or constructive behaviour. The third alternative is to learn to manage it.

Frustrations

We all experience little frustrations everyday but they come and pass, and are forgotten. Waiting at the red light when you are in a hurry to reach your destination can cause frustration but once it turns green, it melts down. Among other smaller frustrations are: you go to a restaurant looking forward to a good time with friends or family but find that it is their closed day. The other restaurant is far away. You feel frustrated but the feeling passes.

Among big frustrations can be that you trained hard for a major sporting event and expected to perform well but just before the event you suffer an injury and are unable to participate.

We undergo frustration when things turn out not quite the way we expected them to, when we cannot accomplish something we set out to do or when we feel cheated, foiled, thwarted or baffled. Frustration may also arise out of our inability to take a decision when it is necessary and important or perform a task. But we must remember that frustrations are not something that can be shut out of our life.

Guilt

The beauty of life is, while we cannot undo what is done,
we can see it, understand it, learn from it and change
so that every new moment is spent not in regret, guilt, fear,
or anger, but in wisdom, understanding, and love.

—Jennifer Edwards

Guilt is a form of self-punishment. The situations that made us feel guilty have their genesis in culture or in the family values. It is a reaction to an event or situation, and when it motivates us for a constructive activity, it is both healthy and useful. For example, you were abrasive or rude to a dear friend. As a result of your words and actions, you hurt her and bruised her self-esteem. You feel guilty, and as a corrective measure, you apologise to the person or do a good deed to help the person in order to overcome your guilt.

You can develop a sense of guilt when you feel that you have betrayed or compromised on an internal value of your own or the trust of the other person. You may also think that you deserve punishment for this. These thoughts can cause anxiety, leading to stress. When you are feeling guilty, the important question is whether it is of healthy or unhealthy nature.

There is a possibility that you may distort your feeling of guilt and start believing that your behaviour is bad or you are a bad person. This is an unhealthy aspect of guilt. Healthier form of guilt is remorse. Remorse is an undistorted and objective awareness that you have wilfully and unnecessarily acted in a hurtful manner towards yourself or another person. You also realise that in doing so you have violated your ethical standards. Remorse differs from guilt because there is no implication that your transgression indicates that you are inherently bad or evil, or immoral. If you are experiencing remorse, you feel bad about your action or behaviour, but there is no sense of self-deprecation.

There are people who may feel vaguely guilty even when there is nothing to feel guilty about. Some people may feel guilty when they feel happy or about something good that has happened.

Some individuals carry a sense of guilt that is no longer valid or appropriate. Guilt that is located in your subconscious is always manifested indirectly. So when you are not aware of your guilt feeling or do not consciously admit or own it, you may be creating other unexplained problems for you. You may feel depressed or tense. You may not take interest in socialising. You may lose your temper more frequently than earlier. The smartest method to determine whether guilt is behind such behaviour is to engage in some reflection, either on your own or with the help of others. In the process, you may find yourself striking on the real issue at hand.

Some people turn their feeling of guilt into anger as this is the easier thing to do rather than admitting it.

Once you realise you are feeling guilty, you should analyse the situation that triggered the guilt and decide whether your guilt feelings are really appropriate. If you decide that your sense of guilt is proper, own up to it. Take responsibility for your actions and do the needful. Then let go of that feeling and move on.

Phobias

Fear is natural. We all have some fears that may be termed as reasonable and appropriate. A phobia by contrast is irrational and inappropriate. A person with intense phobia will be willing to rearrange her whole life to avoid the situation that may trigger the phobia. And, under the circumstances, sometimes, such people may end up causing more stress and tension to themselves.

Fear vs. Phobia

A <u>fear</u> can be explained as a normal response to genuine danger.

A <u>phobia</u> is a 'marked and persistent fear that is excessive or unreasonable, cued by the presence or anticipation of a specific object or situation'.

Many people use the words fear and phobia as substitutes. These words are not synonyms and they do not describe the same condition. It is important to know the difference between fear and phobia, because it shows us what we are up against. Being afraid is normal while having a phobia is pathological. Phobias are unreasonable fears, that is, fears that everyone—including those who suffer from them—considers incomprehensible, absurd or even childish.

Fear is actually common and when we experience it, we usually tend to avoid a potential danger. That is why this mechanism was passed on from generation to generation. It played a significant role in our survival. It uses our own experience to determine if a current situation is dangerous or not.

When it comes to fear, the source is a potential risky or dangerous situation. For example, if you are walking on the edge of the rooftop, there is always a chance to fall. It is absolutely natural to be afraid, because rationally speaking you can fall and suffer a serious injury or worst. The source of fear resides in a healthy and rational judgement. The source of phobia is a distorted and irrational way of thinking.

But as a sensation, fear is not that intense. Remember that the only purpose of fear is to signal a potential danger, not to *paralyse* us. On the other hand, phobia has a *crippling* effect on us. When we are face to face with our worst phobic stimulus, we feel like our blood freezes. Everything seems unreal and our entire attention is focused on whatever is causing the phobia. It is a very unpleasant sensation. Phobia is a result of your own irrational thoughts. It happens in your head.

In case of fear, the most common reaction is avoidance. You simply decide to escape the potentially dangerous situation by stepping back or going around. Actually, there is not much to say about how people react when they are scared. It is a perfectly typical and natural reaction.

Worrying

> 'Worrying does not take away tomorrow's troubles;
> it takes away today's peace'.

Worrying is a state of anxiety, concern or unease about something, real or imaginary. It is a natural part of the human condition. We all experience worry. We know that nagging feeling that something is wrong and the persistent anxiety that it produces. It has historically played a vital role in our survival and it helps us cope with many of the challenges we face today. At the same time, worry, that is too intense, too frequent and too unrelenting, can definitely cut down on your happiness and enjoyment of life.

It is like a rocking chair—it will give you something to do but it will not get you anywhere. Worrying reflects your attempts to mentally cope with your concerns and fears. You can view this as the thinking part of anxiety with no action. While you wait for the result of the interview for a job in which you had appeared earlier, you experience a sinking feeling in your stomach, especially if you need the job desperately.

Worrying is obviously not a pleasant emotion, but it is actually an essential, normal and instinctive emotion that has been hardwired into humans to help us survive. We worry about something because we perceive it as a threat to our existence and worry causes us to focus on it and protect ourselves from that threat.

A way to find out about your worrying profile is to ask yourself the following questions:

- Do you worry about things that are not real or immediate threats?
- Are you more anxious than relaxed?
- Are you more unhappy than happy?
- Do you have difficulty enjoying yourself because you worry so much?
- Are you unwilling to take reasonable risks?
- Do your worries interfere with your normal activities?

If you answered 'no' to the above questions, then you are likely a healthy worrier, so keep doing what you are doing because you will be sensitive to real threats, do what is reasonable to live a happy life and you will not drive yourself crazy. However, if you responded 'yes' to the questions, then you are probably an unhealthy worrier and you will want to take some steps to relieve yourself of that unnecessary burden.

Another thing that can cause the volume of your worrying to go up several notches is to worry about worrying. You can make yourself even more miserable by thinking that you are the only one in the world who worries about the things you worry about. If you can accept that worrying is just a routine part of life and everyone does it, then you can keep the volume of your worrying to a more manageable level.

Sometimes, there is no immediate solution to the worrying (e.g., waiting to hear whether you got a job you had applied for) and you just cannot get your worrying out of your mind. In this case, the best strategy is to distract yourself the best you can from the worry. Whether reading a book, watching a movie, hanging out with friends or exercising, if you are focused on other activities, you are bound to worry less. Even better, if you can do things that produce an emotional experience diametrically opposed to worrying, namely anything that makes you feel positive, happy, excited or relaxed, you will counter the negativity and anxiety that accompanies worrying. This is no panacea, but it can provide you with a beneficial respite, even if temporary, from your worries.

Personality Traits and Attitudes

Perfectionists tend to set high goals for them and they are not willing to accept anything less than complete or perfect success or achievement.

And often their goals are neither reasonable nor realistic. They are so concerned about meeting the goal and avoiding the dreaded failure that they cannot enjoy the process of growing and striving. If they do not reach their target, they consider this as a failure causing them stress.

Perfectionists are far more critical of themselves than high achievers. They tend to spot tiny mistakes and imperfections in their work and in themselves, as well as in others and their work. They are more judgmental and hard on themselves than on others when 'failure' does occur. And this is a cause for stress.

The following statements or questions will help you understand how some personality traits or attitudes contribute to stress:

- Over-planning each day: Do you feel the need to stick to a strict schedule? Do you live in fear of falling behind or overlooking a task?
- Doing several things at once: With too much to do and not enough time, it is easy to think that 'efficient' means doing everything at once. He who chases two rabbits catches neither.
- Extreme need to win: Do you feel like a failure if you do not come out on top—even when the only competition is your own expectations?
- Excessive desire for advancement: Highly stressed people need confirmation from outside sources that they are doing okay and performing well.
- Inability to relax without feeling guilty: Do your weekends become opportunities for 'accomplishment' and 'getting something done'.
- Impatience with delay or chronic urgency: When you are under pressure, everything in life takes on urgency and the additional burdens to get everything done as fast as possible.
- Over-commitment: Are you chronically late or forgetful of commitments? Does your schedule cause problems in personal or professional relationships?
- Highly competitive drive: Have you forgotten what it is like to have fun for fun's sake? Have you 'grown up' so much that playtime actually causes you anxiety?
- Compulsion to overwork: Is your office more familiar to you than your backyard? Do you find yourself missing out on what you might otherwise deem 'meaningful'?

Locus of Control

The term 'locus of control' refers to whether you feel your life is controlled by you or by forces outside you. Those with an internal locus of control feel that they have choices in their lives and control over their circumstances. On the other hand, those with an external locus of control feel more at the mercy of external events. Not surprisingly, those with a more internal locus of control tend to feel happier, more free, and less stressful. On the other hand, those with an external locus of control are more susceptible to stress, as they feel powerless to change their own circumstances, which just adds to their stress load.

EXTERNAL STRESSORS

Relationship Issues

Positive relationships with family members and friends can make your life rewarding, satisfying and meaningful. On the other hand, if the relationships go sour, it can make your life draining and difficult.

Stress can both be a cause and a consequence of unhappy or strained relationship. If you are stressed due to personal or work-related problems or situations, your relationships in the family or within your social circle are likely to be adversely affected. If you are unable to manage your external stresses, your interactions and communication with your family members and friends will not be normal. It will be influenced by your emotional and physical state. On the other hand, strained relationships with family members, especially your spouse or friends can also become a big source of your stress and take a heavy toll of your health and mental state. This personal stress will affect your work performance as well.

In a family, relationship between the parents and the young ones is often guided by the extent of control and authority the parents exercise over the actions and behaviour of their children. Young people may get stressed as they resent this approach or due to fear of admonishment, criticism or reproach.

Stresses at Workplace

While some workplace stress is normal, excessive stress can interfere with your productivity and performance—and impact your physical and emotional health. Often, your ability to deal with stress can mean the difference between success and failure at work. You cannot control everything in your work environment, but that does not mean you are powerless—even when you are stuck in a difficult situation. Whatever your work demands or ambitions, there are steps you can take to protect yourself from the damaging effects of stress and improve your job satisfaction.

Job stress is widely experienced and so pervasive that it has been found to affect people from all types of workplaces, regardless of the status and social–economic background. And because so much of our lives are spent at workplace, job stress can create stress in other areas of life as well. For example, when people are stressed at work, they may have less patience when not at work, and relationships may suffer; they may have less energy when not at work and let exercise go by the wayside; they may feel so much stress at work that they experience burnout or depression.

Stress is not always bad. Stress within your comfort zone can help you stay focused, energetic and able to meet new challenges in the workplace. Stress is what keeps you on your toes during a presentation or alert you to prevent accidents or costly mistakes at work. However, in today's hectic world, the workplace can often seem like an emotional roller coaster. Long hours, tight deadlines and ever-increasing demands can leave you feeling worried, uncertain and overwhelmed by stress. However, when stress exceeds your comfort zone, it stops being helpful and can start causing major damage to your mind and body as well as your job satisfaction and performance. But no matter what you do for a living, or how stressful your job is, there are plenty of things you can do to reduce your overall stress.

Unclear work or conflicting roles and boundaries can cause stress, as can having responsibility for people. The possibilities for job development are important buffers against current stress, with under-promotion, lack of training and job insecurity being stressful. There are two other sources of stress or buffers against stress: relationships at work, and the organisational culture. Managers who are critical, demanding, unsupportive or bullying create stress, whereas a positive social dimension of work and good team working reduces it.

An organisational culture of unpaid overtime or 'presenteeism' (the practice of persistently working longer hours and taking fewer holidays than the terms of one's employment demand, especially as a result of fear of losing one's job) causes stress. On the other hand, a culture of involving people in decisions, keeping them informed about what is happening in the organisation and providing good amenities and recreation facilities reduce stress. Organisational change, especially when consultation has been inadequate, is a huge source of stress.

CAUSES OF STRESS AT WORKPLACE

Lack of Control

A basic human requirement is our need for a reasonable degree of autonomy in conducting our affairs, whether at workplace or in our personal life. At the workplace, that means having the freedom to make our own decisions about how we approach our own job, of course, on the basis of our job description and within the overall working or operational procedures of the organisation. We do expect to exercise some control over the way we work. We prefer to be judged by results, outcomes and objectives met, rather than to be micromanaged in precise detail and expected to conform exactly to organisational procedures. We have a need to influence the outcomes of work we are involved in; a need to *put our own stamp on* the things we do; a need to make a difference because of who we are; a need to *matter*. At some workplaces, supervisors and those responsible to oversee your work are always breathing down your neck and they can drive you mad by their intrusive style. While some people may be able to cope with it but for many of us this becomes a cause for stress as we may find ourselves without an alternative choice.

A feeling of powerlessness is a universal cause of job stress. When you feel powerless, you are prey to depression's travelling companions, helplessness and hopelessness. You do not alter or avoid the situation because you feel nothing can be done.

You have an overwhelming feeling that you are just responding to others' demands. Your work schedule, timelines and tasks are set by others and you have no say in what you do. You feel that you have little control on your work and the way you approach your responsibilities and tasks. Common to this work situation are complaints of too much responsibility and too little authority, unfair working practices and inadequate or unclear job descriptions. You may be overwhelmed by a sense of rudderless drift.

Also, inability to influence decisions that affect your job—such as your schedule, assignments or workload—could lead to job burnout. So could a lack of the resources you need to do your work.

Work-life Imbalance

The ever-present upwards trend in working hours shows no sign of letting up. And the work is not limited to the working hours only. It gets extended to home as well. More often than not, you are constrained to put extra hours to complete the tasks left unfinished during the long working hours or prepare for the next day's work. To make matters worse, the latest communication technology takes over—there is periodic buzz of the mobile phones and the arriving e-mails on your laptop or desktop. These diversions never allow you to enjoy a few relaxed hours of work-free life. Sometimes tongue-in-cheek remarks of the spouse and the demands of the children ensure that there is an overload of stress at home also. In some cases, this strains family relationship.

And, it is not just hours on the job that keep us from home, family and leisure. Commuting, entertaining friends of the organisation, networking with colleagues, work-related travel and workshops and job-related training, all take their toll, creating more annoyance and stress. Pressures from family obligations compete with work commitments and vice versa. There are times when we are unable to give fullness of attention to either, resulting to an overload of stress.

Thus, our lives are sharply divided into segments that compete for our time, energy and attention. Failure to fulfil these obligations is, in the final analysis, one of our deepest causes of stress, with dismal consequences. We become disintegrated. The burnout will be sooner than later.

Responsibilities–Skills Mismatch; Dissatisfaction with the Work Itself

Remember the old saying, 'Find a job you love and you will never work another day in your life'. Most people spend about 25 per cent of their adult lives working. If you enjoy what you do, you are lucky. But in the present-day world, regardless whether you are in a developing country like India or living in a country with an advanced economy, it is not easy to find a job that you love. We all have to make compromises.

When you work with an organisation, you have a job profile that details your work-related responsibilities. While you would have accepted the job fully aware of the responsibilities it will carry, in the longer run you may feel that there is a mismatch between your job-related skills and the requirements of the job. In this situation, there are two possibilities. One, you may feel that your skills are like a square peg in a round hole and there is no sync between the two. In such situations, you are not able to give your best and this affects the outcomes of your efforts. However, you may hang on to the job for other reasons, such as financial benefits, difficulty in finding an assignment consistent with your skills, regardless of the frustration and stress it is causing you.

Another scenario is when you are either short of the skills required for performing the job effectively, or the level of skills is far above the ones required. While, in the first case, you may have a feeling of inadequateness, leading to frustration; in the second case, you may feel that your skills are not being fully utilised and you may feel dissatisfied with the job assignment. Both situations may become a source of occupation-related stress, giving rise to lack of motivation, dissatisfaction, lethargy and negativity.

If you are stuck in a job that does not match your natural talents and aspirations, it is important to recognise that fact and move on. You are a misplaced person; and this is one of the biggest causes of stress possible in the workplace.

Unclear or Inadequate Job Description

Every personnel should have a specific, written job description. Simply negotiating one does more to dispel a sense of powerlessness than anything else we know. It is a contract that you help write. You can object to that and insist on what you do want. If there is a compromise, it is because you agreed to it. With a clear job description, your expectations are spelled out and you set out to realise them. Also, what your bosses or the management expect from you by way of deliverables in activities and tasks, and standards of performance, are also clearly expressed and understood by you. It is important that your job should be a source of satisfaction, optimum utilisation of your skills and dignity. Job description generally spells out what the management or the organisation expects from you by way of performance and deliverables in terms of activities, projects and programmes. If you are unclear about the degree of authority you have or what your supervisor or others expect from you, you are not likely to feel comfortable at work.

Mismatch in Values

Regardless of the organisation you are working with, corporate, social development agencies or government departments, there are certain values, beliefs and ideals attached to the work, whether explicitly expressed or not. The work culture of an organisation is one way of emphasising these values, and the employees, regardless of their position and responsibilities, are expected to respect this work culture and uphold these values. It is likely that your values and ideals, and those of the organisation for which you work do not match. Up to a point, you may be willing to compromise and concede. However, in cases where either you are very passionate about your values or you find that the divergence is substantial, you may continue in the job for reasons beyond your control but will find the going very tough and stressful.

Lack of Positive Work Environment

Work environment is a broader term that encompasses a number of elements or factors that guide the organisation to its objectives. Some key elements are:

- Decision-making structures in which you feel that your views and opinions are heard and valued
- There is a sense of shared purpose and commitment to the organisation's philosophy, mission, objectives and activities
- There is objective performance review and hard work, and positive outcomes are recognised and rewarded; there is positive reinforcement; support and opportunities for improving below-par performances
- Job responsibilities offer adequate scope for learning and professional growth
- Effective channels of intra-organisational communication
- Active and accountable leadership or management
- Relationship between functionaries is not limited to professional transactions; it is perceived as a strong support mechanism when dealing with personal problems
- Teamwork is valued
- Camaraderie

If some or more elements are absent from the organisational functioning, your physical and mental health will take a heavy toll.

Efforts–Rewards/Outcomes Imbalance

We have a basic human need for respect and recognition. We yearn to *belong*. We want to be accepted and valued by others, to be appreciated for who we are and for what we do. This need can be especially strong when it comes to our work, because we *define who we are* largely through our job, our profession. 'I'm a professor', 'I'm a Manager', 'I'm an executive'.

In our lives, we play different roles, fulfil diverse responsibilities and are engaged in a variety of activities. These roles and activities all afford us opportunities for gaining recognition and for feeling valued. Our overall sense of self-worth improves when others admire us for our contributions or achievements in these areas. But for many of us, our chosen work, career or profession is crucial in forming our self-image. We therefore feel the need to be appreciated and respected *as a practitioner* of our chosen type of work.

One of the biggest causes of stress at work can be the feeling that, no matter how hard you work, and no matter how good your results are, *you are just not appreciated*. Not for your effort, not for your contribution and not for your unique value as a member of the team. You feel *you may as well not bother*. We all feel this way at times, but if the feeling drags on, it eventually eats into your self-esteem, your self-respect and your confidence in your own ability. Alternatively, you may become resentful, frustrated and angry; feeling you are being overworked, taken advantage of and denied your due. This may be a cause of frustration, leading to mental stress and even lack of motivation in your work.

There may be situations in the pursuit of your job responsibilities, when you feel that the results are not on expected lines. In other words, there is a mismatch between your investment—in terms of efforts, time and resources—and the outcomes. Now these outcomes may be related to the targets you are expected to reach or some other tangible results. If it is a one-off situation, you may take it in the stride, considering it part of your work. However, if this pattern continues beyond a reasonable time and level, the situation may get to you causing you mental stress that can get easily translated into physical complications.

There is another side to this situation. While the results of your efforts may be on expected lines and you may have a sense of fulfilment, you may feel that your efforts are not receiving due acknowledgement and recognition from your superiors—monetary rewards, promotion or a memo of appreciation.

The financial rewards associated with a job are important in terms of lifestyle. They are also often perceived to be an indication of an individual's worth and value to the organisation. Although financial reward may not be a prime motivator, it could become a factor if there are other negative aspects of the job.

Dysfunctional Workplace Dynamics; Relationship Issues

Quite aside from the complexities of *role* relationships, there is the question of *personal* relationships at the workplace. Conflicts in social relationship can be a significant source of stress. Young employees get into multiple relationships, with peers from the same sex or from opposite sex. However, if these relationships, especially with colleagues from the opposite sex, are strained for whatever reasons, it can create stress. The problem gets further accentuated because you see these colleagues everyday at the workplace and there may not be any way that you can avoid them.

Sometimes, we cannot know with confidence and clarity just exactly how we 'fit in' to the larger picture in the organisation. Job descriptions, role statements, organisation charts, mission statements and all manner of documentation may exist. Unwritten 'rules' may abound. But reality can be much more complex. Management people, supervisors and colleagues may interpret role boundaries and responsibilities in their own ways, and they would not always be clear or consistent with us about where they think we, or they, fit in the context of the organisational framework or goals. They may draw their own boundaries around our roles and what we can do for them, giving rise to ambiguity and creating muddy areas we must live with as we cultivate our relationships.

We each have our own *comfort zone* when it comes to tolerating role conflicts and ambiguities. The daily dance around these issues can become one of the biggest causes of stress at work for some individuals. Lack of clarity in our reporting lines is another reason we, sometimes, experience conflicting or contradictory job demands. There may be multiple people who are keen to supervise our work. Sometimes, we may find ourselves reporting to more than one supervisor or manager, perhaps for different projects or programmes, or for various aspects of our tasks.

It is not unusual for you to have a supervisor or boss who is determined to make your life difficult, regardless of your performance. This can be a major cause of stress. For many of us experiencing 'Sunday evening blues' is a reality—with overbearing boss, undermining or intimidating colleagues and hostile work environment.

As human beings, we all need relationships. We spend a large part of our lives in the workplace, and so our relationships with our boss, our co-workers and our subordinates are important. These relationships can be rewarding and energising, or they can be difficult, draining and stressful. Positive relationships with co-workers can motivate and encourage you and help make your work a satisfying and meaningful experience. Unsatisfactory relationships at work can be one of your biggest causes of stress.

If you feel isolated at work and in your personal life, you might feel more stressed. Personal *isolation* in the workplace can be one of the worst experiences. This can be physical (working on your own) or emotional (being socially outcast). To feel comprehensively isolated in this way would be one of the biggest causes of stress in the workplace.

Sometimes, you may find yourself socially excluded by others in the group due to your being *different* in some way—religion, caste, language, your background, state from which you come, etc. It may even be simply because, unlike others, you are a vegetarian.

Anxiety over Career Advancement Prospects

If you find that the organisation does not have opportunities for growth and career advancement, you feel you are stuck in a hole and are going nowhere. You have an overwhelming feeling of professional stagnation. Fear of failure to climb the ladder of career success can become one of your biggest causes of stress.

However, we must realise that being career-centred is healthy if it is in balance with other areas of your life. This has to be matched by your desire to work on your professional competence and willingness to learn new things in the job. It can be a very positive and energising state, providing motivation and meaning, and a focal point for your life. We see this especially in people whose driving force is a passion for purpose and contribution, rather than simply personal ambition. Unbridled and unrealistic ambitions are one of the biggest causes of stress related to our work.

Some people strive for success beyond their inner needs and known capabilities, just to come up to the expectations of others—family members, friends, colleagues, etc. The sad thing is that you may well be completely *wrong* about others' expectations anyway. We easily read too much into minds of those around us. This crushing desire to conform to social expectations is one of the biggest causes of stress for many people. You may also start comparing yourself with those friends who have climbed the ladder of professional success and have reached higher positions. This comparison can be very stressful if you are still languishing way down the ladder. You suffer from a sense of inadequacy and despair. Pause for a moment and consider how they have reached there—may be through hard work and their competence.

Fear over Job Security

One factor that has brought about one of today's biggest causes of stress related to work is *erosion of the concept of job security*. With the government jobs shrinking and the corporate in India taking over, the scenario has changed considerably. In this highly competitive world, the job situation has become an arena for intense competition.

Fear of unemployment is one of the biggest causes of stress in our state-of-the-art world. Add to this fear of loss of face with family, friends and you have a perfect situation for stress.

Although we are getting into a 'performance culture', yet even if you are giving an above-par performance, you are not sure of job security in return. You live in a state of constant anxiety. You avoid going for a holiday because you fear that when you return, you may get the 'pink slip' (metonym for termination of employment) or some colleague may succeed in usurping your position in the organisation.

Work Setting

Sometimes your work setting creates physical stress because of noise, lack of privacy, poor lighting, poor ventilation, poor temperature control or inadequate sanitary facilities. Settings where there is organisational confusion or an overly authoritarian, laissez-faire or crisis-centred managerial style are all psychologically stressful. If nothing helps and the working environment remains stressful, exercise your avoidance options and get a new job. Job-hunting can be stressful, particularly in times of high unemployment, but being ground down day after day by work is far worse.

GENERAL STRATEGIES TO MANAGE STRESS

Reflection and Self-talk

One of the key techniques available to you for relief from stress is reflection and self-talk. However, an essential prerequisite is that this reflection has to be very objective, open-minded and unemotional. If you are not ready or unwilling to take a detached view of the situation, this strategy can offer little help to you. In fact, it may complicate the matter further as you may not be able to unravel the situation. Reflection or self-deliberation also means that you should be prepared to accept your share of the blame if the analysis suggests that. However, it does not mean that you should get into a mode of self-reproach. This way, you will only be shifting the source but you may not get any relief. A realistic approach will be to engage in an appropriate thought process but then take necessary steps to come out of the stressful situation, as proposed by your review. Mere reflection may be adequate in a minor stress but if it is more deep-rooted and the source is more complicated, suitable action offers the ultimate solution. Only then, you can hope to get relief from your stress. This is a very important strategy in the management of stress.

As you ponder over the situation, you may engage in a lot of self-talk. When you talk to yourself, you start unravelling the problem, looking for reasons that you might not have discerned otherwise. Remember, self-talk has to be a serious dialogue with you. If you conduct it in a superficial way, you only betray yourself and nothing will come out of this effort. Some part of you may, sometimes, even become the devil's advocate. This will help considering the situation from different standpoints or perspectives.

When you engage in self-talk, you must ask yourself these questions:

- Does the situation or the problem warrants me to get stressed?
- Who is to be blamed for this stress and what is my share in getting stressed?
- What do I do to get out of this mess?
- What are my options and which one I take?

Communication

When you are in stress, you may want to be alone as you may feel that it is better to be all by yourself. There is also the concept of 'victim syndrome'.

By confining your emotions to yourself, you will only aggravate and prolong your stress. You may continue to suffer unless you have practised this before successfully. It is, therefore, advisable that when you find the situation difficult to cope with by yourself, you should communicate and interact with people as much as you can. Many people feel that they should stop communicating with those who are viewed as the source of the stress. This may be right if you are convinced that no useful purpose will be served by communicating with these people as a starting point but this cannot be the norm. Many a time, however, you may find that contrary to your understanding, the person who supposedly caused the stress may herself become the source of relief. This may be a workable strategy with those with whom you have close relations and you will not feel uncomfortable interacting or communicating with them despite the strain that has come in the relationship due to your stress.

Alternately, you may wish to communicate with those who you feel will be able to extend help and support in your hour of stress. Obviously, these will be the people with whom you are close enough to seek their assistance. You approach them with the hope that they will be able to provide you insights into the problem that you are unable to see or offer a solution to the problem you are facing. When under stress, the sense of reasoning and enquiry often gets impaired and, consequently, you may not be able to understand the dimensions of the situation that would offer explanation or give clues to its solution. Others may be able to provide better insights or clues into your problem, thus, helping you lessen your stress. In many cases, communicating or sharing your woes by itself can also provide some relief to you. Sharing often lessens the intensity of the problem or the impact of a difficult situation.

Family and Friends

In India, as in most Asian countries, family is an important institution in one's life. Despite considerable changes in its structure and roles, it still remains the social institution that can help immensely when you get into stressful situations. For certain problems—especially those involving major changes or disappointments—no one is in a better position to provide practical and concrete help in times of crises. The person from a really supportive family does not have to go through it alone. A family that praises you when you achieve something and supports you when you fail or suffer from disappointments has the potential of providing encouragement when you need it.

Close and confiding relationships have been found to reduce or buffer the stress connected with life's major changes as well as the cumulative effects of daily hassles and problems. Researches indicate that people in crisis who enjoy contact and support from others tend to maintain high morale but also suffer from fewer physical symptoms than those who do not have their support base. Social support helps to alleviate feelings of dissatisfaction, depression or anxiety generated by various types of stress.

Engage in Activities That Give You Pleasure

Engage in activities that give you pleasure and enjoyment, taking your mind off the immediate problem or stress. For instance, go for a long walk, listen to music, visit a friend or go to a club. You may also go for some games and sports. This should not be considered as an escapist strategy or a temporary diversion. True, the problem may not get solved by this action but, possibly, by diverting your mind from the problem for some time, you may give yourself an opportunity to ponder over it and you may be able to get better understanding of the situation. It is possible that when you return to the situation, you may look at it with a different perspective and in a much positive way. A positive frame of mind may not only give you some relief from the stress but also help you in getting to the solution or find options to deal with the problem. Remember, a relaxed body can give you a relaxed mind.

Management of Time

Many stresses can arise out of lack of time management or an organised life. For instance, you have to catch a flight and you have to finish a lot of paperwork that you have to take with you for the meetings. As you are rushed, you are likely to get stressed. Perhaps, a better time management could have saved you a lot of hassles and resultant stress. Some people are in the habit of leaving things

for the last hour, regardless whether they are going for travel or for an important event in the same city. This can create avoidable stress. By organising things better, you could have saved yourself from stress. It is, therefore, important that in your day-to-day life, personal or work-related, you should exercise better control of your life by managing your time and organising your tasks and activities.

Assertive Behaviour

You should be assertive in expressing yourself. An assertive response means that you are in a position to express yourself clearly and calmly without getting excited or agitated. You do not back down even in the face of disagreement without losing your composure. You do not sulk. Development of these skills will help you bring down the level of stress in your life.

(Cross-reference: for more details, see Module 2 titled 'Interpersonal Communication')

THINGS YOU CAN DO TO AVOID OR MANAGE STRESS

Find time to engage in physical activities. It does not necessarily mean that you go to gym. It only implies that when you are engaged in physical activities, your mind gets diverted and your body and mind join together to help you shift attention from a particular activity and relax. Once you do it over and over again, you will create conditions to lessen your stress or even prevent it.

Practise relaxation by prayers or meditation. These are not related to any particular religion or philosophy. Find a place where you can sit quietly and comfortably. Reduce sensory distractions to the minimum. Breathe slowly and evenly. Concentrate on your breathing and let your mind and body rest. Find a focus in a physical object, figure or words. This will help.

Ability to manage stress is closely linked with your self-esteem and self-confidence. It is, therefore, important that you remain constantly in contact with your self-esteem and self-confidence and persuade yourself to raise their levels to meet new and challenging situations that have caused the stress.

Be positive. For every negative thought, find two positive ones. Positive thinkers are in a better position to avoid stress and if at all they get into a stressful situation, they find it easier to ease out of it. Engage in positive self-talk and look at the proverbial silver lining in dark clouds. You can pick something positive in seemingly difficult situations and unhappy circumstances.

Do not consider every problem as if the whole life depends on it. If you make every single disappointment or failure as a matter of survival or raise the stakes inappropriately high, the problem may get disproportionately bigger resulting in avoidable stress.

When faced by a problem or issue that appears to be complex, big and insurmountable, try to break it into smaller manageable parts and you may find that it ceases to be so complicated or difficult. It may look solvable or doable, reducing or even preventing stress.

When faced with a multitude of tasks, try to set priorities. This will also help in management of time, thus, giving you better ways to attend to the activities that need to be dealt with on an urgent basis, reducing stress.

You must constantly attempt to develop your coping skills. Talk to people who have more experience in tackling similar problems, attend special workshops meant for the purpose or go through literature on the topic. Learning comes from doing and doing reflects learning.

Perception is amazingly important to stress. You can generate unnecessary stress or eradicate it by modifying your state of mind. This is, however, a conscious effort. Once you start practising it, it will become a part of your *persona* and you will develop attitudes that will stand you in good stead when faced with difficult or stressful situations.

Before retiring for the day, give yourself time to reflect over the day's events, recalling those issues, persons or situations that have given you cause for worry, frustration and disappointment. Go over them carefully and take a reality check whether these were worth worrying about. Consider your stakes in each one of them. Those worries or problems that do not deserve to become the source of your tension or stress the next day should be dumped or at least put aside lower in your list. You must tell yourself that tomorrow is another day and this could mean a new beginning for you. Seize this moment and work on this. Life can become better for you.

There are things that you cannot change but you worry about them and this gives you tension. Make an honest appraisal and convince yourself that what I cannot change I should accept them. This world does not run on the basis of my needs and desires. Say a silent prayer, 'Oh god! Give me the serenity to accept things that I cannot change; ability and desire to change things that I can and wisdom to know the difference'. Learn the art of letting go. Accept your limits. That, however, does not mean that you should not constantly endeavour to widen the base of your coping abilities and prepare yourself to face new challenges.

Avoid brooding. Many a time, our past frustrations and tensions do not allow us to relax when they do not mean anything to us any longer. Past is important as it shapes your present and future but those who continue to live in the past find it difficult to move forward or progress. They consciously or subconsciously bring stress in their life.

At least once a week do something good for yourself. Celebrate your accomplishment and reward yourself for it. Be kind and gentle with yourself. This does not mean that you should not engage in self-analysis and self-criticism, but remember to love yourself.

Learn to accept things that are not perfect. Your goal may be perfection but remember it is an elusive goal. Once you are satisfied that you have put in your best, learn to relax and accept the result. It is important that you compare with your own potential and assess how you have developed your coping skills. This will give you cause to celebrate. This is the way life is and it must be enjoyed that way.

SUGGESTED GUIDELINES FOR CONDUCTING THE SESSION

Three exercises have been suggested for this module. These exercises are designed to bring out all aspects of stress, relevant to the participants. The first exercise will help you deal with the concept of 'stress' and its negative and positive dimensions.

Before taking up the second exercise, you should provide detailed inputs, elaborating on internal and external stressors. You may draw from the trainer's notes, integrating the material with your own experiences. Reinforce your presentation with examples from everyday life, relevant to the participants.

The second exercise will help you bring into discussion the strategies one adopts to cope with stresses. Here also you can draw from the trainer's notes to discuss how the participants can prepare themselves for coping with their day-to-day stresses.

As part of de-stressing, you may introduce participants to physical exercises such as deep breathing, meditation, walking around, listening to music, etc. (see handout for the participants). You may also explore local resources (a yoga institute or a yoga expert) for organising special sessions on de-stressing for the group.

It is suggested that you may also refer the group to some sections of the module on 'Positive Thinking' that they will find relevant.

Exercise 3 is designed to help the participants find out what personality traits are helpful in coping with stress. As part of your summing-up of the discussion on the exercise, you can refer to the point 'Personality traits and attitudes' under the section on 'Internal Stressors'.

EXERCISE 1

STRESS—POSITIVE AND NEGATIVE IMPLICATIONS

Objectives

At the end of the exercise, the participants will be able to:

- Understand the meaning of stress
- Become aware of positive and negative aspects of stress

Time allocation

About 1 ¼ hours (including your inputs between two parts of the exercise)

Materials required

Training aids and tools required for explaining the topic as part of your introductory talk, your detailed inputs and for summing-up; flip charts and writing markers for displaying key points emerging out of the participants' responses to the brainstorming part of the exercise and sharing of the partners of the dyads; white board and markers.

Steps in conducting the exercise

- Introduce the exercise, informing the group that it will be conducted in two parts. First part will be through brainstorming in the group; and the second part will be conducted through dyads.
- Invite the participants to share their understanding of 'stress', as we experience it in our day-to-day life, family, social circle or workplace. As they give their understanding of 'stress', note down their responses on the flip chart. At this stage, do not comment on the responses but you may ask for clarifications, if needed.
- After most of the participants have shared, use their responses to provide your inputs.
- Once the group has a fairly good understanding of 'stress', introduce the concept of positive and negative stress and elaborate. Check whether the group has fully grasped the difference between positive and negative stress.
- Next, divide the group into dyads. Each partner of the dyad shares an event or situation related to positive stress and one which could be termed as negative stress. Inform the dyads that the information is confidential unless they want to share it.
- Assemble the group and invite those who wish to share their sharing.
- Elaborate and give your inputs. Sum up and close the exercise.

EXERCISE 2

STRESSFUL EVENTS IN YOUR LIFE AND YOUR RESPONSE

Objectives

At the end of the exercise, the participants will be able to:

- Understand the dynamics of stress that they have experienced
- Become aware of various strategies that can be adopted to cope with the stress

Time allocation

About 1 ½ hours

Materials required

Training aids and tools required for explaining the topic as part of your introductory talk and for summing-up; flip charts and writing markers for displaying key points emerging out of the discussion based on the responses of the participants to the exercise; copies of the worksheet for the exercise (one for each participant); white board and markers.

Steps in conducting the exercise

- Refer back to the discussion the group had on stress and how it impacts our life. Explain the objective of the exercise, emphasising that it aims to bring out certain stressful events or situations that we encounter in our day-to-day life and help the participants understand the implications of these events and situations to their life.
- Distribute the worksheet. As this is an individual exercise, ask each participant to complete it by recalling one stressful event—related to family, workplace or social circle—that had affected them emotionally. Brief the participants as under:
  - o Give a brief description of the event or situation that caused the stress
  - o How did it impact you—emotionally, behaviourally and physically?
  - o What was your immediate response?
  - o How did you cope with it?
  - o Be brief in your response
  - o You have 30 minutes for completing the worksheet
  - o You may not share your response, if you do not wish to
- After everyone has completed the worksheet, invite those who wish to share their responses. Encourage the participants to talk openly about their stresses and what they did to manage them.
- Provide your inputs as you proceed with the participants' sharing. Sum up and close the exercise.

WORKSHEET

Stressful Events and Your Response

Description of the event _____

_____

_____

Source of stress _____

_____

_____

Impact on you _____

_____

_____

Your response _____

_____

_____

HANDOUT FOR THE PARTICIPANTS

Some Exercises for De-stressing

Deep breathing

Any yogi knows that the breath—known as *pranayama* or life force—plays an important role in nourishing the body, and medical researchers agree. Breathing exercises—or just taking a few deep breaths—can help reduce tension and relieve stress, thanks to an extra boost of oxygen. While shallow breathing—a marker of stress—stimulates the sympathetic nervous system, deep breathing does the opposite. It stimulates parasympathetic reaction that helps us to calm down.

Visualisation

A short visualisation is an easy way to get back to centre. Health researchers the world over recognise the power of 'guided imagery' to elicit a relaxation response. Simply make yourself comfortable in a chair, at your desk or in a room, and then try to picture a peaceful scene—mountains or hills, a beach, a lovely green forest, etc. You may visualise yourself in the company of a person whom you love dearly.

Nadi Shodhana or 'Alternate Nostril Breathing'

How it is done: A yogi's best friend, our breath is said to bring calmness, balance and unite the right and left sides of the brain. Starting in a comfortable meditative pose, hold the right thumb over the right nostril and inhale deeply through the left nostril. At the peak of inhalation, close off the left nostril with the ring finger, and then exhale through the right nostril. Continue the pattern, inhaling through the right nostril, closing it off with the right thumb and exhaling through the left nostril.

Relax Your Body at Work

The following body-centred exercises work well in an office setting, as all you need to do is sit forward on a chair with your feet flat on the floor. You may increase the number of repetitions as your body grows stronger and more flexible. Take a few minutes at the end of the exercise to sit comfortably, noticing your breath and releasing tension with each exhalation. You'll be ready to return to work feeling more comfortable and refreshed.

Here are some good relaxation exercises for the office:

Feet and Legs

With legs outstretched

- Alternate curling and stretching the toes. Repeat three times and relax.

- Alternate flexing (bending) and extending (stretching) the whole foot at the ankle. Repeat three times.
- Rotate the ankles to the right as if drawing circles with your toes. Repeat three times.
- Rotate the ankles to the left. Repeat three times.

Arms and Hands

With arms extended out in front of you:

- Move your hands up and down, bending from the wrist. Repeat three times.
- Alternate stretching your fingers, then making a fist. Repeat three times.
- Rotate your wrists three times, first to the right, then to the left. Relax. Repeat three times.

Shoulders

Either sitting or standing:

- Raise your right shoulder up towards your ear. On the exhale, release your shoulder down. Repeat three times.
- Move your right shoulder forward. On the exhale, return it to the starting position. Repeat three times.
- Move your right shoulder back. On the exhale, return it to the starting position. Repeat three times.
- Repeat the sequence on the left side.
- Bring both shoulders up towards your ears, tense and then drop your shoulders down as you exhale. Repeat three times.

Head and Neck

Hold each of the movements described below, take three easy breaths and relax tension with each exhalation, then return your head to the upright centre position before doing the next movement.

- Drop your chin to your chest. Feel the weight of your head stretching out the back of your neck. Hold.

- Look as far as you can over your right shoulder. Hold.
- Look as far as you can over your left shoulder. Hold.
- Drop your right ear to your right shoulder. Hold.
- Drop your left ear to your left shoulder. Hold.

EXERCISE 3

STRESS AND PERSONALITY SELF-TEST

Objective

At the end of the exercise, the participants will be able to:

- Find out about their personality traits that help in either prevention and/or in coping with stress or contribute to producing stress or stressful situations

Time allocation

About 1 ¼ hours

Materials required

Training aids and tools for your inputs; flip charts and writing markers for posting the points emerging out of sharing by the participants; copies of Stress and Personality Self-test worksheet, score or answer sheet and handout on Type A Personality Traits and Type B Personality Traits (one copy for each participants of the worksheet, score or answer sheet and handout for the participants); white board and its markers.

Steps in conducting the exercise

- Give a brief talk on how personality traits can help you prevent or cope with stress; and these traits can also contribute to creating more stress for people. However, at this point in time, do not elaborate as this may condition their responses.
- Explain the exercise and distribute copies of the worksheet. Ask them to go through the instructions before recording their responses. Give them enough time to complete the exercise.

- After the participants have completed the task, distribute copies of score or answer sheet and the handout. Ask them to calculate and record their scores, and find out about their personality type in the context of stress management.
- Invite some participants to share their scores (only on voluntary basis) and offer clarifications, where necessary.
- Using the content of the exercise and participants' responses, provide inputs on how personality traits are connected with stress (you may draw from the relevant section from trainer's notes).
- Sum up and close the exercise.

STRESS AND PERSONALITY SELF-TEST

Worksheet

Instructions: The following 20 personality traits have been identified as crucial to either producing or helping to prevent stress. The two sets of traits represent two extreme positions that an individual can take. However, most of us are somewhere in between these two positions. Your task is to circle the number that describes *your position* with respect to that particular trait. As this is an individual self-assessment test, you should be honest and sincere if you wish to enhance your abilities to cope with stress.

Don't mind leaving things temporarily unfinished	1 2 3 4 5 6 7	Must get things finished once started
Calm and unhurried about appointments	1 2 3 4 5 6 7	Never late for appointments
Not competitive	1 2 3 4 5 6 7	Highly competitive
Listen well, let others finish speaking	1 2 3 4 5 6 7	Anticipate others in conversation, interrupt, finishing their sentences
Never in a hurry, even when pressured	1 2 3 4 5 6 7	Always in a hurry
Able to wait calmly	1 2 3 4 5 6 7	Uneasy when waiting
Easy-going	1 2 3 4 5 6 7	Always going at full speed

Take one thing at a time	1 2 3 4 5 6 7	Try to do more than one thing at a time. What's next?
Slow and deliberate in speech	1 2 3 4 5 6 7	Vigorous/forceful speech, use a lot of gestures
Relaxed	1 2 3 4 5 6 7	Hard driving
Express feelings openly	1 2 3 4 5 6 7	Hold feelings in
Have a large number of interests	1 2 3 4 5 6 7	Few interests
Satisfied with life	1 2 3 4 5 6 7	Ambitious
Never set own deadlines	1 2 3 4 5 6 7	Often set own deadlines
Feel limited responsibility	1 2 3 4 5 6 7	Always feel responsible
Never judge things in terms of quantity, just quality	1 2 3 4 5 6 7	Quantity is more important
Casual about work	1 2 3 4 5 6 7	Take work very seriously
Not very precise	1 2 3 4 5 6 7	Very precise, careful about detail
Concerned with satisfying yourself, not others	1 2 3 4 5 6 7	Want recognition from others for a job well done
Slow doing things	1 2 3 4 5 6 7	Fast doing things

Source: Adapted from Relay for Life (https://www.cancer.org/involved/fundraise/relay-for-life.html) and Stress Management for Health Course (http://stresscourse.tripod.com/).

STRESS AND PERSONALITY SELF-TEST

Stress and Personality Type

Score or Answer Sheet

Add up the scores you have given to the 20 traits in the worksheet.

Traits with regard to **Personality A** or **Personality B** are given in the handout for the participants.

Score: 110–140 **Type A**	You are in the high-risk category with regard to stress. This can lead to physical and/or emotional problems. You need to take strong measures to reduce stress
80–109 **Type A**	You are in the risk zone and should be careful. You should take strong measures to reduce stress
60–79 **Type AB**	You belong to a mixed category between Type A and B. This is a healthier pattern, but you have the potential to slip into Type A Personality behaviour and should recognise this
30–59 **Type B**	You are generally relaxed and cope *adequately* with stress
0–29 **Type B**	You are relaxed and fully capable of coping *very well* with stress

HANDOUT FOR THE PARTICIPANTS

Stress and Personality Self-test

Stress and Personality Type

Type A personality traits	Type B personality traits
Must get things finished	Do not mind leaving things unfinished for *a while*
Never late for appointments	Calm and unhurried about appointments
Excessively competitive	Not excessively competitive
Cannot listen to conversations, interrupt, finish others' sentences	Can listen and let the other person finish speaking
Always in a hurry	Never in a hurry even when busy
Do not like to wait	Can wait calmly
Very busy at full speed	Easy-going
Trying to do more than one thing at a time	Can take one thing at a time

Type A personality traits	Type B personality traits
Want everything to be perfect	Do not mind things not quite perfect
Pressurised speech	Slow and deliberate speech
Do everything fast	Do things slowly
Hold feelings in	Can express feelings
Not satisfied with work/life	Quite satisfied with work/life
Few social activities/interests	Many social activities/interests
If in employment, will often take work home	If in employment, will limit working to work hours

Module 6

Positive Thinking

Many of us do not realise the value of our attitudes and thought processes in guiding and shaping our life. However, the need for it cannot be over-emphasised. This module, therefore, sets out the blueprint for adopting and developing a positive way of thinking and acting. As in other modules, the focus is more on helping the participants develop a way of life that reflects positivity and alacrity to lead a healthy, confident life.

Specifically, this module deals with the following key areas:

- Understanding positive thinking
- Manifestations of positive thinking and attitude
- On way to developing a positive attitude!

Expected Outcomes from the Module

At the end of the session on this module, the participants will be able to:

- Understand various aspects of positive thinking and a positive way of life
- Develop necessary guidelines and a plan of action for themselves to adopt and engage in constructive and positive self-talk and reduce the influence of negative thoughts and views about themselves, their actions and behaviour

UNDERSTANDING POSITIVE THINKING

Man often becomes what he believes himself to be. If I keep on saying to myself that I cannot do a certain thing, it is possible that I may end by really becoming incapable of doing it. On the contrary, if I have the belief that I can do it, I shall surely acquire the capacity to do it even if I may not have it at the beginning.

—Mahatma Gandhi

Whenever we are in the midst of a problem and appear to be worried, those who are concerned about us counsel us to 'be positive'. While, sometimes, we tend to act in accordance with their encouraging words, at other times, we are so overwhelmed by our problem that we remain in that emotional state, or return to it after a brief swing to the other side. Despite these exhortations and persuasions, it is a fact that the power of these words or their significance in life is neither communicated in a meaningful way nor is understood in a serious manner by the persons who are downhearted and despondent.

In the present-day stressful world, where people are often confronted with problems that they find difficult to cope with, *positive thinking* and *positive attitude* have acquired considerable meaning and substance. The increasing importance of adopting positive thinking as a code of our life-style is also evidenced by the growing volume of literature and a number of courses that are being offered on the subject. Positive thinking has become a key concept in most personal development programmes.

However, it is necessary to understand that effective positive thinking that brings desired results is much more than just repeating a few positive words or a situational attempt to convince yourself that all is going to be well. It has to be your overarching mental attitude influencing your words, actions and behaviour, in fact, steering your life and environment. It should bring about significant change in the manner in which you approach people and situations that you confront in your day-to-day life. It has to be integrated with other aspects of your *persona*: a way of life.

Positive thinking is the idea that has the potential to change your life. This idea may sound a bit soft and fluffy. There are many who contend that just owning good thoughts will not change the world and, therefore, discard the whole idea. However, research shows that positive thinking really does have a scientific basis. You cannot change the world, but you can change how you perceive it and how you react to it. And that can change the way that you feel about yourself and others, which can, in turn, have a huge effect on your physical and emotional well-being.

Positive thinking does not mean that you keep your head in the sand and ignore life's less pleasant situations. Positive thinking just means that you approach unpleasantness in a more positive and productive way. You think the best is going to happen, not the worst.

Positive thinking is also motivational. It provides you with an impetus to deal with life in a constructive way. It provides you direction and helps you set life objectives that are forward-looking. It can also stimulate you to make stronger and more persistent efforts to realise these goals. Your ability to succeed gets enhanced. Remember that having a positive mental attitude is indispensable for reaching new heights of success and translating your dreams into achievements.

One of the best ways to define a positive mental attitude is having a 'constructive and positive response to adversity'. It is only when you are confronted with a setback or harsh conditions that you really know if you have a positive attitude or not. Anyone can be positive when things are going well. It is only when things are going against you or not according to your expectations that you are in a situation to demonstrate to yourself and others that you have a positive character and personality.

To understand the effect of positive thinking, it is necessary to think about the impact negative thinking has on your life. First, you should try to train your mind to avoid negative thoughts. Constant negative thinking can produce stress and, if allowed to go un-coped, can lead to more serious problems, like depression.

Happy people—those with a positive outlook on life—are not just happier but also seem to achieve much more. While success may lead to happiness, it is equally true happiness also leads to success.

Positive thinking is not valued by all. Some consider it as unrealistic and unworkable idea and scoff at people who propagate or profess it. On the other hand, there are a growing number of people, who accept positive thinking as a fact and believe in its effectiveness. There are more people who want to develop positive thinking and, as a result, this subject is gaining popularity, as evidenced by the amount of literature being generated on it.

Indeed, some studies show that personality traits such as optimism and pessimism can affect many areas of your health and well-being. The positive thinking that typically comes with optimism is a key part of effective stress management. And effective stress management is associated with many health benefits. If you tend to be pessimistic, do not despair, you can learn positive thinking skills.

Positive thinking often starts with self-talk. Self-talk is the endless stream of unspoken thoughts that run through your head. These automatic thoughts can be positive or negative. Some of your self-talk comes from logic and reason. Other self-talk may arise from misconceptions that you create because of lack of information. If the thoughts that run through your head are mostly negative, your outlook on life is more likely pessimistic. If your thoughts are mostly positive, you are likely an optimist—someone who practises positive thinking.

(Cross-reference: to know about how positive talk helps in de-stressing, see Module 5 on 'Management of Stress')

MANIFESTATIONS OF POSITIVE THINKING AND ATTITUDE

The positive thinker sees the invisible, feels the intangible,
and achives the impossible.

—Winston Churchill

It is not always possible to recognise or decipher positive attitude in an individual. It expresses itself in behaviour and actions of an individual and the way she conducts her interactions with people. If you are a person with positive outlook and thinking, you:

- Demonstrate high level of optimism in your thoughts, actions and in promoting your relationships. You persevere in your pursuit of happiness and success in whatever you attempt.
- Remain constantly motivated to accomplish the goals and objectives you have set for yourself. In fact, you are forever looking to set new goals and standards for your performance in all fields.
- Are not overwhelmed or deterred by the enormity or extent of the problem you confront while undertaking a task or activity. You regard them as challenges. You believe in yourself and in your ability to overcome problems and adversities, and learn not to give up.
- Display a high degree of self-esteem and self-confidence through your body language or your overall demeanour.

- Are constantly looking for solutions to the problems that you may confront in your endeavours. This helps you engage in creative and constructive thinking. You become resourceful.
- Are not only looking for opportunities to grow and develop yourself but also ensure that you remain fully prepared to make optimum use of them.
- Are willing to take initiative and not afraid to take calculated risk wherever you consider necessary and appropriate, in pursuit of your goals. You appear to be in control of yourself, your efforts and the environment in which you work.
- Display a conspicuous spirit of enthusiasm and zeal. You enjoy your work and the relationships that you develop with others.
- Are generally cordial and pleasant, willing to strike warm relationships with people who come in contact with you. You are liable to win respect of people around you.

ON WAY TO DEVELOPING A POSITIVE ATTITUDE!

I am in charge of how I feel and today I am choosing happiness.

—Likainen Parketti

Positive thinking is good. But you should not try to use it to block out everything negative that happens in your life. Sometimes, bad stuff happens, and you will feel down about it. It is no good pretending that you are not feeling despondent or low. Remember forced positive thinking can be counterproductive. What you need to avoid is developing disaster or failure scenario—the 'my life is a total disaster' or 'I am surrounded by misfortune' tapes that play in your head. The best way to do that is *not* to tell you that life is perfect but, instead, recognise what has gone wrong but set it in proper perspective. For example, 'Yes I am having a bad day, but tomorrow will be better. I will go home now and I will be able to think of the solution to the problem in the morning when I am less tired'.

In order to turn the mind towards the positive, some inner work is required, since attitude and thoughts do not change overnight. You may try the following:

- Read about the subject, think about its benefits and persuade yourself to try it. The power of your thoughts provides you the vigour and energy that will shape your life. This moulding is usually done subconsciously, but your effort should be to make the process a conscious one. Even if the idea seems strange, give it a try. You have nothing to lose, but only to gain

- Ignore what other people say or think about you, if they discover that you are changing the way you think
- Use your imagination to visualise only favourable and beneficial situations
- Use positive words in your inner dialogues or when talking with others
- Smile a little more, as this helps to think positively

Once a negative thought enters your mind, you have to be aware of it, and endeavour to replace it with a constructive one. If the negative thought returns, replace it again with the positive one. It is as if there are two pictures in front of you, and you have to choose to look at one of them, and disregard the other. Persistence will eventually teach your mind to think positively and to ignore negative thoughts.

In case you experience inner resistance and difficulties when replacing negative thoughts with positive ones, do not give up, but keep looking only at the beneficial, good and happy thoughts in your mind.

It does not matter what your circumstances are at the present moment. Think positively, expect only favourable results and situations, and circumstances are likely to change accordingly. If you persevere, you will transform the way your mind thinks. It might take some time for the changes to take place, but eventually they will.

Engage in Positive Self-talk

It is important that you start talking to yourself in a positive and optimistic way. You will observe that it is not about lamenting your failures or travails endlessly or finding excuses or justifying them. It is about conveying to you a message that failures and problems are part of life, finding what really went wrong and looking for answers within you.

Try to explain things to yourself in a different way, and you will see a difference in your attitude. Make positive self-talk your normal mode of functioning and you will experience big positive changes in your life.

Sample the following to start with. You may add to this list as you move on and progress:

- It is okay to make mistakes. Everyone does that. This will help me to learn and grow but I promise myself that I will not repeat it.
- I may not be performing as well as others (in certain activities), but I am good at these (certain other activities). Anyway, I have come a long way and will continue my progress.
- This is only a temporary setback/problem/adversity and will pass. After all, everybody faces problems one time or the other. It is going to be fine with me.
- Why not me? It was someone else facing similar problem but, perhaps, today it is my turn. After all, I have enjoyed happy moments earlier. Then I did not ask, why me? Everyone has ups and downs. There will be times when things go awry and make me feel unhappy. I will face this situation as best as I can. Surely, I will come out of it.
- This is not something that I should get unusually upset about. After all, life is much bigger than this.
- I do not have to struggle on every front at the same time. I can choose where I need to focus my efforts to confront now. I will move to other areas later after I have won my battle on this front.
- I am doing the best that I can with what I have right now. I will find out where I lack and explore every opportunity to improve further.
- I cannot control what other people say, do, think or feel. So why should I worry about it. I have control over my actions and behaviour.
- True, I had some problems in the past but it is now history. I have learnt my lessons from those experiences. I have moved on and I will continue to do so. I cannot let my past haunt me and mess up my present and future.

Meditation or Yoga

To develop positive thinking, it is important to uncover your inner self—the *you* that lives inside—and promote a sense of stillness and connection. An effective way of accomplishing this is 'mindfulness meditation'. Meditation can give you a sense of calm, peace and balance that benefits both your emotional well-being and your overall health. It can reduce the day's stress, anxiety and worry, restoring your calm and bringing inner peace and contentment. Remember, meditation and Yoga are not related to any religion.

People who meditate tend to show more 'mindfulness', or ability to live in the present, which is closely associated with positive thinking. And these benefits do not end when your meditation session ends. Meditation can help carry you more calmly through your day and may improve even certain medical conditions.

Yoga is also very relaxing and will help ease your mind. It is a meditation of the body. In yoga, our bodies help to 'anchor' us in the present. Yoga takes your focus away from your thoughts and brings your attention to your breath—inhaling and exhaling—and body changes.

A particularly useful paradigm for those struggling with anxiety or depression is to hold a challenging pose (such as downward-facing dog, plank or warrior) and to bring attention to the discomfort—embrace it and breathe through it. When we experience a depressive or anxious state, we feel that it may never end, that the pain will not lift.

Anyone can practise meditation. It is simple and inexpensive, and it does not require any special equipment. And you can practise meditation wherever you are—whether you are out for a walk, riding the bus, waiting at the doctor's office or even in the middle of a difficult business meeting.

International Yoga Day—21 June

It was in recognition of health-related benefits of yoga that the United Nations General Assembly (UNGA) passed a resolution on 11 December 2014 to celebrate 21 June annually as the International Yoga Day. In his address to the UNGA, on 24 September 2014, Hon. Prime Minister Narendra Modi said

> Yoga is an invaluable gift of India's ancient tradition. This tradition is 5,000 years old. It embodies unity of mind and body; thought and action; restraint and fulfilment; harmony between man and nature; a holistic approach to health and well-being. It is not about exercise but to discover the sense of oneness with yourself, the world and the nature. By changing our lifestyle and creating consciousness, it can help in well being. Let us work towards adopting an International Yoga Day.

Seek the Company of Positive and Happy People

We affect, and are affected by the people we meet, in one way or another. This happens instinctively and on a subconscious level, through words, thoughts and feelings, and through body language. Man is known by the company he keeps but you can turn it around and say 'that man is influenced by the company he keeps'.

It is often said that you will have a similar level of health, income and lifestyle as the people you spend the most time with. So if you want to be fit then start hanging out with fit people...want to start a business then hang out with business owners. And if you want to be positive, make sure you are hanging out with positive people.

Positive and negative thinking are contagious. Therefore, it is important to have a positive support group to help one another through difficult times. Surrounding yourself with positive people will help you stay positive when in a negative situation. There are plenty of negative people out there; avoid them! Their negative attitudes will only bring you down and be counterproductive to what you are trying to achieve by practising positive thinking.

Read Positive Quotes

There are plenty of famous people and celebrities who have extolled the virtue of 'positive thinking and attitude'. Read their thoughts and quotes on positive thinking, and you will feel stimulated.

The pessimist sees difficulty in every opportunity.
The optimist sees opportunity in every difficulty.

—Winston Churchill

See the positive side, the potential, and make an effort.

—Dalai Lama

Watch your thoughts, they become words.
Watch your words, they become actions.

Watch your actions, they become habits.
Watch your habits, they become your character.
Watch your character, it becomes your destiny.

—Anonymous

You can't live a positive life with a negative mind.

—Anonymous

Accept Problems and Find Solutions

Being positive does not mean that you have to be oblivious to problems. Positive people have constructive criticisms to improve conditions. If you are spending time to indicate problems in people or situations, put in just as much effort into suggesting solutions. Instead of pointing out all of the things that are wrong, offer ways to make it better.

When confronted by a problem, look at it as a challenge and an opportunity to improve and grow. There is no use whining or nitpicking about it. If you are overwhelmed by the enormity of the problem, its complexity, or find that many issues and questions are intertwined, try to unknot them. Break it into recognisable smaller problems or issues. This will give you an opportunity to look at specifics, facilitating solutions. You may pick up one issue or question at a time and focus your efforts to resolve it before moving to the next one.

There are no dead ends, only redirections. Although we might try, there are very few things in life that we have complete control over. We should not let uncontrollable occurrences from the outside turn our inner to mush. What we can control is the effort that we put in and when we are convinced that we have given our best, there is no reason for regret. Have fun with challenges; embrace them as adventures instead of attempting to resist an experience for growth.

Sometimes you win and sometimes you learn.

—Robert Kiyosaki

Be Grateful for What You Have; Count Your Blessings

Sometimes one single event can ruin an entire day, and an unpleasant interaction or experience at night can overshadow the enjoyable parts of our day. With this awareness that our mind tends to cling to the negative, we can intentionally focus on the good parts of our day to offset this imbalance. Try writing down five things that you feel grateful for everyday and see how your attitude changes. Science has found that gratitude can significantly increase your happiness and protect you from stress, negativity, anxiety and depression. Being grateful helps appreciate what you already have.

Even in the worst of times, most of us realise that we still have things in our lives for which we are grateful. Voice those blessings! Practise gratitude. Talk about the things you are grateful for with your closest friends, your support group. Keep a gratitude journal to capture the thankfulness you feel for what you have on a daily basis. Actively acknowledging what you are thankful for will help you to always have a gratifying mind and heart, even when bad things happen.

We often take what we have in life as granted and deserved and crib about those things that we do not have, are deprived of it or not in a position to obtain. We tend to overlook our achievements and count our failures.

Another small thing that you can try is to keep a diary of positive and happy experiences that happen in your life on a daily basis; or you could write a blog focusing on positive experiences. In a study, a group of undergraduates were asked to write about an intensely positive experience everyday for a full week. Amazingly, their moods turned for the better, affecting their physical health as well.

Replace 'Have to' with 'Get to'

Do you ever notice how many times we say that we *have to* do something? I *have* to go to work. I *have* to write an article for the magazine; I *have to* take my family for shopping. I *have* to attend the parent–teacher meeting. Now change this one little word *have* to *get* and see what happens. I *get* to go to work; I *get* to write an article for the magazine; I *get* to take my family for shopping; I *get* to attend the parent–teacher meeting. Your attitude quickly changes from needing to just fulfil obligations to being grateful for the things that we become accustomed to having: a job to support you and your family; carrying out a professional commitment; the joy of shopping with the family; pleasure of fulfilling my responsibility as a parent. Try to make this change when you are thinking to yourself and you may feel and appear happier and less stressed.

Develop Positive Counterstatements to Refute Negative Self-talk

Instead of always putting yourself down in your head, think of some things you actually like about yourself. What are your strengths, what are you good at? Developing counterstatements requires you to have some degree of belief in their veracity. Keep your counterstatements in the here and now, instead of saying 'I am not good enough' try saying 'I am capable. I am good at _____. I accept myself the way I am'.

Thinking poorly about ourselves gets us nowhere and is extremely self-limiting. Decide today to turn off the negative self-talk channel in your mind and develop your true potential.

Learn to Accept What is Beyond Your Control to Change

There are a lot of things happening around you on a daily basis that are unpleasant and are a source of unhappiness and even stress to you. Think of your personal attributes that consciously or subconsciously make you feel unhappy or miserable, such as your height, your complexion, your face, etc. In some cases, these physical attributes may even dent your self-esteem and self-confidence. Now turn to some other things in the environment—personal or official—that are big turn-offs for you and about which you are continually grumbling, thus giving rise to negative emotions and stress. For example, your neighbourhood is very noisy; everyday you are caught in traffic snarls or you have a boss who is very intimidating. You have to ask yourself: what among these are within my control and I can change; what is that that is beyond my control and I cannot change? Then say a silent prayer in your mind: Bless me with the ability to change the things that I can change; the courage to accept the things that I cannot and the wisdom to make a distinction between the two. See if this makes a difference to your outlook of life.

Do Not Get Dragged into People's Complaints and Grievances

Your day was going pretty well and then you get to work and your co-worker cannot stop complaining about the hot weather. You did not really think about it before she brought it up and now you find yourself agreeing and joining in on the complaint fest of how sick you are of this hot weather. In a month, you will be pulled into complaints about how it is too hot. Do not fall into the trap. A study done at the Warsaw School of Social Psychology shows that complaining leads to lower moods and negative emotions, decreases life satisfaction and optimism, and is detrimental to social adaptation, leading to emotional and motivational deficits. You might find that your co-worker will complain less without the validation of someone else having the same complaint.

There are people who are complaining or have something negative almost about everything—weather, colleagues, boss, political situation, traffic on the road, about people in general. You may not share these insinuations, thoughts and views but you start getting drawn into these situations and circumstances that offer only negativity. This affects your mood and even attitude.

Avoid Reacting to Every Action and Behaviour of Others

A lot of things happen around you all the time—some that affect you directly, and others that may not have much to do with you but you get influenced by them through observation and by experiencing them. It is likely that some of them may evoke negative emotions in you or lead to stress, particularly those that affect you. However, there are many things that are happening around you that have the potential to set off negative emotions in you but are inconsequential as far as you are concerned. You have to ask yourself a simple question: Do I need to take notice of all these things that are happening around me? And the answer should be definite 'No'. If you start responding—emotionally or otherwise—to everything that you experience and observe, you can make your life miserable. You will be loaded with a lot of negative emotional baggage. There are things that you should let go by and move on.

Do Not Label Yourself

Another thing that you must try to avoid is labelling yourself with negative words such as fool, failure, unfortunate, etc. This labelling will deter you from attempting to do things and hold you back from addressing them.

There are people who find solace in labelling themselves as this absolves them of the responsibility to try and come out of their adverse situations. This provides them security from action and gives them justification for inaction or inappropriate behaviour. People with negative thoughts tend to adopt behaviour or engage in actions that best describe these labels. Desire for change dies down or is suppressed. Children whose parents constantly scold them or put them down by using such epithets come to believe their description as correct. With low self-esteem, these children have little hope of changing and they make little effort in improving themselves.

Stop Playing the Victim

You should learn to take responsibility for whatever you are and what you get from life. Many people act as victim to draw attention of the people around them and to gain empathy or sympathy. They may not openly say that they are 'victims' but indirectly send message that they are being treated harshly by people and circumstances around them. They are stuck in their own web and do not progress in life. Work on the following don'ts to avoid getting into the 'victim act':

- *Do not* pity yourself and act as a defenceless person
- *Do not* compare yourself with others negatively
- *Do not* put down others and find fault with them in order to enjoy a fleeting sense of superiority
- *Do not* blame others for all your woes and problems
- *Do not* feel powerless; you can make or break your destiny
- *Do not* consider everyone around you as untrustworthy

Think of the Health Benefits of Positive Thinking

Researchers continue to explore the effects of positive thinking and optimism on health. Health benefits that positive thinking may provide include:

- Increased life span
- Lower rates of depression
- Lower levels of distress
- Better psychological and physical well-being

- Reduced risk of cardiovascular diseases
- Better coping skills during hardships and times of stress

One theory about health benefits is that having a positive outlook enables you to cope better with stressful situations, which reduces the harmful health effects of stress on your body. It is also thought that positive and optimistic people tend to live healthier lifestyles.

Start the Day with Positive Words About You

You should start your day with positive words such as, 'This is another day of opportunity and challenge and I look forward to it'; 'I like myself'; 'I am a competent person' and 'I can do it'. These are personal and positive affirmations that will build your levels of self-confidence and self-esteem. Drive these new positive thoughts deep into your subconscious by repeating them constantly to you. At times, you may find this funny or even childish but once you programme it into you, you will realise that it is very reassuring and helpful, removing negativity from your thoughts.

Have Fun and Enjoy Lighter Moments of Life

In today's hectic and complex world, many of us find it difficult to grab time and take life in a non-serious and cool way. We are so much caught in the humdrum of day-to-day activities that joy, humour and relaxation do not have a place in our routine. Many of us have forgotten to smile. Remember that joy, celebration and humour bring positivity in life. Therefore, find reasons to spend time and celebrate with family, friends and colleagues. It could be just a leisurely walk or shopping for groceries with the family, having an evening out with friends, going to a movie or just having a casual conversation with family or friends. These brief moments of fun and togetherness will help take the focus away from serious matters of life and stir up positive emotions.

Summation

When you are mulling over a situation, problem or event, you have the choice of considering positive and negative aspects of it. If you deliberately choose the positive thought to dwell upon, you keep your mind optimistic and your emotions upbeat. Since your thoughts and feelings determine your actions, if you keep your words and thoughts affirmative, you will automatically be a more dynamic person and move more rapidly and progressively towards your goals.

When you are not able to resolve a problem and a feeling of frustration starts to grip you, you must either do something more constructive about it or learn to accept it. After all, it is not possible to overcome all the difficulties you face or solve all the problems you encounter. A positive approach helps you recognise that and you will not feel despondent. Negative thinking will instigate negative emotions and you may constantly feel bad and not do anything about it. You tend to go in a perpetual state of limbo, causing frustration and even distress to you. Instead of seeing problems as an integral part of life and seeking to manage them as best as you can, people with negative thinking may overreact and blow things out of proportion. They tend to magnify the problems to assure them that the problem is so big that it cannot be resolved. Negative thoughts, therefore, are the beginning of misery and getting upset over circumstances of life.

There are times when we do not realise that we are going through negative thoughts as we take them in the stride and never pause to analyse our thought process. We may not consciously get into a mode of negative thoughts but our feelings will describe them. If we get overwhelmed by problems and get into a mode where we do not find a way out, we invite negative thoughts and attitude. You not only continue to mull over a particular situation but let it overwhelm you. Pessimism, fatalism and depression are some of the indicators of negative emotions and thoughts.

Many of us are resistant to changes in our lives. What we must do is learn to accept that change will happen. Have you not heard that 'the only constant in life is change'? There is a lot of truth to that, as we continually go through changes, whether good or bad. Accepting that changes are a part of life can help us to relax and be more accepting. Try to look for the positive aspect. For example, if you are in a bad job situation, what do you do? Accept it and try to make it better? Possibly. Or maybe this is the chance to make a change for yourself and look for that job you really want.

Back at you: If you have struggled with negative thoughts, how did you overcome it and go on to reach your full potential?

SUGGESTED GUIDELINES FOR CONDUCTING THE SESSION

This module addresses issues related to positive thinking and attitude in our personal or work-related life.

Two exercises have been suggested for this module. Both these exercises aim to promote positive thinking and attitudes in the participants and in order to help them, three self-improvement instruments have been provided as handouts. These are:

- Manifestations of positive attitude
- Positive and negative self-talk
- Evaluating and fighting negative thoughts

These instruments aim to help the participants dispel negativity and develop positive attitude. You may also like to pick up certain points from these instruments and discuss them with the participants.

You may consider two options for your inputs: Make a detailed presentation on various aspects of positive thinking and how an individual can work on it; or give an introductory talk on some selected areas of positive thinking and give thorough inputs before or after the exercises, as you consider appropriate.

Here, it is necessary to emphasise that this topic lends itself to high level of participation of the group. Therefore, they should be encouraged to share their thoughts, concerns and queries about the topic and you should prepare well to respond to them.

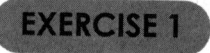

EXERCISE 1

FIGHTING NEGATIVE FEELINGS OR EMOTIONS

Objective

At the end of the exercise, the participants will be able to:

- Develop an attitude that will enhance their ability and potential to fight negative feelings or emotions.

Time allocation

About 1 ¼ hours

Materials required

Training aids and tools required for explaining the topic as part of your introductory talk and for summing-up; flip charts and writing markers for displaying key points emerging out of the discussion based on the responses of the participants to the exercise; copies of worksheet and the handout for the exercise (one for each participant); white board and markers.

Steps in conducting the exercise

- Explain the objective of the exercise and distribute the worksheet and the handout. Instruct the participants to complete the first part of the exercise—describing the three situations and indicating the negative feelings or emotions they generated.
- After the first part is completed, ask them to go over the handout carefully and complete the second part of the exercise—identifying those questions that could have helped them to fight the negative feelings or emotions and describing how.
- Invite some participants to share their responses and analyse them to bring out key issues related to positive thinking, as part of personal development.
- Sum up the discussion drawing from the responses of the participants and giving your inputs.

Worksheet

Fighting Negative Feelings or Emotions

Think of three key situations—related to the family, friends and colleagues or work-related area in your life—that you have confronted and which gave rise to negative feelings and emotions (anger, sadness, hatred, guilt, fear, frustration, worry, etc.). Go over the questions given in Handout A and identify those that relate to the situation and could have helped you in fighting these negative feelings and emotions, and adopt a more positive and healthy attitude.

Description of the situation _____

_____

_____

Negative feelings _____

Questions that could have helped you fight the situation (item numbers from the handout) and how?

.

_____

_____

_____

Description of the situation _____

_____

_____

Negative feelings _____

Questions that could have helped you fight the situation (item numbers from the handout) and how?

_____

_____

_____

Description of the situation _____

_____

_____

Negative feelings _____

Questions that could have helped you fight the situation (item numbers from the handout) and how?

_____

_____

_____

HANDOUT FOR THE PARTICIPANTS (A)

Exercise 1

Fighting Negative Feelings or Emotions

1. Was I minimising my strengths and positive qualities? Was this because I was not aware of them?
2. Was I overlooking or missing out on the positive aspects of other people or in situations that I was confronting?
3. Was I overreacting or blowing things out of proportion and focusing on those that brought unhappiness to me?
4. Was I giving undue attention to small and insignificant things, making myself more unhappy and dejected?
5. Were my negative perceptions right and accurate?
6. Were my fears or apprehensions about possible consequences of the situation for me real or imaginary?
7. Was the situation or event that gave rise to negative emotions less important than I originally thought?
8. Was I focusing on facts that were not relevant to this immediate situation?
9. Did I consider the option of accepting the situation as the circumstances were beyond my control?
10. Was I underestimating my abilities and potential to handle this situation? Was it because I was not sure whether I could use them effectively in this situation?
11. Did I not consider that I had faced similar situation earlier and came out of it successfully? If so, what made this situation different from the previous one?
12. Did I consider the same advice for myself that I have been giving to friends who faced similar situations?

13. Did I deliberate whether the situation could be interpreted or viewed in a manner that would have made me feel better?
14. Was I making assumptions about people and situations based on my predispositions, without any supportive evidence or facts?
15. Was I exaggerating my limitations and weaknesses in facing the situation?
16. Was I physically and mentally not prepared to face the situation?

EXERCISE 2

POSITIVE ATTITUDE AT WORKPLACE

Objectives

At the end of the exercise, the participants will be able to:

- Develop appropriate responses to situations that challenge their positive attitude
- Know about the ways that may help in bringing about positive change in negative members of your team
- Use techniques to minimise the impact of negative members on team morale

Time allocation

About 1 ½ hours

Materials required

Training aids and tools required for explaining the topic as part of your introductory talk and for summing-up; flip charts and writing markers for displaying key points emerging out of the discussion in the subgroups; copies of the subgroup discussion/assignments (one for each participant); copies of participants' handouts 1.2 and 3 (one for each participant of each handout); white board and markers.

Steps in conducting the exercise

- Refer to your earlier inputs on positive thinking and attitude, and introduce the exercise emphasising that our positive attitude will help us deal with a variety of situations that we confront at our workplace
- Divide the group into subgroups of 6–8 participants each, and brief them about the triple assignments, making the following points:
  o The handout lists the tasks for the subgroup
  o Although the three tasks relate to the workplace, they are to be discussed separately
  o Total time allocation for the three assignments is about one hour; you are free to allocate time for each task
  o Discussion on all three topics are to be completed within the allocated time
  o Each subgroup will present brief report on each of the assignments, highlighting key points for presentation to the larger group
- Assemble the group and ask the subgroups to make presentations, separately for each task
- After all presentations are completed, elaborate on the points that have emerged from the discussions and sum-up

HANDOUT FOR PARTICIPANTS

Topics for Subgroup Discussions

Task 1: There are situations at the workplace that seem to challenge your positive attitude or undermine it. Your task as a subgroup is to consider a frequently encountered situation and suggest how you will deal with it. It is important that after quick sharing, you select only one situation and discuss it.

Task 2: In any team or group that works together, there are members who often display negative thinking and attitude. As a team leader, what specific techniques you will use or steps you will take to change the thinking of such people and make them more positive in their outlook?

Task 3: Sometimes, members with negative attitude and thinking impact the functioning of the entire team and affect other members as well. As the leader of the group, what steps you will take to minimise this adverse influence on the team?

(Total time allocation—about one hour)

HANDOUT FOR THE PARTICIPANTS (1)

Self-improvement Instrument for the Participants

Manifestations of positive attitude

(If you wish to assess your own positive attitude and thinking, the following signals and pointers offer some guidelines. On a scale of where 10 is the highest and 1 is the lowest, you rate yourself. It is important that you are honest in your assessment. You may share your ratings if you so wish)

If you are a person with positive outlook and thinking, you:

- Demonstrate high level of optimism in your thoughts, actions and in promoting your relationships. You persevere in your pursuit of happiness and success in whatever you attempt.
- Remain constantly motivated to accomplish the goals and objectives you have set for yourself. In fact, you are forever looking to set new goals and standards for your performance in all fields.
- Are not overwhelmed or deterred by the enormity or extent of the problem you confront while undertaking a task or activity. You regard them as challenges. You believe in yourself and in your ability to overcome problems and adversities and learn not to give up.
- Display a high degree of self-esteem and self-confidence through your body language or your overall demeanour.
- Are constantly looking for solutions to the problems that you may confront in your endeavours. This helps you engage in creative and constructive thinking. You become resourceful.

- Are not only looking for opportunities to grow and develop yourself but also ensure that you remain fully prepared to make optimum use of them.
- Are willing to take initiative and not afraid to take calculated risk wherever you consider necessary and appropriate, in pursuit of your goals. You appear to be in control of yourself, your efforts and the environment in which you work.
- Display a conspicuous spirit of enthusiasm and zeal. You enjoy your work and the relationships that you develop with others.
- Are generally a cordial and pleasant person, willing to strike warm relationships with people who come in contact with you. You are liable to win respect of people around you.

HANDOUT FOR THE PARTICIPANTS (2)

Self-improvement Instrument for the Participants

(Below are some of the things that people with positive or negative attitudes say. Look at the difference and start talking to yourself in constructive ways, if you are not doing it already)

Positive Self-talk

- It is okay to make mistakes. This will help me to learn and grow but I promise myself that I will not repeat it.
- I may not be performing as well as others (in certain activities) but I have come a long way and will continue my progress.
- This is only a temporary setback/problem/adversity and will pass. I will be okay. After all, everybody faces problems one time or the other.
- Why not me? If I have enjoyed happiness and satisfaction earlier, there will be times when things go awry and make me feel unhappy. I will face this situation as best as I can.
- Life might be hard right now but happy things are around the corner.
- This situation or problem provides me an opportunity to learn to face difficulties and grow.

- This is not something that I should get unusually upset about. After all, life is much bigger than this.
- I do not have to struggle on every front. I can choose where I need to focus my efforts to confront and fight my battles.
- I am doing the best that I can with what I have right now. I will find out where I lack and explore every opportunity to improve further.
- I cannot control what other people say, do, think or feel.
- The past is history, and I need to move on. I cannot continue living in the past. I have learnt my lessons and I will not repeat the mistakes I committed.
- You will observe that it is not about lamenting your failures or travails endlessly or finding excuses or justifying them. It is about conveying to you a message that failures and problems are part of life, finding what really went wrong and looking for answers within you.
- Try to explain things to you in a different way, and you will see a difference in your attitude. Make positive self-talk your normal mode of functioning and you will experience big positive changes in your life.

Negative Self-talk

People who are in negative mode tend to explain unhappy situations or problems in a manner that they put themselves in vulnerable position. They assume the mantle of a helpless person, who is more exposed to the vagaries and problems of life than others. Sample the following:

- You are inclined to convince yourself that *only* you are always the target of unhappy or unfortunate happenings.
- You may develop a fatalistic attitude, condemning yourself to continuing misfortune and feeling; you tell yourself that your life will always be like this and there is no possibility of things getting better.
- You may be predisposed to blow up a relatively small unhappy incident and tell yourself that it is always going to be like this.
- When good things happen to you, you are likely to attribute the success to external factors, such as luck or someone else's efforts and trivialise your own efforts or role in making it happen.

- You believe that your happiness is a temporary phenomenon and adversity may be just around the corner.
- When something goes well you tell yourself that at least this went well. It is more like a relief or an escape from something that could have gone wrong.

HANDOUT FOR THE PARTICIPANTS (3)

Self-improvement Instrument for the Participants

Evaluating and Fighting Negative Thoughts

In fighting pessimistic and depressing thoughts, you must raise certain questions for you and attempt to find honest and frank answers. This is the way you will be able to engage yourself constructively in dispelling negative emotions and beliefs. You must, however, remember that it will not be enough to find answers to these questions. You must also commit yourself to action if you really want to come out of this unhealthy situation. The following questions may also help you in this exercise but you can supplement the list by adding more questions in accordance with your situation and circumstances.

- How does this thought affect me emotionally? Am I feeling unhappy, depressed or upset? Am I frustrated?
- Am I minimising my strengths and positive qualities?
- Am I overcoming or missing out on the good in other people or in situations that I am confronting?
- Am I overreacting or blowing things, especially those that bring unhappiness to me, out of proportion?
- Am I giving due attention to trivialities and insignificant things, making myself more miserable?
- Am I overgeneralising by using the words such as always, never, nobody, everyone, everything, more often than necessary?
- Am I ascribing motives to people without a firm basis or facts?
- Are my negative perceptions right and accurate?
- Are my fears or apprehensions about future events or situations real or imaginary?

- Is the event that gave rise to negative emotions less important than I originally thought?
- Am I focusing on facts that are not relevant to this immediate situation?
- Do I need to learn to accept this situation as circumstances are beyond my control?
- Am I underestimating my abilities and potential to handle this situation?
- Have I not come out of a similar situation successfully earlier? If so, what makes this different?
- What advice or suggestion would I make to a friend who is going through a similar situation?
- Is it possible to view the situation in another way? How else can I interpret it that will make me feel better?

Module 7

Critical Thinking and Creative Thinking

This module deals with two key life skills—critical thinking and creative thinking. Critical thinking is an important ability in the repertoire of an individual. Many of us form our views and opinions on the basis of perceptions of others, certain assumptions and hearsays. We do not make an attempt to verify the facts or check the authenticity of assumptions or veracity of hearsays. And this can, sometimes, lead to a lot of complications in our everyday life—in our relationships, performance at the workplace, etc. Critical thinking emphasises on this. Another important skill covered by this module is creative thinking that stimulates 'out of the box' thinking, engages our imagination to devise new and innovative ways to carry out our tasks and provide new perspectives to the issues that we confront in our daily life.

Specifically, this module focuses on the following areas:

- Understanding critical thinking
- Some prominent features of critical thinking
- What critical thinking is not?
- Three parts of critical thinking
- Critical thinking—its application in our day-to-day life
- Skills in critical thinking
- Profile of a critical thinker
- Understanding creative thinking
- Creative thinking versus critical thinking
- Improving your creative abilities
- Creative thinking skills
- Profile of a creative thinker

Expected Outcomes from the Module

At the end of the session on this module, the participants will be able to:

- Understand the meaning of critical thinking and creative thinking and appreciate its significance in everyday life
- Develop their ability to critically analyse issues and situations that they confront in their everyday life
- Develop their creative thinking and power of imagination

Education is not the learning of facts, but training the mind to think.

—**Albert Einstein**

All of us are constantly engaged in thinking. This is our day-to-day activity. However, generally speaking, our thinking is considerably influenced by our biases, distorted view of things and people, partiality and uninformed or downright prejudice. In other words, there is a subjective element in our thinking process. It is recognised that the quality of our life and that of  what we produce, make or build depends precisely on the quality of our thoughts. It is, therefore, important that we should make a conscious and systematic effort to bring in more method, reason and rationality to reach excellence in our thought process. This will help improve the quality of our life and bring in more positivity in our interaction with people.

UNDERSTANDING CRITICAL THINKING

Critical thinking features prominently in all the skills or abilities that learners are expected to acquire through the type of education being provided. One who cannot think may not be able to solve even the smallest problem. We now live in a world of problems—social, economic, political, plurality-related, science- and technologically-related, etc. It only takes a sound mind, a mind imbued with reflective thinking, which can engage in deep analysis, to come up with causes of the problem at hand and generate possible solutions or options to arrive at a decision to solve or get out of the problem.

Various specialists and experts have put forward a range of definitions of critical thinking, depending on their perspectives, experiences and contexts. Some are:

- Critical thinking, in general, refers to higher order of thinking that questions assumptions.
- It is a way of deciding whether a claim is true, false or sometimes true and sometimes false or partly true and partly false.
- Some describe it as 'thinking about thinking'.
- Critical thinking is that mode of thinking—about any subject, content or problem—in which the thinker improves the quality of his or her thinking by skilfully taking charge of the structures inherent in thinking and imposing intellectual standards upon them.
- More recently, critical thinking has been defined as the process of purposeful, self-regulatory judgement, which uses reasoned consideration to evidence, context, conceptualisations, methods and criteria.

However, for our distinct purpose and understanding, it is possible to identify from these definitions, the following core elements:

- It is a scientifically correct, intellectually sound, evidence-based and systematic process...
- of skilfully and actively...
- examining, evaluating and deciding...
- on the validity, relevance, truth and reasonableness...
- of assumptions, perspectives, information, concepts, beliefs, thinking and values...
- that have been generated by observations, experience, reflection and communication...
- and are part of our day-to-day life and basis of our behaviour and actions

Critical thinking, therefore, gives due consideration to the evidence, the context of judgement; the relevant criteria for making the judgement well;

the applicable methods or techniques for forming the judgement; and the applicable theoretical construct for understanding the problem and the question at hand. Critical thinking employs not only logic but also broad intellectual criteria such as clarity, credibility, accuracy, precision, relevance, depth, breath, fairness and significance. In contemporary usage, the word 'critical' may connote expressing disapproval, which is not always true of critical thinking. A critical evaluation of an argument, for instance, might conclude that it is valid.

Critical thinking is the intellectually disciplined process of actively and skilfully conceptualising, applying, analysing, synthesising and/or evaluating information gathered from, or generated by, observation, experience, reflection, reasoning or communication, as a guide to belief and action. In its exemplary form, it is based on universal intellectual values that transcend subject matter divisions: clarity, accuracy, precision, consistency, relevance, sound evidence, good reasons, depth, breadth and fairness.

Critical thinking of any kind is never universal in any individual; everyone is subject to episodes of undisciplined or irrational thought. Its quality is, therefore, typically a matter of degree and dependent on, among other things, the quality and depth of experience in a given domain of thinking or with respect to a particular class of questions. No one is a critical thinker through and through, but only to such-and-such a degree, with such-and-such insights and blind spots, subject to such-and-such tendencies towards self-delusion. For this reason, the development of critical thinking skills and dispositions is a life-long endeavour.

Critical thinking may be seen as having two components:

- Skills to generate and process information and beliefs
- Habit and attitude of using those skills to guide behaviour, based on intellectual commitment

These components should be contrasted with:

- Mere acquisition and retention of information alone; this is because it involves a particular way in which information is sought and treated
- Mere possession of a set of skills, because it involves the continual use of them
- Mere use of those skills (as an exercise) without acceptance of their results

Consequent upon the foregoing, it may be summarised, therefore, that critical thinking is self-guided, self-disciplined, self-directed, self-monitored and self-corrective thinking, which attempts to reason at the highest level of quality in a fair-minded way.

SOME PROMINENT FEATURES OF CRITICAL THINKING

Critical Thinking is Reflective

Critical thinking is different from just thinking. It is meta-cognitive. It involves thinking about your thinking. If I enter a social studies course where one of the topics to be studied is conformity, it is likely that I already have views about conformity: what it is, how prevalent it is and what influences people to conform or not conform. I have these views even if I have not formulated them explicitly for myself. Each view is an example of thinking, but not necessarily an example of critical thinking. Critical thinking starts once I reflect on my thinking: Why do I have these views about conformity? Since my views are really conclusions, what evidence are they based on? How do other people look at conformity differently? What are their views based on? How can I tell which are more accurate, their views or mine? To reflect on these questions is the path to critical thinking.

Critical Thinking Involves Standards

Critical thinking involves having my thinking measure up to criteria. I can think about something accurately or inaccurately. I can use evidence that is relevant to an issue or irrelevant, or somewhere in between. When I reason out and try to understand the main ideas in a course I am taking, I can do so on a superficial level or I can try to understand them deeply, trying to get at the heart of the matter.

Accuracy, relevance and depth are examples of standards or criteria. The words *critical* and *criteria* come from the same root, meaning 'judgement'. For my thinking to be *critical* thinking, I have to make judgements that meet criteria of reasonableness.

Critical Thinking is Authentic

Critical thinking, at its heart, is thinking about real problems. Although you can reason out puzzles and brain-teasers, the essence of critical thinking comes into play only when you address real problems and questions rather than artificial ones. Critical thinking is far more about what you actually believe or do. It is about good judgement. Puzzles and narrow problems may help occasionally when you want to hone or practise special skills, but even those skills help only if you consciously transfer them to real-life settings. Honing your skills at guessing the endings of murder mysteries is not likely to be good preparation for becoming a criminal investigator. In murder mysteries, all the clues are provided, the murderer is one of the characters and someone (the author) already knows the murderer's identity. None of that is so in a criminal investigation.

Real problems are often messy. They have loose ends. They are usually unclear: clarifying and refining them are part of thinking through them. They often have no single right answer. But there are wrong answers, even disastrous answers: there may not be any unique right person to take as your partner in life, but there are certainly people it would be disastrous to choose.

Critical Thinking Involves Being Reasonable

There are no sure-fire rules of reasoning. That is, no rules are so foolproof that they guarantee your reasoning will be successful. There are guidelines, even 'rules', sometimes, but these always need to be followed thoughtfully, not by rote. You need to apply them with sensitivity to context, goals or practical limitations—a whole bunch of realities. For thinking to be critical thinking, it must be reasonable thinking.

Compare critical thinking to driving a car. There are rules for good driving, but merely following the rules would not make you a good driver. To be a good driver, you have to follow the rules *mindfully*. What does that mean? It means, for example, following the rules while being aware that the purpose of sticking to the lane is to allow traffic to flow more smoothly and reduce chances of ramming into other vehicles. Notice that this is an open-ended list of what a mindful driver is aware of while driving.

We often long for sure-fire, step-by-step procedures; and the more personally important or threatening a situation is, the more we want foolproof rules. But there are no rules that guarantee our thinking will be correct—and that is especially true in very important or threatening situations. There are no rules to tell us if our reasoning is correct, precisely because we must use our reasoning to evaluate rules rather than vice versa.

The only way we can decide whether to follow certain rules is if we use our best reasoning to determine that those rules are reasonable, that they lead to reasonable results when followed. Critical thinking is 'self-correcting', at least partly, because it is the court of last resort. There is no level of greater certainty beneath it that we can use to evaluate our reasoning.

WHAT CRITICAL THINKING IS NOT

A number of widespread misconceptions about critical thinking can throw off your understanding of critical thinking and influence the way you develop in your thinking skills.

Critical Thinking is Not Negative

The word *critical* often has negative overtones. A 'critical person' is one who does a lot of fault-finding. To 'criticise' someone usually means to say something negative. A 'critic' is often thought of as someone who is against something.

However, the word *critical* in 'critical thinking' has no negative connotations at all. It is related to the word *criteria*: it means thinking that meets high criteria of reasonableness. To learn to think critically is to learn to think things through and to think them through well: accurately, clearly, sufficiently, reasonably. Some people have proposed the term *effective thinking* as a synonym for 'critical thinking', and using that term can help in removing negative overtones. Critical thinking does involve making judgements. Unfortunately, the term *judgement* has also acquired negative connotations in certain contexts. To be judgmental is certainly not to be a critical thinker, and the judgements a critical thinker makes are far removed from being judgemental *per se*. These are reality-based and not value-based.

We cannot exist without making judgements. We make judgements all the time, whether we know it or not. People sometimes say, 'I just want to accept people the way they are—myself included—without making judgements about them'. There can be a lot of wisdom in that approach. It can mean, for example, 'I am going to accept people as having the feelings they have, and the reactions they have, without condemning them for it'. That is, refraining from making judgements often means refraining from making harsh value-based judgments. But it cannot be generalised to mean not making judgements at all. To accept people's feelings and reactions as they are, involves making a judgement—the judgement that those indeed *are* their feelings and reactions. Critical thinking comes in directly because accepting people as they are presupposes making accurate, clear, relevant judgements about what their feelings and reactions are. That is accepting people as they are, rather than imposing preconceptions on them.

Another aspect of negativity is that sometimes sensitivity to negative feedback gets in the way of critical thinking. Suppose someone makes a judgement about what you have said; that it is inaccurate or unclear, or not relevant to the question asked. Maybe the person even personalises it, criticising you when she is actually talking about your statement or remarks. The person might say *you* are unclear or inaccurate. Maybe the person even says it harshly.

Critical Thinking is Not Emotionless Thinking

One of the most widespread myths about critical thinking, and one of the most harmful too, is that critical thinking is somehow opposed to emotions. According to this myth, the best way to think critically is to be devoid of emotions or, if emotions arise, to put them aside, do not let them influence your conclusions. The image in this myth is of someone coldly rational, someone who puts aside her feelings in order to be 'logical'.

This is one of the most misleading myths, and it is all the more damaging because there is a grain of truth in it. Some emotions do indeed get in the way of critical thinking: rage and panic, for example. It is extremely difficult for people to think clearly about a decision when they are enraged. Often, the only reasonable thing they can do in such circumstances is to put off action until the rage subsides, maybe helping it to abate by exercising, or by deep breathing or by not letting the same enraging thoughts keep repeating in their head.

So some emotions can interfere with critical thinking. But certain other emotion-laden states help with critical thinking: the love of truth is an example. So are the joy of discovery, anger at biased presentations of information and fear of making an unreasonable decision when something very important hangs in the balance.

There is another area in which emotions are essential to critical thinking. Emotions often give us data, and much of the time, it is foolhardy to ignore that data. The reasonable thing to do, however, is neither to ignore the data of your emotions nor to give them too much weight.

If we think of desires as intertwined with emotion, then the tie between critical thinking and emotions is even stronger. That is because, in the end, it is not possible to engage in critical thinking without desires and their attendant emotions. Unless I have goals—desires, things I want, things I am emotionally attached to—I have no reason to think critically, no reason to take action X rather than action Y.

THREE PARTS OF CRITICAL THINKING

Full-fledged critical thinking involves three parts, which are as follows:

- First, critical thinking involves asking questions. It involves asking questions that need to be asked, asking good questions, questions that go to the heart of the matter. Critical thinking involves *noticing* that there are questions that need to be addressed.
- Second, critical thinking involves trying to answer those questions by reasoning them out. Reasoning out answers to questions is different from other ways of answering questions. It is different from giving an answer we have always taken for granted but never thought about. It is different from answering impressionistically (that reminds me of...), answering simply according to the way we were raised or answering in accordance with our personality. It is also different from answering by saying the first thing that comes into our mind and then using all our power of reasoning to defend that answer.
- Although asking questions is necessary to begin critical thinking, merely asking the questions is not enough; the questions need to be answered (or at least addressed). Often we raise questions only to worry about them, to torment ourselves or even to put off action, instead of trying to answer them by thinking them through.
- It is easy to misunderstand questions about reasoning. Thus, you might interpret the second item listed as implying that critical thinking is opposed to the way you were raised, but that is not what it means. What critical thinking is opposed to *is* acting in the way you were raised, without examining it. For example, someone raised in a family where violence and abuse were acceptable, or where blind conformity to authority was taken for granted, should not simply follow those values.

- Reasoning itself is drawing conclusions on the basis of reasons. *Good* reasoning, therefore, is drawing conclusions on the basis of reasons and giving due weight to all relevant factors. Relevant factors include the *implications* of drawing those *conclusions*, the *assumptions* on which the reasoning is based, the *accuracy* of the reasons used, the *alternatives* available and a number of other elements.
- Third, critical thinking involves believing the results of our reasoning. Critical thinking is different from just engaging in a mental exercise. When we think through an issue critically, we internalise the results. We do not give merely verbal agreement: we actually believe the results because we have done our best to reason the issue out and we know that reasoning things out is the best way to get reliable answers. Furthermore, when we think critically through a decision about what to do in a situation, then what follows the reasoning is not just belief, but action: Unless something unforeseen occurs, we end up taking the action we concluded was most reasonable.

CRITICAL THINKING—ITS APPLICATION IN OUR DAY-TO-DAY LIFE

There are many positive and constructive uses of critical thinking. Some of them are indicated below:

- Critical thinking gives us insights into issues that are central to a problem and helps us understand its various dimensions. This helps in the processes of problem-solving and decision-making. Thus, critical thinking serves as a way of taking up problems of life.
- It does not automatically involve disapproval or negation of what it is examining. It only emphasises critical analysis and evaluation.
- It clarifies goals, examines assumptions, discerns values, evaluates evidence, accomplishes actions and assesses conclusions.
- It helps us in figuring out what to believe or what to do and do so in a reasonable and reflective way.
- It also helps us in understanding the validity of an argument and deciding whether it is based on true premises and information and, thus, worthy of acceptance.

- In formulating a workable solution to a complex personal problem, deliberating as a group about a course of action to take or analysing assumptions and the quality of methods used in scientifically arriving at a reasonable level of confidence about a given hypothesis.
- We are able to integrate new and revised perspectives into our ways of thinking, behaving and doing things and willingness to foster criticality in others.
- Reading, writing, speaking and listening can all be done critically or uncritically.
- Critical thinking is crucial for becoming an accomplished reader and substantive writer.
- We might evaluate an argument presented by a speaker as worthy of acceptance and whether based on true premises and valid information.

SKILLS IN CRITICAL THINKING

Critical thinking

Skills	Action
Analysing	Separating or breaking a whole into parts to discover their nature, functions and relationships. 'I studied it piece by piece' 'I sorted things out'
Applying Standards	Judging according to established personal, professional or social rules or criteria. 'I judged it according to...'
Discriminating	Recognising differences and similarities among things or situations and distinguishing carefully as to category or rank. 'I rank ordered the various...' 'I grouped things together'
Information Seeking	Searching for evidence, facts or knowledge by identifying relevant sources and gathering objective, subjective, historical and current data from those sources 'I knew I needed to lookup/study...' 'I kept searching for data'.

(continued)

(*continued*)

Skills	Action
Logical Reasoning	Drawing inferences or conclusions that are supported in or justified by evidence 'I deduced from the information that...' 'My rationale for the conclusion was...'
Predicting	Envisioning a plan and its consequences 'I envisioned the outcome would be...' 'I was prepared for...'
Transforming Knowledge	Changing or converting the condition, nature, form or function of concepts among contexts 'I improved on the basics by...' 'I wondered if that would fit the situation of ...'

Source: http://cct.wikispaces.umb.edu/ and http://umb.libguides.com/CCT

PROFILE OF A CRITICAL THINKER

Critical thinking requires a complex combination of traits, competencies and characteristics. These are:

Rational and Logical Thinking

We are thinking critically when we:

- Rely on reason and rationale rather than on emotions and sentiments
- Require evidence and substantiated data and information, ignore no known evidence and follow the leads given by all available evidence
- Are concerned with finding the best and most logical explanation

Self-awareness

We are thinking critically when we:

- Recognise our own assumptions, prejudices, biases or points of view
- Weigh the influence of motives and bias

Honesty and Objectivity

We are thinking critically when we:

- Recognise our emotional impulses, selfish or ulterior motives and other modes of self-deception

Open-mindedness

We are thinking critically when we:

- Evaluate all reasonable inferences
- Consider a variety of possible viewpoints or perspectives
- Remain open to alternative interpretations
- Accept a new explanation, model or paradigm because it explains the evidence better, is simpler, has fewer inconsistencies or covers more data
- Accept new priorities in response to a re-evaluation of the evidence or reassessment of our real interests and
- Are not judgemental and do not reject seemingly inappropriate or unpopular views out of hand

Discipline

We are thinking critically when we:

- Are precise, meticulous, comprehensive and exhaustive
- Resist manipulation and irrational appeals

Sound Judgement

We are thinking critically when we:

- Recognise the relevance and/or merit of alternative assumptions and perspectives
- Recognise the extent and weight of evidence

To sum up:

Critical thinkers are sceptical by nature. They are unwilling to accept things at the face value and approach texts with doubt and caution, and doubt in the same way as they consider spoken remarks.

They are active, not passive individuals. They are ready to ask questions and engage in the analysis of the responses. They consciously apply tactics and strategies to uncover meaning of what they confront and enhance their understanding.

They do not take an egotistical view of the world. They are open to new ideas and perspectives. They are willing to challenge their beliefs and investigate competing evidence or views of others.

Critically Thinking People

- Think critically consistently; attempt to live rationally, reasonably and empathically
- Are keenly aware of the inherent flawed nature of human thinking when left unguided and unchecked
- Strive to diminish the power of their egocentric and sociocentric tendencies
- Use the intellectual tools offered by critical thinking such as concepts and principles that enable them to analyse, assess and improve thinking
- Work diligently to develop the intellectual virtues of intellectual integrity, intellectual humility, intellectual civility, intellectual empathy, intellectual sense of justice and confidence in reason
- Realise that no matter how skilled they are as thinkers, they can always improve their reasoning abilities and that they can at times fall prey to mistakes in reasoning, human irrationality, prejudices, biases, distortions, uncritical accepted social rules and taboos, self-interest and vested interest
- Strive to improve the world in whatever ways they can and contribute to a more rational and civilised society. At the same time, they recognise the complexities that are inherent in doing so

- Avoid thinking simplistically about complicated issues and strive to appropriately consider the rights and needs of relevant others
- Recognise the complexities in developing as thinkers, and as such get committed to life-long practice towards self-improvement
- Exemplify the Socratic principle: 'The unexamined life is not worth living', because of their belief that many unexamined lives together result in an uncritical, unjust and dangerous world

(*Source:* Paul & Elder, 2008)

UNDERSTANDING CREATIVE THINKING

Creative thinking means thinking about new things or thinking in new ways. It is 'thinking outside the box'. Often, creativity in this sense involves what is called lateral thinking or the ability to perceive patterns that are not obvious. The fictional detective Sherlock Holmes used lateral thinking in one famous story when he realised that a dog *not* barking was an important clue in a murder case.

Some people are naturally more creative than others, but creative thinking can be strengthened with practice. You can practise creative thinking by solving riddles, by becoming aware of and letting go of your assumptions and through play—anything unstructured and relaxing. Even daydreaming can help.

Creative people can devise new ways to carry out tasks, solve problems and meet challenges. They bring a fresh and sometimes unorthodox perspective to their work and can help departments and organisations to move in more productive directions.

In schools and even in universities, the students are asked to be creative in their thoughts. This highlights a need to be original and to 'think outside of the box'.

If a person is continuously paying attention to the limitations and boundaries, it is quite difficult to be creative. Creative thinking is non-judgemental and expansive. There is no end to creative thinking. In fact, it can be said that the sky is the limit for creative thinking. This is the specialty of creative thinking. It allows the person to break away from the usual barriers and imagine the unimaginable.

Creative thinking is not selective; the mind is free to think anything creative. Unlike in the case of critical thinking where you are bound to make some choices, in creative thinking it is different. Various kinds of choices are not made in the case of creative thinking. In fact, creative thinking aims at generating new and thought-provoking ideas. This is why one can claim that creative thinking is all about imagination and imagery. Hence, it is best suited to creative arts such as poetry and painting.

Most of us are not natural creative thinkers. Telling oneself and the team *to be creative* does not usually yield results. Some special techniques are required to help us use our brains in a different way—to change our usual thinking process. The issue with creative thinking is that almost by definition any idea that has not already been examined is going to sound crazy. But a good solution will probably sound crazy at first. Unfortunately, that is why we often would not put it forward.

To sum up:

- *Creative thinking* involves creating something new or original
- *Creative thinking* is imaginative, generates many possible solutions and is divergent
- *Creative thinking* is a way of looking at problems or situations from a fresh perspective that suggests unorthodox solutions (which may look unsettling at first)
- *Creative thinking* can be stimulated both by an unstructured process such as brainstorming and by a structured process such as lateral thinking

There are, however, certain blocks to creativity or creative thinking:

- Fear of trying something new, making mistakes and failing
- Feeling that in the eyes of family members, friends and colleagues, they may appear to be foolish or stupid; fear of being criticised
- Feeling that by trying something new and innovative, they might be challenging certain traditions of the group or the community; or, worse, they might get associated with certain taboos

CREATIVE THINKING VERSUS CRITICAL THINKING

Creative thinking is divergent, critical thinking is convergent; whereas creative thinking tries to create something new, critical thinking seeks to assess worth or validity in something that exists; creative thinking is carried on by violating accepted principles, critical thinking is carried on by applying accepted principles. Although creative and critical thinking may very well be different sides of the same coin, they are not identical (Beyer, 1987).

Creative thinking and critical thinking are two expressions that show the difference between them when it comes to their inner meanings. Creative thinking is going beyond the limitations and being original and fresh in one's ideas. Critical thinking, on the other hand, is more evaluative in nature and analyses a particular thing. Hence, one can conclude that while creative thinking is generative in purpose, critical thinking is analytical in purpose. This is one of the main differences between creative thinking and critical thinking.

Critical thinking is selective, but creative thinking is not selective. The mind is free to wander about in creative thinking, but in the case of critical thinking it is not so.

IMPROVING YOUR CREATIVE ABILITIES

- Keep track of your ideas at all times. Many times ideas come at unexpected times. If an idea is not written down within 24 hours, it will usually be forgotten.
- Pose new questions to yourself everyday. An inquiring mind is a creatively active one that enlarges its area of awareness.
- Keep abreast of your field. Read the magazines, trade journals and other literature in your field to make sure you are not using yesterday's technology to solve today's problems.
- Engage in creative hobbies. Hobbies can also help you relax. An active mind is necessary for creative growth.
- Have courage and self-confidence. Be a paradigm pioneer. Assume that you can and will indeed solve the problem. Persist and have the tenacity to overcome obstacles that block the solution pathway.
- Learn to know and understand yourself. Deepen your self-knowledge by learning your real strengths, skills, weaknesses, dislike, biases, expectations, fears and prejudices.

- Learn about things outside your specialty. Use cross-fertilisation to bring ideas and concepts from one field or specialty to another.
- Avoid rigid, set patterns of doing things. Overcome biases and preconceived notions by looking at the problem from a fresh viewpoint, always developing at least two or more alternative solutions to your problem.
- Be open and receptive to ideas (yours and others). New ideas are fragile; keep them from breaking by seizing on the tentative, half-formed concepts and possibilities, and developing them.
- Be alert in your observations. Look for similarities, differences as well as unique and distinguishing features in situations and problems.
- Adopt a risk-taking attitude. Fear of failure is the major impediment to generating solutions which are risky (i.e., small chance of succeeding) but would have a major impact if they are successful. Outlining the ways you could fail, and how you would deal with these failures, will reduce this obstacle to creativity.
- Keep your sense of humour. You are more creative when you are relaxed. Humour aids in putting your problems (and yourself) in perspective. Many times, it relieves tension and makes you more relaxed.

(*Source:* http://cct.wikispaces.umb.edu/ and http://umb.libguides.com/CCT)

CREATIVE THINKING SKILLS

1. **Suspending advocacy of your own idea to push for another person's concept:** It is helpful to be able to come into a creative situation and demonstrate your willingness to champion another person's idea. It can open the way to getting others to support your thinking as well.

2. **Putting your own idea to the same test you apply to an idea from someone else:** When it comes to propagation of your own ideas, it is easy to be a hypocrite. Some people apply all kinds of hurdles to others' ideas while letting their own thinking slide by unchallenged in your own mind. This is unhealthy and even unethical; do not become somebody known for doing this.

3. **Combining two different ideas and making them better (not muddled) as one idea:** Ability to dissect two ideas, pull out highlights of both ideas, putting them together as something new and still maintaining the innovativeness of the ideas is a great skill to have.

4. **Letting someone else take 'ownership' of your idea in order to build support for it:** This skill really tests whether you believe so strongly in an idea you are willing to let someone else step up and take it on as their own idea to see it prevail. The key to seeing your idea win out can be letting somebody else be the vocal proponent for it.

5. **Displaying the patience to wait for someone else to say what needs to be said so all you have to do is agree:** It is tempting to jump in right away and make all the points you feel necessary in a creative discussion before anyone else talks. At times though, patience and silence are called for when it becomes clear someone can and will express your perspective, more appropriately than you can.

6. **Sticking to your guns amid challenges to a creative idea, which makes solid strategic sense:** There are many creative ideas, which, while being really cool, have nothing to do with what you are trying to achieve and how you should be achieving it. When confronted with others who are passionately arguing for highly creative yet hardly strategic concepts, make and remake your case if you are convinced that the idea you are advocating is on the mark, strategically.

7. **Looking for new creative skills to develop in yourself and those around you:** Not only do you want to make yourself stronger creatively at every juncture, it is in your best interests to help improve the creative performance of your overall team. Creative meetings are a great opportunity to spot gaps and to identify your own creative shortcomings. Inventory what you saw and observed, and after a creative meeting, get to work to fill these gaps.

(*Source:* Brown, 2016)

PROFILE OF A CREATIVE THINKER

Good Communicators

- Creativity and confidence are expressed in many ways through both listening and communicating
- This is why creative thinkers are good communicators

- Collaboration is also important for this kind of thinking, and good communication is essential for work performance as a part of a team

Open-minded

- An open mind is a mind that appreciates criticism, is ready for new solutions and ideas, and is not afraid of evaluating ideas
- A person who is open-minded is willing to learn from both successes and mistakes, being able to grow and develop

Risk-takers

- Exploring new ideas and strategies is impossible without risk-taking as a willingness to face challenges and accept change
- Creative thinkers are resilient, and they are not afraid of taking a chance, knowing that one needs to be brave when exploring innovative and original ways of thinking about and solving problems
- They know that leaving a comfort zone is sometimes necessary to succeed, even if it means facing the unknown

Knowledgeable

- To develop an understanding of things and situations, you need a background story
- Knowledge allows creative thinkers to see the full picture, which is why they know a lot about the sector they work in
- They are experts in what they do, and the concept of life-long learning is what they base their expertise on

Flexible

- Abilities to adapt to changes and think outside the usual patterns are parts of creative thinking, which is why being flexible is a characteristic trait of creative thinkers
- They welcome changes; they are not afraid of changing their method of work, and they are good at working with others

Ask Questions

They are intensely curious. They are always asking questions. They ask questions like 'Why?' very much like children do all the time. Then they ask, 'Why not?' 'Why can't we do it?' 'Even if it hasn't been done before, can it be done now?'

Practise Zero-based Thinking

- They practise 'zero-based thinking' all the time. They continually ask themselves, 'If I were not now doing what I am doing, knowing what I now know, would I start?'
- And if the answer is no, they cut their losses, discontinue what they are doing and start doing something else. It is absolutely amazing how many people persist in something that they would not even get into if they had to do it over again. And they wonder why they are making so little progress.

Willing to Change Their Mind

They have a willingness to change. They recognise that in a world such as ours, the unwillingness or inability to change is fatal. They prefer to be in charge of their lives rather than being caught up in the flash flood of change that is inevitable and unavoidable. The words of the truly flexible person, the person who is willing to change, are simply, 'I changed my mind'. According to researchers, fully 70 per cent of the decisions you make turn out to be wrong in the long run. This means that you must be willing to change your mind and try something else most of the time. Mental flexibility is the most important quality that you will need for success in the present-day world.

Admit When They Are Wrong

They are willing to admit when they are wrong or make mistakes. Research shows that 80 per cent of people burn up most of their mental and emotional energy defending their stand and in not admitting that they made a wrong decision. Truly intelligent, highly creative people are open-minded, fluid, flexible and willing to both change their mind and admit that they are wrong when their earlier decisions turn out to be incorrect.

Desire to Learn

Highly creative people can say, 'I don't know'. They recognise that it is impossible for anyone to know anything about everything, and it is very likely that almost everyone is wrong to some extent, no matter what they are doing. So when someone asks them a particular question that they do not know the answer to, they admit it early and often. They simply say, 'I don't know'. And, if necessary, they go about finding the answer. Here is an important point. No matter what problems you have, there is someone, somewhere who has had the same or similar problem and who has already solved it and is using the solution today. One of the smartest and most creative things you can do is to find someone else, somewhere, who is already implementing the solution successfully and then copy him or her.

Goal-oriented and Focused

They are intensely goal focused. They know exactly what they want. They have it written down very clearly. They visualise it on a regular basis. They imagine what their goal would look like if it were a reality today. And the more they visualise and imagine their goal as a reality, the more creative they become and the faster they move towards achieving it.

No Inflated Ego

They have less ego involvement in being right. They are more concerned with what's right rather than who is right. They are willing to accept ideas from any source to achieve a goal, overcome an obstacle or solve a problem.

SUGGESTED GUIDELINES FOR CONDUCTING THE SESSION

One exercise is suggested for developing critical skill of the participants. However, it is important that before the participants are engaged in working on the exercise, you must provide them comprehensive understanding of the concept of critical thinking through your presentation. You may particularly refer to the sub-topics such as application of critical thinking, abilities for critical thinking and profile of a critical thinker. As the concept may be new to at least some of the participants, they may have a number of queries and points to get clarification on. Therefore, ensure that the group moves with you on the discussion.

In addition to the main exercise, four mini-exercises on creative thinking are also included. These are like on-the-spot exercises. You may decide to conduct them at the time you consider appropriate. There is also a handout for the participants on 'Techniques for Creative Thinking'. This can also be used by you for discussion on this sub-topic. If you choose, you may demonstrate these techniques also through on-the-spot exercises. This will help the participants understand these techniques better.

EXERCISE

DEVELOPING CRITICAL THINKING

Objective

- To help the participants develop their ability to critically analyse issues and statements on the basis of some definite criteria.

Time allocation

1 ½ hours

Material required

Training aids and tools required for your presentation; flip charts and writing markers for displaying key points emerging out of the discussion based on the responses of the participants to the exercise; worksheet and the answer sheet for the exercise; white board and markers.

Steps in conducting the exercise

- Introduce the exercise by referring to your presentation. Clarify that this is an individual exercise and the participants are expected to think clearly before they record their responses in the worksheet
- Distribute worksheet and let the participants work on the task, keeping in view the instructions given in the worksheet. After they have completed the task, distribute the answer sheet and ask them to compare their responses with those given in the answer sheet
- Bring them back in the plenary and ask them to share their responses, identifying the problems they faced in giving right answers. Process the reactions and observations of the participants and give your observations and inputs on the basis of your presentation
- Sum up the discussion and close the exercise

DEVELOPING CRITICAL THINKING

Worksheet

The following are some guidelines for critical thinking:

1. Ask questions; be willing to wonder
2. Define the problem
3. Examine the evidence
4. Analyse assumptions and biases
5. Avoid emotional reasoning
6. Do not use either/or thinking or overgeneralise
7. Consider other interpretations
8. Tolerate uncertainty

Each of the statements below violates at least one of the guidelines for critical thinking. On a separate sheet of paper, identify the guideline that was violated and give a brief explanation for your choice. It is possible that some of the statements may violate more than one guideline.

1. Since we have never been visited by extraterrestrials, and have had no communication from outer space, we can safely assume that intelligent life exists only on our own planet.

2. It is pretty obvious that smoking marijuana causes people to crave more potent drugs such as cocaine and heroin. Statistics show that almost all the people who become addicted to drugs smoked marijuana before they began using more potent drugs.

3. You are either for us or against us.

4. I get disgusted with my science classes. We study the 'principle of this' and the 'theory of that'. Are not there any laws? Why cannot scientists make up their minds and stop acting like they do not know anything for sure?

5. People tend to become forgetful as they get older. This is just one of the natural consequences of aging, and it would be a waste of time to look for specific causes or ways to prevent the problem.

6. People of different ethnic backgrounds just cannot live harmoniously in the same neighbourhood. Almost everyone I have talked to thinks the same way. This is a gut feeling, and we are not likely to be wrong.

7. The increase in violence by adolescent gangs in this country is just another result of the liberal thinking that has more sympathy for criminals than for their victims.

8. Why are the people in this class so much better looking and intelligent than people in other introductory classes?

9. I looked at several issues of the *Journal of Parapsychology*, a periodical that publishes research on psychic phenomena. Every article confirmed the existence of extrasensory perception (ESP), so I do not understand why most psychologists are sceptical about it.

10. Let us just make up our minds and buy one or the other of the houses. I am tired of thinking about it, and all this investigation and indecision is making me nervous.

DEVELOPING CRITICAL THINKING

Answer Sheet

1. Oversimplification (6). An example of either/or thinking. Since you cannot prove a negative, you must also consider other interpretations (7) for the absence of contact with other planets.

2. Consider other interpretations (7). A causal relationship between marijuana use and use of other drugs is assumed. There is no

information on people who smoked marijuana who did not 'move on' to more potent drugs.

3. Oversimplification (6). An example of either/or thinking. Maybe I'm indifferent.

4. Tolerate uncertainty (8). The student seems more interested in answers than in 'truth'.

5. Ask questions; be willing to wonder (1). Statement shows a lack of willingness to search for causes and cures.

6. Avoid emotional reasoning (5). 'Gut feelings' can be wrong.

7. Consider other interpretations (7).

8. Analyse assumptions and biases (4). The question has a built-in assumption. Is the assumption biased?

9. Examine the evidence (3). Perhaps the journal publishes only studies that support the existence of psychic phenomena.

10. Tolerate uncertainty (8). The statement suggests making a hasty decision to escape the discomfort of uncertainty.

MINI-EXERCISE 1

CREATIVE THINKING (WORLDLY WORDS)

Work on some skills using metaphor and choosing words carefully with this fun, challenging exercise.

Note for the trainer:

- Total time for the exercise is about 30 minutes
- You may form your rules for sharing
- This is an individual exercise but you can conduct it in dyads as well

Instructions for the participants:

Imagine you live in a world where there are only 10 words you can ever use. You can repeat them as much as you want, but you *cannot ever use any other words*. Write down the 10 words you would choose.

Next, make 3–4 sentences with them in order to communicate something to members of your group. Use feeling and gesture to help them understand you. You can measure their understanding by writing your actual intended meaning below the sentence. Remember, you have only got 10 words to use, so choose them well!

WORKSHEET

Your 10 words:

1. _____

2. _____

3. _____

4. _____

5. _____

6. _____

6. _____

7. _____

8. _____

9. _____

10. _____

Create sentences with them here:

1. _____

    Actual meaning: _____

2. _____

    Actual meaning: _____

3. _____

    Actual meaning: _____

4. _____

    Actual meaning: _____

MINI-EXERCISE 2

CREATIVE THINKING (CREATIVE USES OF AN OBJECT)

Note for the trainer:

- This is a brainstorming exercise. Each participant writes the name of an object or thing of everyday use on a slip of paper and drops it in a box. Mix the slips and randomly draw slips from the box and give one each to the participants
- Distribute worksheet and put a 15-minute timer for the exercise
- This is an individual exercise but you can conduct it in dyads as well

Instructions to the participants:

Instruct the participants that they must now come up with as many *new uses for your object as you can*. Write them down or sketch them out in the box. Be as creative as you can!

WORKSHEET

My Object: _____

MINI-EXERCISE 3

CREATIVE THINKING (CREATE RULES FOR ALL)

Note for the trainer:

- Put a 15-minute timer for the exercise
- Provide worksheet to the participants
- You may use any method for sharing

Instructions to the participants: The rules and laws we have in life are meant to guide us and protect us and to keep order in our society. Imagine that you get to make three rules that *everyone in the country must follow*. What rules would you make and why? This is an individual exercise.

WORKSHEET

Rule no. 1 _____

I chose this rule because _____

_____

Rule no. 2 _____

I chose this rule because _____

_____

Rule no. 3 _____

I chose this rule because _____

_____

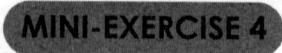

CREATIVE THINKING (WHAT I CHOOSE TO GIVE UP; AND WHAT I CHOOSE TO HAVE?)

Note for the trainer:

- Put a 20-minute timer for the exercise
- Provide worksheet to the participants
- Ask for volunteers to share their responses

Instructions to the participants

Part of life is being able to strike a healthy balance between our needs and our wants. It is also about focusing on what we consider to be truly important. Imagine you can have *any three things that you want*. In return, you must *give away three things that you already have*. What do you want and what will you give away, and why?

Worksheet

What I choose to have?

1. _____

2. _____

3. _____

I would want these things because…

1. _____

2. _____

3. _____

What I would give away?

1. _____

2. _____

3. _____

I would give up these things because…

    1. _____

    2. _____

    3. _____

HANDOUT FOR THE PARTICIPANTS

Discussion Tool for the Trainer

Techniques for Creative Thinking

Brainstorming

- This technique includes thinking about something and putting down all the ideas that come to your mind—regardless how silly or unrelated they might seem at first.
- In this ocean of ideas, you are bound to find one that will stand out, one that will be tangible and innovative.
- Used as an individual or group practice, brainstorming is a great way to develop creative thinking and problem-solving.
- It encourages thinking in a different way and exploring many options that might be applied in that situation.
- The more options come to your mind, the more potential you will have to find great ideas.

Mind mapping

- Mind mapping is the process of connecting the dots.
- While brainstorming involves putting all the ideas down as they come to your mind, mind mapping is about arranging your thoughts, thinking in a logical way, using associations, recognising patterns and creating an order.
- All that cluster of ideas from brainstorming should come together in mind mapping.
- This exercise engages both left and right hemisphere of the brain; it encourages you to think about the relationship among aspects and ideas.
- It also has a positive influence on organisational skill.

Reframing

- Since reframing focuses on analysing the same situation or a problem from a different perspective, it is a great exercise for developing creative thinking.
- Reframing means changing the frame of things, so you will need to take a look at a problem or a situation in a different way, to be able to come up with a new, innovative approach.
- Explore other meanings of things, analyse the context and spread the perspective to spot new opportunities and expect potential obstacles.
- Again, this exercise and way of thinking are applicable in many professions nowadays.

Envisaging the futures

- The goal of this exercise is to train your mind to anticipate future based on the images of today.
- Start with the current situation.
- Regardless if you are using images or data to understand it, try to think about future and where you want future to take you.
- Through this process, you will need to create bridges from present to future, and this is where creativity comes in useful, as ideas to overcome gaps become solutions that will take you to desired future and help you achieve your goals.

Role-play

- The technique of using role-play is a good way to change the way you are thinking and explore the situation from a different perspective.
- Creative thinking encourages you to be open-minded, so when using this method, you will try to think about the situation from the point of someone else.
- You need to reframe your way of thinking to see a different perspective of things, to change the perspective and find new solutions that go over your limits and overcome your personal style of problem-solving.
- Assuming a new role encourages you to come up with solutions that might not be typical for you, but they are what you need for creative problem-solving.

Module 8

Empathy

Empathy is one of the key life skills that shape our communication and interaction with others, especially those who are going through a difficult period in their life. This module aims to discuss various aspects of this important skill. Here also, the focus is on helping the participants learn about their own empathy-related behaviour and skills.

Specifically, the module deals with the following topics:

- Understanding empathy
- Elements of empathy
- Types of empathy
- Using empathy effectively

Expected Outcomes from the Module

At the end of the session on the module, the participants will be able to:

- Get an understanding of various aspects of empathy and empathetic behaviour
- Assess their own empathetic behaviour and the skills they possess

---

I call him religious who understands the sufferings of others.

—Mahatma Gandhi

UNDERSTANDING EMPATHY

According to Rogers (1995), 'an empathetic way of being with another person has several facets'. These are as follows:

It means entering the private perceptual world of the other and becoming truly at home in it. It involves being sensitive, moment by moment, to the changing felt meaning which flows in this other person, to the fear or tenderness or rage or confusion or whatever the other person is experiencing.

It means to temporarily live in the others' perceptual world and moving in it delicately without making judgements.

It means sensing meanings of which the other is scarcely aware, but not trying to uncover totally unconscious feelings because this can be too threatening.

It includes communicating your sensing of the person's world as you look with fresh and unfrightened eyes at elements of which he or she is fearful.

It means frequently checking with the other person as to the accuracy of your sensing and being guided by the responses that you receive.

You are a confident companion to the person in his inner world. By pointing to the possible meanings in the flow of the other person's experiencing, you can help him to focus on this useful type of referent. This way, the other person can experience the personal meanings more fully and move forward in the experiencing.

Some other psychologists have also defined 'empathy':

Gallo (1989) stated: '...an empathic response is one which contains both a cognitive and an affective dimension...the term empathy is used in at least two ways; to mean a predominantly cognitive response, understanding how another feels, or to mean an affective communion with the other'.

Haynes and Avery characterise empathy as '...the ability to recognise and understand another person's perceptions and feelings, and to accurately convey that understanding through an accepting response'.

And, the *American Heritage Dictionary of the English Language* defines empathy as '...understanding so intimate that the feelings, thoughts, and motives of one are readily comprehended by another'.

Daniel Goleman, author of the book *Emotional Intelligence*, says that 'empathy is basically the ability to understand others' emotions. He also, however, notes that at a deeper level, it is about defining, understanding, and reacting to the concerns and needs that underlie others' emotional responses and reactions'.

Tim Minchin noted that 'empathy is a skill that can be developed and', as with most interpersonal skills, empathising (at some level) comes naturally to most people.

Empathy is, at its simplest, awareness of the feelings and emotions of other people. It is a key element of emotional intelligence,[1] the link between self and others, because it is how we as individuals understand what others are experiencing *as if we were feeling it ourselves.*

It may not always be easy, or even possible, to empathise with others but, through fine people skills and some imagination, we can work towards more empathetic feelings. Research has suggested that individuals who can empathise enjoy better relationships with others and greater well-being through life.

There is an important distinction between empathy, sympathy and compassion. Both compassion and sympathy are about feeling *for* someone: seeing their distress and realising that they are suffering. Compassion has taken on an element of action that is lacking in sympathy, but the root of the words is the same. Empathy, by contrast, is about experiencing those feelings for yourself, as if you were that person, through the power of imagination. It goes far beyond sympathy, which might be considered 'feeling for' someone. Empathy, instead, is 'feeling with' that person through the use of imagination.

ELEMENTS OF EMPATHY

Understanding Others

This is, probably, the most important element of empathy. In Goleman's words, 'sensing others' feelings and perspectives, and taking an active interest in their concerns'. Those who do this:

- Tune into emotional cues. They listen well and also pay attention to non-verbal communication, picking up subtle cues almost subconsciously
- Show sensitivity and understand others' perspectives

---

[1] Retrieved on 2 November 2017, from https://www.skillsyouneed.com/general/emotional-intelligence.html

- Are able to help other people based on their understanding of those people's needs and feelings

Developing Others

Developing others means acting on their needs and concerns, and helping them to develop to their full potential. People with skills in this area usually:

- Reward and praise people for their strengths and accomplishments, and provide constructive feedback designed to focus on how to improve
- Provide mentoring and coaching to help others to develop to their full potential
- Provide stretching assignments that will help their teams to develop

Leveraging Diversity

It means being able to create and develop opportunities through different kinds of people, recognising and celebrating that we all bring something different to the table. It does not mean that you treat everyone in exactly the same way, but that you tailor the way you interact with others to fit with their needs and feelings.

People with this skill respect and relate well to everyone, regardless of their background. As a general rule, they see diversity as an opportunity, understanding that diverse teams work much better than teams that are more homogenous.

People who are good at leveraging diversity also challenge intolerance, bias and stereotyping when they see it, creating an atmosphere that is respectful towards everyone.

TYPES OF EMPATHY

Psychologists have identified three types of empathy: cognitive empathy, emotional empathy and compassionate empathy.

Cognitive Empathy

Cognitive empathy is about understanding someone's thoughts and emotions in a very rational, rather than emotional, sense. Effectively, cognitive empathy is 'empathy by thought', rather than by feeling. It is basically being able to put yourself into someone else's place and see their perspective on issues and matters that are mutually important. Therefore, many do not consider it empathy.

It is a useful skill, particularly in negotiations, for example, or for managers. It enables you to put yourself in someone else's shoes, but without necessarily engaging with their emotions. It does not, however, really fit with the definition of empathy as 'feeling with', being a much more rational and logical process.

Emotional Empathy

Emotional empathy is when you quite literally feel the other person's emotions alongside them, as if you had 'caught' the emotions. It is also known as 'personal distress' or 'emotional contagion'. This is closer to the usual understanding of the word 'empathy', but more emotional.

Emotional empathy is good because it means that we can readily understand and feel other people's emotions. This is vital for those in caring professions, such as doctors and nurses, to be able to respond to their patients appropriately. It also means that we can respond to friends and others when they are distressed.

Emotional empathy can be bad, because it is possible to become overwhelmed by those emotions, and, therefore, unable to respond. This is known as *empathy overload*. Those with a tendency to become overwhelmed need to work on their self-regulation, and particularly their self-control,[2] so that they become better able to manage their own emotions.

Compassionate Empathy

Finally, compassionate empathy is what we usually understand by empathy—feeling someone's pain and *taking action* to help. The term is also consistent with what we usually understand by compassion. Like sympathy, compassion is about feeling concern for someone, but with an additional move towards action to mitigate the problem. Compassionate empathy is the type of empathy that is usually most appropriate.

---

[2] Retrieved on 3 November 2017, from https://www.skillsyouneed.com/ps/self-control.html

As a general rule, people who want or need your empathy do not just need you to understand them (cognitive empathy); they certainly do not need you just to feel their pain or, worse, to burst into tears alongside them (emotional empathy). Instead, they need you to understand and sympathise with what they are going through and, crucially, either take, or help them to take, action to resolve the problem, which is *compassionate empathy*.

Finding the Balance

Cognitive empathy can often be considered *under-emotional*. It involves insufficient feeling and, therefore, perhaps too much logical analysis. It may be perceived as an unsympathetic response by those in distress. Emotional empathy, by contrast, is *over-emotional*.

Too much emotion or feeling can be unhelpful. Feeling strong emotions, especially distress, takes us back to childhood. More or less by definition, that makes us less able to cope, and certainly less able to think and apply reason to the situation. It is very hard to help anyone else if you are overcome by your own emotions. Therefore, in exercising compassionate empathy, we can find the right balance between logic and emotion.

We can feel another person's pain, as if it was happening to us, and, therefore, express the appropriate amount of sympathy. At the same time, we can also remain in control of our own emotions and apply reason to the situation. This means that we can make better decisions and provide appropriate support to them when and where it is necessary.

USING EMPATHY EFFECTIVELY

Put aside your viewpoint, and try to see things from the other person's point of view: When you do this, you will realise that other people most likely are not being evil, unkind, stubborn or unreasonable—they are probably just reacting to the situation with the knowledge they have.

Validate the other person's perspective: Once you 'see' why others believe what they believe, acknowledge it. Remember: acknowledgement does not always equal agreement. You can accept that people have different opinions from your own, and that they may have good reason to hold those opinions.

Examine your attitude: Are you more concerned with getting your way, winning or being right? Or is your priority to find a solution, build relationships and accept others? Without an open mind and attitude, you probably would not have enough room for empathy.

Listen: Listen to the entire message that the other person is trying to communicate. Listen with your ears—what is being said and what tone is being used? Listen with your eyes—what is the person doing with her body while speaking? Listen with your instincts—do you sense that the person is not communicating something important? Listen with your heart—what do you think the other person feels?

Ask what the other person would do: When in doubt, check up with the person about her position. This is probably the simplest, and most direct, way to understand the other person. However, it's probably the least used way to develop empathy.

Practise these skills when you interact with people. You will likely appear much more caring and approachable—simply because you increase your interest in what others think, feel and experience. It is a great gift to be willing and able to see the world from a variety of perspectives—and it is a gift that you can use all of the time in any situation.

SUGGESTED GUIDELINES FOR CONDUCTING THE SESSION

Before you take up Exercise 1, the Empathy Quotient (EQ) Test, for the participants, you may use the method of brainstorming for eliciting responses on the participants' understanding of the concept of empathy. However, it is suggested that while you may give a general overview of the concept to the group and how it is relevant to our life, you should not elaborate, taking care that the discussion does not influence their responses to the EQ test.

After they have completed the EQ test and done the scoring, you may distribute the Handout 1 to the participants that catalogues definitions of empathy by eminent psychologists. Now you may give further elaboration on these definitions, responding to their questions and clarifying their doubts.

Now is the time to return to the EQ test. You may now invite those participants who may wish to share their scores of the EQ test. As some of them come forward to share their scores and the interpretations, they may have some queries on the statements included in the test. It is, therefore, suggested that you should go through every statement in the test so that you are fully prepared for this discussion.

Before you take up Exercise 2, you may make another presentation on other aspects of empathy that have been discussed in the trainer's notes—elements of empathy, types of empathy and using empathy effectively. You may plan another presentation on other aspects of empathy or you may defer it until after the completion of Exercise 2.

EXERCISE 1

EMPATHY QUOTIENT (EQ) TEST

Objective

At the end of the exercise, the participants will be able to:

- Find out about their empathetic skills or profile

Time allocation

About 1 ½ hours

Material required

Training aids and tools required for introducing the exercise and your inputs; flip charts and writing markers for displaying key points emerging out of the discussion based on the responses of the participants to the exercise; copies of EQ test worksheet and the handout on scoring sheet and interpretation for the exercise (one for each participant); white board and markers.

Steps in conducting the exercise

- Introduce the exercise and ask the participants to follow the instructions for giving their responses to the statements in the test
- Distribute copies of the worksheet and inform the group that time allocation for completing the test is about 45 minutes
- After all participants have completed the worksheets, distribute the scoring and interpretation sheet and ask them to calculate their scores

- Inform the participants that discussion on the results of the test and the statement will be taken up later after other presentations
- Sum up and close the exercise

EMPATHY QUOTIENT TEST WORKSHEET

The EQ is intended to measure how easily you pick up on other people's feelings and how strongly you are affected by other people's feelings.
(*Source:* Scott)

Please read each of the 60 following statements very carefully and rate how strongly you agree or disagree with them by circling your answer. Some of the statements may refer to others' opinions about you. In such cases, you reflect, make a quick self-appraisal and give your response.

There are no right or wrong answers or trick questions.

Take the Test

1. I can easily tell if someone else wants to enter a conversation.	Strongly agree	Slightly agree	Slightly disagree	Strongly disagree
2. I prefer animals to humans.	Strongly agree	Slightly agree	Slightly disagree	Strongly disagree
3. I try to keep up with the current trends and fashions.	Strongly agree	Slightly agree	Slightly disagree	Strongly disagree
4. I find it difficult to explain to others things that I understand easily, when they don't understand it first time.	Strongly agree	Slightly agree	Slightly disagree	Strongly disagree
5. I dream most nights.	Strongly agree	Slightly agree	Slightly disagree	Strongly disagree
6. I really enjoy caring for other people.	Strongly agree	Slightly agree	Slightly disagree	Strongly disagree
7. I try to solve my own problems rather than discussing them with others.	Strongly agree	Slightly agree	Slightly disagree	Strongly disagree
8. I find it hard to know what to do in a social situation.	Strongly agree	Slightly agree	Slightly disagree	Strongly disagree
9. I am at my best first thing in the morning.	Strongly agree	Slightly agree	Slightly disagree	Strongly disagree

(*continued*)

(*continued*)

10.	People often tell me that I go too far in driving my point home in a discussion.	Strongly agree	Slightly agree	Slightly disagree	Strongly disagree
11.	It doesn't bother me too much if I am late meeting a friend.	Strongly agree	Slightly agree	Slightly disagree	Strongly disagree
12.	Friendships and relationships are just too difficult, so I tend not to bother with them.	Strongly agree	Slightly agree	Slightly disagree	Strongly disagree
13.	I would never break a law, no matter how minor.	Strongly agree	Slightly agree	Slightly disagree	Strongly disagree
14.	I often find it difficult to judge if someone is rude or polite.	Strongly agree	Slightly agree	Slightly disagree	Strongly disagree
15.	In a conversation, I tend to focus on my own thoughts, rather than on what my listener might be thinking.	Strongly agree	Slightly agree	Slightly disagree	Strongly disagree
16.	I prefer practical jokes to verbal humour.	Strongly agree	Slightly agree	Slightly disagree	Strongly disagree
17.	I live life for today rather than the future.	Strongly agree	Slightly agree	Slightly disagree	Strongly disagree
18.	When I was a child, I enjoyed cutting up worms to see what would happen.	Strongly agree	Slightly agree	Slightly disagree	Strongly disagree
19.	I can pick up quickly if someone says one thing but means another.	Strongly agree	Slightly agree	Slightly disagree	Strongly disagree
20.	I tend to have very strong opinions about morality.	Strongly agree	Slightly agree	Slightly disagree	Strongly disagree
21.	It is hard for me to see why some things upset people so much.	Strongly agree	Slightly agree	Slightly disagree	Strongly disagree
22.	I find it easy to put myself in somebody else's shoes.	Strongly agree	Slightly agree	Slightly disagree	Strongly disagree
23.	I think that good manners are the most important thing a parent can teach their child.	Strongly agree	Slightly agree	Slightly disagree	Strongly disagree
24.	I like to do things on the spur of the moment.	Strongly agree	Slightly agree	Slightly disagree	Strongly disagree

25. I am good at predicting how someone will feel.	Strongly agree	Slightly agree	Slightly disagree	Strongly disagree
26. I am quick to spot when someone in a group is feeling awkward or uncomfortable.	Strongly agree	Slightly agree	Slightly disagree	Strongly disagree
27. If I say something that someone else is offended by, I think that that's his or her problem, not mine.	Strongly agree	Slightly agree	Slightly disagree	Strongly disagree
28. If anyone asked me if I liked their haircut, I would reply truthfully, even if I didn't like it.	Strongly agree	Slightly agree	Slightly disagree	Strongly disagree
29. I can't always see why someone should have felt offended by a remark.	Strongly agree	Slightly agree	Slightly disagree	Strongly disagree
30. People often tell me that I am very unpredictable.	Strongly agree	Slightly agree	Slightly disagree	Strongly disagree
31. I enjoy being the centre of attention at any social gathering.	Strongly agree	Slightly agree	Slightly disagree	Strongly disagree
32. Seeing people cry doesn't really upset me.	Strongly agree	Slightly agree	Slightly disagree	Strongly disagree
33. I enjoy having discussions about politics.	Strongly agree	Slightly agree	Slightly disagree	Strongly disagree
34. I am very blunt, which some people take to be rudeness, even though this is unintentional.	Strongly agree	Slightly agree	Slightly disagree	Strongly disagree
35. I don't tend to find social situations confusing.	Strongly agree	Slightly agree	Slightly disagree	Strongly disagree
36. Other people tell me I am good at understanding how they are feeling and what they are thinking.	Strongly agree	Slightly agree	Slightly disagree	Strongly disagree
37. When I talk to people, I tend to talk about their experiences rather than my own.	Strongly agree	Slightly agree	Slightly disagree	Strongly disagree
38. It upsets me to see an animal in pain.	Strongly agree	Slightly agree	Slightly disagree	Strongly disagree
39. I am able to take decisions without being influenced by people's feelings.	Strongly agree	Slightly agree	Slightly disagree	Strongly disagree

(*continued*)

(*continued*)

40. I can't relax until I have done everything I had planned to do that day.	Strongly agree	Slightly agree	Slightly disagree	Strongly disagree
41. I can easily tell if someone else is interested or bored with what I am saying.	Strongly agree	Slightly agree	Slightly disagree	Strongly disagree
42. I get upset if I see people suffering on news (TV) programmes.	Strongly agree	Slightly agree	Slightly disagree	Strongly disagree
43. Friends usually talk to me about their problems as they say that I am very understanding.	Strongly agree	Slightly agree	Slightly disagree	Strongly disagree
44. I can sense if I am intruding, even if the other person doesn't tell me.	Strongly agree	Slightly agree	Slightly disagree	Strongly disagree
45. I often start new hobbies but quickly become bored with them and move on to something else.	Strongly agree	Slightly agree	Slightly disagree	Strongly disagree
46. People sometimes tell me that I have gone too far with teasing.	Strongly agree	Slightly agree	Slightly disagree	Strongly disagree
47. I would be too nervous to go for a ride on a big roller coaster.	Strongly agree	Slightly agree	Slightly disagree	Strongly disagree
48. Other people often say that I am insensitive, though I don't always see why.	Strongly agree	Slightly agree	Slightly disagree	Strongly disagree
49. If I see a stranger in a group, I think that it is up to them to make an effort to join in.	Strongly agree	Slightly agree	Slightly disagree	Strongly disagree
50. I usually stay emotionally detached when watching a film.	Strongly agree	Slightly agree	Slightly disagree	Strongly disagree
51. I like to be very organised in day-to-day life and often make lists of the chores I have to do.	Strongly agree	Slightly agree	Slightly disagree	Strongly disagree
52. I can tune into how someone else feels rapidly and intuitively.	Strongly agree	Slightly agree	Slightly disagree	Strongly disagree
53. I don't like to take risks.	Strongly agree	Slightly agree	Slightly disagree	Strongly disagree
54. I can easily work out what another person might want to talk about.	Strongly agree	Slightly agree	Slightly disagree	Strongly disagree

55. I can tell if someone is masking his or her true emotions.	Strongly agree	Slightly agree	Slightly disagree	Strongly disagree
56. Before making a decision, I always weigh up the pros and cons.	Strongly agree	Slightly agree	Slightly disagree	Strongly disagree
57. I don't consciously work out the rules of social situations.	Strongly agree	Slightly agree	Slightly disagree	Strongly disagree
58. I am good at predicting what someone will do.	Strongly agree	Slightly agree	Slightly disagree	Strongly disagree
59. I tend to get emotionally involved with a friend's problems.	Strongly agree	Slightly agree	Slightly disagree	Strongly disagree
60. I can usually appreciate the other person's viewpoint, even if I don't agree with it.	Strongly agree	Slightly agree	Slightly disagree	Strongly disagree

SCORING AND INTERPRETATION SHEET

How to work out your EQ score:

Score two points for each of the following items if you answered 'strongly agree' or one point if you answered 'slightly agree': 1, 6, 19, 22, 25, 26, 35, 36, 37, 38, 41, 42, 43, 44, 52, 54, 55, 57, 58, 59, 60.

Score two points for each of the following items if you answered 'strongly disagree' or one point if you answered 'slightly disagree': 4, 8, 10, 11, 12, 14, 15, 18, 21, 27, 28, 29, 32, 34, 39, 46, 48, 49, 50.

All other questions are not scored.

Add up your scores for both sets of questions

What your score means

0–32 = You have a lower than average ability for understanding how other people feel and responding appropriately.

33–52 = You have an average ability for understanding how other people feel and responding appropriately. You know how to treat people with care and sensitivity.

53–63 = You have an above average ability for understanding how other people feel and responding appropriately. You know how to treat people with care and sensitivity.

64–80 = You have a very high ability for understanding how other people feel and responding appropriately. You know how to treat people with care and sensitivity.

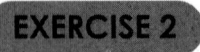

EXERCISE 2

DEVELOPING EMPATHETIC SKILLS

Objectives

At the end of the exercise, the participants will be able to:

- Enhance their understanding of empathy
- Learn the five skills to develop empathy

Time allocation

1 ½ hours

Materials required

Training aids and tools required for explaining the topic as part of your introductory talk and for summing-up; copies of Handouts I and IA; flip charts and writing markers for displaying participants' responses; white board and markers.

Steps in conducting the exercise

- Recall your discussion on empathy and brief the group about the exercise
- Elaborate on the five skills (also the steps) that are essential part of empathetic behaviour:

    Watch and listen—verbal communication; more importantly body language; how is the person feeling; words matching body language; what are the words saying?

    Remember—when in the past you felt the same way? When did something like this happen to you?

    Imagine—imagine how you might feel the same way in the situation. Validate the wide range of emotions that come up, for example, I felt like crying; I was embarrassed

Ask—Ask how the person is feeling; are you ok? What happened to you? How do you feel? How are you doing?

Show you care—Through words and actions; I am sorry you are feeling that way. Encourage them. How can I help? Let us get help. I am here for you.

- Invite two participants to volunteer—one to play a person who is going through a problem and the other to show empathetic behaviour—to demonstrate all the skills or steps necessary for empathetic behaviour. Give some time to the second volunteer to go through the Handout I and prepare for the role of an empathiser.
- Choose a situation or a scenario, relevant to the participants. For example, the boss ridiculed me in front of other colleagues; or family or social relationship problems.
- Provide time for the role-play—15–20 minutes and give necessary instructions to other members of the group about what they have to observe and give feedback later.
- Assemble the group and ask the group members and the two volunteers: Did it happen the way it should have? Were all the skills used and in logical order?

HANDOUT FOR THE PARTICIPANTS I

Empathy Skill Development

Steps	Ways to help you (Skills) Understand how people feel Show someone you care	Purpose
1.	**Watch and listen** to the person	To know what happened to someone and observe feelings (see Feeling Column; Handout IA)
2.	**Remember** when you felt the same way or something similar happened to you	To check whether this experience or feeling has happened to you before
3.	**Imagine** how you might feel or felt during your experience	To know your own feelings

(continued)

(*continued*)

Steps	Ways to help you (Skills) *Understand how people feel* *Show someone you care*	Purpose
4.	**Ask** what the other person is feeling?	To understand (care) how someone else is feeling
5.	**Show you care**	To learn different ways to tell people that they are important, respected and valued
		Say: What happened? Are you okay? Do you want to talk about it?
		Do something: To show that you care about that person

Source: Project Happiness (Adapted from *Understand and care* by Cheri Meiners, Free Spirit Publishing).

HANDOUT FOR THE PARTICIPANTS IA

Feelings Column

Happy Feelings	**Sad Feelings**
Content	Hurt
Excited	Disappointed
Good	Down
Joyful	Lonely
Pleasant	Sorry
Proud	Unhappy

Angry Feelings	**Other Feelings**
Furious	Confused
Grumpy	Worried
Mad	Frustrated
Mean	Impatient
Revenge	Jealous
Upset	Delighted

Module 9

Problem-solving and Decision-making

This module deals with different aspects of problem-solving and decision-making—in groups and as individuals. The aim is to help the participants get fully familiar with the factors, processes and the dynamics involved in decision-making and the process of problem-solving.

Specifically, this module focuses on the following areas:

- Understanding decision-making
- Understanding problem-solving
- Process of problem-solving and decision-making
- Decision-making methods
- Steps in problem-solving and decision-making
- Participatory decision-making—core values
- Individual decision-making
- Factors that influence individual decision-making
- Individual decision-making under stress—strategies

Expected Outcomes from the Module

At the end of the session on the module, the participants will be able to:

- Understand the dynamics of problem-solving and decision-making
- List the steps that one follows in problem-solving and decision-making
- Get fully acquainted with the factors that influence individual decision-making

UNDERSTANDING DECISION-MAKING

Decision-making can be understood to be a process by which members of a group arrive at a decision, judgement or conclusion through a process of deliberation. It is one of the most critical applications for the performance of the group.

Decision-making should be considered as means rather than an end in itself. It is a process that leads to action for achieving some desired results. Thus, decisions are responses to problems and issues, based on your ability and opening up new opportunities.

Every decision is the outcome of an active process influenced by many forces. Thus, decision-making is the progression of thought, analysis and deliberation that results in certain course of action and accomplishments. The quality of the decision depends on the process and the assessment of the incriminating forces that are at play not only at the time of decision-making but they also influence its implementation. Thus, the value of the decision is to be assessed not only in terms of the soundness of the decision in 'here and now' situation but also in the context of its implementation potential. The question that needs to be asked is 'Is it a realistic decision capable of being implemented and producing desired results?'

Decision-making is not a fixed procedure, but it is a sequential process. In most situations where decisions are required, we may go through a number of stages that help us think through the problem and develop alternate strategies. The stages do not follow a predetermined or rigid pattern and are specific to a particular problem or issue. The importance of these stages lies in our ability to structure the process in a meaningful way. The process also depends on the nature and complexity of the problem, availability of time and mental skills of the decision-makers. The critical point is that decision-making is more than an act of choosing; it is a dynamic process.

Some decisions are very complex and require not only large amount of information but also in-depth deliberations and analysis. Several options may be considered before a final decision is taken. On the other hand, there are decisions that are relatively simpler. The group may only be faced with the task of deciding whether a proposal is to be accepted or rejected. In such cases, the choice is limited to the option that is placed before the group. Its task is cut out in discussing the pros and cons of the implementation of the proposal.

UNDERSTANDING PROBLEM-SOLVING

We come across numerous problems routinely in our life and we resolve many of them without giving much thought or making a special effort. We tend to pass some others, as they do not affect us. There are problems that we face in our family life, in our relationships, physical health or in choosing or pursuing an academic course or career.

However, there are times when we find ourselves confronted by problems that defy solution or have the potential of testing our skills to the limit. In such situations, we have two options. The first thing we attempt to find out is to what extent the problem impacts us. In case we realise that the problem does not affect our life immediately, we can be persuaded to ignore the problem or defer it to a later date when we will be in a better position to address it. On the other hand, if we find that the problem has the potential of affecting us in a major way—physically, emotionally, socially or financially—we are constrained to take action soon enough to ensure that there are no damaging consequences for us. In such cases, we have no choice but to take it head-on.

We are drawn into an active process of problem-solving when we are confronted by a problem that we find difficult to resolve. As mentioned earlier, we will resort to this course of action only when we recognise that the problem is important for us and finding solution to it is imperative. We are aware that we will ignore the problem only at our own peril.

PROCESS OF PROBLEM-SOLVING AND DECISION-MAKING

(Note: We all are well aware that problem-solving is closely linked to decision-making and there are a lot of common elements in the two processes. Therefore, to avoid overlap, we will discuss the processes together indicating specific distinguishing aspects, where necessary.)

Problem-solving has its origin in the past. A problem is associated with a situation, an issue or a person suggesting that something that has gone wrong in the past and must be managed in the present with an eye on the future of the group. It is more precise and objective than decision-making. Decision-making, on the other hand, is rooted in the present with a look into the future for resolution.

A decision is a commitment to a course of action selected from several alternatives. In problem-solving as well, there may be situations when we are faced with several possible solutions to a problem and we need to decide on the most effective course of action. We have to take the best option and this is a crucial decision. Thus, we go into the process of decision-making. Here the problem-solving and decision-making seem to be merging with each other.

When we are faced with a situation or a problem where taking timely and appropriate decision is imperative, we look back at our experience and examine how we have faced similar situations earlier and what decisions we took on those occasions. These past experiences provide us some norms and procedures that we can use for finding solution to the problem and taking a decision. In addition to our own prior experience, these norms may be drawn from the family, our social or professional groups, or derived by observing people who are close to us. All these can provide us some clues and guidelines. Therefore, in many cases, such decisions are made without expending much time. There is something routine, repetitive or predictable about this decision-making as we are inclined to follow some standard procedures and take a tried course of action. These may be termed as programmed decisions.

However, when the problem is not of a routine nature and contains elements that we have not earlier confronted or if it is complex and extremely important, it requires a different or perhaps, a unique solution. Thus, non-programmed decisions are for novel and unstructured problems. And this requires creative problem-solving. Coping with non-programmable decisions is a formidable task, regardless of the stage of life we are in. It is, however, open to us to seek the help of persons on whom we have confidence, including family members and peers.

DECISION-MAKING METHODS

Decision by Authority

There are occasions when the leader of the team or group takes a unilateral decision, using the power and authority vested in her. In such cases, she is totally accountable for the decision. Unless there is complete trust in the leader, it is likely that such decisions do not get full acceptance of other members of the group and they may not cooperate in implementing it. In worst-case scenario, the disgruntled members may even resort to creating conditions for its failure. Such decisions can generate discontent that may simmer and affect the harmony and functioning of the group. It can also lead to intra-group conflicts.

Decision by Minority

There are situations when a small group of members of the decision-making group exert their influence over the majority of the group. This may be considered appropriate if these few members are experts on the issues that are central to the problem or have more stakes than others. If not properly handled, this method may create resentment and hostility among members if there is a perception that this strong-willed and vocal minority is not allowing others to participate in the decision-making process or are suppressing opposition to their point of view.

The Democratic Process

This is perhaps the most popular method because it is based on democratic principles—respect for the viewpoints of all and dignity of individuals. The decision is the outcome of active discussion and participation by most members of the decision-making group and there is a general feeling that they had the opportunity to present their views and the decision is based on collective wisdom of all members.

Decision by Consensus

Consensus can be understood as a process of group decision-making, whereby the entire group can come to an agreed and collective decision on a position on an issue or solution to a problem. The input and ideas of all participants are gathered and synthesised to arrive at a final decision acceptable to all. Through consensus, we are not only working to achieve better solutions but also creating greater commitment and ensuring better implementation. Every member is accountable not only to the group but also to herself. It also promotes group harmony and cohesion. However, for this method to succeed the prerequisites are as follows: conducive environment within the group, mutual trust and commitment to work through the process. The flip side of this method is that, in some cases, the decision arrived at through consensus may not be the 'best' decision.

STEPS IN PROBLEM-SOLVING AND DECISION-MAKING

Before you launch yourself in the process of problem-solving, you may attempt to seek answers to the following questions:

- What are the stakes for the group as a whole and members individually?
- If the group is not in a position to resolve the problem, what are the likely consequences of it?
- What is the gravity of the problem?
- How it affects the group and members, and what are the aspects that are likely to be most affected?
- Is it a short-term problem or can have long-term repercussions?

Once these replies are collated and analysed, you are ready to initiate the process of decision-making and problem-solving. You may consider the following steps that are common to both the processes.

Willingness to Engage in the Process

The first step, obviously, is that members of the formal or informal group (or the concerned individuals) recognise that a problem or an issue exists and express their willingness to engage in the process of finding solution to the difficulty or taking a decision on the issue or the matter on the table. The group should be willing to devote time and effort to arrive at a solution or decision. It is important that you approach the decision-making process with a positive attitude and confidence, and view the situation as an opportunity and a challenge. You should be convinced that there is a solution to the problem and with a little hard work, you will be able to find one or take the decision that is in the best interest of the group. You should have faith in your ability.

Setting the Criteria and Establishing Framework

The group must set out the criteria and establish the broad framework within which the decision will be taken or the solution to the problem explored. This means boundary spanning and identifying the limiting factors—resources, time factor, etc. This provides the basis for the exercise. This will also help the group members to be more constructive and rational in presenting their viewpoints and making suggestions. Thus, the decision will be more realistic and practical.

Defining the Problem and Analysing it

The process of problem-solving or decision-making begins when you recognise the problem and define it in a manner that will facilitate the process. If problem is not identified clearly and properly, problem-solving or decision-making may become an ineffective exercise and, therefore, the action that follows will be unproductive. It is, therefore, of prime importance that you get fully familiar with the details that are necessary for finding the solution or taking a decision. Problem identification, though, is not easy. It is not unusual for people to be unsure of the problem. They may have vague idea about it but may not be clear about the specifics or pinpoint exactly the nature and dimensions of the problem. Sometimes, we may be tempted to regard the manifestations or symptoms as the problem. Therefore, what is perceived as the cause of a problem or the problem itself may actually be only a symptom. So we start on a wrong foot.

Sometimes, things seem obvious, but it is important that you gather as much information as possible about the problem, and make sure that the problem you are trying to solve is the 'real' problem. It is also likely that you persuade yourself to define the problem in a manner that you find easy to deal with. In such cases, you may be focusing on a problem that is not the 'real' problem. It is a check-step to ensure that you do not answer a side issue or only solve the part of the problem that you find convenient or expedient to solve.

If the problem appears to be complex and overwhelming, you must break it down to smaller parts for better understanding of different aspects of it and of the issues involved. You may end up having not one but several related problems. This will ensure that your response answers the right problem. If you discover that you are looking at several related problems, then prioritise which ones you should address first.

In most cases, it may be advisable to check your understanding of the problem with those who either have knowledge of similar situations or are part of the decision-making exercise. So we start with a common understanding of the problem and there is less chance of us going wrong.

It is amazing how much we do not know about what we do not know. Therefore, in this phase, it is critical to get input from other people who have either knowledge of the problem or are the affected persons.

Generating Options

Once the problem is defined and you have thorough knowledge of the environment into which the decision or the solution must fit, it is time to generate a number of possible options. The persons involved in the exercise should brainstorm all solutions or alternatives, regardless of their merit or feasibility. If we can suspend judgement or evaluation (of the ideas or suggestions) for the time being, the members of the decision-making group may be encouraged to be more creative and innovative. As a result, we may get a thorough list of options from which we will choose the best one. Very often, an idea, which would have been discarded or ignored immediately, when evaluated properly, can be developed into a superb solution. At this stage, you should not prejudge any potential solutions but should treat each idea as a new idea in its own right and worthy of consideration. Screening can be done later.

During this stage, you should ask yourself, 'What have I done in this situation in the past, and how well has that worked?' If you find that what you have done in the past has not been as effective as you would like, it would be useful to generate some other solutions that may work better. Even if your action or behaviour in the past has worked like you wanted it to, you should think of other solutions as well, because you may come up with an even better idea. When you start to think of possible solutions, do not limit yourself. Think of as many possible options as you can, even if they seem unrealistic. You can always reject implausible ideas later.

Evaluating the Options and Making the Decision

Now you are ready to narrow down some of the options that you have generated in the previous step. You can sort out which are most relevant to your situation and which are realistic and manageable. It is important that you examine each of the options and consider its strengths and weaknesses, and assess potential consequences of each option, if implemented. You should also consider the likelihood that each option has in terms of your being able to achieve the goals that you set for yourself in the context of finding the solution. As you start to narrow down your choices, remember no solution to a problem is perfect and all will have drawbacks, but you have to choose the one that appears to be most workable and credible. You still have the option of revising the solution if it does not work the way you want it to. Specifically, you may examine the following:

- Weigh the limiting factors of each of the desirable options.
- Draw up a comparative statement for the options with regard to their feasibility and against the other criteria set out by you before the exercise.
- Identify the risk factor that each option carries in the event of its implementation.

Implementing the Decision

Implementation is a crucial part of the decision-making process. Once a decision is arrived at or solution is chosen, it should be shared with those who are likely to be associated with its implementation or affected by it. You must, however, make sure that when you are ready to implement this solution, you and all others are wholeheartedly committed to the task and are willing to give their best. If some preparatory work is required for its implementation, you should be ready to put in the necessary efforts. Also, make sure that all the resources—human, time and finances, if any—required for its implementation are in place before you undertake its implementation. It will be useful to draw a schedule for action. Assign responsibilities and set up a mechanism for continuing monitoring, accountability and feedback.

Monitoring Implementation of the Plan or the Decision

During this stage, you should continue to examine the chosen solution and the degree to which it is 'solving' the problem. If you find that the solution is too hard to implement or it is just not working, revise it, modify it or try something else. Trying to solve a problem is not always an easy task and, sometimes, it may take several solutions before something works. But, do not give up hope, because with perseverance and your best effort, many difficult decisions and solutions can be effectively implemented.

Evaluating the Decision

The main function of the follow-up is to determine whether or not the problem has been resolved. Just because you have worked your way through the problem-solving process, it does not mean that by implementing the possible solution, you automatically solve your problem. So evaluating the effectiveness of your solution is very important. You can refer to the following questions:

- How effective was that solution?
- Did it achieve what we wanted?
- What consequences did it have on the pre-decision situation?

If the solution was successful in helping you solve your problem and reach your goal, then you know that you have effectively solved it. If you feel dissatisfied with the result, then you can begin the steps again. Look for more alternatives. Viewing problem-solving as a cycle may help you recognise that it is a way of searching for a solution. If you have solved the problem, you have found an effective solution.

PARTICIPATORY DECISION-MAKING—CORE VALUES

In any discussion that involves decision-making that may have far-reaching impact on the life of the people represented in the group taking decisions, there are some core values that must be recognised by all those participating in the discussion.

Full Participation

The participants are encouraged to speak up and say what is in their minds. They are willing to raise difficult and even controversial issues without a fear of rebuttal. They learn how to share their ideas even when they are not fully convinced about their relevance and usefulness to the group. As a result, the group becomes more functional, more adept at discovering and acknowledging the diversity of opinions and backgrounds inherent in it.

On the other hand, in a typical group that does not encourage participation of all members, self-expression is generally constrained. People are reluctant to share views or opinions that may be considered as irrelevant or inappropriate in the group. In such groups, the most highly regarded comments are those that are precise and articulated in clear words and in the most polished manner. Thinking out loud is treated with impatience; people get annoyed with those whose remarks are considered vague or poorly stated. This discourages free expression and participants carefully evaluate their thoughts before expressing them. There is no spontaneity in discussion. This self-imposed censorship reduces the quantity and quality of participation overall. A few people end up doing almost all the talking, repeating themselves over and over again. As a result, in many groups, the views of these few people dominate those of others and are deemed to be the views and opinions of the entire group, when the reality is otherwise.

Even in a participatory decision-making group, if some members take well-known positions and express easily comprehensible and familiar views, a workable decision may be quickly reached and the process of decision-making may be swift. However, when a group is struggling for a workable solution to the problem, a participatory group will open up the process and encourage more divergent thinking. What does it look like in action? It looks like participants making 'out-of-box' or unusual suggestions that stimulate the thinking process and encourage others to come up with new, innovative thoughts. An environment is created in which people feel free to state half-formed thoughts that express unconventional, but, perhaps, valuable perspectives. Participants are willing to take risks and bring out controversial or contentious issues. And it looks like a group where participants encourage one another to do all these things.

Mutual Understanding

In order to reach a sustainable agreement, the members of the group need to understand and acknowledge the legitimacy and value of one another's needs, views and goals. This basic sense of acceptance and appreciation is what creates an environment in the group that helps in developing innovative ideas that incorporate everyone's points of view.

In a normal discussion, persuasion is much more common than mutual understanding. The views of the 'other side' are dissected point by point for the purpose of refuting them. Little effort, if any, is put into understanding the meaning and substance of the views and discovering the deeper reasons for actions and behaviour of others. Even when it appears unlikely that persuasion will change anyone's mind, some participants may continue to press home their points, hoping that their reiteration will enhance the possibility of their acceptance by the group. They start believing that their expression and style are central to the discussion. In such situations, many participants may even stop listening to each other, except to prepare for a rebuttal.

The process involved in building a shared framework of understanding means taking the time to understand everyone's perspective in order to find the best idea. To build that framework, participants spend time and effort questioning each other, getting to know one another and learning from each other. They are willing to put themselves in each other's shoes. The process is laced with intermittent discomfort; some periods are tense, some stifling; but the group persists and does not give up. Over time, many people gain insights into their own positions and viewpoints on the issues under discussion. They may discover that their perspectives are based on inaccurate or inadequate information; their thoughts are outdated or irrelevant to the discussion or driven by their biases or stereotypes about the 'other side' or they are only fulfilling their own agenda and not that of the group. And through this process of self-reflection and an attempt to get insights into their actions, behaviour or verbal communication, the participants may get into a mode of promoting better understanding of one another and feel convinced that most of them are working towards achieving a mutual goal.

Inclusive Solutions

Inclusive solutions are not compromises but they emerge from the integration of everybody's perspectives, views and opinions. Typically, an inclusive solution may involve the discovery of an entirely new option acceptable to the group members. In many cases, inclusive solutions are not obvious. They are the result of persistent and sincere efforts of the participants. As they learn more about each other's perspectives, they become progressively more capable to integrate their goals and needs with those of others in the group. This leads to innovative, original thinking.

These are solutions that take on board the views of not only the most articulate and influential members of the group but also of the shy, the disenfranchised and the weak. All the participants leave the discussion with a feeling that they have also made their contribution in arriving at the solution of the problem or in deciding upon a course of action. Everyone feels that her views are reflected in the final outcome of the discussion.

On the other hand, in groups where participation is not emphasised, discussions seldom result in inclusive solutions. More commonly, the more articulate will present their views forcefully and the discussion may just centre round these views. Participants will form and give opinions for or against these views. Everyone expects that one side will get what they want and the other side will not. This may ultimately lead to disenchant-ment of, at least, some of the participants. In such situations, other views and opinions are often not even expressed. In cases where there are disa-greements, it is expected that the person who has the most authority will resolve them. Some groups settle their differences by majority vote, but the effect is similar. In either case, it is likely that the final decision may exclude the views, needs and goals of the minority.

Shared Responsibility

In participatory group decision-making, members feel a strong sense of responsibility not only for creating and developing sustainable agreements but also for their sincere and effective implementation. They develop a sense of purpose in the entire process and, therefore, make every effort to give and receive inputs before final decisions are taken. They also recognise the need for ensuring that the proposals or decisions they have endorsed are fully implemented. They feel accountable not only to the group and other members but to themselves also and are willing to face consequences of their decisions. This contrasts sharply with situations in some other groups where all members of the group suffer the consequences for the decisions made by a few influential participants.

The operational value in a business-as-usual discussion is dependent on leadership it is not a shared responsibility. The person-in-charge or the leader is expected to run the discussion, set ground rules, monitor its progress and generally take full responsibility for all aspects of the process of decision-making. If there are doubts or questions, they are either not encouraged or, if expressed, are dealt with as a matter of routine business and not with any seriousness. There is an overwhelming desire to move on and complete the business.

In order for an agreement to be sustainable, it needs everyone's support. Understanding this principle leads everyone to take personal responsibility for making sure they are satisfied with the proposed course of action. Every member of the group, in other words, recognises that she is an owner of the outcome and has equal stakes in implementing it. Thus, members voice objections even when doing so will delay the group from reaching a decision. Moreover, the commitment to share responsibility is evident throughout the process: in the design of the agenda, in the willingness to discuss and co-create the procedures they will follow, and in the overall expectation that everyone will accept and take responsibility for making their meetings work.

INDIVIDUAL DECISION-MAKING

Regardless of what stage of life or situation an individual is in, she is often called upon to take decisions in personal life. This is, in fact, an important part of life and as it becomes more complex and one is faced with diverse situations and difficult options, decision-making acquires more crucial significance.

There are some decisions that do not pose any dilemma or encounter any problem and can be taken by an individual without any constraint or delay. In fact, sometimes, we take decisions without actively engaging our mind. These are simple and straightforward decisions. There are also situations when decision-making becomes relatively easy because our choices are limited or circumstances help us in the process.

On the other hand, there are certain decisions that involve considerable mental and emotional application. We have to take into account or consider a number of incriminating or associative factors, elements or situations before taking a decision. Such choices have the potential of creating certain degree of stress or anxiety in an individual, depending on the level of risk involved in translating a particular decision into action or its likely consequences. Decision-making becomes more difficult if it requires us to come out of the existing comfort zone—in terms of our life or relationship with people around us. And that is the big dilemma.

There are decisions that have immediate or short-term relevance but there are others that have far-reaching impact on the life of an individual. This forces us to be cautious and judicious. In such situations, we may land ourselves in a big predicament. We may not be able to determine what option to take. Sometimes, we postpone decision-making that may result in further aggravating the situation or making it more difficult to take decision later. However, there are situations when we leave the decision-making to the circumstances or the situation itself, taking a back seat or adopting a laid-back attitude and watch things unfold. There is a lurking hope that the situation will take its own course and take the decision for us.

FACTORS THAT INFLUENCE INDIVIDUAL DECISION-MAKING

Decision-makers are influenced by many forces, operating at the conscious and subconscious levels. While some of them may be termed as psychological factors or personality traits, there are other elements that can play a significant role in certain situations and in some specific areas of decision-making. For instance, financial conditions, concern for relationship, concern for job, etc.

Several individual dissimilarities influence the decision-making process. Some of these differences influence only certain aspects of the process, while others affect the entire process. However, each may have an impact and, therefore, must be understood to appreciate fully individual decision-making as a process.

Values

In the context of decision-making, values are the guidelines that a person uses when confronted with a situation where choices must be made. The effect of values on the decision-making process is profound:

- In establishing objectives: it is necessary to make value judgements regarding the selection of opportunities and the assignment of priorities.
- In developing alternatives: it is necessary to make value judgements about the various possibilities.
- In choosing alternatives: the values of the decision-maker influence which alternative is chosen.
- In implementing decision: value judgements are necessary in choosing the means for implementation.
- In the evaluation and control phase: value judgements cannot be avoided when corrective action is taken.

Propensity for Risk

When we talk about our propensity for risk-taking in decision-making, we are indeed considering the level of risk involved in taking a particular course of action. In our day-to-day life, all of us take some degree of risk and many a time we do this without bothering to ponder over the extent of risk involved or the consequences of taking that decision. However, risk-taking assumes considerable significance or becomes a dominating factor in decision-making when the fallout or outcomes can be significantly harmful or even damaging.

Propensity for taking risk varies not only between people but also within an individual from situation to situation. It is common knowledge that some people are more predisposed to taking risk than others due to a number of family-related, social or psychological factors. Similarly, there are situations or time when a person is more ready to take risk than, perhaps, at other times. It depends on the likely fallout or pay-off of the decision. Our difficulties get further multiplied when we are about to enter uncharted territory; the outcomes of the course of action we are about to take are not clearly evident; or we are unsure even of our ability to carry the decision to its logical end.

Those with a fair degree of aptitude and preparedness to take risk or low aversion to it are inclined to establish different objectives, set out varied standards of evaluation and select different alternatives than those with high aversion to risk-taking. While being conscious of the possibility of failure or its likely disagreeable consequences, they attempt to focus more on positive aspects of their action. They convince themselves of the benefits of success rather than the harmful effects of failure. On the other hand, those with low propensity for risk tend to opt for decisions that provide them more security of action. Before taking decisions, they look for safeguards against the possible ill effects or insurance against failure.

Decision-makers vary greatly in their propensity for taking risks: the optimum decision-maker takes risks by assuming that the outcome will always be favourable. This one specific aspect of personality strongly influences the decision-making process.

A decision-maker who has a low aversion to risk establishes different objectives, evaluates alternatives differently and makes different choices than another decision-maker in the same situation who has a high aversion to risk. The latter attempts to make choices where the risk or uncertainty is low or where the certainty of the outcome is high. Many people are bolder and advocate greater risk-taking in groups than as individuals. Apparently, such people are more willing to accept shared risk as members of a group.

Personality

Decision-makers are influenced by many psychological forces, both conscious and subconscious. One of the most important of these forces is personality. Decision-makers' personalities are strongly reflected in the choices they make. The following are some of the variables:

- Personality variables include the attitudes, beliefs and needs of the individual
- Situation variables pertain to the external, observable situations in which individuals find themselves
- Interactional variables pertain to the momentary state of the individual as a result of the interaction of a specific situation with characteristics of the individual's personality

The most important conclusions concerning the influence of personality on the decision-making process are as follows:

- It is unlikely that one person is equally proficient in all aspects of the decision-making process. The results suggest that some people do better in one part of the process, while others do better in another part.
- Such characteristics as intelligence are associated with different phases of the decision-making process.
- The relation of the personality to the decision-making process may vary for different groups on the basis of such factors as sex and social status.

Potential for Dissonance

It is not unusual for many of us to take a decision and then start ruminating whether the decision was correct and appropriate. We may begin to harbour doubts and have second thoughts about the choice. Such anxiety is related to a lack of consistency or harmony among various aspects of an individual, such as attitudes, beliefs, values and so on, after a decision has been made. This can be described as post-decision anxiety or cognitive dissonance. For some of us, this misgiving or uneasiness may not last long and after some self-talk and self-convincing, the worry may dissipate and we may reconcile and feel comfortable with our decision. However, for some, this state of disquiet or of deep-seated concerns is likely to be more agonising when any of the following conditions exist:

- The decision is psychologically or financially important.
- There are a number of foregone alternatives.
- The foregone alternatives have many favourable features.

When dissonance occurs, people can reduce it by admitting that a mistake has been made. Unfortunately, many individuals are reluctant to admit that they have made wrong decisions. They are more likely to use any of the following methods to reduce their dissonance:

- Seek information that supports their decisions
- Selectively perceive (distort) information in a way that supports their decisions
- Adopt a less favourable view of the foregone alternatives
- Minimise the importance of the negative aspects of the decisions and exaggerate the importance of the positive aspects

While each of us may resort to some of these behaviours in our personal decision-making, at one time or the other, however, if we continue to engage in this behaviour, this can be emotionally harmful. It is, therefore, important that we guard against these tendencies.

Your Emotional and Physical Health

A key factor that plays a significant role in decision-making is your emotional and physical health. If we are not in the pink of our emotional health, the vision may get blurred and we are not in a position to take rational decision on a course of action. We may lose contact with ground realities. This can severely affect our ability to make the right choice and adversely cramp our decision-making ability.

Role Conflict

All of us play multiple roles in life depending on the responsibilities that we are expected to carry. Sometimes, these conflicts may arise because of divergent interests associated with these roles.

(Cross-reference: for more details, see Module 4 'Intrapersonal and Interpersonal Conflicts')

Conflicting Messages or Suggestions

In taking a decision, you may get suggestions and advice from people representing different points of view and interests. These suggestions can even be conflicting. These inconsistencies and conflict of interest can put you in a difficult position, depending on the nature of relationship you have with these people and the consideration you give to them individually or collectively.

Once you are aware of these discordant notes, you should organise yourself in a manner that leads to better role clarification and understanding of different messages being communicated to you. This will definitely enhance your decision-making competency.

(Cross-reference: for more details, see Module 4 'Intrapersonal and Interpersonal Conflicts')

INDIVIDUAL DECISION-MAKING UNDER STRESS—STRATEGIES

There are five ways we make decisions under stress. These are:

Ignore the Problem

- When faced with a decision under stress, the easiest thing to do is nothing. Individuals who ignore the problem are actually saying 'The risks are not serious if I don't take any corrective action'.
- **Consequences:** This causes the initial stress from the situation to subside and little or no stress will be caused by the problem. Their ability to achieve a low level of stress can lead to complacency, lowered performance and ignoring a serious safety risk.
- **Decision strategy used:** They may *minimise* problems, settling for shortcuts and deviations from established practices.

Minor Protective Action

- If the individual feels the risks are too high to ignore the problem, the next easiest thing to do is the absolute minimum. Individuals who use minor protective actions are actually saying 'I can't ignore the problem but the risks seem low if I select the most available alternative or protective action'.
- **Consequences:** This causes the stress to subside substantially. Something they failed to consider usually catches them by surprise.
- **Decision strategies used:** Individuals may continue to employ the first alternative that appears to solve the problem, without looking at all the alternatives (*muddle*). They may often consider only the minimum requirements (*minimise*). They also may look (*scan*) for just those things they think are important.

Avoid the Problem

- Avoidance happens when the individual realises they cannot ignore the problem and that the most available alternative may cause problems also. The individual knows that a better alternative is available, but chooses to avoid the problem to reduce stress. 'There may be a better way, but it is not realistic to hope that I will find it!' or 'I may not want to know the answer'.
- **Consequences:** Avoiding the problem reduces the stress but does nothing to solve the problem.
- **Decision strategies used:** Anything that stimulates anxiety or other painful feelings is avoided. The individual *denies* the problem exists. To reduce the stress further, individuals may *moralise*, blaming others and 'passing the buck' for their predicament.

Panic or Confusion

- If an individual can see that real danger is rapidly approaching and can see no route of escape, it is easy to assume that 'There does not appear to be sufficient time to solve the problem'.
- **Consequences:** Stress becomes so high the individual is unable to process information effectively. This may be evidenced by confusion, even with simple tasks, and panic in some situations.

- **Decision strategy used:** The individual *denies* the problem can be solved.

These four strategies for decision-making may be good when:

- We are busy and must ignore a problem?
- Doing the minimum allows us handle more important problems?
- Avoiding some problems lets us get on with more important things?

Making a *conscious* decision to solve a problem is good. When we do this, the questions asked above describe ways we can prioritise alternatives, not ways we cope.

Coping generally works at the *subconscious* level. We do not think about it. That is what makes these four ways risky. Subconsciously, we are trying to reduce the stress and not solve the problem.

Avoiding Ineffective Coping or Decision-making

To avoid these ineffective ways of coping make decisions a *conscious* process. When faced with a problem, keep the following in mind:

- Do not ignore any problem
- Select a course of action that meets the minimum requirements to work but can lead to bigger problems
- Regardless of how bad the situation looks there is always something you can do
- No matter how close the danger is, there is always time to do something

Vigilance

Vigilance is a *conscious* mental process that is alert to potential problems. It gives you the time and information needed to *optimise* decisions (the **Decide** model). Individuals who are vigilant have:

- A constant belief that sufficient time exists to solve the problem
- High confidence in ability to find a solution to the problem
- A number of alternatives to decide from based on careful search and appraisal
- Team members who remain vigilant and use the optimising strategy have the lowest potential for mishaps

Showing the Relationship Between Human Error Potential, Decision Strategies and the Ways We Cope

Coping pattern	Decision strategies	Error potential
Ignore	Minimise	High
Minor protective action	Muddle	Moderate high
	Moralise	Moderate low
Avoidance	Deny	High
	Moralise	Moderate high
Panic or confusion	Deny	High
Vigilance	Optimise	Low

Source: Team Coordination Training Student Guide (8/98).

SUGGESTED GUIDELINES FOR CONDUCTING THE SESSION

Two exercises have been suggested for this module. You may open the session with a brief interaction with the group through brainstorming exercise, inviting the participants to share their understanding of the processes of decision-making and problem-solving. This can be followed by a detailed presentation on process of decision-making and problem-solving, using appropriate training aids. Now the group is ready for the role-play.

For Exercise 1, you are expected to prepare a 'case situation' that will help the participants fully understand the processes of decision-making and problem-solving. It is, therefore, important that you prepare the case with necessary details that will ensure that all the key aspects of these two processes are fully brought out. The success of this exercise will, to a considerable extent, depend on how this case situation is written. After Exercise 1 is completed, give another presentation on 'participatory decision-making' and its core values. Ensure that the group is moving with you. Encourage the participants to get fully involved in the discussion, by processing their earlier experiences.

Now introduce the topic of individual decision-making, preparing the group for the individual exercise. As mentioned in the steps for conducting the exercise on individual decision-making, prepare for your presentation at the time of discussion on the responses to the exercise. Conduct Exercise 2.

After the exercise is completed, ensure that all the topics covered under this module are discussed.

EXERCISE 1

PROCESS OF PROBLEM-SOLVING AND DECISION-MAKING IN A GROUP

Objective

At the end of the exercise, the participants will be able to:

- Get comprehensive insights into the process of problem-solving and decision-making in a group

Time allocation

About two hours

Material required

Training aids and tools for introducing the topic and the exercise; flip charts and writing markers for displaying key points emerging out of the feedbacks given by the two subgroups on the exercise and for your summing-up; white board and markers.

Steps in conducting the exercise

- Introduce the topic and the exercise. Inform the participants that the success of the exercise depends on how sincerely they participate in the role-play. Refer to your presentation on the problem-solving and decision making process and suggest that the subgroups should keep in view various steps that a group must go through for a sound and realistic decision.
- Divide the participants into two subgroups. Inform the group that the exercise will be in two parts. To start the exercise, one subgroup will take up the given situation (prepared by you in advance as

indicated in the 'Suggested Guidelines for Conducting the Session') and engage in discussion to arrive at a solution or a decision that is practical and can be implemented. The other subgroup will sit in the outside circle (behind the discussion group) and observe the proceedings, noting how the process is progressing. They may give particular attention to the following:

- o To what extent the steps necessary for taking a decision or solving a problem were followed
- o What different roles the participants were playing while the session was on
- o The level of enthusiasm and commitment to the exercise
- o Role of the moderator or discussion leader
- Inform the subgroup that discussion time for each will be 40 minutes.
- Now reverse the roles. The discussion subgroup becomes the observer subgroup and the observer subgroup becomes the discussion subgroup. Accordingly, the sitting arrangement is also changed. Another situation is given to this new subgroup. The observers will take notes on the same points.
- The subgroups are recalled for the plenary. Both the subgroups are given opportunities to share their experiences—as part of the discussion group and as the observer subgroup—highlighting the key learning points. You may collate the points and sum up the discussion.

(Note for the trainer: If there is constraint of time, you may limit the exercise to first part only)

EXERCISE 2

INDIVIDUAL DECISION-MAKING

Objective

At the end of the exercise, the participants will be able to:

- Get fully acquainted with the complexities of taking a decision when faced with a dilemma—need to decide from several options to address a situation or problem

Time allocation

About 1 ¼ hours

Material required

Training aids and tools required for your presentation, for summing-up, and for your inputs; copies of the worksheet (one for each participant) for individual exercise; flip charts and writing markers; white board and markers.

Steps in conducting the exercise

- Brief the participants about the exercise and its purpose. Inform them that this is an individual exercise and they have to recall a particular situation when they were confronted with several alternative actions to solve a problem or take a decision. It may be related to their personal life (family, social group, education-related) or to their workplace (10 minutes).
- Distribute the worksheet and ask them to complete it.
- Call them back to the plenary and invite them to share their responses as recorded in the completed worksheet. Using the material generated by the exercise; elaborate on the factors that influence individual decision-making.
- Sum up and close the exercise.

INDIVIDUAL DECISION-MAKING

Worksheet

Instruction: You need to be brief to the point and frank in recording your responses

1. Describe briefly the situation that you confronted for taking a personal decision

    _____

    _____

    _____

2. What were the options available to you?

_____

_____

_____

3. Pros and cons of each option

_____

_____

_____

4. What was the decision? State reasons and indicate whether you received help from others.

_____

_____

_____

Section B

Delivering an Effective Training Programme

- Beginning an Active Training Programme
- Creating and Maintaining Learning Environment
- Planning a Training Session—Writing a Session Plan
- Question–Response Approach—A Tool for Promoting Participation
- Using Training Methods Effectively

I

Beginning an Active Training Programme

OPENING THE PROGRAMME

In keeping with the level and status of the programme, the training agency may organise a formal opening. However, the programme is deemed to begin when the participants assemble in the room where most of the training activities will be conducted and the training team opens the proceedings in accordance with the programme schedule.

TASKS FOR THE TRAINER

Devolving Ownership of the Programme to the Participants

The first session is very important not only for the training team but also for the participants and the training itself. It sets the course and direction for the programme and creates an environment likely to influence its delivery.

The first task is to explain some basic elements or features of the programme. One of your key objectives is to generate interest in them and arouse their curiosity about the training. Remember, this initial enthusiasm and inquisitiveness can be translated into motivation, which, in turn, will enhance their participation.

Take the participants through the programme and explain the rationale behind including the modules in the programme, and briefly indicate how development of these competencies will help them grow and become a more proficient and successful person, and a more responsible and productive member of the society. Engage them in a process of consultation and discussion that enhances their commitment to the programme and makes them aware of their responsibilities and obligations towards the programme and the training team. Emphasise that the training will be participant centric and they are the point of convergence of all efforts of the trainers. They are its immediate *beneficiaries*. By taking this line of discussion, you make them active partners in the training.

Inform the group of the overall methodology you wish to adopt for the programme and, where necessary, make a mention of the training instruments and exercises that will form part of this methodology. This explanation enables the participants to fully understand the path the training will take and its meaning and relevance to them.

The theme of the training itself will raise the curiosity level of the participants and, undoubtedly, they will have a number of queries and concerns. Take some time to address them. Here is an opportunity for the training team to win the participants' confidence and foster a good, functional relationship and set up a process of collaboration and cooperation. Do not miss it.

Blending the Group into a Cohesive, Functional Unit

Your next task is to initiate action that helps blend the participants into a functional, cohesive group. Remember that for creating an appropriate learning environment, it is important to build mutually supportive and healthy relationships in the group. For this training, trust and sound rapport among the participants are essential prerequisites. You can lay the first brick by organising activities that promote interaction among the participants and, thus, initiating the process of establishing sound interpersonal relations. If the participants are from diverse social and cultural backgrounds, this task assumes greater importance. For this purpose, you may carry out a few exercises, depending on the level and background of the participants. In cases, where they are from the same organisation, this aspect may be limited to a few introductory exercises.

II

Creating and Maintaining Learning Environment

The primary responsibility for creating a stimulating and motivating environment that promotes the learning process rests with you and your colleagues in the training team. Even if the programme begins on a positive note and the participants are energised and are full of enthusiasm, they can easily get dispirited and dissuaded if the training environment is not maintained at that level. The challenge for you, therefore, is to *establish and maintain* that climate throughout the programme. It is one thing to start with a bang and another to sustain that momentum and vigour throughout its duration. The gains of the initial stage in *creating a will to learn* should not be frittered away as the programme moves on.

ELEMENTS OF HEALTHY LEARNING ENVIRONMENT

Learning environment has three key elements—emotional, intellectual and physical—though they are not exclusive to one another. There is constant interplay of these elements, each one influencing the other, and the final outcome that emerges is the learning environment. For instance, an emotionally assuring environment can stimulate the desire for learning. If the participants enjoy warm and mutually supportive relationship with the trainer and among themselves, they will be able to contribute and participate in training activities with greater zeal and enthusiasm, shedding their fears or inhibitions. Similarly, a physically relaxing environment can be mentally stimulating.

Emotional Component

The participants feel comfortable and emotionally relaxed, in the sessions and in informal settings in the training programme.

There is high level of trust and goodwill among members of the group. There is also openness and transparency in their behaviour and actions, and sincerity of purpose and intent. No one has a hidden agenda.

There is positive and invigorating bonding between the group, on the one hand, and the trainers, on the other.

The trainers are approachable, in the sessions and outside in informal settings. The participants do not feel inhibited to raise queries, ask for clarifications and express their concerns on training-related issues.

The group is high on self-esteem. There is an element of self-belief and confidence in the participants.

Intellectual Component

Participants are able to respond spontaneously and readily to the learning stimuli—from the trainers or other participants. They feel motivated to participate meaningfully in the training activities.

The participants are helped to establish personal learning objectives and encouraged to make sustained efforts to achieve them. Participants should engage in self-reflection to become aware of what they know and what they do not in the context of training content (where am I now? Where do I want to go? Where and how will I use the learning?)

The participants are helped to process their experiences in their day-to-day personal and workplace life and relate them to the discussion and learning in the sessions.

They have a keen desire for growth and change, based on the learning accruing from the training. They do not wait for opportunities to learn but are keen to *explore or create* them.

The participants look forward to the next training activity with enthusiasm, curiosity and expectancy.

They demonstrate a sense of purpose in their contributions to the discussion.

There is *healthy* competition among the participants to perform and contribute.

Physical Component

Physical surrounding of the room where most of the sessions are organised are conducive to learning. There are no unwanted distractions.

The participants feel comfortable during sessions, stimulating them to participate with enthusiasm with a keenness to learn and contribute.

Living conditions for the participants are appropriate to their level and background.

Environment of the programme provides opportunities for relaxation and reflection.

YOUR BASIC TOOLS FOR CREATING LEARNING CLIMATE

Your own training style; level of your training skills; your knowledge about the subject matter of training; values and attitudes towards training and the training group; your level of bonding with the group as a whole and with individual participants.

The training methods, exercises and instruments you propose to use in delivering the training.

Interactive process in the group and to the extent you have been able to develop bonding within the group.

The participants' learning styles and their learning skills.

Physical environment and infrastructural facilities.

STRATEGIES TO PROMOTE LEARNING CLIMATE IN A TRAINING PROGRAMME

Creating learning climate is not something that can be achieved through some basic do's and don'ts. There is no *mantra* or a short answer to this question. It is the result of several measures and approaches that you adopt and follow them throughout the programme.

Motivate Participants

It is not enough to facilitate and provide inputs; you must also create a motivating climate. Model a high performance ethic. An important motivation tool with you is your own level of energy and enthusiasm and your knowledge about the topic(s) you handle during the training. This will add meaning and substance to the learning process.

Participants assume responsibility for their learning. They also decide what they wish to learn and how they propose to integrate learning into their personal and work-related behaviour and actions.

Use different approaches, processes, activities and ways of involving the participants. Keep in mind that an informal and relaxed atmosphere helps create readiness and openness to learning and willingness to participate actively and meaningfully.

Establish support system in the group as key to risk-free participation.

Build Participants' Confidence and Self-esteem

Treat the participants with respect and courtesy. You will find that they reciprocate.

Open their eyes to their own worth. Make them aware of what they already know about the areas covered by the modules, their intellectual capabilities, their skills and their experience with people.

Establish Yourself Personally and Professionally with the Group

Establish yourself with the participants professionally and on a personal level. You must build trust and goodwill. Your credibility will be assessed by the participants in two ways—your professional competence and ability to deal with the topics under the programme and sincerity of purpose, honesty and openness.

As early as possible, you need to become a *trusted source* of learning and a *reliable ally* in realising their learning objectives. They should have confidence in your capabilities.

You have to lead by example upfront. Demonstrate that you are enjoying your work, relaxed, fully committed to the success of the programme, and willing to take up the challenges in the interest of the programme.

Use Appropriate Training Methods and Techniques

In delivering the modules, you have opportunities to use a variety of techniques, exercises and other training instrument. These techniques should stimulate active participation and ensure that the training remains participant-centric. An important ingredient in promoting the learning process is the use of a variety of learner-friendly training techniques that stimulate active participation and reduce *learning fatigue*. Make the process of self-discovery and personal growth an interesting process.

Consolidate Learning Periodically

If learning is not put together and communicated to the group at regular intervals, it can be lost in the plethora of training activities and intense involvement of the participants. You must, therefore, aim to periodically bring out the key learning points from the sessions and indicate how this learning may help them in their personal as well as work-life. Putting together bits and pieces of learning into recognisable and useful learning packages gives more meaning to training, keeping the participants' motivation at a high level.

You should also encourage them to engage in a process of reflection and assessment to identify areas of learning that might not be so apparent.

Remember that some learning also takes place at the subconscious level. You need to bring it out and underscore its importance.

This process of reinforcement of learning will also help the participants in internalising learning and integrating it with their experience and earlier learning to optimise results.

Attend to Small Details about the Programme

Besides the use of basic tools, you can also enhance the learning process by attending to the *nuts and bolts* of the programme. Make sure that no time is wasted. Start and finish the session on time. Breaks between the sessions should be regulated, enabling the next activity to start on time.

Give clear and precise instructions for group or individual assignments and encourage them to carry out these tasks with diligence and commitment, in accordance with the instructions.

Begin Where the Participants are and Keep Moving at Their Pace

Determine at what pace the group is prepared to move with you in the process of discussion and learning, and organise training activities and your presentation accordingly. A prerequisite for this is your understanding of their level of knowledge and experience, and their learning styles.

Keep the discussion as close to ground realities as possible. Give examples with which the participants are familiar. Use their experiences to engage them in productive and meaningful deliberations, leading to consolidation of the outcomes.

Use simple, clear and unpretentious language, easily understood by most of them, especially when you are introducing new ideas or making suggestions with regard to their personal or professional life.

III

Planning a Training Session— Writing a Session Plan

WHAT IS A SESSION PLAN?

A training session plan—also called a learning plan—is an organised description (or guidelines) of the inputs (in terms of the topic), activities and resources that you will use to guide a training group towards a specific learning objective.

It can be as simple as a brief outline, or more complex, with scripts, prompts and lists of questions that you plan to ask or expect from the training group.

Your session plan should be in harmony with the overall framework and methodology of the training programme.

It should be in sync with the general tenor and flow of other sessions, especially the one preceding it or following it.

Write in a language and style that you are familiar with and understand.

WHY DO YOU NEED A SESSION PLAN?

As you plan, you visualise each step of the session. This helps you ensure that you have prepared everything that you need to do, and that you will be able to present it in a logical order. You will also be able to identify points that might be tricky for people to understand.

After your session, you can use your plan to work out what went well— and what did not. This assessment will be useful in planning future sessions.

It may take time to create an effective training session plan but the efforts are always worthwhile. You, the training team and the training group will benefit from this preparation. A well-prepared session plan will boost your confidence.

It will be invaluable for a substitute trainer if, for some reasons, you are not available for the session.

It is helpful for co-facilitating.

Session Plan Format

Session Title .... **Topic** ....

Sub-topics	Learning Objectives	Information/ Knowledge/ Skills/Attitudes	Training Methods	Time Allocation	Resources Required	Measuring Outcomes	Special Remarks
List the sub-topics/ issues that you would like to cover during the session	Write down the learning objectives for the session, if necessary, for each of the sub-topics you propose to cover	Indicate training outcomes in terms of information, knowledge, competencies, etc.	List the training methods, techniques and instruments you would use for delivering the session

Write down instructions or specific guidelines that you would follow in carrying out the training activity

Write if there are any do's and don'ts | Indicate the duration of the session, where necessary, for each training activity | Resource materials used for planning the session

Resources and support materials needed for the delivery (audiovisual aids, printed materials, etc.)

Co-trainers and support personnel

Logistical requirements including extra discussion rooms, transport, etc. | Write down indicators you would use to measure how well objectives were achieved | Indicate special conditions, features or aspects that the trainer should keep in view while planning or conducting the activity |

IV

Question–Response Approach—
A Tool for Promoting Participation

When we talk about questions in the context of training, we are not referring to a question–answer session at the end of a presentation or lecture, which is assumed to be mandatory. Here, we discuss the question–response approach as a tool to enhance participation, promote the learning process, energise the group and make the presentation more interesting and useful.

In any training programme, adult participants bring with them a baggage of knowledge and/or experience. In the context of life skills training, the question–response approach assumes far greater importance than other training approaches because the adult participants bring with them a substantial repertoire of deeply embedded behaviour patterns, values, attitudes, etc.

QUESTIONS–RESPONSE APPROACH CAN BE HELPFUL IN MANY WAYS

While it stimulates learning and makes the process of learning more interesting and useful, it can help in promoting interaction among the participants. A question posed or doubt raised by a participant can generate interest in other members of the group and, sometimes, even elicit response from some of them. Some participants may relate with the questioner as they could have similar doubts or views about the issues or topic under discussion, but, for some personal reasons, were reluctant to ask the question themselves. This may become the basis of further interaction among these participants and help develop bonds between them. This can even extend to other participants and lead to better cohesion in the training group.

This technique can also help in establishing a good functional relationship between the training group, on the one hand, and the trainer or the training team, on the other. It helps in promoting interactive process between the trainers and the group, more specifically the participant(s) asking the question(s). If the questions asked are relevant to the discussion and provide an opportunity to the trainer to elaborate further on her presentation, the trainer is likely to connect with the participants better. It is seen that if the questions do not put the trainer in an uncomfortable position (in responding to them) she will enjoy this interaction with the participants. This will contribute to nurturing a healthy relationship between the group and the trainer. However, it is equally true that if the questioner's intentions are perceived to be suspect by the trainer, the question can trigger a negative vibe between the two. This can have unhealthy consequences for the training itself. Therefore, the trainer should be on guard.

Regardless of who initiates the process, question–response technique should be deemed as a key aspect of feedback system. Questions from the participants help the trainer in gauging her own performance and finding out to what extent she was able to communicate effectively with the participants, in the context of her presentation or expressing her views on a topic or an issue. The tenor of the question, its contents and the questioner's body language will indicate the level of understanding and comprehension of the participants of the discussion. Question asked by a participant can be used by the trainer to assess whether similar doubts on the discussion are shared by others as well by redirecting it to other members of the group, preferably by rephrasing. This will also help the trainer ensure that she moves with the pace of the participants. These clues will help the trainer modify the contents, level and the pace of the presentation.

Question–response interaction, if pursued discerningly, can also provide clues to the trainer for assessing the level of knowledge of the group and for finding out the dimensions that they are aware of with regard to the topic under discussion. The trainer will also be able to get some indication on how the participants are in a position to relate the contents of the training to back home situation or the practical aspects of their work. As a trainer, you would have noticed that, sometimes, questions are asked keeping in mind the application of the learning to personal life and work situations. This is a clue you should not miss.

Effective and timely questioning by the trainer does not allow the participants to sit back. They remain alert and active throughout the session. Question–response approach is a very useful tool to regenerate interest when you find it sagging. It encourages a process of thinking, reflecting and responding, making the group an active partner in the training process. A single question either from a participant or a trainer can spark an interesting discussion that can create an environment that assists in the learning process.

Question–response interaction can generate energy and interest in the group. Your task as a trainer is to ensure that this energy and enthusiasm do not dissipate and are diverted to enhance participation and promote learning.

It can generate an environment that is learner-friendly and thus helps many participants feel more relaxed in the session. It can also generate energy and interest in the group that can be appropriately harnessed by the trainer for enhancing participation and generating interest and curiosity. This energy will have to be diverted to generate enthusiasm and interest in the group thus enhancing participation.

Sometimes, the questions may also set direction for further discussion in the group on the topic.

Some seasoned and experienced trainers may even take the option of building up the session on the basis of this question–response approach. However, if you take this option, you should be reasonably confident of your facilitative skills and your knowledge of the topic. You must also ensure that the questions are appropriately framed and worded to help you realise your objective.

A pertinent question recognised by the group and the trainer can infuse or reinforce confidence in the participant. This can encourage others to also express themselves freely. Remember, self-confidence is generally infectious.

When a trainer responds to a question to the full satisfaction of the group, she grows in self-confidence and this also enhances her credibility with the group. Effective handling of the questions also contributes to her professional growth. The ability to respond to questions can make her an accomplished trainer brimming with confidence and enjoying better standing with training groups and co-trainers.

Questions by the participants may provide opportunities to elaborate or clarify some of the points. This is helpful not only to the trainer but also for the group and in taking the learning process forward. It induces a process of reflection, analysis and collation.

Depending on the type of questions asked or the manner it is used, this technique can also help you in providing linkage of one point to another, ensuring a better flow of your presentation.

Sometimes, you may toss a question just to draw out the silent and shy participants from their shell.

There are occasions when questions can be used as icebreakers or openers for a session.

QUESTION–RESPONSE TECHNIQUE—GUIDELINES TO ENHANCE ITS USEFULNESS

Keeping in view the importance of this approach in training, it is necessary for the trainers to know how to make optimum use of it in enhancing participation and making the group more active and participatory. Some suggestions are as follows:

Right at the beginning of your presentation or the session, you should inform the group that you wish to follow question–response approach and you expect the participants to stop you at any point in time and put forward their views or ask a question. You may also make it clear to them that you also have the right to stop at any point and get the views of the group on the issue under discussion. This will keep the group in an 'alert' mode.

Do not let a few participants monopolise the question–response inter-action. Remember that this approach is to enhance participation and make the group an active partner in the learning process. It is, therefore, your responsibility to ensure that most of the participants, if not all, become active in the process, otherwise you will defeat the very purpose of using this technique. If the group is heterogeneous, it is all the more impor-tant that you encourage questions and responses from a cross-section of the participants representing different levels of experience and knowledge. This will ensure that various dimensions or perspectives of the issue are brought in the discussion, benefiting the group.

You should develop a positive attitude towards questions. Do not dread them. This is your ultimate test as an accomplished and effective trainer. Welcome them enthusiastically and thank the participants for asking questions. You will find yourself growing in stature and confidence.

Some trainers may feel that they will lose their credibility if they do not answer every question. It is not the case. Even the group does not expect it. The important point, however, is that no question should be ignored or sidelined. It is the test of your ability how you turn the question over to the group while you reflect on possible response. If some other partic-ipants try to respond to the question, provide them the opportunity. You get breathing time and it is possible that as others attempt to put together a response or express their views, you may get some clues or ideas in build-ing your own response. Do not try to win a brownie point but be generous to acknowledge the contributions of these participants.

Remember never to make up an answer that you feel is not the right one. Also, avoid twisting and turning the question or deliberately trying to misinterpret it. It is always a better option to admit that you do not have a proper response and widen the scope of the discussion by directing the question to the group. One way of handling 'off-the-wall' question from the participants is to tell the group *let me get back to you* and post it on the white board or a flip chart labelled 'parking lot'. However, you should not resort to this option too often otherwise the group may take a dim view of your ability to field questions and respond effectively.

Do not give a long-winded or unintelligible response. As far as possible, be specific and brief. If you feel that the question can trigger more substantive discussion, inform the group and introduce the new points that may have emerged from the discussion. It will be wrong to extend your answer to include additional views because the group may not realise that you are now adding some more points. You may say, 'This question opens up a new area or this question has brought in another perspective that requires some elaboration', and then proceed to do it. However, ensure that the question and your response do not take the group away from the core discussion.

As a rule of the thumb, do not be judgemental on the intention and motive of the questioner. You must give him or her the benefit of the doubt. However, if you are convinced of negative or hostile undertone of the question or the questioner, you should attempt to take the sting out of it by rephrasing it for a more objective and meaningful discussion. You should do it subtly and ensure that you are in full control of your emotions and body language. Once you get the nod of the group on the rephrased question, the questioner will find it difficult to disagree.

Regardless of the merit, timing or relevance of the question, you should give your attention to the questioner and the question. There are instances when participants' questions or responses may lack focus, coherence or may not be even relevant to the discussion. Due to language limitation, some of them may find it difficult to properly phrase the question or use the right words. They may not even be able to properly articulate what they want to say. Treat such questions or responses graciously. Do not deride the participant, dismiss the question or use sarcasm. You may hurt the dignity of the participant and this may be unacceptable to some other participants also. You will end up a loser. Also, do not get frustrated or irritated. This is indeed the test of your patience and tact in handling somewhat unpleasant situations.

Your best bet is to listen to the question or response carefully and try to make sense of it without appearing to be doing so. Where possible, help by rephrasing or taking out some positive points from the participant's question or response. As far as possible, make use of the participants' words and phrases. This sends a message to the participants that you value their questions and even legitimises their way of asking questions. Check with the participant and then move on. In doing this, be careful that you do not appear to be condescending or trying to convey a message that the questioner could not word it properly. Bring the onus on you by saying, 'Let me try to understand what you mean by this'; or 'I am sorry I did not get it. Please let me know if this is what you wanted to say'.

If the question appears to be challenging or attacking you, do not take it personally and decide to give it back to the participant in similar language and tone. This is not a wise course of action and can be counterproductive. Avoid this approach and try to diffuse the situation through a relaxed posture, by using your sense of humour or by redirecting the question to the group, thus widening the scope of the discussion.

Remember that question–response approach is aimed to benefit the group and not just a few participants. It is, therefore, important that the questions and the responses, regardless whether they originate from you or the participants, should be deemed as the 'property' of the group. This is the essence of this approach. After all, this transaction uses group time, not just of the participant, asking question or giving a response. If the question remains that of the participant alone, there may be resentment of other participants and they may consider it a waste of time of the group.

Equally important is that your response should also be addressed to the group and not just the questioner. While it is important to ask the questioner whether he or she is comfortable with the response, you should also take the group's nod before moving on.

During question–response transaction, you should be fully in control of yourself. The participants should get the message that you are feeling good about it and enjoying this exchange. In encouraging or welcoming questions, you should not sound superficial or faking interest.

While keeping an eye on the time factor, you should not appear to be hurrying things. This will send a negative message to the group.

You should make it a practice to repeat the question, whether asked by a participant or by you, particularly when you consider it important for your presentation and the learning process.

TRAINERS' INNER RESTRAINTS WITH RESPECT TO QUESTIONS

These are some of the negative perceptions or restraints some trainers have about questions from the participants. You need to check on this and engage in some self-reflection. This will help you grow as a trainer.

An Actual Dislike of Questions

Some trainers simply have aversion for questions during a session for no apparent reason. This could be their mindset or just an upshot of some unpleasant previous experience. However, questions are an important aspect of any training session and if you wish to be an accomplished trainer, you should not shy away from questions by the participants.

Question Viewed as a Challenge

Questions or articulation, especially when they appear to be reflecting a point of view that is either different or in conflict with the one expressed by the trainer, may be considered as a challenge to the knowledge and experience of the trainer. There are trainers who do not like to be confronted on their views or opinions. Some may even go beyond this position and feel that this 'challenge' could undermine their authority and status as a trainer within the group by encouraging others to take similar stance. You need to check on your attitude by engaging in some self-reflection and apply necessary correctives.

Lack of Preparation or Self-confidence

Those trainers who are not fully confident of their knowledge about the topic may have fear of exposure through the questions. They feel that if they are not able to respond to the question to the satisfaction of the questioner or other participants, they may lose their credibility. The question may expose their ignorance or lack of knowledge about the topic or the issue. They may also suffer from anxiety that the participant may upstage them before the group, affecting their position.

Some trainers may also be apprehensive about questions as they are concerned with the fact that in responding to the question, they may be unwittingly drawn into a discussion that they do not want to and may be forced to say things that they wish to avoid. Some may even feel that by responding to the question, it is likely that they may open new issues for discussion for which they are not prepared and they may not be able to manage.

Attitude Towards the Questioner

A trainer's suspicion and attitude towards some participants may also drive her to a position of unease or discomfort with either the question or the questioner. Many trainers are quite comfortable when a 'friendly' participant asks a question but are not in the right frame of mind when some participant who is not considered friendly asks a question, regardless of the importance and relevance of the question. This bias can act as a deterrent for the trainer. Watch out.

Question as a Distraction

You may also feel that the question may take the group away from the focus of the discussion. You fear that once you start responding to the question, it may not be easy to maintain the interest and momentum that have been generated in the discussion. There is some merit in this concern but what is important here is to consider the extent to which the question is related to the discussion. You must take a call on your ability to handle the question and the questioner deftly, and, yet, maintain the level of interest and energy in the group. This is a challenge for you.

Waste of Time

A trainer may feel pressure of time in completing the assigned task in a training session and this may result in 'resentment' against those who 'waste' time by asking questions.

QUESTIONS ABOUT QUESTIONS

Should the trainer toss out a question for a voluntary response or at a particular participant by name?
It may embarrass the participant and discourage others from thinking and responding. In some cases, it may be appropriate especially if you are sure that there is greater chance of getting the response. You can later bring in other participants also.

How do you involve those who never volunteer?

Ask them to write answers, draw lots, go alphabetically and call numbers. You can think of other methods but it is important that you attempt to involve most participants.

Should you repeat the question to ensure that everyone has understood it?

The answer is yes. But look for the body language of other participants and find out whether the wording of the question is comprehensible. Otherwise also it will help transfer the ownership of the question to the entire group and not limited to the questioner.

What if the respondent gives you a wrong answer, especially if she is a high-status participant?

Broaden out to other members of the group. Use the group as the corrective resource and do not do it yourself.

What if I do not understand the answer?

Check with the participant. Repeat what you have understood. But for your lack of understanding, do not put the responsibility on the participant. Tell her that you are trying to get the import of what she said but if she can help in that. She will feel delighted and help you out.

How do I deal with slow, rambling, disorganised response?

Do not put down or deride the participant. Help the participant articulate better by 'supplying' words or rephrasing. You also have the option of asking some other participant to summarise the thoughts. But remember you should not belittle the participant.

What if no one responds to my question?

It might be too simple a question that no one is ready to respond. Group may not be sufficiently enthused; no one knows the answer; perhaps no one had understood the question; they do not want to waste time answering question; time is not opportune for the question. So, check on these possibilities and take the call accordingly.

How do I deal with irrelevant, distracting questions?

Do not express your irritation or disappointment openly, try to find some positive point in the question, toss the question to the group and try to get their comments, just check with the questioner how does that relate to the discussion that we are having but do not be intimidating, tell that you have not really understood the question and ask the questioner to repeat it. She may get the message.

What if no one is able to answer, should I do it myself?
Wait for some time; rephrase the question; add a bit of humour and relax the group. Then decide what to do.

What do I do if I do not know the answer?
Admit that you do not have an answer at the moment; check whether any other participant has the response; do not bluff and or give wrong answers; this is worse than not answering at all.

How do I deal with a question that is really a statement or an opinion?
Tell the questioner: good point but can you rephrase the question that you wish to ask.

Do I handle a question on something that was covered 10–20 minutes back?
There is no bar that a participant cannot ask question about something that was covered some time back. Remember this. Just check whether others also have a related question. If so, go ahead and respond to it but quickly return to what you are handling now.

V

Using Training Methods Effectively

LECTURE

The lecture is, by definition, words spoken by the trainer. It is thus a verbal symbol medium. This is the oldest method of training in which the trainer, by virtue of his or her knowledge and expertise in a field, presents orally, in a direct and often unilateral manner, the subject matter. In most cases, it implies a one-way communication. In this method, the possibility of significant learning is greatly diminished by the lack of interaction not only between the trainer and the participants but among the participants as well.

As a training method, the purpose of the lecture is, in fact, specific and limited. In the continuum of information, understanding, knowledge, skills/competencies, behaviour or attitudes, the lecture method is effective only where it seeks to transmit information or intellectual understanding, as part of the learning process. Generally speaking, it offers a relatively passive and uninspiring experience to the participants. However, if the trainer has an unusual talent to stimulate and keep the audience engaged through excellent verbal communication skills, sheer personality or by establishing a warm and positive relationship with the participants during the course of the lecture, there may be unexpected and productive results. Thus, lecturing holds a premier place as an established method of training.

Why and When to Use the Method

The most obvious application is where there is a large group needing information or knowledge about certain concepts, theories and issues, and participation is not possible because of the sheer size of the group. The timing can be worked out with considerable degree of accuracy, with an assurance that the trainer will be able to cover the ground she intended to within the stipulated period.

The main attraction of lecturing as a method of training is its deceptive simplicity and the control over the session and the participants it purportedly gives to a trainer. Coverage and preparation of the lecture can be predetermined and once prepared, the lecture can be delivered by even a stand-in and repeated any number of times. A trainer can derive considerable satisfaction from her performance as she holds the direct responsibility for its preparation and delivery.

Usually, in a lecture, the participants are expected to listen carefully and reflect on the subject and clear their doubts either during or after the lecture. It has a number of variations and can be used in combination with other methods of training, perhaps, with greater effectiveness.

Because of the live voice and manner, and the ambience generally associated with the presentation of the lecture, the trainer can make facts come alive, making the session more inspiring and full of vitality.

Why and When Not to Use the Method

In the lecture method, it is assumed that the participants can by themselves, through reading and informal discussions, bridge the gap between the contents of the lecture and realities in their personal life and at their work situation. Intellectual understanding of the issues will be translated into action. However, this assumption may not be valid. There is no assurance that the participants will be willing to invest further time and effort to build on the knowledge transmitted by the lecture.

Also, as the method does not stimulate thinking or actively involve the participants, the understanding of various issues that the lecture may generate in the participants is often not very lasting and after a certain length of time, the participants may not be in a position to recall much of what was said during the lecture.

In most cases, the onus for the success of the method lies with the trainer and its effectiveness. Also, to a considerable extent, its effectiveness depends on the personality of the trainer and the manner of presentation. There are few opportunities to apply correctives midway through the lecture if things are not going the way the trainer would have wanted them to.

The process of lecturing calls for motivation and commitment on the part of the individual. Lecturing by itself addresses neither the individual nor the social or emotional dimensions of this process.

It is a non-participatory, passive medium that does not allow two-way communication. Although it is relatively a simple method, its simplicity can be deceptive because the emphasis can be on contents, effective delivery and presentation of the contents, rather than on learning.

The lecture method also develops a sense of dependence on the trainer. Some participants may be inclined to accept the trainer's views and opinions as gospel and make it part of their own understanding. They may not feel the need to go through a process of thinking, analysing, choosing and discarding or accepting.

The very qualities of a good lecture threaten its value as a training method, that aims to develop the potential and understanding of the participants. The more complete and logically consistent the argument, the more erudite its derivation. The more appealing its delivery, the more it tends to be 'bought' as the final answer or view.

The lack of involvement of the participant leaves the trainer without any feedback on the extent the materials is absorbed and the inputs are comprehended by the participants. Unless the entire presentation is fully understood and assimilated, the sequence and sense of the lecture may be lost.

Enhancing its Usefulness

In spite of criticisms by the advocates of participatory learning, the lecture method still has its place in certain training situations, provided the trainers are willing to bring about some changes in the manner it is delivered.

For this method to be successful and effective, a key factor is the trainer. It demands a high level of skills from her. If the object of the lecture is transmission of information and understanding of issues, it is necessary for the trainer to possess the requisite knowledge and information in the subject and that she is perceived as such by the participants. The quicker the trainer is able to establish her credibility with the group, the better it is for the delivery of the lecture.

Good lecturing skills are a prerequisite for a good presentation. If the trainer is skilled in interacting with the audience and creating a climate suited to learning, the message will be effectively transmitted.

Trainer may build in participatory element in the lecture. The skilful use of audience involvement and providing encouragement to the participants to interact can turn the lecture into a dynamic learning experience for everyone, including the trainer. It can be transformed into a process of two-way communication. There is no good reason why the participants cannot interrupt the trainer during the lecture and ask for a clarification or raise a query. Further, all the questions need not be from the participants. Nothing prohibits the trainer from asking questions of the group or interacting with it during the lecture. This approach can also fulfil the need for a feedback.

The trainer should not feel inhibited to use visual aids to emphasise, highlight or elaborate a point. However, important thing is that the aids should be appropriate and produced ably. Remember, training aids should not be allowed to take over from you.

If readings and assignments about a topic or a subject precede the lecture, the trainer can present the facts in the context of such readings, making the lecture learner-friendly, turning it into an understandable whole. The trainer can also help the participants synthesise and analyse facts and focus on relevant aspects.

Handouts could also be used albeit with some care and discretion. They are a valuable means of consolidating and supplementing information provided in a lecture. But they should be suitably designed and produced, and used at the right time to make them more effective. If handouts are distributed at the beginning or during the lecture, the group (as also the trainer) can get distracted and the participants may get so engaged in reading through them that they may disregard the trainer or the lecture. If the participants find that the lecture is only repeating or restating what is incorporated in the handouts, they are likely to be less attentive to what is being said in the session. Therefore, while the lecture may be based on handouts they should not be repeating the contents of such material. One suggestion could be that a framework of the lecture could be provided before the lecture is delivered to enable the participants to follow the contents easily and, later, handouts may be given out to supplement the lecture. This will also ensure that the learning the participants acquire is more lasting.

Perhaps another functional approach is to provide the framework of the lecture before the lecture commences (as suggested above) but under each subhead leave some space to enable the participants to write key points of the lecture that they find interesting and worthwhile.

The effectiveness of the lecture method also depends on its place among other methods in the same programme. The lecture holds greatest promise when it is a response to the questions and concerns of the participants, raised in earlier discussions, fieldwork or other experiences. It can also be effectively used as a prelude to other experiential methods such as role-play, case study, simulation games, laboratory training or field visit.

The length of the lecture is an important factor in its effectiveness. Studies have shown that 20 or 30 minutes may be the maximum time that a lecturer can hold the attention of the participants effectively. However, if the lecture is interspersed with some interaction with the participants and occasional use of visual aids, this period may be extended considerably.

GROUP DISCUSSION AS A METHOD OF TRAINING

This is a popular method with most of the trainers because of its adaptability and wider application. It can be used as a stand-alone method or in combination with other training methods. It can take the form of the whole group sitting together and discussing a topic or the larger group divided into subgroups or syndicates. Group discussion aims at a structured but informal exchange of knowledge, ideas and perceptions among the participants on any issue, topic or sub-topic. It induces a high level of participation, enhancing the involvement of the group in the learning process.

Objectives of Group Discussion

Broadly speaking, group discussion can be organised with two ends in view. It can be *process-oriented* where the emphasis is on promoting interaction among the participants, encouraging them to open up and express themselves freely and frankly or *result-oriented* where the stress is on concrete and specific outcomes or results. These two objectives, however, are not exclusive to each other, and, in most cases, the trainers set up small groups with these dual purposes. Specifically, a group discussion may be organised with one or more of the following objectives:

- Produce a range of options or solutions, addressing a particular problem or an issue.
- Generate a pile of ideas by examining issues in greater depth, looking at different dimensions or perspectives of these issues.
- Broaden the outlook of the participants through cross-fertilisation and exposure to new and different experiences and ideas, and enrich their understanding of the issues.
- Develop their skills in interpersonal communication and in expressing their views in a clear and concise manner. Group discussion provides opportunities to the participants to share their views in a relatively secure and nonthreatening environment. To some participants, participation in smaller groups provides confidence for more substantive contribution in the bigger group.
- It is also an effective means of changing attitudes through the influence of peers in the group. Participation in group discussion can help participants develop greater respect for the points of view and opinions of others and become more tolerant.
- It is also a valuable means of obtaining feedback for the training team on self-expression, motivation level and personal traits of the participants and characteristics of the group. Thus, it helps in generating personal data on individuals in a training group.

Tasks for the Groups

Most people feel more comfortable participating in discussion in smaller groups. One variation can be that the group is first divided into smaller groups and then they report to the total group. The process can also be discussed. This can be enriching and valuable for learning of the participants.

In setting up subgroups for simultaneous discussion, you have three broad options:

- All the groups may be given similar tasks or assignments. The purpose is to generate a wide range of ideas, views and opinions on a topic, thus enhancing the scope of discussion or arrive at an array of solutions to a problem.
- The groups may also be given tasks that are related and, in fact, complementary—for instance, aspects of an issue or sub-topics of a bigger topic. The aim is to provide for in-depth discussion on a smaller, more focused area within a relatively shorter time. The group reports may be consolidated to provide a comprehensive perspective on the topic.
- The third option is that the groups are given different unrelated tasks, for later sharing in the plenary.

Your next task is to set out specifically and explicitly the intended outcomes from the exercise. It is important that all members should be clear about these.

The composition of the groups also needs attention. Each group should be properly balanced, with the right proportion and combination of strong contributors, shy introverts, logical thinkers, analysts and happy followers. The size of the group is also crucial to a good and effective discussion.

The group should select its own discussion leader but once this has been done, your task is to brief the leader on his or her role to lead the group to the desired objectives.

Dynamics of a Discussion Group

The group may not fully perceive the objectives and meaning of the deliberations or comprehend the issues that need to be focused upon. Therefore, the task may not be carried out on the desired lines.

If the group is large, all the members may not get the opportunity to participate and contribute to the discussion. This defeats the very purpose of using this method to promote participatory training.

A few individuals who are more articulate and can communicate well may dominate the discussion and succeed in imposing their views on the group. Therefore, their ideas may be reflected as the views of the entire group. On the other hand, as this is a group task, some members may take it easy and just take a back seat and not participate.

The group may be so overwhelmed by the desire to complete the task in double quick time and to achieve results, that the group process that is central to this method may get ignored or sidelined.

A group discussion can turn into an endless debate unless it is properly organised and controlled. It can turn into a slinging match of arguments and counterarguments between some individuals, with other members reduced to the role of spectators.

Difficulties can arise if the discussion leader is unskilled in guiding the discussion and/or not familiar with the topic or the issues.

Role of the Discussion Leader

Ensure that the objectives of the discussion, set out earlier, are met and the exercise provides a meaningful and fulfilling experience for the members of the group.

Stimulate the members, ensure that the focus of the discussion remains on the issues or the topic and encourage participation by most members of the group. All participants should be persuaded to express themselves freely. And for this he or she needs to generate and sustain an appropriate environment.

Useful contributions should be optimised and inappropriate comments and interventions limited, without discouraging the concerned members.

The leader should not *control* the discussion but *guide* it in a way that it remains on course. The ownership of the process and the contents should be devolved to the group. This will enhance the interest and motivation of the members. He or she must also make sure that the members remain persistently committed to the group task and its objectives.

As mentioned earlier, in any discussion group, some members are inclined to control or dominate the discussion. The leader must skilfully restrain the more aggressive and dominant elements. He or she needs to determine what stimulus, assistance or support is required to make the silent and the reluctant assert and participate more actively in the deliberations.

It is a huge help to the group if the discussion leader, periodically, highlights and summarises key points of discussion. This keeps the focus on the main issues and facilitates the finalisation of the group report.

The discussion leader needs to guarantee that the discussion remains as close to reality as possible. Sometimes, the group may be tempted to move into an unreal world and move away from practical solutions or decisions. The discussion leader has an important role here.

Preparation of Group Reports

Group reports are prepared in accordance with the objectives for which the discussion was set up.

You should provide guidelines to the groups for preparing the group reports. The reports should highlight core points, bringing out the main substance of the discussion. If the reports are prepared in an agreed format, it facilitates presentation and consolidation. The report should be a sincere and correct record of the deliberations.

If the objectives of setting up discussion groups are to promote interpersonal communication among the participants and encourage them to open up and share, reports will focus on these aspects.

Presentation and Consolidation of Group Reports

If group discussion has been held in the subgroups or syndicates, the next step would be to ask these subgroups to present their reports to the total group. You should set out a procedure for presentation and discussion of these reports to make it interesting, less time-consuming and productive. Several variations are possible. In cases where the subgroups have discussed the same topic or issues, it is desirable that each group is asked to display the key points on a flip chart. This can be followed by brief presentation. Thus, each group gets an opportunity to report the essence of its discussion without the fear of getting overshadowed by the group having the first chance for the presentation. It has generally been seen that in such cases, after the first report is presented, the participants lose interest in subsequent presentations, as some of the points may be common. Therefore, it is important that you adopt a strategy that avoids this situation. If the groups have discussed different topics or issues, you have a number of options. You may adopt any procedure, appropriate to your requirements.

BRAINSTORMING

Brainstorming is a specialised form of discussion method that can be used in a training situation. Many trainers believe that brainstorming means a random and unstructured way of generating ideas and solutions. It is not so. Brainstorming is certainly not a straightforward method of decision-making or problem-solving. At the heart of this method is the principle that as ideas or solutions are proposed, comments and evaluation are suspended until the time this step is completed and the group is ready to move on to the next step of analysis. It is also based on the premise that it is not good to shoot down an idea or proposal without properly considering its merits and demerits in an unbiased manner. Another posit on which this method is based is the principle of synergy and creative thinking. It is possible to generate more ideas collectively than the sum of the ideas that would be produced individually.

Objectives of the Method

Generating a wide range of solutions or options in solving a problem, address-ing an issue/situation or in taking a decision, thus stimulating creativity in the group.

Developing a positive attitude among the participants by encouraging them to listen carefully to others, suspend judgement and outright rejection of their ideas and refrain from negative comments without considering care-fully their merits and demerits.

Encouraging shy and reluctant participants to share their ideas and views without the fear of getting an immediate negative reaction from other colleagues. The members can become open about their thoughts and viewpoints.

Promoting attitudes that will help the participants work more effec-tively in groups.

Steps in Organising a Brainstorming Session

Learning in this exercise occurs because participants discipline their inputs to the discussion. Control occurs through instructions and through the discussion leader. The following are the steps in organising the session:

Generation of Ideas

The starting point is to generate a large number of ideas within a short span of time. Thus, there is a comparatively greater emphasis on quantity and encouraging members to think and be *creative* in generating new ideas, proposals or options. Quality or merit is assessed later lest it should inhibit or even stifle the process of generation of ideas. It is the task of the discussion leader to ensure that this basic principle is not violated. No discussion should be permitted, except to clarify a thought or statement. It is likely that some of the ideas put forward by the members may be totally outlandish. But, sometimes, a sound solution may emerge from proposals that, at the outset, may appear to be impractical or inappropriate. These ideas may be further worked upon by the group and refined to make them more relevant, in line with the criteria set out by the group and acceptable to it.

Amending Ideas

The discussion leader can intervene if the ideas expressed need to be amended through elaboration, editing or consolidation. He or she also has the task to assist those who are not in a position to appropriately articulate their views. If certain ideas are repeated, the discussion leader can bring this to the attention of the participant and ask for another option. He or she should, however, avoid any analysis at this stage. The leader should also ensure that ideas expressed earlier should not be opposed or repudiated.

Posting All the Ideas on a Flip Chart

It will be helpful to post all the ideas generated through this exercise on a flip chart or white board. This will reinforce the contributions of those who have provided their views earlier and serve as a point of reference and an encouragement for those who follow.

Analysing Ideas

Once all the ideas are posted, the discussion leader should proceed to analyse them, going in chronological order. It is necessary that until this step, the discussion leader should make it clear that judgement is suspended and the merits and demerits are not expressed. The analysis takes place in light of the objectives of the exercise and the criteria set by the group. All factors, which could have any bearing on the final decision of the group, should be duly considered.

Consolidation of Ideas or Action Planning

Once all the views and ideas put forward by the participants have been analysed, assessed and accepted, it is time to consolidate them and arrive at conclusions. In case the objective was to generate suggestions and proposals as part of decision-making process, now is the time to shortlist those that have received broad acceptance of the group. Once again, members' views are considered for finalising the decision through consensus.

CASE STUDY METHOD

The case study method is very popular with the trainers. It samples a real-life situation in the field and provides an opportunity to the participants to learn on the basis of a summary of a well-documented series of events, incidents and circumstances, centring round an organisation, problem, a situation or an issue. It demonstrates in a 'live' and realistic way, the complex or multidimensional nature of a situation or a problem in which a number of individuals, factors or circumstances are at play.

It helps the participants to familiarise themselves with facts, situations and dilemmas that they might face in their real life, especially with regard to their job responsibilities. A discussion on a case study can highlight their assumptions, experiences, attitudes, preferences and ways of functioning, giving them an opportunity to correlate these with those of the others in the group. It helps a participant to understand the situation from the perspective of wider organisational interests and not merely from his or her own standpoint.

The case study method, thus, provides a frame of reference for the participants.

Objectives of the Method

The objectives for using case study as a method of training vary in accordance with the learning objectives for the session or the topic.

It stimulates analytical, in-depth discussion with a view to presenting a multifaceted or an integrated perspective of the situation for better understanding, guidance and action by the participants. This will also help them develop a wider outlook of the situation and issues that they are likely to face in their life situations. They have an opportunity to view the problem or the issues not only from their own limited perspective but also from the point of view of others as well.

This method can also be used as an exercise in decision-making or problem-solving. It develops participants' ability to think, decide and choose appropriate course of action. They learn to respond to a problem or situation, taking into account all circumstances rather than going by a particular approach or style.

As a case study incorporates description of people and situations taken from real-life events with which the participants are familiar and can even identify with, this method also promotes exploration and awareness of one's attitudes, values and patterns of job or personal behaviour.

It helps in developing knowledge of skills in dealing with particular situations that they may confront in their job.

Guidelines for Using the Method

Effectiveness of the use of the method depends on its relevance to the learning objectives of the session, level of the trainer's skills in using the method and the ability of the participants to participate meaningfully and productively in the discussion.

It is desirable that a case study should be based on genuine data and situations. Otherwise, the participants will not identify with the details given in the case and this may dilute learning. However, in the absence of good case studies for a wide range of purposes and groups, sometimes, the information is concocted, although it might be presented as facts in a fairly convincing way.

If the case deals with a real situation, you should usually know the actual outcome in order to enable you to compare and contrast the participants' findings and conclusions. Since the true outcome may not be the most expedient or desirable, you should encourage the participants to explore various options that might be available rather than directing their efforts towards searching for the right response or predetermined conclusions.

When dealing with certain problems or situations in the field, it is quite unrealistic to assume that there is only one response to a situation. There area always different ways of looking at a situation.

Before the case study method is introduced, it may be useful to prepare the participants by exposing them to basic concepts likely to be emphasised in the case study and providing relevant theoretical inputs. Ideally, this method should be preceded by a sound theoretical and conceptual discussion on the issues that are likely to be highlighted in the case study.

Steps for Writing a Case Study

The first step in writing a good case study is to set out the learning outcomes, as the case will be structured on the basis of what you want to get out of this training activity.

The next step is to identify the problem or issues that you wish to deal with in the case. It is advisable to focus on one or two situations or problems. If you include a number of issues, the participants may get confused and this affects discussion.

The materials that you wish to use for the case should relate to everyday operations of the participants. It is generally useful to collect more materials than you will use in writing the case study. The materials that you have not used for the case will help during the discussion as the participants seek clarifications and raise queries pertinent to the case. You should be ready to respond.

Arrange the data and information in a logical structure or scheme. Determine opening statements for the facts of the case. This gives you an outline and a broad framework for the case. Ensure that you highlight the issues and the situations. If you find that two situations or problems are running concurrently, review and keep the focus on one problem.

You are now ready to write the first draft. Add more details and information to the outline that you have prepared. These details should assist the participants in fully comprehending the situation as it unfolds in the case. Avoid superfluous details. Be as specific as possible.

Write in simple and easy language. Do not use complicated words. Write short sentences. One paragraph should lead to the following in an easy flow of the narration.

Once the body of the case is completed, you may write the introductory paragraph(s). Very briefly, you should spell out the parameters and the principles within which the case is to be viewed, analysed and discussed. You should also set the scene for the case, giving relevant and adequate information on the organisation or the individuals who constitute the subject of the case.

Go over the case to ensure that important details are not missed.

Once you have finalised the case, go back to the first step about the learning outcomes and what you want to get out of the training activity. These expected outcomes will help you formulate questions and statements that outline the scope and provide guidelines for discussion on the case. Effectively, this will be the assignment for the group.

Presentation and Discussion

You are a key player in this exercise and, therefore, it is imperative that you possess the necessary skills for conducting the session. You should be thoroughly familiar with various discussion methods and techniques. However, your interventions should be kept to the minimum—only when the situation demands—and your comments should be brief and specific. You should refrain from expressing opinions and your own viewpoints on the issues under discussion. It is, however, important that you maintain control of the session, while allowing for maximum participation of the members. The extent to which the group is able to achieve the learning objectives depends largely on how well you conduct the discussion.

A key prerequisite for you to conduct an effective discussion is that you should be fully conversant with all aspects of the case. In fact, as indicated earlier, you should have full and complete materials, even fuller than required for the case, in order to be in a position to respond to the queries and clarifications of the participants. This is necessary in order to lead the group to the desired objectives for the session.

It is desirable that as part of the preparation for the session, you should read the case thoroughly, well in advance of the session, and grasp all the facts of the case and the main points for guiding the discussion on the right lines.

As leader of the discussion, your role is to help the participants, individually and collectively, in clarifying their understanding of the persons and the situations mentioned in the case. They should be able to analyse the decisions and actions indicated in the case and draw inferences from them. You then have to build on the participants' contributions, making appropriate derivations and highlighting key points.

It is important to adequately prepare the group for the exercise. Give the participants enough time to read the case before the exercise begins. Encourage them to get familiar with the facts and other details of the case and grasp important points for discussion.

You must have a clear idea about who among the participants has the ability to initiate discussion and which other members are capable of playing different roles—seeking clarifications, raising queries, analysing situations and issues, providing insights into certain aspects of the case, giving impetus to the discussion when the group appears to be slackening and bringing the group back on course if it seems to be moving out of the parameters set for the discussion. These inputs are necessary for a meaningful and productive discussion.

You should be aware of and in contact with your personal biases and prejudices on the issues likely to be covered by the discussion. If this does not happen, you may consciously or subconsciously influence the discussion, thus inhibiting free flow of ideas and viewpoints.

For wider participation, you may consider dividing the group into smaller subgroups. This facilitates more in-depth consideration of the issues. The subgroups may be given different sets of tasks and their conclusions and decisions may be further discussed in the plenary session for broader consensus and integration.

As part of summing up, at the end of the discussion, you should collate the key points—issues, points of views, inferences and suggestions for action—that have emerged during the discussion and reorganise them into concepts, generalisations and learning outcomes. Do not forget that the case was a means to bring out certain learning that will help the participants approach their work and personal life in future with greater understanding of the problems and better insights into dynamics associated with similar life situations. This will enhance their ability to deal with various organisational scenarios and conditions.

PREPARING AND USING TRAINING SUPPORT MATERIALS

Training support materials are usually used in combination or in support of other training methods. The main objective for using these materials is to enrich the presentation or promote the learning process. These materials add variety to the presentation, making it interesting and easy to comprehend.

Training support materials may be of different types and forms. These can be classified into two broad categories.

- Audiovisual materials
- Printed materials

Audiovisual Materials

What Constitutes Audiovisual Materials?

- Images, pictures, graphics, diagrams, etc., presented through black and white boards, flip charts, cards, printed chart; transparencies projected through overhead projectors; slides projected through slide projector.
- Motion visuals including films, video cassettes, filmstrips or other materials projected through monitor or screen.
- Models or objects for three-dimensional presentations.
- Audio materials played through cassettes or tapes.

Principles of Using Audiovisual Materials

You must draw out a clear plan of presentation, decide on how the materials will be used and the manner in which these could be blended or combined with verbal presentation. You must ask yourself the following questions:

- What will the presentation add to the programme or the training strategy? Will it provide useful variety?
- Will the participants be able to relate to the materials? Is it appropriate to their intellectual level?
- Are the resources worth spending?
- Does it take into consideration the sensitivities of the participants?
- Will it generate a good discussion?

Your prime concern should be the relevance of these materials to the learning objectives for the training activity and the participants should be able to see the justification for use of these materials. You may be tempted to use these materials to generate or sustain the interest of the participants or to do something out of the routine. Do not use this method as a gimmick.

Check your own ability and competency to use these materials.

The materials should comply with the principles of adult training and be consistent with the overall environment of the programme.

Much of the success of this method depends on how it is integrated into the proposed training activity. Some materials generate excellent discussions but some others require a lot of assistance and direction from you.

Maintain a consistent format rather than mixing several different ones. Avoid using too many different types of materials in one presentation.

An important principle is that you should not overdo it otherwise it will defeat the purpose of using these materials.

Preview all audiovisual aids before presentation.

Printed Materials

- Handouts
- Learning aids
- Workbooks
- Instructional modules
- Assignment sheets
- Manuals
- Pamphlets
- Study guides

This list is not exhaustive and you may add more varieties of printed materials.

Developing Training Support Materials

The first task for you is to decide whether the training activity or the presentation that you are planning requires support materials, and, if so, what are your appropriate options.

Once you have established the need, it is imperative to make the purpose clear. The purpose should be directly related to the learning objectives for the training activity or a presentation for which the materials will provide support. If the purpose is to prepare the participants for the training activity or your presentation or to provide a context or some basic information on the topic likely to come up for discussion, you may choose to prepare printed materials, such as handouts, assignment sheets, workbooks, learning guides, etc. However, if the purpose is to emphasise certain points and help in the learning process, you are looking for some audio or visual aids to support you in your presentation.

Once you are clear about these basics, you must decide on the content of the message you wish to convey to the participants. What do I want to emphasise? How can I say this so the participants grasp the key points and do not get lost in details? In what ways will the material assist in my presentation? These are the questions you need to answer.

One of the key considerations in deciding on the type of materials you wish to use is the message you wish to communicate and the content of the materials. You also need to know about the general composition of the group, status of the participants, their level of comprehension, their sensitivities, if any, etc.

You must be aware of the resources at your command. What equipment you will require? Do you need the support of other team members in using the support materials? What is the time allocation for the presentation? Answers to these questions will also help you prepare the support materials.

Prepare the content of your presentation keeping in view the support aids you are using. Remember that support materials are there only to assist in your presentation or the training activity. These cannot be substitute for your inputs as a trainer or your knowledge about the subject matter.

Decide at what point of time in your presentation, you will introduce the audiovisual aids.

Determine the pace of putting up the support materials, keeping in view the level of comprehension of the participants and the learning objectives.

Make the materials attractive. In case of visual materials, ensure that they are visible to all participants. Also, make sure about the clarity of voice and sound for audio materials.

References[1]

Advanced Life Skills. *7 traits of highly confident people.* Retrieved 28 September 2017, from http://advancedlifeskills.com/blog/7-traits-of-highly-confident-people/

Allport, G.W. (1948). The genius of Kurt Lewin. *Journal of Social Issues, 4.*S1: 14–21.

Armesh, H. *Decision making.* Retrieved 28 September 2017, from https://www.scribd.com/document/165957720/483-Hamed. Malaysia: Multimedia University.

Arrington, P. (2008). *Stress at work: How do social workers cope?* NASW Membership Workforce Study, National Association of Social Workers. Retrieved 8 November 2017, from http://workforce.socialworkers.org/whatsnew/stress.pdf

Australian Curriculum, Assessment and Reporting Authority. *Critical and creative thinking.* Retrieved 9 November 2017, from https://www.australiancurriculum.edu.au/f-10-curriculum/general-capabilities/critical-and-creative-thinking/

Bacon, T.R. (2011). *The elements of power: Lessons on leadership and influence.* New York: AMACOM American Management Association.

Baker, M., Rudd, R., & Pomeroy, C. *Relationships between critical and creative thinking.* Retrieved 9 November 2017, from http://citeseerx.ist.psu.edu/viewdoc/download?doi=10.1.1.576.9835&rep=rep1&type=pdf

Ballesteros, D., & Whitlock, J. (2009). *Coping: stress management strategies.* Retrieved 28 September 2017, from http://www.selfinjury.bctr.cornell.edu/documents/coping-stress-man-strat.pdf

Beyer, B.K. (1987). *Practical strategies for the teaching of thinking.* Boston, MA: Allyn & Bacon.

Bishop, S., & Taylor, D. (1992). *50 activities for interpersonal skills training.* Amherst, MA: HRD Press.

Blanchard, K., & Johnson, S. (1983, October). *The one minute manager.* New York, NY: The Berkley Publishing Group.

Bookbinder, L.J. *Empathy and listening skills and psychological hugs.* Retrieved 28 September 2017, from http://www.psychological-hug.com/index.htm

Brown, D., & Kusiak, J. *Creative thinking techniques.* Retrieved 28 September 2017, from http://www.modernanalyst.com/Resources/Articles/tabid/115/ID/63/PageID/219/Creative-Thinking-Techniques.aspx

Brown, M. (2016, July). All Posts, Collaboration, Communication, Creativity, Implementation, Innovation, Strategic Thinking, Strategy, Tools. Brainzooming.

---

[1] Besides these references, the author drew extensively from the training materials developed by him on various aspects of personal development/self-improvement, as part of his work as a trainer for training programmes organised by national and international agencies for different target groups, spread over four decades.

Caroselli, M. (2010). *50 activities for developing critical thinking skills*. Amherst, MA: HRD Press Inc.

Chapin, J. (2013, May). *7 tips for building trust and rapport rapidly*. Retrieved 7 November 2017, from http://www.completeselling.com/7-tips-for-building-trust-and-rapport-rapidly/

Charter for Compassion. *Empathy is essential: The 'soft skill' that engages the whole brain*. Retrieved 28 September 2017, from https://charterforcompassion.org/empathy-is-essential-the-soft-skill-that-engages-the-whole-brain

Coastal Training Technologies. *Motivation: Igniting exceptional performance*. VA, Virginia Beach: Coastal Training Technologies Corp.

Community of Human Resource Management. (2010). *Conflict prevention and conflict avoidance—Are they the same?* CHRM: The author.

Davenport, B. *Self-awareness: What is it and why do you need to seek it?* Livebold& Bloom. Retrieved 8 November 2017, from https://liveboldandbloom.com/07/relationships/self-awareness-what-is-it-and-why-do-you-need-to-seek-it

DCU. (2007–2008). *Learning to learn: Creative thinking and critical thinking* (Compiled by Ann Coughlan). DCU Learning Resources. Retrieved 9 November 2017, from https://www4.dcu.ie/sites/default/files/students/studentlearning/creativeandcritical.pdf

Decision Innovation. *Personal decision making*. Retrieved 28 September 2017, from http://www.decision-making-solutions.com/personal_decision_making.html

Dewe, C. *11 tips for maintaining your positive attitude*. Lifehack: The author. Retrieved 28 September 2017, from http://www.lifehack.org/articles/communication/11-tips-for-maintaining-your-positive-attitude.html

Division of Mental Health, WHO. (1994). *Life skills education for children and adolescents in schools. Pt.3, Training workshops for the development and implementation of life skills programmes*. Geneva: WHO.

Docucu Archive. (2016, February). *Conflict management styles assessment*. Retrieved 28 September 2017, from http://www.docucu-archive.com/view/ddc0e634eaa277a645029f537e5304ff/Conflict-Management-Styles-Assessment-IREM.pdf

Doyle, A. (2017, February). *Decision making skills (with examples): How the decision making process works*. Retrieved 28 September 2017, from https://www.thebalance.com/decision-making-skills-with-examples-2063748

Drucker, P. (2002). *The effective executive*. New York, NY: PerfrctBound™/ HarperCollins Publishers Inc.

Elliot, A.J., & Covington, M.V. (2001). Approach and avoidance motivation. *Educational Psychology Review, 13*. Retrieved 28 September 2017, from https://link.springer.com/article/10.1023/A:1009009018235

Emergency Capacity Building (ECB) Project. (2007). *Building trust in diverse teams: The toolkit for emergency response*. Oxford, UK: Oxfam GB.

Ennis, R.H. *The nature of critical thinking: Outlines of general critical thinking dispositions and abilities*. Retrieved 28 September 2017, from http://www.criticalthinking.net/longdefinition.html

Exforsys Inc. (2007, April). *Traits of a self-confident person*. Retrieved 9 November 2017, from http://www.exforsys.com/career-center/self-confidence/traits-of-a-self-confident-person.html

Fienberg, S.E., & Makov, U.E. (1998). Confidentiality, uniqueness and disclosure limitation for categorical data. *Journal of Official Statistics, 14:* 385–397.

Garber, P.R. (2008). *50 communications activities, icebreakers, and exercises.* Amherst, MA: HRD Press, Inc.

Global Digital Citizen Foundation. *The critical thinking workbook: Games and activities for developing critical thinking skills.* Retrieved 9 November 2017, from http://www.schrockguide.net/uploads/3/9/2/2/392267/critical-thinking-workbook.pdf

Gnoul, M. *Decision-making—Team coordination training student guide.* Retrieved 28 September 2017, from http://www.academia.edu/4700380/DECISION-MAKING_6_-1_Team_Coordination_Training_Student_Guide_8_98_

Goleman, D. (1998, January). *Working with emotional intelligence.* New York, NY: Bantam Books.

Greene, K., Derlega, V.J., & Mathews, A. (2006). Self-disclosure in personal relationships. In Anita L. Vangelisti & Daniel Perlman (Eds.), *The Cambridge handbook of personal relationships* (409–428). Cambridge: Cambridge University Press.

Haden, J. (2014). *9 qualities of remarkably confident people.* Retrieved 28 September 2017, from https://www.inc.com/jeff-haden/9-qualities-of-remarkably-confident-people-th.html

Harrin, E. (2015, 8 January). *15 top skills project managers need.* PM Perspectives Blog. Retrieved 7 November 2017, from http://www.esi-intl.co.uk/blogs/pmoperspectives/index.php/15-skills-project-managers-will-need-2015/

Harvey, J., & Technical Information Service. (2007, December). *Effective decision making.* London: Chartered Institute of Management Accountants.

Innovations for Maternal Newborn & Child Health. (2012, December). *Stress management training: Facilitator's manual.* Retrieved 8 November 2017, from http://studylib.net/doc/8652045/stress-management-training--facilitator-s-manual

Isen, A.I., & Reeve, J. (2006, July). The influence of positive affect on intrinsic and extrinsic motivation: Facilitating enjoyment of play, responsible work behavior, and self-control. *Motivation and Emotion, 29*(4). Retrieved 9 November 2017, from http://citeseerx.ist.psu.edu/viewdoc/download?doi=10.1.1.469.3320&rep=rep1&type=pdf

Johnson, D.W. (1940). *Reaching out: Interpersonal effectiveness and self-actualization.* Needham Heights, MA: Allyn & Bacon.

Jourard, S. (1964). *The transparent self.* New York, NY: Van Nostrand Reinhold.

Katib, M.E. *Critical thinking.* Retrieved 28 September 2017, from https://www.studocu.com/en/document/hogeschool-rotterdam/critical-thinking/summaries/critical-thinking-summary-summary-chapter-1-2/524058/view?has_flashcards=0

Klinic Community Health Centre. (2010, January). *Stress & stress management.* Retrieved 8 November 2017, from http://hydesmith.com/de-stress/files/StressMgt.pdf

Lakhani, D. (2011). *Persuasion: The art of getting what you want.* Hoboken, NJ: John Wiley & Sons.

Lambert, J., & Magees, S. (2000). *50 activities for conflict resolution.* Amherst, MA: HR Development Press.

Lewicki, R.J., McAllister, D.J., & Bies, R.J. (1998). Trust and distrust: New relationships and realities. *Academy of Management Review, 23*(3). Retrieved 9 November 2017, from http://citeseerx.ist.psu.edu/viewdoc/download? doi=10.1.1.159.8876&rep=rep1&type=pdf

Lewin, K. (1935). *A dynamic theory of personality.* New York, NY: McGraw-Hill.

Lipman, M. (1988). Critical thinking—what can it be? *Educational Leadership, 36*(1): 38–43.

Maehr, M.L., & Meyer, H.A. (1997). Understanding motivation and schooling: Where we've been, where we are, and where we need to go. Educational Psychology Review, 9(44): 371–409.

Mar, A. (2016, July). *87 soft skills (the big list).* Simplicable. Retrieved 7 November 2017, from https://training.simplicable.com/training/new/87-soft-skills

McShane, S.L. (2004). *Effective interpersonal communication exercise.* Toronto: McGraw-Hill Ryerson Limited.

Michie, S. (2002). Causes and management of stress at work. *Occupational and Environmental Medicine, 59*(1), 67–72.

Mind Tools. *Communication skills—Become a skilled business communicator.* Retrieved 28 September 2017, from https://www.mindtools.com/pages/main/communication_skills.htm

————. *Building rapport—establishing strong two-way connections.* Retrieved 28 September 2017, from https://www.mindtools.com/pages/article/building-rapport.htm

————. *Building self-confidence—preparing yourself for success!* Retrieved 28 September 2017, from https://www.mindtools.com/selfconf.html

————. *Stress management—Manage stress. Be happy and effective at work.* Retrieved 8 November 2017, from https://www.mindtools.com/pages/main/newMN_TCS.htm

————. *How to make decisions—Making the best possible choices.* Retrieved 28 September 2017, from https://www.mindtools.com/pages/article/newTED_00.htm

————. *Empathy at work: Developing skills to understand other people.* Retrieved 28 September 2017, from https://www.mindtools.com/pages/article/Empathyat Work.htm

Modell, C., Beaver, W., Broch, M.H., & Herzog, M.A. *Stress management training workshop (TI 051-Thematic).* The Clearinghouse for Structured/Thematic Groups and Programs, The University of Texas at Austin. Retrieved 28 September 2017, from https://www.cmhc.utexas.edu/clearinghouse/files/TI051.pdf

Morin, A. *10 tips to make positive thinking easy.* Lifehack: The author. Retrieved 28 September 2017, from http://www.lifehack.org/articles/communication/10-tips-make-positive-thinking-easy.html

National Institute for Educational Development (NIED). (2014). *Life skills facilitators' training manual.* Retrieved 9 November 2017, from http://docplayer. net/43633096-Life-skills-facilitators-training-manual.html

Nolan, J. *Creative thinking and idea generation.* Careers Service. Retrieved 28 September 2017, from http://docplayer.net/20909006-Creative-thinking-and-idea-generation.html. Newcastle University.

Norouzi, B. (2015). *Skills for improving critical thinking and argumentation course.* Retrieved 28 September 2017, from http://www2.it.lut.fi/wiki/lib/exe/fetch. php/courses/ct60a7000/spring2015/1/critical_thinking_and_argumentation_ materials-behnaz_norouzi.pdf

Office Oxygen. *Communication and listening exercises.* Retrieved 28 September 2017, from http://blog.trainerswarehouse.com/communication-exercises/

Online Counselling College. *10 personality traits of a confident person.* Retrieved 28 September 2017, from http://onlinecounsellingcollege.tumblr.com/post/ 27716724125/10-personality-traits-of-a-confident-person

Pardee, R.L. (1990). *Motivation theories of Maslow, Herzberg, McGregor & McClelland: A literature review of selected theories dealing with job satisfaction and motivation.* Retrieved 8 November 2017, from https://eric.ed.gov/?id= ED316767

Paris, C. (2014, March). *6 listening skills exercises to promote stronger communication.* Course Categories.

Parry, C., & Nomikou, M. *Life skills: Developing active citizens.* British Council. Retrieved 28 September 2017, from https://www.britishcouncil.gr/sites/ default/files/life-skills-manual-english.pdf

Paul, R. & Elder, L. (2008). *The miniature guide to critical thinking concepts and tools.* Tomales, CA: Foundation for Critical Thinking Press.

———. (2012). *Critical thinking: Tools for taking charge of your learning and your life* (3rd ed.). Boston, MA: Pearson Education/Prentice Hall.

———. *Critical thinking: Learn the tools the best thinkers use.* Upper Saddle River, NJ: Prentice Hall.

Perloff, R. M. (2003). *The Dynamics of persuasion: Communication and attitude in the 21st century.* Hillsdale, NJ: Lawrence Erlbaum Associates.

Pettry II, D.W. *Building social skills through activities.* Retrieved 10 January 2018, from http://www.dannypettry.com/ebook_social_skills.pdf

Riley, L. *Five strategies for managing employee conflict.* Retrieved 8 November 2017, from http://www.aglobalreach.com/wp-content/uploads/2012/04/Conflict-Management_5-Strategies.pdf

RN Central. (2009, 12 October). *100 positive-thinking exercises that will make any patient healthier & happier.* Retrieved 7 November 2017, from http://www. rncentral.com/nursing-library/careplans/100_positive_thinking_exercises_to_ incorporate_into_your_life/

Rogers, C. R. (1995). *A way of being.* New York: Houghton Mifflin Harcourt.

Rogers, C. (2012). *On becoming a person: A therapist's view of psychotherapy.* New York: Houghton Mifflin Harcourt.

Rosseau, D.M., Sitkin, S.B., Burt, R.S., & Camerer, C. (1998). Not so different after all: A cross-discipline view of trust. *Academy of Management Review, 23*(3): 393–404.

Rozakis, L. (1998). *81 fresh & fun critical-thinking activities.* New York, NY: Scholastic Professional Books.

Scannell, M. (2010). *The big book of conflict resolution games: Quick, effective activities to improve communication, trust and collaboration.* New Delhi: Tata McGraw-Hill.

Scheffer, B.K., & Rubenfeld, M.G. (2000). A consensus statement on critical thinking in nursing. *Journal of Nursing Education, 39*(8), 352–359.

———. (2001). Critical thinking: What is it and how do we teach it? *Nursing* (current issue).

Schutz, W. (n.d.). *Schutz's interpersonal needs theory & business communication.* TECEP Managerial Communications: Study Guide and Test Prep/Business courses. Retrieved 9 November 2017, from http://study.com/academy/lesson/schutzs-interpersonal-needs-theory-business-communication.html

Scott, A.T. (n.d.). *Communication skills & empathy.* Retrieved 28 September 2017, from http://cpd.yolasite.com/resources/Communication%20Skills%20%26%20Empathy.pdf

Self-help Groups-Neighbor to Neighbor. (2001). *Managing stress—Session 5* (Reviewed by Colleen Jolly). Ames, IA: Iowa State University Extension. Retrieved 8 November 2017, from http://www.wellnessproposals.com/stress/stress-pdfs/self-help-group-session-managing-stress.pdf

Shapiro, Lawrence E. (2004). *101 ways to teach children social skills.* Retrieved 28 September 2017, from http://www.socialskillscentral.com/free/101_Ways_Teach_Children_Social_Skills.pdf. The Bureau for At-Risk Youth.

Skills You Need. *Effective decision making—A framework.* Retrieved 28 September 2017, from https://www.skillsyouneed.com/ips/decision-making2.html

———. *7 ways to boost your self-esteem.* Retrieved 28 September 2017, from https://www.skillsyouneed.com/rhubarb/boost-self-esteem.html

———. *Assertiveness—An introduction.* Retrieved 28 September 2017, from https://www.skillsyouneed.com/ps/assertiveness.html

———. *Building confidence.* Retrieved 28 September 2017, from https://www.skillsyouneed.com/ps/confidence.html

———. *Building rapport.* Retrieved 28 September 2017, from https://www.skillsyouneed.com/ips/rapport.html

———. *Decision making.* Retrieved 28 September 2017, from https://www.skillsyouneed.com/ips/decision-making.html

———. *Interpersonal communication skills.* Retrieved 8 November 2017, from https://www.skillsyouneed.com/ips/interpersonal-communication.html

———. *Interpersonal skills self-assessment.* Retrieved 28 September 2017, from https://www.skillsyouneed.com/ls/index.php/343479

———. *Positive thinking.* Retrieved 28 September 2017, from https://www.skillsyouneed.com/ps/positive-thinking.html

———. *Recognising and managing emotions.* Retrieved 28 September 2017, from https://www.skillsyouneed.com/ps/managing-emotions.html

Skills You Need. Elements of empathy. In *What is empathy?* Retrieved 28 September 2017, from https://www.skillsyouneed.com/ips/empathy.html

Smith, M.J. (1982). *Persuasion and human action: A review and critique of social influence theories.* Belmont, CA: Wadsworth.

Sponge (UK). (2017, March). *Empathy: The soft skill that delivers hard results.* Retrieved 28 September 2017, from https://spongeuk.com/insights/2017/03/empathy-soft-skill-delivers-hard-results

The Center for Building a Culture of Empathy and Compassion. (2013). Increasing empathy. In *Manual: Empathy training.* El Cerrito, CA: The Centre for Building a Culture of Empathy and Compassion.

The Critical Thinking Community. *Defining critical thinking.* Tomales, CA: Foundation for Critical Thinking Press. Retrieved 28 September 2017, from http://www.criticalthinking.org/pages/defining-critical-thinking/766

The Foundation Coalition. *Understanding conflict and conflict management.* Retrieved 9 November 2017, from http://fc.civil.tamu.edu/publications/brochures/conflict.pdf

The Levels of Communication; Microsoft PowerPoint Presentation.

Tilus, G. (2012, December). *6 critical thinking skills you need to master now.* Rasmussen College.

Time-Management-Guide.com. *Decision making skills and techniques.* Retrieved 28 September 2017, from http://www.time-management-guide.com/decision-making-skills.html

Topping, D.M., Crowell, D.C., & Kobayashi, V.N. (Eds.). (1987). *Thinking across cultures: The third international conference on thinking.* Hillsdale, NJ: Erlbaum.

Trinity College. (2003, January). *Interpersonal skills module—Exercises and handouts* (Compiled by Tamara O'Connor). Generic Skills Integration Project (GENSIP). Dublin: University of Dublin, Ireland.

Tubesing, D., & Tubesing, N. (Eds.) (1983). *Structured exercises in stress management: A whole person handbook for trainers, educators and group leaders* (Volume 1). Duluth, MN: Whole Person Press.

UNICEF. (n.d.). *Life skills: A facilitator's guide for teenagers.* Retrieved 28 September 2017, from https://www.unicef.org/eapro/Life_Skills__A_facilitator_guide_for_teenagers.pdf

University of Massachusetts. *7 steps to effective decision making.* Retrieved 28 September 2017, from https://www.umassd.edu/media/umassdartmouth/fycm/decision_making_process.pdf

van Warmerdam, G. *Exercises and activities for developing self awareness.* Retrieved 28 September 2017, from https://www.pathwaytohappiness.com/sessions_summary.htm

———. Self image. In *Changing self image.* Retrieved 8 November 2017, from http://www.pathwaytohappiness.com/self_image.htm. Santa Barbara, CA.

———. *Self-awareness exercises.* Retrieved 28 September 2017, from https://www.pathwaytohappiness.com/sessions_summary.htm. Santa Barbara, CA.

van Warmerdam, G. *Self awareness*. Retrieved 8 November 2017, from https://www.pathwaytohappiness.com/self-awareness.htm. Santa Barbara, CA.

———. *The pathway to happiness is through self awareness*. Retrieved 9 November 2017, from http://www.ashtarcommandcrew.net/profiles/blogs/the-pathway-to-happiness-is-through-self-awareness-teacher-gary

Wafula, K. *Developing critical thinking skills*. Orientation Lecture Series: Learning to Learn. Retrieved 8 November 2017, from https://www.academia.edu/24876103/Orientation_Lecture_Series_LEARNING_TO_LEARN_Developing_critical_thinking_skills_Learning_Centre_Orientation_Lecture_Series_LEARNING_TO_LEARN_Developing_critical_thinking_skills_Defining_critical_thinking. Learning Centre.

Walsch, N.D. (2014). *A way to self-awareness*. Spiritlibrary. Retrieved 9 November 2017, from https://spiritlibrary.com/neale-donald-walsch/a-way-to-self-awareness

Wax, D. *10 skills you need to succeed at almost everything*. Lifehack: The author. Retrieved 28 September 2017, from http://www.lifehack.org/articles/featured/10-skills-you-need-to-succeed-at-almost-anything.html

WebMD. *Stress management—Ways to avoid stress*. Retrieved 28 September 2017, from http://www.webmd.com/balance/stress-management/stress-management-avoiding-unnecessary-stress#1

Whalen, D.J. (1996). *I see what you mean: Persuasive business communication*. New Delhi: SAGE Publications.

Whitbourne, S.K. (2014, December). *4 ways to improve your emotional communication*. Retrieved 28 September 2017, from https://www.psychologytoday.com/blog/fulfillment-any-age/201412/4-ways-improve-your-emotional-communication

Wood, J.T. (2016). *Interpersonal communication: Everyday encounters*. (8th ed.). Boston, MA: CENGAGE Learning.

Xerox Corporation. (2013). *Stress management: Tips, insights, and tactics*. Retrieved 8 November 2017, from http://www.office.xerox.com/latest/XOAFL-19U.pdf

About the Author

Devendra Agochiya has over three decades of rich and varied experience of working with national and international organisations engaged in the fields of youth and social development, training, empowerment and management. He has worked for 12 years (1969–1980), in senior professional positions, with an international NGO in New Delhi—International Youth Centre. He has worked for about 18 years with the Youth Affairs Division of the Commonwealth Secretariat—first as the Regional Director for Asia and then as Head of the Division based in London, the headquarters of the Secretariat. He has been actively associated with the planning and delivery of a wide range of training programmes for a variety of target groups, including policy makers, senior government and non-government officials, business executives and young people in India and other Commonwealth countries. He is presently working as a freelance consultant with a number of national and international agencies in training and development and related areas.